MW00834731

Collected
Bodhi Leaves
Publications

Volume IV

Numbers 91 to 121

BPS Pariyatti Editions

BPS Pariyatti Editions
An imprint of Pariyatti Publishing
www.pariyatti.org

Published with the consent of the original publisher.

First BPS Pariyatti Edition, 2017
ISBN: 978-1-68172-517-8 (hardback)
ISBN: 978-1-68172-333-4 (paperback)
ISBN: 978-1-68172-087-6 (PDF)
ISBN: 978-1-68172-085-2 (ePub)
ISBN: 978-1-68172-086-9 (Mobi)
LCCN: 2017910765

Typeset in Palatino Pali

Triple bodhi leaf cover image used with permission from Keith Carver Photography: www.keithcarverphotography.com

KEY TO ABBREVIATIONS

A	Aṅguttara Nikāya
Ap	Apadāna
Bv	Buddhavaṃsa
Cp	Cariyāpiṭaka
D	Dīgha Nikāya
Dhp	Dhammapada
Dhs	Dhammasaṅgaṇī
It	Itivuttaka
Ja	Jātaka verses and commentary
Khp	Khuddakapāṭha
M	Majjhima Nikāya
Mil	Milindapañha
Nett	Nettipakaraṇa
Nidd	Niddesa
Paṭis	Paṭisambhidamagga
Peṭ	Peṭakopadesa
S	Saṃyutta Nikāya
Sn	Suttanipāta
Th	Theragātha
Thī	Therigātha
Ud	Udāna
Vibh	Vibhaṅga
Vin	Vinaya-piṭaka
Vism	Visuddhimagga
Vism-mhṭ	Visuddhimagga Sub-commentary
Vv	Vimānavatthu

The above is the abbreviation scheme of the Pali Text Society (PTS) as given in the *Dictionary of Pali* by Margaret Cone.

The commentaries, *aṭṭhakathā*, are abbreviated by using a hyphen and an "a" ("-a") following the abbreviation of the text, e.g., *Dīgha Nikāya Aṭṭhakathā* = D-a. Likewise the sub-commentaries are abbreviated by a "ṭ" ("-ṭ") following the abbreviation of the text.

The *sutta* reference abbreviation system for the four Nikāyas, as is used in Bhikkhu Bodhi's translations is:

AN	Aṅguttara Nikāya
MN	Majjhima Nikāya
J	Jātaka story
Mv	Mahāvagga (Vinaya Piṭaka)
Cv	Cullavagga (Vinaya Piṭaka)
SVibh	Suttavibhaṅga (Vinaya Piṭaka)
DN	Dīgha Nikāya
SN	Saṃyutta Nikāya

Contents

Buddha-Bush

Seeing Dhamma in Nature

Bhikkhu Khantipālo

Bodhi Leaves No. 91

First published: 1982

A Few Words Explained

Dhamma: Law, Path or Way, righteousness, virtue, moral precepts, states of mind, conditioned events, and the Unconditioned Element (Nibbāna).

Deva: god, deity, a divine being so born according to the *kamma* made, but impermanent as all other beings.

Dukkha: pain, anguish, what is unsatisfactory, whether gross suffering or subtle.

Kamma: intentional action originating in mind and manifesting through speech and body actions, either wholesome or unwholesome, and having the potential results respectively of happiness and suffering.

Wat: a Buddhist monastery.

Buddha–Bush

Seeing Dhamma in Nature

On Living on the Edge

How easy it is to be complacent, how hard to feel all the time that this world is the edge! Complacency is helped by the way things are arranged: in cities, neat orderly houses in rows with neat gardens in front and neat curtains in the windows. But why is it arranged like this? This is what satisfies most peoples' craving for security. It looks secure, so it must be secure. Behind that facade of orderliness though, there is always the jungle. A garden illustrates this very well: take a neatly trimmed lawn with orderly rose beds and let it do its own thing for a month, a year, twenty years. You know what happens—it starts by looking overgrown, then weedy, and then the forest reasserts itself and within fifty years there will be tall trees which bear no signs of human order. Houses are like that too: without attention they decay and fall down. Bodies are like that too, they do the same. And the mind, if not looked after, soon becomes a jungle of greed, hatred and delusion.

As this is so, should we not remind ourselves of the nature of this world? If we live in a relatively well-ordered city (though they're going out of gear more and more), shouldn't we remind ourselves: "It doesn't last! Not permanent? Unsure! Insecure!" If we don't do this then we just settle down and become more complacent. And though decay, disease and death are threatening all the time we pretend that they don't concern us. We can take it easy and enjoy the security of our well-ordered lives. Don't be fooled by it!

Living in the country can open one's eyes to the disorder and to the chanciness of this life. Though there is a kind of order in plants and animals, it is based on "strongest grows, weakest dies" and the web of supporting conditions, any part of which can disappear leading to starvation and death. Human life, too, depends on such a web and only one link has to go for life to be disrupted. Look into that and get rid of complacency!

Here in Australia the bush emphasises how precarious existence is. The countless eucalyptus trees all around, the many kinds of "gum" trees that so typify this country, have leaves full of volatile oils. So do a lot of the bushes that grow under them. Then if one chooses to live in the seclusion of the bush, one chooses too a very high fire risk. Actually such fire is necessary for the regeneration of Australian forests but it often leads to the death of humans. The gums all sprout again and the rest of the bush shoots up from underground tubers or regenerates from seed, but human beings and their buildings can't do that.

Maybe you say: "It's crazy to live in such a place. It's not safe!" But then the question is: "Where is a safe place?" Knowing insecurity and practising Dhamma every day, one is reminded of disease, decay and death, which leads to true security: that of the mind which can't be shaken by the worldly conditions. And how is it possible to make the unstable eight conditions of the world[1] sure and unchanging? Look at the uncertainty, live on the edge and don't be afraid of it.

Book-heads

Sometimes they come here—book-heads—they know it all, every Buddhist book.

They say that they want to practise meditation but all they do is display their theories. What trouble! Here it is quiet, with wind in the gums and cicadas at their never-ending song, teaching Dhamma all the time. Rocks worn away and split apart and the bush that grows between, teach even more silently, but book-heads can't see that. They're full of *yāna*s and *vāda*s (yes, and *ekayāna*[2] too!) so that there is no room for Dhamma. How heavy their heads must be with all that load of books and words but they don't put it down. Not even for a moment.

---

1 Gain and loss, fame and infamy praise and blame, happiness and unsatisfactoriness (*dukkha*).

2 *Yāna* = vehicle, *vāda* = way *ekayāna* = one vehicle.

Bright and Beautiful Plus Dark and Ugly

People who visit often say: "Oh, what a wonderfully beautiful place you have here." And that is true because this valley with its surrounding rocky hills all covered with trees is very beautiful. There are our groves of smooth-barked apple with incredibly twisted limbs and trunks which vary from smooth silver-grey to pure apricot and all shades between. Very beautiful, yes. But then we ask, "Why see only one side? Why see only the beautiful?" All so beautiful, but all so terrible too. The beauty of the trees is subject to the hunger of termites and borers, fungus and old age. The insects, birds, wallabies, and wombats all live on other living beings or plants. Living means eating; eating means killing. If these beings are not looking for their next meal—and they usually are— they are about to become the next meal of another. You say it is nature? Then one must recognize that nature is not only bright and beautiful but also dark and ugly. And of course this body, too, is subject to both sides, youth and old age, health and disease, life and death. Admiring the beauty of the Wat—and elsewhere—has a disadvantage, that is of attachment, clinging and craving. Looking also at the other side where there is decay, disease and death has a great advantage—dispassion grows and one can let go easily.

Tenacity

All these plants around here, such as the felted flannel-flower, cling tenaciously to cracks in the rocks. People say: "How tenacious they are!" thereby praising them. But think a minute about tenacity in everyday life, how it depends on desires and how its outcome is possessiveness leading to avarice, the need to guard, and so to weapons and fighting, and you will see tenacity in a different light. Just as generations of flannel-flowers have clung tenaciously—but with a hard battle for existence—to the rocks and sandy cracks, so people cling and will not let go. But what should one let go of? Some people want to let go of even good things before they have ever practised them. "Oh, I have renounced my attachment to meditation so I don't have to practise it now." Such lofty virtue! Giving up what one has not got—who cannot do that! But the letting go of evil, unwholesome mental states and the speech and body actions that they give rise to, that is difficult. Be tenacious in Dhamma but let go of what is not Dhamma.

Spinners

In the early morning when mist fills the valley and the dew has been heavy, the ground, grass, bushes and trees are covered in pearl-sprinkled nets of silk of innumerable kinds. What precision and what marvellous energy to produce it all in a single night. Nets of death, nets of destruction! One must look, too, at the other side. They are only for catching breakfast. And the beautiful beasts who have created them—spiders are two million or so to the acre—have poison to paralyze their victims and then dissolve out their innards and suck them dry. Well now, that's a different picture! And it gets worse if you look into it. Female spiders are usually larger than the males and some even eat their mates in the sexual embrace. Gruesome indeed, but that's how the spider-world keeps going. So what should one do? Just look at the beauty of the spider webs (and perhaps marvel at the supposed creator's plan) or see the grim struggle for life which lies behind the veneer of the mind's imposed concepts of beauty? If one knows thoroughly the terror and fear which pervades animal life, and intrudes into human exigency quite frequently, one will give up such notions as "creator" and "divine plan" and awake in oneself great compassion for all living beings so afflicted by diverse sufferings.

Impermanence

Crack … crump! On a perfectly still day, a huge tree or a large limb has come down. Wood weakened by fire, eaten by white ants, and down it comes, unexpectedly. So too, in this life the major events of impermanence cannot be predicted and the unexpected can always happen. If one goes around with one's life nicely planned out, or just complacent with the flow of pleasures, how shocking these things can be. You have to be aware of impermanence all the time, otherwise there is bound to be *dukkha*.

Ants

Imagine yourself ant-size, though even they come very big and very small. You are busily looking for something dead or dying to clear up and take back to the nest. Suddenly the earth beneath you shakes, sudden shade falls and an enormous object lands just near you. It seems to tower to the sky. You stagger back in fear, blind fear of being crushed but it is already gone and the earth-tremors subside. How can ants, even granting them enough intelligence, conceive of human beings—they are too big. They can be known only as fearful intrusions into the ceaseless business of the ant world. This might lead humans to think that perhaps there could be beings so vast in proportions and different in form that they cannot conceive of them. And there are of course. And how small then are humans and their works!

Control

Human cities give the impression that we can control everything: switches turn on electricity, gas-taps release gas. The grass in the gardens has tidy edges and the municipal trees are regularly pruned. And then the starter (usually) starts the car's motor (and how irritated we get if it doesn't), while trains and buses run to schedule (unless affected by increasingly frequent strikes). So by and large we are in control—aren't we? But come to a place like this where there are hundreds of acres of bush in every direction. It is not under any human control at all. It does its own thing with no reference to human beings. No doubt this is why some people cannot bear to live in such a place. Obviously, a human being is not on top of it all here. A person can fit in by adaptation, otherwise there are two possible courses: go back to the well-controlled city which is not fearful, or chop down all the trees and make some fields—human order in all this natural disorder. Then he's in control again, isn't he? But look again. Even in the safest cities how can the floods of decay, disease and death be completely controlled? Who can even pretend to control death? And everywhere the four great elements, earth, water, fire and air, how much can they be controlled? The exterior ones every now and again let humanity know that they are not controlled at all, as in earthquakes, floods, bushfires and high winds. These four are what this body is made of too …

Birds

We have them in all sizes and varieties with an amazing range of calls. Even on the stillest cold winter night there is an occasional harsh owl-screech or the repetitious "mopoke" echoing. At other times there are always plenty of bird noises. Watch one for a while. The little head darts this way and that, even when there is no food involved. Well certainly it is looking for food, endlessly, until death. But what else? It looks for enemies. It is frightened, full of fear. Even when humans do nothing to cause fear, as here in the Wat, the birds' heads turn ceaselessly and though there is no danger, off they fly. Fear rules the animal world even more nakedly than it does the human.

Enlightened Kookaburras[3]

He laughs long and loud, again and again,
What does he laugh at on this grey day?
An abundance of lizards gone down his throat?
It cannot be so with this cold and rain.
Perhaps he laughs making light of troubles,
Sure he has plenty though quite simple ones,
Not the complications of human beings though.
Their greeds and their hatreds, elaborate evasions,
Curious and contorted self-justifications.
Is he laughing since rid of this heavy burden.
Or just out of habit hoping the rain's stopped?
In the last analysis his laughing is man-made,
A mind-made overlayjust interpretations,
Surely a thing he might well laugh at!
Trees aren't troublesome,
Grevilleas just grow themselves;
She-oaks sigh and sough
But humanity means hassles.
Whoever heard of a lazy lambertia?
When did a wattle ever tell a lie?
And gums though twisted never distort things
But humans though straight are twisted inside.
Ferns don't intrude, they grace small spaces.
They aren't conceited or opinionated;
Humans how different with cravings and hates.
But trees just aren't troublesome.

---

3 Kookaburra, a large and gregarious species of the kingfisher family peculiar to Australia. Its "laughing" cacophony morning and night usually raises a smile.

Undertakers

They are the world-wide firm dressed in sober hues and fully experienced in the clean and proper disposal of bodies for several tens of millions of years—but humans aren't allowed to use these very natural undertakers. So, not at all deterred by this loss of business, they go about the animal world where they undertake to dispose of all bodies, big and small, very efficiently. They can do so because they are so much more ubiquitous than the human variety—and, by contrast, they do it for free! Do you know who they are?

Night Silence

The moon, nearly full, shines from a hazy sky through the twisted maze of branches. Though a summer night, yet it is so quiet, perhaps an odd "gloop" by a frog, a little cicada sound sometimes, occasionally the screech of an owl, or more rarely the weird scream of a possum. So quiet that if you just stand still and look at it all, or close your eyes and listen, there is the intense ringing soundlessness all around, and it goes on and on. Then comes the reflection: "What marvellous good *kamma* has been made to be able to live like this, in such a place conducive to Dhamma-practice?" How one then appreciates the worth of the Dhamma which has led to this solitude in the bush. This solitude which can be enjoyed and used, while so many come here to savour the taste of the Dhamma in these peaceful surroundings.

Nature, Mother or Murderer?

When you look at it closely you wonder. Romantics call nature a mother but then they do not care to look closely. Hindus with their imagery of black-tongued, blood-drinking, skull-bedecked Mother Kali (the Black One) really have an image closer to reality but then that raises all sorts of quite unsolvable problems. If she is a mother, why create such a bloody mess as nature; surely her creation should evince a mother's compassion? But she is bloody and ravening … It will be better not to label nature with any sex-tag, for a stem father-God is hardly a more reassuring figure! It all just happens according to *kamma* which produces the innumerable variety of births. And since most of them that we can know about are without any great distinction regarding intelligence, they are the result of unwholesome *kamma*—they live in a world of endless conflicts. Listen to these impressive words of the Buddha:

> "What is dark kamma with dark ripening? Here someone produces (kammic) bodily, verbal and mental processes (bound up) with affliction.[4] By doing so, that person reappears in a world of affliction. When that happens, afflicting contacts[5] touch that person. Being touched by these, one feels afflicting feelings entirely painful as in the case of beings in hell. Thus a being's reappearance is due to a being (in the past); one reappears (is reborn) owing to the kammas one has performed. When one reappears, contacts touch one. Thus I say are beings heirs of their kammas. This is called dark ripening."[6]

As the Buddha said, more beings are reborn this way than in the good destinies, such as human birth. It's no good saying: "I've a human soul now and can't descend to animal birth"—how comforting if it were so! If a human being is no longer up to human level regarding conduct—and some humans do worse things than animals, then why should there be no possibility for animal birth? And the animals, footless, two-footed, four-footed or manyfooted—they don't appreciate this forest as beautiful; for them it's a full-on struggle to keep alive. They would certainly not agree with the romantics' Mother Nature and be more inclined to agree with the Hindus' Mother Kāli—that is, if they could think such ideas. But they have no time for that. Food, mating and avoiding enemies takes up all their time. Oh, the *dukkha*! Open your eyes to this and awake the great compassion for all these creatures trapped in the terrible round of existence.

So Easily Upset

Meaning this body. Of course most people's minds are that way too but that can be trained away with Dhamma. The body's fragility however was emphasized by a recent incident of

---

4 Defiled kinds of *kamma* (rooted in greed, aversion, delusion) and expressed through body speech and mind.

5 Painful 'touches' through eye, ear, nose, tongue, body mind.

6 Condensed from Ven. Nyanamoli's translation of the Dog-Duty Ascetic Discourse of Majjhima-nikāya (see *Middle Length Sayings*, 57).

snakebite. Though we have been here nearly three years there have been no cases of this until now. People are always told, "If you have mindfulness with your feet and loving-kindness in your heart you are unlikely to disturb snakes." And it worked well. Just for safety—as there are children running round—there are "snake-stations" with bandages in jars and splints to immobilize the affected limb, all marked by a smiling white serpent on a red ground who says "METTA." But a resident was bitten in long grass and did not even see the creature concerned. Anyway, as recommended, she put on a pressure bandage and lay down until discovered shortly afterwards. The hospital said it was a small bite perhaps by a small snake but it caused quite a bit of bodily pain. Only such a very little poison! And others were affected too—the driver who rushed the sick lady to hospital, the ferryman who sped us across the river and the police car which preceded us and cleared the road. Just a little bit of poison to upset the body. How frail it is and how easily upset. Something to think about …

In the Middle

"In the Middle" is the description of the Buddha's Dhamma. It does not mean halfway compromises but refers to the fact that one practising Dhamma never goes to extremes—not emotionally, intellectually or in views, speech or actions. From this one can easily know that there are plenty of humans who have no idea of the Middle Way. And there must be a lot of *deva*s who have never heard of it too, that is, if Buddhist tradition regarding their influence on weather is more accurate than the mere scientific patterns of physical change accepted by most people now. Capricious *deva*s who go on holiday! So that Australia is gripped by a few years' continuous drought, and who then return, carelessly directing colossal storms into the arid interior so that enormous floods ensue, lakes suddenly appear, rivers usually of sand fill with the roar of water and whatever crops and animals did not die of drought are swept away … Even in the more temperate parts, the pattern can still be one of droughts and floods, though more moderately. The creeks dry up and water is reduced to a trickle, as month follows month and the heavens hold only the bright sun and moon, no clouds. A last, when the garden is no longer cultivated for lack of water and there are talks of trucking in water for drinking (washing has long been done by "bucket bath"—one-bucket equals one bath—or even "cat-lick" passing a damp towel over the body), rain falls enough to stave off extremities but not to fill the creeks. And so it goes on until finally, in a gigantic storm lasting some days, so much water falls that the road is washed out, the ferryboats are carried downstream, trees and rocks block highways, people are cut off for days, and of course the creeks flow and there is enough water. Drought, according to the Buddha, has as one cause that human beings don't keep the Five Precepts … well there are some of those! If this is combined with the capriciousness of weather deities, it might account for the lack of keeping in the middle as far as our climate is concerned. What to do about it? Convert the *deva*s to Dhamma-practice? A big job with a rather unseen audience. Turn the humans in the direction of Dhamma? An even bigger job …

Logorrhoea

They come with sad faces, strained, troubled, worried or anxious—all suffering from that common disease of the mind, logorrhoea. In case you don't recognize this word (though you know its body-relation, diarrhoea), it means a flow of words, the never-ending flow of words that goes on and on. Because of it there is madness, grief and remorse. Like other diseases, when it is not treated it becomes worse. So they come for the treatment, a meditation weekend or ten-day course so that the mad mind stops, or at least slows down. They get away from the causes of their sufferings—business worries, family strife, loss of what is dear, dissatisfaction with life generally or general ennui, and come to this very quiet and secluded place where they are up early in the morning to meditate, and continue to do so walking and sitting throughout the day. Twice a day they hear the Dhamma and afterwards there is ample time to ask questions and find out, "How does this apply to me?" Once a day they can go and ask the teachers questions in private. Between nine and ten each night, the days finish with loving-kindness meditation and then a lot of very tired meditators sleep very soundly. First and second days pass and usually a few are afflicted with 'second-day blues'—"I can't do it. It's too difficult!" But most of them stay. Then things start getting easier as the mind becomes gentler and more relaxed. The logorrhoea is easing up. Even the country noises of birds and cicadas (and the occasional distant baby) no longer seem mountainous obstacles to concentration; in fact with growing loving-kindness towards all living beings the noises become a joyful part of meditation. And as that dread disease disappears, how happy faces become! Years and wrinkles disappear. Grimaces are replaced by smiles. So wonderful when logorrhoea stops! And if it stops for long periods of time so that there is just bright wordless awareness, then real rapture and bliss are experienced. People wonder then why they always thought that this disease was the normal state.

All for what?

This summer the raked area round the *sālā* (meditation hall) has seen an amazing invasion of thousands of low-flying flies. Their circling low over the ground has filled the *sālā* with a constant hum. They dig out holes in the sand and crawl in, perhaps to lay their eggs, and they roll about in tangled balls of bodies, indulging in some dipterous orgy. All this is the revered effort to keep the species going. And what does this mean? This means keeping the body going. While flies' minds have few concerns apart from this, human minds have more. But then, think about it. Isn't so much of life just keeping this body going? There's "getting up, washing, dressing, eating, urinating and excreting, going to work … for money for this body's clothes, shelter and medicines … relaxation and enjoyment and finally lying down when this body is tired." It looks although most of this life can be spent, as flies spend their lives, concerned with the body. The Buddha calls it "to live following the body" (*kāyanvyatā*). No one thinks much about this because it is the common thing to do. And it is fairly satisfactory while the body works well … but what happens when it doesn't? Suppose there is an accident, or the onset of old age, or of serious illness … what then? One has lived "following the body" all the time and now it shows its impermanent nature. There are no resources in heart and mind to deal with this, for such materialists have never looked into themselves. The inside is dry and barren; there is no confidence in good Teachings, no loving-kindness, no insight into the transitoriness of everything. Faced with crises like these, such people grieve and lament; they become bitter and remorseful. Their lives may rise up before their eyes and with sorrow they think, "What was it all for? What purpose has it?" And if they are hardened cases, they may come up with the answer, "No purpose. It's just the blind drive of nature to keep going." So, hopelessly, they die. Just like the transient flies, here today and gone a few days after. But why not look into this impermanence? For all life is about that, without any exception. Then one would not "live following the body" any more, nor lament when serious sufferings arose regarding the body. And of course, one would know what it was all about.

Conflict

Selfish desires produce it. More selfish desires, more conflict. You can see it everywhere, especially in the world of humans where desires are assiduously being cultivated by business interests so that one will buy more and increasingly complex things. Stir up the desires! And the ad-men know how to do it—quite easy because desire is an underlying tendency and just waits for arousing. But our desires conflict with those of others, so human society divides into more and more parties and factions, sects and groups, all at loggerheads with one another. Conflicts multiply from day to day and governments have a more and more difficult task to keep the peace between all these parties. Even in a peaceful place like Wat Buddha-Dhamma there are conflicts because this is the desire-world where all beings are beset by desires, not only humans. Our gardeners wanted to supply the kitchen with fresh vegetables and fruit grown without poisonous sprays but the garden fence was low. Wallabies-hopped over, wombats dug under … all to sample these various (to them) exotic tastes. They certainly desire to eat our vegetables. So, as the least harmful way of preventing this, the lay community built a high fence, wallaby-proof and buried rocks along it, only partly wombat-proof! The animals' desires conflicted with our desires—a simple case where our desires were not especially selfish and their desires could be limited without causing them harm.

Then there was another example: rats got into the new house. At first it was just one or two and no-one took much notice. But they invited all their relatives and multiplied at such a prodigious rate that there was never a time without a scurrying of rats. Holes appeared, and rat droppings. That house contains a large library of Buddhist books assembled over many years and the rats started to pay them some attention, not alas to their wisdom content but as food! One of the lay people then made a number of cage-type rat traps. But we found that it was against the law to take live rats (they are black rats and therefore classed as vermin) from one place to let them go elsewhere. At this point, the conflict arising from desires became acute! Let them stay in the house? Then we have to move out with all our things! Or they have to go! Their desires and ours were quite different and not reconcilable. Our notice-boards inform people: "Buddhist Monastery. All living beings protected. No shooting or fishing." But due to the law we could not keep to this completely. In this world it is sometimes so; one party may desire peace, yet the other will not agree to it. One should not be too idealistic about this world, where due to conflicting desires, there will never be complete and lasting peace. One just has to minimize one's selfishness, and so minimize the conflicts. Everyone can do that.

Noise-Silence (1)

Once there was a rather mad, meditating architect who was bent on building a completely silent meditation centre. His idea, inherited from others, was that there must be no noise to disturb meditation, so he designed a meditation hall which would be soundproof. As it was airproof, too, this meant air-conditioning machinery would be necessary ... and this makes a noise. Apart from this, it was pointed out to him that though the centre was to be rurally located, there were such noise risks as tractors, milk-trucks and, if you can escape from all of these, there are birds. No, there were to be no bird-noises in the meditation hall! Fortunately, the place never even got started. It would have been a disaster! So much costly building to isolate meditators from the world they have to live in and come to terms with. Here in the Wat it's different. It is true that we have no agricultural noises to contend with because we are isolated completely by miles of national park and crown land—all of it wild bush. But all that bush is full of living beings both day and night, all making their special noises. For example, Ten-Mile Hollow has a large and flourishing tribe of kookaburras which sound off many times at dawn and dusk and are liable to break into long cacophonies of "laughter" at any time between. The meditation hall is certainly not kookaburra-proof; in fact as its walls are vertical half-logs, there are necessarily plenty of spaces between them, apart from windows and doorway. This provides cooling breezes in summer but means that a few blankets are needed for winter. Even meditators can't have it just as they want it all the time! So, bird songs and screeches and all sorts of other noises drift into the hall. A good meditator just takes it in stride, notices it and lets it go. Or if concentration is even better, those noises are not even noticed. When it comes to the time for loving-kindness meditation then the presence of all those living beings "footless and two-footed, four-footed and many-footed" gives something else, apart from humans, to direct it towards. Because of this, living-beings nearby have no fear of the meditation hall and its inhabitants. Only the other night, a portly wombat scratching around near the hall continued to do his thing though I was only ten feet from him. This is how it should be in world at large.

Noise-Silence (2)

Noise should not be thought of as a break in silence. Neither is silence an absence of noise. For even in the most silent of silences, there is still sound. Go into a dry cave and sit down: you can hear silence. Maybe it is the sound of molecules of air on the eardrums or perhaps it is just the sound of one's own hearing system. Just by going places, it can never be escaped from. But on the interior journey this subtle sound can be used as something to be aware of when outside noises fade away, and even "head-noises" have been stilled. As concentration improves, though, it is necessary to recognize this sound as impermanent, subject to variation, arising and passing away. It should not be clung to as "holy vibrations." Even that sound must be let go of. Then what is there?

Mindfulness

When *bhikkhus* or Buddhist monks walk on almsround, they do it barefoot. One goes much more silently, and of course it emphasizes non-possession and renunciation. The other day, coming back from my alms-gathering, I was climbing to the brow of a hill, taking the shortcut back to my hut. It had been raining and blowing for several days and the ground was littered with dead twigs and branches, so it was necessary to be careful where the bare feet were placed. Suddenly, one of the grey smooth eucalypt branchlets looked different. Only three feet away, I stopped and gazed at it.

Half a minute went by. Then the branch shot off into the grass at the side of the track. A young brown snake dozing in the sun. Quite poisonous. Good for mindfulness though!

Empire-building

We stake our claims. We make our fences. "Inside that belongs to me—I can do, more or less, what I like with it." Though the human world may agree to respect our ownership, there are many nonhumans who will not; they may have their own boundaries, and they may not recognize ours. And the more boundaries we put up, the larger our frontiers and the more extensive our possessions, the more we are forced to "defend" our empire. The words of the Buddha come to mind:

> "Thus it is that dependent on feeling there is craving, on this is dependent seeking, on this, gaining; on this, discriminative thought; on this, desire and passion; on this, tenacity; on this, possessiveness; on this, avarice; on this, guarding; and many evil, unwholesome things come into being such as resorting to sticks and weapons, quarrels, brawls, disputes, recriminations, malice and false speech—all this is dependent on guarding—thus these many evil, unwholesome things come into being."

A case in point is our meditation hall. Even that has to be defended against the onslaught of various small beings. On the hottest summer days the stink-ants go mad. You can see them climbing everywhere with a remarkable frenzy. Now ants and meditators don't agree well. The former like movement and like to move unmoving bodies, while the latter prefer stillness. Because of this the brick pillars under the hall must be wrapped with lamp-oil soaked rags to deter the ants and even then they find cunning ways to get in. They do not at all recognize the human boundaries there, and think that mining meditators' sweat and flesh is quite legitimate.

But when autumn comes, the ants quieten down while the local black rat population gets busy. They like to make themselves a snug den before winter comes. Then meditation cushions are in danger of their contents being taken (and even the canopy above the main Buddha-image is chewed). Human beings, rather aggressive animals on the whole, do not like any other species challenging their primacy—so do away with the rats, or whatever. But the trouble is not the rats; it is the empire-making which the Buddha calls "mine-making." Whenever this body is regarded as "mine" there is trouble, particularly when it shows how it is not-mine by disease, decay and death. How much more when other "possessions" are so regarded. More possessions means more trouble—unless one changes the mine-making mind.

Obsessions

After the forenoon meal, the last in a Buddhist monk's day, the alms bowl of grey is washed and then dried in the sun's heat for a few minutes. In that time, or even before that while the meal is still on, the March flies come buzzing and settle on the warm grey iron. They feed on blood, yet they walk slowly and perhaps in a rather puzzled way over the iron's hot surface, feeling it with their forelegs and trying vainly to insert their proboscis. They have quite an obsession with dark coloured things it seems. Could it be that they associate this colour with the gray fur of the local rock wallabies? Though a human being with plenty of blood sits nearby, they are not interested in him but return again and again to the hard grey, bloodless iron. If we pity them for their ignorance, what shall we say of more intelligent humans who though they get no happiness, only frustration, out of obsessions, yet return to them again and again. And the worst of that is that the obsessions become stronger each time they are returned to. To use another illustration for this: when someone goes for a walk in the miles of bush around here, he will leave almost no trace. Only a very good tracker could say, "A person has been this way." The bushes close behind, the wiry grasses and sedges spring into place again. But suppose a person begins to go the same way every day. At first, there will be just a little trampling and flattening; later a path is made. And a track may appear there still later as bushes are slashed for human convenience. It may even become a road or a superhighway, given time and development. It is the same in the mind. There too, pathways can be worn … habit patterns set up. And these also become wider and easier to use as they get more traffic. The Buddha cautions one not to make the pathways of greed, hatred and delusion stronger than they are already, for such mental paths are easy to fall into and they lead downwards to deterioration. The pathways of unwholesomeness can become obsessions, and then where do they lead but to misery?

— §§§ —

Radical Buddhism and Other Essays

Leonard Price

Bodhi Leaves No. 92

First published: 1982

Radical Buddhism

Buddhism comes West as a vast body of teaching, and we who receive it are often awed by its abundance, its complexity, and its subtlety. Where is the centre, the real thing we should fix on? Or is there a real thing at all to be apprehended? History shows that Buddhism can and will accommodate itself to new cultures, and will flourish according to the perceptiveness and energy of its new adherents. Now in the West our perceptiveness and energy are put to the test to grasp the "real thing" by which this religion lives—its radicalism.

The Buddhas only point the way, and the way they point is a difficult one through the perfection of morality, concentration, and wisdom to the freedom from suffering called Nibbāna. It is a way of action. A path is useless without the will to follow it, and good intentions alone are futile. To make the journey, the roots of mental defilement must be torn out entirely; the old illusions we live by must be shattered; the mind must seek the light. It is a radical way, because the Buddha enjoins us to give up what is before, give up what is behind, and give up what is in between. Then and only then will the wheel of birth-and-death be knocked from its axis.

Those of us in the jaded and desperate West who hear the resonance of truth in the teachings of the Buddha must hear also that urging to act, to start an inner rebellion against our ancient sloth and stupidity. Yet the more we ponder, the more we recognize the enormity of the task, and an understandable reaction is to set about re-defining just what has to be done and just how prudent it might be to fling ourselves into action. The danger here—so typical in our comfortable and seductive society—is to forget the radical imperative of suffering and try to make over Buddhism into a tame amalgam of platitudes suitable for pleasant contemplation—praising it in order to avoid practicing it. Indeed, Buddhism is rational, patient, deep in wisdom, but should we then just bask in its reflected light?

Complacency is death. If, out of custom and timidity, Western Buddhists turn their religion into a museum piece, or worse, a hobby, they lose the essence. It is easy enough to settle for an undemanding status quo, a modicum of calm, a pleasant sense of harmonious living, and it is easy enough to postpone or forget any effort to break the shackles of old delusion, believing that one need not strain when the road will likely be long. But in accommodating too much to personal or societal expediency we cheapen our ideals and slide further from the disturbing implications of the Noble Truth of Suffering. We may even take the Buddhist vision of *kamma* as an indication that "everything is as it should be." But everything is not as it should be. Everything is in fact miserable. If we are complacent we blind ourselves, and there is no safety in blindness.

In the radical view of the Buddha, *saṃsāra* is no cosmic merry-go-round, but a terrible juggernaut of birth and death dragging beings through endless cycles of woe. "Free yourselves!" says the Buddha. All lives and events are variations on the theme of suffering. All are without substance, endurance, permanence—merely a web of emptiness, void upon void. The "self" that everyone spends so much time defending and nurturing is pure fiction. "Dismiss it," says the Buddha. The world will not conform to our wishes and to presume otherwise is folly; the disciple must cease clinging to it and proceed along the path to the end of suffering. The root problem is craving, and the radical solution is the destruction of craving through wisdom.

The sober truths taught by the Buddha, squarely faced, present us with problems and choices. Are we to assume that every Buddhist ought to be off grunting in a cave, sweating his way toward enlightenment? Is this the radical conclusion? Actually, the dilemma is not so formidable. The Buddha taught gradually, according to the capacity of his hearers to understand and practice. Every person should devote himself to the teaching as far as he is able. The goal is ultimately the same for all, though progress along the path depends on the individual. The Dhamma of the Buddha will lead us to the safety of Nibbāna, and it will also sustain us along the way. What matters is always to bear in mind where we are and where we are headed.

The radicalism of the Buddha is probably no more difficult for Westerners to comprehend than for anyone else, yet we are especially concerned with it now, because the teaching is only just now settling into our culture and its future direction is uncertain. It is a critical time for the religion. The fundamental teachings must not be neglected, lest we take to wearing our religion like warm slippers and doze into mediocrity. Understood rightly, the Noble Truths are profoundly disturbing. They compel us to act, to pursue the ideal of emancipation no matter how difficult the journey appears. Buddhism truly goes against the stream of the world and demands an uncommon vigour of the disciple. How well we respond depends on individual choice and ability, but what matters most is the recognition that a response is called for, that a path does exist, and that the goal can be achieved.

Understanding the basic teachings, Western Buddhists should be wary of tendencies to turn Buddhism into an instrument of secular reform, or a philosophical playground, or an esoteric hobby. Before all else, there is suffering and the path to the end of suffering. There is no safety in faddishness, complacency, or the compulsive intellectualism that hungers for truth but eats the menu instead of the dinner.

To reach the truth, to reach deliverance, we are told to give up what is before, give up what is behind, and give up what is in between. The essence of Buddhism is to let go of everything, to cease clinging desperately to transient, woeful, empty phenomena. The disciple who acts on this breathtaking advice may find the bottom dropping out of this fictitious world. So be it! Thus begins the journey.

The Baited Hook

Though seldom stated in so many words, a cherished belief of all human beings is that happiness lies in the satisfaction of our desires. All our actions are usually predicated on this seemingly self-evident fact. We are devoted to obtaining the objects of our desire; we consider it our right, our duty, and indeed our highest aspiration to get what we want, to obtain what we think will bring us enjoyment, satisfaction, or "fulfilment." We are accustomed to asking one another, "What do you want out of life?" believing that if we can settle on some clear vision of happiness, and go after it, then all will be well.

Unfortunately, experience has a way of overturning our theories. Those manifold objects we yearn for prove troublesome to capture; when captured they yield less pleasure than expected; when held onto they decay and cause us grief. Then we are driven to turn for relief toward other enticements and thereby renew the cycle. Somehow we believe that if only this search for gratification is conducted correctly, if only the right objects are selected, if only we can have a little luck to add to our efforts, then we can certainly attain that permanent happiness that now eludes us. Badly thumped by fortune, we doggedly tell ourselves, "Yes, it's worth all the pain," and turn a swollen eye toward fresh delights.

But is it worth all the pain? Consider a succulent worm bobbing just below the surface of a pond, attracting the attention of a hungry fish. In a flash the fish swallows the worm, only to discover the hidden hook, the barb that rips into its innards and causes it terror, suffering, and ultimately death. The worm is attractive, but it delivers little satisfaction to the fish. Such is the nature of sense pleasures. Those objects of eye, ear, nose, tongue, body, and mind that we find so alluring are more likely to cause us misery than happiness, and the surprising truth is that it is not so much our choice of objects that is at fault, but the mere act of choosing in the first place, since all phenomena of this world are in reality flawed, connected to suffering, and unreliable.

According to the Buddha, true happiness is not to be found in the deceptive sense-pleasures of the world—not in wine or wealth or roses. No matter how hard we try, we can never reach security as long as we persist in wrong views of the desirability of this or that sensual object. Without a clear understanding of the nature of phenomena our search is doomed from the outset. Our first task must be to confront the facts that the universe does not exist for our amusement and that such pleasures as we customarily derive from it are false, impermanent, and unworthy of our interest. While the Buddha does not deny the existence of enjoyment in world, he points out that all worldly pleasure is bound up with suffering, inseparable from suffering, and sure to give way to suffering. Therefore in embracing the pleasant we cannot help but embrace the unpleasant. Our craving prevents us from realizing these facts by continually projecting a false appearance on the world, convincing us that the tempting objects around us can actually be possessed and squeezed dry of some satisfying essence. Without the intervention of wisdom, craving will keep us running from one disappointment to another. Though we have many times taken the bait of sense-pleasure and suffered the inevitable pull of the hook, each new worm that comes wiggling through the water excites the heedless man.

The Buddha teaches that the solution to the terrible union of pleasure and pain is not to struggle hopelessly to split them apart, but to view the whole contaminated mass with detachment. All phenomena share the same characteristics of impermanence, unsatisfactoriness, and unsubstantiality, so it is futile to single out some objects for liking and others for loathing. The whole cast of mind that sees things in terms of liking-and-loathing must be abandoned in favour of the detached observation called "mindfulness." Clearly, if the bait hides a hook we do best to curb our appetites.

Forsaking attachment to sense-pleasures is a logical application of the Four Noble Truths, yet even among those who subscribe to the teachings of the Buddha there can be found a deep-seated reluctance to move from theory to practice. The hold which craving has over our minds is so tenacious that we tend to straddle the abyss between truth and illusion, hoping to live in both with some fast philosophical footwork. For example, may we not propose that sense-pleasures are not in themselves harmful and may therefore be enjoyed in moderation? We may propose it, but we are apt to justify thereby any craving that enters our heads. As long as one regards any experience as personal or desirable, one remains mired in ignorance. There are pleasant, unpleasant, and neutral feelings arising in the mind; they come and they go; they are to be observed, not sought after, because it is such seeking or craving that sustains the round of suffering.

Another common notion is that Buddhism may be employed to beautify life by making the individual more appreciative of the "harmony" of the universe. This is false on two counts. Firstly the

Buddha did not aim to put a pleasing, comforting face on things, but to educate the individual to the ultimate worthlessness of suffering-dominated, conditioned existence. Secondly, the only "harmony" discernible here and now is the implacable and impersonal law of cause and effect—not the blissful oneness beloved of poets.

A third erroneous notion is that sense-pleasures may be pursued full speed if they are part of worthy efforts and worthy goals. This is a self-serving rationalization. While mundane aspirations may be quite wholesome in conception, as long as they provide a surreptitious vehicle for craving they are flawed. For the proper development of insight one needs to get rid of the idea of an ego or self that enjoys, possesses, and appropriates. The noble-minded man is detached from both ego and world. He acts for the welfare of himself and others without thought of reward or gratification. He is indifferent to results; he is not swayed by the pleasant and the unpleasant.

In considering the lure and danger of sense-pleasures, it is not difficult to see that most of us will ultimately defend our indulgences, not from logic but from the blind urge, "I want." What harm, we reason, can there be in a little innocent delight? To clarify: the harm lies not in the sensation but in the deluded mind that fastens onto the sensation and clings to it obsessively. What behoves the diligent Buddhist is to get beyond the whole idea of liking and disliking, to set it aside, to cease entertaining it—in order to advance to the fruitful fields of direct insight.

Suppose then, that we acknowledge the danger of the baited hook and agree that the restless, craving mind is a source of suffering. What do we do about it? Often we complain, "I can't help myself! I know it's dangerous but I can't help it." Anyone who has tried to oppose his own ravenous appetites for pleasure, amusement, or gratification knows this sense of helplessness. A mind long accustomed to grasping is not dissuaded by mere rational arguments; it goes its own way, chewing up one experience after another in a hopeless search for happiness. So what is to be done? The trouble here, as is so often the case, is one of self-deception. Although we may say we understand the danger of sensual obsession and the advantage of restraint, our weakness shows that in fact we do not. Wisdom is simply incompatible with defilement. As long as we are willing to compromise with our obsessions we have not fully understood the Buddha's teaching about the nature of reality. We may recognize intellectually that craving and clinging lead to suffering, but we have not penetrated to a direct experience of the truth. Much work remains to be done; we can't simply throw up our hands and plead weakness.

If we truly recognize the hazards of succumbing to the baited hook, we must resist its enticements. Yet the Buddha does not recommend a stubborn, stoical self-abnegation. The disciple must deal with the problem intelligently. Escape from suffering does not depend on obliterating or denying sense-pleasures but on seeing them for what they are through the systematic practice of mindfulness. In ordinary life we are generally too caught up in gaining and losing to give sufficient attention to the elements and dynamics of the process. We are borne along on these ancient waves only because of compulsive habit. To stop our headlong career it is essential to develop and apply mindfulness, to cultivate scrupulous attention toward even the most mundane habits and desires. Steady mindfulness, intensified in meditation, reveals that the mind is a ceaseless torrent of thoughts, feelings, perceptions, and mental impressions—never still for an instant, never stable enough to be considered substantial or enduring. What we loosely term the "external" world is likewise a blur of evanescent phenomena, all changing with incredible speed, arising and vanishing with no beginning or end in sight. Where then is the object that is truly desirable? Gone! Lost to view in the instant. Where is the one who desires? Gone! Thought succeeds thought, effect succeeds cause in a tumble of empty foam, with a desiring "self" nowhere to be found. Mindfulness discerns these truths directly, examining and breaking down experience until the "permanent" is understood as impermanent, until the "pleasant" is understood as unsatisfactory, until the "self" is understood as empty and unreal.

As with all of the truths taught by the Buddha, these three characteristics of existence must be realized through direct insight—not just through the ruminations of the intellect. The practice of mindfulness can lead us to such insight if we undertake the task with patience and impartiality. One who luxuriates in craving will remain twisting between misunderstood suffering and imagined pleasure, but one who recognizes danger will shun the baited hook and seek the bare facts of reality beneath the dazzling magic show of the senses.

By avoiding the baited hook of sense-pleasures we do not, as is sometimes maintained, rob life of all its joy. On the contrary, we abandon false satisfaction and approach the true happiness that is born of freedom. We take worldly enjoyment in moderation keeping it in perspective. The wise disciple does not dwell in gloom and try to see the bad side of every experience. If it is pleasant, he notes it as pleasant; if it is unpleasant, he notes it as unpleasant; if it is neutral, he notes it as neutral. Whatever its appearance, he regards it with mindfulness and does not cling to it. He enjoys life simply as he finds it. In so doing, he escapes the peril of hook and line and swims freely toward the end of suffering.

Again and again the Buddha exhorts his followers to be mindful, because the world is burning with greed, hatred, and delusion. Freedom can be won, but not by the careless, infatuated person. The one who attains freedom will be the one who has mindfulness, energy, and the courage to see the canker in the rose.

Meeting the Buddha, Alone, on the Empty Shore

A veneer of credulity and feeble optimism covers the dark preoccupations of our lives. In an age marked everywhere with signs of spiritual decay, we somehow remain ever entranced by new toys, ever receptive to the latest balderdash from noisy charlatans, and ever ready to abandon the present moment for the lure of the next. Let it be rumoured that "self-fulfilment" has been glimpsed in somebody's book or therapy or religion, and immediately a cloud of dust obscures the sun as we stampede into the new territory—only to find ourselves, puzzlingly, still in the same dull company. Do we really want happiness, or only titillation? It's hard to say, because we rarely sit still long enough to examine the matter. Suspecting dimly that life is treacherous, we keep moving fast to avoid calamity.

If we are credulous, we are no less sceptical. We are quick to believe but find belief intolerable. We topple today's idols and from their fragments eagerly assemble tomorrow's. We pace up and down the shores of doubt, rousing one another with shouts of encouragement, but stepping into the river we find the water cold, and promptly conclude there's a better crossing further down.

The water is always cold. Somebody sees a vision over the horizon, and the chilled troops waste no more time at this spot. In our solitary reflections we may notice our inconstancy and regretfully wonder, "Has it always been thus?" If we are Buddhists we are bound to answer, "Yes." This endlessly mutable landscape of disappointment, this lurch and halt of conviction, is called *saṃsāra*. We are accustomed to regarding the "cycle of birth and death" as a remote, cosmic scheme of creation and dissolution. In fact, *saṃsāra* whirls with cyclonic force here in the prosaic moment, here in the wavering and furtive mind. If this is, that is. Out of ignorance rises craving; out of craving rises the whole mass of anxiety and suffering. We deceive ourselves even in our desire for happiness. Our pursuit of pleasure or "self-fulfilment" is also a flight from despair. Uneasy with the deteriorating present, we leap with unseemly greed toward the future, which, fictitious creature that it is, soon fails us and leaves us exactly where we were. The great wheel turns, and has turned, and will turn again.

Freedom from *saṃsāra* does not spring from finding the right teacher or the right temple or the right style of meditations. We must instead begin by discarding false expedients, brief enthusiasms, fashions, platitudes, and most of all, excuses. Self-excuse is just grease for the wheel. Ah, we sigh, if only we had met the Buddha in person! Vain foolishness, this. The Buddha was never to be found in six feet of flesh. In his time and in ours he is only seen in the destruction of the defilements, in the giving up of excuses, evasions, and wilful blindness. If we earnestly strive to distinguish between the false and the true, the shallow and the profound, the path of the Buddha takes shape before us.

But after so many years of quick credulity and quicker doubt, of lukewarm and ambivalent effort, how can we make it across that cold, lonely river of ignorance? If we divest ourselves of false and trivial comforts shall we not be left naked? Indeed we shall. And it is in precisely that condition that we may encounter the Buddha. Buddhism is, after all, a religion of renunciation—renunciation of wrong thoughts, wrong speech, and wrong deeds. When we give up our shabby illusions and the manifold hiding places of the mind we find ourselves naked and ready for the first time to see the world without distortion. Whereas before we may have nominally accepted the reality of impermanence, suffering, and non-self, now we may begin to discern these truths directly and realize our predicament. The old cliché, "The Buddhas only point the way," strikes us with fresh significance. Buddhism demands that we help ourselves, and here on the long, empty shore where we have so often wandered we may at last appreciate the task ahead.

The world around us may be crass and wicked, but not so crass and wicked as our own deluded minds. We feast on the bones of cynicism and are not satisfied. We give new names to iniquity and pursue it in shadows. We mistake the pleasant for the good and perennially follow the easiest course. Then in our accidental nights of fear we stare in bafflement at the four walls and ask ourselves, "Haven't I tried?" Silence replies with silence, and there's nothing left for us but to blunder after a new ghost of happiness, and thereby give the wheel of *saṃsāra* another spin.

Credulity is not faith, nor is scepticism wisdom. The noble follower of the Buddha proceeds with a balanced mind, considering the world as he finds it, shunning the harmful and welcoming the useful. He crosses the flood of *saṃsāra* on the raft of Dhamma, knowing that nobody will make the effort for him. What distinguishes such a person from his fellows is not necessarily brilliance of mind, but plain and simple perseverance, the resolve to follow the true course no matter how long it may take. We can do likewise if we set ourselves firmly on the path.

Delay is the luxury of ignorance. We commonly suppose Nibbāna, the ultimate purity and freedom, to be something infinitely far away and terrifically difficult to reach. We think of the Buddha as long departed. But Nibbāna is near for those who would have it near, and the Buddha is as close as true Dhamma truly observed. What is required of us is to let go of our crumbling, mortal toys and to come down, alone, to the long shore of renunciation. In that exhilarating solitude we may meet the Buddha, whose body is wisdom, whose face is compassion, and whose hand points out the waypoints directly to the deep and hidden purity in our hearts.

April and November

Early spring is a fitting time to consider death, though few of us, alas, appreciate this healthy practice. When the first crocuses and skunk cabbage blunder into the sunshine, the conventional mind waxes bold and brave and salutes the regeneration of the world. We have won through once more, we've got another chance, we shall dawdle barefooted in gardens. Gone is the dark time, the emphatically dead winter of land and heart. We are, surely, about to participate in the general leafiness of things. The gurgling pigeons in the park—formerly wretched pests—excite our fine feelings of sympathy. We are magnanimous at seventy degrees. We have great expectations.

Legions of us swarm the sidewalks with uplifted chins, celebrating what we had no part in making. But there's a certain self-deception here. If the sun burns more beneficently these days is it any of our doing? If it shut down altogether would we be consulted? We may fancy ourselves philosophers improvising on the rhapsody of spring, but we display, in the main, scarcely more independence than the pigeons. We are seduced by the flowers April throws our way and esteem ourselves wise for having noted they are pretty. We find in the loveliness of the season not a theme for true reflection but only a licence for yearning. We indulge without compunction, believing that we are in accord with the sacred law of the moment, when really we continue to flee the present moment and lust for the unborn fixture—some garden of promise yet to bloom.

Better we should turn our minds to dissolution and death— right now in the brilliant season. Any fellow of sound faculties can stroll through late November and remark the transience of vital forces. Ah, withered grass, leaden skies, brief span of happiness! He is moved—having, as he thinks, come to terms with mortality. The same fellow, come the daffodils, is warbling about youth and beauty. But where is the brave heart who sees deeply in spring the bud dying to the flower, the flower to the fruit? Where is he who at close of the year regards the snow-bitten rose and is not cast down? Where is he who lives serenely in fair times and foul? All things shall pass not only in black November but in pastel April as well— a lapsing without pause, a continual perishing of the dear, the unlovely, and the indifferent. Nature suffers no moratorium on decay; it unrolls itself in seasons that we with our predilections for warmth and light, habitually misunderstand, finding gloom this month and gaiety in that.

To dote on April is to despise November. We are caught up in liking and disliking, taking a sip of truth when we can't avoid it and spitting it out at the first opportunity, living tentatively like wine-tasters. We ride the seasons on and ever on to the sweet, cruel music of hope, while the world burns because of us, because we've lit it with the torch of delusion. Should we not now starve the fire to coolness and let be the race of forms we call our life? Change sweeps all forms away, and no one can find peace in his time who does not attend to this universal moving-on.

So then, it is spring and the bluebirds are twittering. Shall we pick our scabs and visit graveyards? Of course not. Let us go on breathing; if the air is sweet, why then, it is sweet. If the rain blows off and the sun slants warm through the willow tree, so be it. Let us sit on the porch and be alive. No need to scourge ourselves or sleep on gravel. No need to curse winter or praise spring. They come and go independently of us: dead grass, dragonflies, thunderstorms, and snow—what scene should we prefer when all are flowing? Reality cannot be seized; it arises when the mind stops grasping. He who lets go is he who is established. He lives in all seasons but serves none.

The Heart Awakened

Three Essays

Eileen Siriwardhana

Bodhi Leaves No. 93

First published: 1982

Muditā

Muditā means appreciative joy at the success and good fortune of others. Evaluation of achievement is a precursor to *muditā,* and appreciation a component of *muditā*. Seeing the good in others and learning to recognise and admire what good there is, is what *muditā* tacitly implies. Laughter and exhilaration are not characteristics of *muditā. Muditā* is joy and appreciation flowing quietly out of the core of one's heart towards others like the waters from a spring flowing outwards from the bowels of the earth. Spontaneous and sincere participation in another's glorious hour is possible only when the quality of *muditā* is developed to its fullest. Genuine joy in the prosperity of others is indeed a rare quality.

The virtue of *muditā* may be best noticed at work in the joy of parents over the success of their offspring, and in the genuine ecstasy of teachers over the success of their pupils, particularly in the latter situation when the threat of the younger eclipsing the older is always imminent. While it is easy to practise *muditā* within the narrow circle of one's family and friends, to identify oneself with the joys and triumphs of outsiders requires deliberate effort. Yet the capacity for doing so is rooted in man's nature. Smiling faces of adults make children respond readily with their own smiles. This potential in the child should be nurtured and activated by parents and educationists. For the seed of *muditā* planted early in a child will grow and blossom and bear fruit in his adolescence and in his adult life. To some extent, man is a product of his environment—with this in mind, adults, parents, teachers and wardens who handle children should be of a cheerful disposition and an appreciative nature.

> If a child lives with criticism,
> He learns to condemn;
>
> If a child lives with hostility
> He learns to fight;

If a child lives with ridicule,
He learns to be shy;

If a child lives with jealousy
He learns to feel guilty;

If a child lives with tolerance,
He learns to be patient;

If a child lives with encouragement,
He learns confidence;

If a child lives with praise,
He learns to appreciate;

If a child lives with fairness,
He learns justice;

If a child lives with security;
He learns to have faith;

If a child lives with approval,
He learns to like himself;

If a child lives with acceptance and friendship
He learns to find love in the world.

Latent in man are both noble characteristics as well as vicious tendencies. It is strange that the vices latent in man seem almost natural and spontaneous, whereas the dormant virtues have to be brought to the surface with great effort. As one advances in years, activating and developing the potential of *muditā* becomes more and more difficult—though not impossible. Seeds will not take root in hard and crusty soil. One has to loosen and soften the soil if one expects shoots from seeds. In children the heart is tender and seeds planted therein will take root early and grow fast. So the best time to activate and develop the positive and saintly tendencies which lie dormant in every human being is during the tender years. When a child receives praise and approbation, he will naturally learn to give it to others for he knows the joy of recognition and appreciation.

Envy and jealousy are the chief opponents of *muditā*, or appreciative joy. These noxious qualities arise partly out of a lack of confidence in one's achievements and one's capacity to achieve. Dislike, boredom—nuances of the Pali term *arati*—may be considered as enemies of *muditā*. The opposite sterling virtues which can vanquish these enemies are loving kindness, *mettā*, and compassion, *karuṇā*. *Muditā* is placed third in the listing of the *brahma vihāras*, for *muditā* is the natural outcome of the two preceding benign mental states. *Mettā* and *karuṇā* are the forces that urge one to alleviate the sufferings of others with purely altruistic motives, expecting nothing in return—not even gratitude. What matters to the Buddhist is the little bit of joy he has brought to another's heart by relieving him of even a little bit of sorrow, of suffering. Little do people realise how a kind word, a warm smile, a loving touch can act as a balm to a sorrow-laden heart. We can now see how *muditā* becomes a natural result of *mettā* and *karuṇā*.

Too often people are much more ready to sympathise with the misfortunes of others than to rejoice with them in their good fortune. Where is a definition of a friend: "What are friends? Are they not dear sweet people who abuse you behind your back and take an inward deep pleasure in hearing of your faults and misfortunes?" We have to take ourselves to task whenever we recognise these psychological perversities within us, and with great effort try to eradicate these unwholesome tendencies which seem to be deep-rooted.

We have to be honest with ourselves and look within. Whenever traces of envy or jealousy enter our hearts, we should recognise the emotion as one which is unwholesome. We should also make an effort not to let it take hold of us. Let us ask this question: Why are we envious? Because someone possesses something we do not. Why do we not have that which we want, that which would give us joy? The answer lies in our own *kamma*. In the light of the Buddha Dhamma no one is to blame but ourselves. The greatest sorrow for a woman is the inability to bear a child. Why accumulate more bad *kamma* by envying those who have children? Unwholesome states of mind such as hatred and anger are said to be the causes of infertility. So why promote such a state in a future birth too by continuing that evil train of thought? This line of thinking, of arguing, needs very great effort. It is not easy. That is why the Buddha praised effort, *viriya*, as a noble virtue. "If it were not possible to do good I would not tell you to," said the Buddha. This mode of thinking helps to eradicate delusion—*moha*. The source of all unwholesome *kamma* is ignorance of *moha*. When the veil of *moha* is lifted, one sees clearly that craving is the source of all sorrows. Craving gives rise to jealousy, envy, covetousness, avarice, greed— all enemies of *muditā*.

Let the fertile woman not look down upon her less fortunate sister who is denied the great joy of motherhood. Let not the one endowed with beauty scorn her plain-looking sister. Let not the wealthy insult the poor. After all, we must remember that this earthly existence is but a short sojourn in our journey through *saṃsāra*. The Buddha says there is no one on earth who has not in a previous existence been a mother, a father, a sister, a brother, a child to us. So let us suffuse the whole world with *mettā*, with *karuṇā* and with *muditā*. This is why the *brahma vihāras* are described as *appamaññā*—illimitables (all embracing). They are so-called because they find no barrier or limit. They embrace all living beings.

Jealousy can poison a man's system, mar his character, and ruin his social relationships. And what is life but a series of relationships? It is only in death that we are alone. Today jealousy and greed for power have poisoned the mind of the world. We now witness jealousy on a global scale. We are destroying each other and our home—the earth. The situation at the present is so very grave that we can no longer talk of individuals or groups or nations. We have to speak for Earth. Carl Sagan, the eminent astronomer, exasperated by the wanton destruction of our beautiful little planet and its resources asks, "Who speaks for Earth?" The practise of *muditā* never seemed to be as important as in the present day. The forces of evil seem to have been unleashed in full measure in human hearts the world over.

Advances in science and technology have been of immense value to man's material progress and development, but the negative by-products of this progress are truly frightening. Destruction of natural resources, pollution, unhealthy rivalry and dangerous competition have reached such colossal proportions that life on earth is threatened. Discoveries and inventions in the fields of science and technology should be for a better and more comfortable life. But now many of those discoveries' are a threat to life itself. It is indeed depressing that the irony of this situation is not considered with sufficient concern. The ills of the world are insidiously increasing so that there is a growing sense of cosmic gloom and defeatism.

Man's predicament as perceived by the modern poet, George Barker, is embodied in the following words:

When will men again
Lift irresistible fists
Not bend from ends
But each man lift men
Nearer again.

Many men mean
Well: but tall walls
Impede, their hands bleed and
They fall, their seed the
Seed of the fallen.

See here the fallen
Stooping over stones, over their
Own bones, but all
Stooping doom beaten.

Whom the noonday wishes
Whole, whom the heavens compel,
And to whom pass immaculate messages,
When will men again
Lift irresistible fists
Impede impediments
Leap Mountains,
Laugh at Walls?

Looking on, dejected and dispirited, is not the solution. We have to struggle to save ourselves and our planet. This is why institutions like the United Nations Assembly exist. Though satisfactory results may not always be forthcoming, the fact that while a section is destroying, inventing weapons of hate, another section of mankind is arguing, demonstrating, petitioning for peace. As long as such forces opposing evil are in existence, there is hope. This means that there is still sympathy and love in men's hearts for their fellow beings. So we must be hopeful. Conflict is eternal; conflict is natural. Conflict helps us to rediscover lost values. We must not see only hatred in conflict. Conflict is the natural prerequisite of a satisfactory solution.

A section of the world today is enveloped by the thick veil of delusion. Hence their inability to see the truth. Failure to perceive the Truth is delusion. So it is with persistent effort and enduring patience that those who wish to be noble and serviceable must sublimate themselves and serve humanity, both by example and by precept. The cultivation of *muditā* and the practise of this virtue can relieve humanity of the suffering it has brought upon itself. Those with right understanding must by personal example work out salvation for themselves and for their fellow beings.

Diligent practise of *muditā* will make a person more amenable, flexible, and understanding. He will learn to live outside himself. He will experience a new kind of happiness, the joy of sharing. This virtue will elevate him to eradicate the cankers of jealousy and egoistic craving; "We" and "ours" will be substituted for "me and "mine." Wholesome camaraderie will build up, and he will gradually embrace the whole world with loving kindness—*sabbe sattā bhavantu sukhitattā*. The ego will gradually disintegrate, and he will gain insight into *anattā*, the Buddha's central doctrine. The fetters of attachment to self will break first, and with it all other fetters of attachment, which will lead him gradually toward renunciation.

The Buddha advocates the sharing not only of material resources, but of spiritual resources as well. The transferring of merit to our dear departed ones is a truly beautiful sharing. Our loved ones who are no more with us physically feel such a sense of joy in the thought that they are not forgotten; the joy that accrues to them by our enlightened acts is *anumodana*.

Mankind is on the eve of a nuclear war. Sure and certain destruction will be the fate of the human race if war breaks out. Now is the hour to muster benign forces within the human heart on a global scale. The virtues of *mettā, karuṇā, muditā* and *upekkhā* must be practised to combat the degrading forces of greed and hatred which cause dangerous divisions. Once the sparks of divinity in men's hearts are released, all divisions of creed, colour, religion and race will recede into insignificance. Then only one creed will be in evidence: the creed of humanity. So let us activate, cultivate, and develop the sublime qualities—*brahma vihāras*. These powers hidden within the human heart are yet untapped, yet it is through these powers that humanity can be saved. This seems to be the way—the only way out of the present entanglement.

> "The inner tangle and the outer tangle—
> This generation is entangled in a tangle.
> And so I ask Gotama this question:
> Who succeeds in disentangling this tangle?"

The answer of the enlightened One given centuries ago embodies the solution to the present tangle. It is, in fact, the answer to every generation—past, present, future. "He who succeeds," says the Buddha, "in disentangling this tangle, is the wise man, established well in virtue, who has developed consciousness and understanding."

Mettā

Mettā is a sincere wish for the welfare and genuine happiness of all beings, without exception. It means that which softens one's heart—a friendly disposition. "Just as a mother protects her only child even at the risk of her own life, even so should one cultivate loving kindness towards all living beings." It is not the passionate love of the mother that is stressed here, but her sincere selfless wish for a genuine welfare of her child.

Mettā transcends all boundaries of caste, class, race and religion. It is limitless in size and range (*appamaññā*); it has no barriers, no discriminations.

Think of the number of instances during a day when your actions are coloured by discrimination. When your unfortunate servant boy accidentally breaks an article, you shout at him. When your own child does it, you tolerate it. That servant boy is also somebody's child who, through bad *kamma*, has come under your roof to do your menial work—to do your bidding.

When you strike a blow across your dog's back for trampling your flower bed, do you realise the unwholesome state of your mind at the moment of such action? You may even be a person who recites the *gāthā*s and the *sutta*s, who goes to the temple, who observes the Eight Precepts, who listens to sermons, who gives alms. But at the moment of such discriminating actions you have turned away from the Dhamma.

At some time you may bide the time, waiting for an opportunity to take revenge on someone who has slandered you. During that period of waiting—please think of the Buddha. Enact in your mind's eye the story of Ciñcā Māṇavikā or the courtesan Sundarī. Then your little embarrassments and heartaches will fade into insignificance.

Mettā is described as a divine state (brahma-vihāra) which cannot co-exist with anger or hatred.

> "Hatreds never cease through hatreds in this world.
> Through love alone they cease.
> This is an eternal law."
>
> (Dhammapada verse 4)

Goodwill, loving kindness, benevolence and universal love are suggested as the best renderings of the Pali word *mettā*. A point to be clarified here is that *mettā* is not synonymous with ordinary affection. The world cannot exist without mutual affection. Between parents and children, between husbands and wives, between teachers and pupils, between friends, exist varying degrees of affection. This affection is natural, and *mettā* has to be cultivated. A benevolent attitude is the chief characteristic of *mettā*. One who practises *mettā* is constantly interested in promoting the welfare of others—not only in his family and friends. Such a person is sincere when he says: "May all beings be happy."

Another very important point that should be clearly understood is that in exercising *mettā*, do not ignore yourself. How often do you say, "Oh, I got so angry with myself" or "I can never forgive myself"? Some hasty words or actions on your part fill you with resentment towards yourself. Remorse, though a fine corrective, is an extreme form which can bar your progress when indulged in again and again. There are times when you may even make yourself mentally and physically ill. So the most important person to make friends with is yourself.

Remorse, regret, diffidence and hopelessness are negative tendencies the existence of which can never result in a friendly disposition towards oneself. *Mettā* is a positive quality. Unless you feel friendly toward yourself, you cannot be friendly towards others. To the world outside you may appear to be well-disposed towards others and give the impression of possessing a benevolent, magnanimous nature. But be aware of yourself. Be honest with yourself. Honesty is the starting point towards self-purification.

> "To thine own self be true
> And it must follow as the night the day
> Thou canst not be false to any other man."
>
> (Shakespeare)

All men have their frailties. What is meant by making friends with oneself does not mean that we expect to find within ourselves only that which is good and perfect. We talk about understanding people. Let us understand ourselves first. Let us recognise our strong points and feel satisfied about them. Let us recognise our failings, and strive towards lessening or eradicating them.

> "Whoever looks for a friend without imperfections will never find what he seeks."
>
> (Cyrus the Great)

> "A faithful friend is a sturdy shelter.
> He that has found one has found a treasure."
>
> (Sirach 6:14)

> "He who throws away a friend is as bad as he who throws away his life."
>
> (Sophocles)

Let us not throw away our lives by throwing away that friend that is in us.

"I" or "myself" should be the central or starting point. *Mettā* radiates from oneself to others, so it is very important to feel a sense of goodwill, friendliness, well-being towards one-self. This is a subtle point which has to be clearly understood.

The Buddha radiated *mettā* equally towards his adversary Devadatta, Yasodharā his royal wife, and Paṭācārā the demented woman, his royal father King Suddhodana and Sopāka the humble low-caste youth.

Mettā then should be extended towards friend, foe and mere acquaintances alike. The identification of oneself with all beings (*sabbe sattā*), making no difference between oneself and others is the culmination of *mettā*. The ideas of "me" and "mine" are building blocks of barriers. *Mettā* dissolves barriers and loosens all constraints. With the diligent practise of *mettā*, division evaporates and humanism is realised. Such a mind is free from ill will, and this freedom is bliss or *sukha*.

Ill will is the antithesis of *mettā*. Anger, hatred, aversion are related qualities. *Mettā* cannot co-exist with such unwholesome attitudes. Disparaging, condemning and belittling others is possible only through ill will. Pointing out another's faults with the intention of leading him towards good does not mean a lack of *mettā*. Parents, teachers and elders often have to resort to various methods of correction and reform where the young are concerned. But one has to be very watchful when one is engaged in such activity. The motive has to be analysed carefully. Elders sometimes react in anger. At such moments one must question oneself: Was it to avert a disaster to the other that one acted so? Or was it merely giving vent to one's own anger which oppressed one?

A mother who could not convince her son that the path through the jungle was unsafe and that he should take a safer route exclaimed in despair, "May a bear maul you!" The son departed and the mother radiating *mettā* towards her son, hoped and prayed that no harm should befall him. Though the jungle was infested with wild animals, the loving kindness which radiated from the core of the mother's heart towards her son was a weapon against the fierce jungle beasts. *Mettā*, one has to understand, is a powerful weapon against evil—and protects one from many pitfalls in life.

Mettā is a constructive healthy force with the power of combating hostile influences. Just as anger can produce toxic effects on the system, benign thoughts can produce soothing health-bringing physical effects. Many instances in the Buddha's life illustrate the fact that the peaceful thought vibrations of the Buddha produced salutary effects, so much so that the intoxicated elephant Nālāgiri and the wild Aṅgulimāla were completely subdued. The magnetic power of *mettā* is indeed deeply rewarding. *Mettā* has a liberating influence on the one who possesses it and on the one to whom it is extended.

In our day-to-day lives with its trials, tribulations and complexities, the art of being friendly is fast disappearing. We act like automatons. We are so wrapped up in ourselves, in our own affairs, that we hardly think it is necessary to spend time over anything that is not connected directly to ourselves and our affairs.

We must teach our young the value of a friendly disposition. We must do it by example more than by precept. In our homes, in our schools, in our places of work, if this simple quality of friendliness is allowed to pervade the atmosphere, our corner of this earth can be a little haven—a true home.

Let us fill our hearts with *mettā*, and let us make our hearts a home where peace and love and friendship will dwell.

"I read within a poet's book
A word that starred the page:
'Stone walls do not a prison make
Nor iron bars a cage!'
Yes, that is true, and something more,
You'll find wherever you roam
That marble floors and gilded walls
Can never make a home.
But every home where Love abides
And Friendship is a guest
Is surely home, and home sweet home
For there the heart can rest."

(Richard Lovelace)

Getting Hold of Myself

I told myself never to do certain things:
Never to fly into a rage when things have gone wrong,
But something is simmering inside me;
Then I try to get hold of myself
But I can't!

Never moan and lament over loss and disaster,
But something is writhing inside me;
Then I try to get hold of myself
But I can't!

Never be elated over triumphs and victories,
But something is dancing inside me;
Then, too, I try to get hold of myself,
But I can't!

Exasperated,
I try and I strive
But I can't!

I just can't get hold of myself,
Can you?
If you can, please let me know how
Yes, I can.
And you can, too,
If you turn to the Buddha.

"Irrigators lead the waters.
Fletchers bend the shafts.
Carpenters bend the wood.
The wise control themselves."

(Dhp 80)

Just as a water-course is dammed and directed through channels towards a chosen direction, so too the mind must be bent and consciously directed towards good, towards virtue, towards righteousness.

To amass wealth, to dig up the treasures from the bowels of the earth, man makes laborious efforts and spends enormous sums of money, but to dig up the invaluable treasures of the mind, man makes little or no effort. But to make the effort man has first to realise, he has first to understand the mysterious and mighty potentialities hidden within his mind.

On the other hand, if, though well aware of the natural destructive forces within him, man makes little or no effort to curb them, he thereby causes untold misery to himself and to others.

Latent in man are both saintly characteristics and destructive tendencies. It is strange that too often the vices latent in man seem almost natural and spontaneous, whereas the dormant virtues have to be brought to the surface with great effort. It is worth noting that every vice possesses its opposite, a noble virtue which may not appear to be natural and automatic, yet which lies within the range of every person.

And so man lives enveloped in miseries of various types. Man is never happy, never satisfied, always frustrated, always wanting something more, something new. His mind is constantly in turmoil, and the misfortune is that he thinks that this has to be the natural condition common to all. This is delusion, or *moha*.

> "Blind is the world.
> Few are those who clearly see.
> As birds escape from a net,
> few go to the blissful state."

(Udāna)

It is a pity that man does not realise that all these fears, sorrows, phobias and miseries are mind-made—and can be eliminated. A man can live in a constant state of bliss and joy devoid of unnecessary sufferings and live life to its fullest if only he would live the word of the Buddha, for the word of the Buddha embodies peace. This is why the arahats often uttered:

> "Calm in mind,
> Calm in speech,
> Calm in deed,
> who rightly knowing is wholly freed,
> perfectly peaceful and equipoised."

(Dhp 317)

A desert traveller with parched lips and burning soles will be gladdened on hearing that an oasis is not far off. But he will not experience real joy until he tastes its waters with his lips, and dips his soles in the cool waters. In like manner the word of the Buddha gladdens our hearts, but we should not stop until we have tasted the bliss of that noble state which is the panacea, the only panacea, for all the ills of the world.

> "There is no medicine comparable to the Dhamma.
> Taste of it.
> Drink it, O monks."

(Dhp 205)

The Dhamma is to be lived, not merely to be read about or listened to. Listen. Think. Practise.

In our day-to-day lives, in the course of being engaged in our daily chores, we should think of the innumerable times when we have neglected the word of the Buddha. Yet the incense chamber of the Buddha should be created within our hearts, and that fragrance must pervade every thought, every word, every action of our waking life.

"Purify your mind," said the Blessed One. Now think of the numberless unwholesome thoughts that daily pollute the mind. We speak and we act impulsively, rashly. Our words and our actions are often harsh; we cause pain of mind to others, which in turn brings on remorse. A whole train of unwholesome thoughts are unleashed as a result of our inability to control our mind. We get angry. That anger even results in chemical changes in the body which can be injurious to our health, and to the well-being of others. And then we repent for a lifetime a few words uttered impulsively.

So, realising the unhappiness we bring upon ourselves and the suffering we cause others, we must first understand and accept the fact that we are not on the right path. What is the remedy? Do not let the mind drift. Take hold if it. Cultivate it. What is cultivation? It is meditation. It is a process of mind cleansing. What are the steps leading to purification of the mind, which is the heart of the Buddha's message?

1. To know the mind—that is so near to us; and is yet so unknown.
2. To shape the mind—that is unwieldy and obstinate, and yet may turn to pliant.
3. To free the mind—that is in bondage all over, and yet may win freedom here and now[7]

To know the mind one has to watch it from moment to moment. Take a few minutes off your daily chores and sit down in a quiet place and be mindful of your thoughts. Watch carefully the thought processes coursing incessantly through your mind like

7 *The Heart of Buddhist Meditation*, by Nyanaponika Thera, BPS, Kandy

the rising and falling away of the ocean waves, but continuous—in a never-ending flow they arise and they fall away. Recognise each thought as pleasant or unpleasant, as the nature of the thought may be. We have to be honest with ourselves. We must recognise jealousy as jealousy, know it to be unwholesome, cast it aside and substitute its antidote or opposite—which is appreciative joy or *muditā*.

We can gradually increase the period of watching by a few minutes each day. After some time we will find that when watching and perceiving, all shades and nuances of thought pass through our mind. With practise, this process will become automatic, natural and effortless, even while we are engaged in our daily activities. This is as it should be—a very desirable condition for our wellbeing, for then we will be constantly mindful. An action performed with mindfulness will be a skilful action. The result, or *vipāka*, of such action will be pleasant and good. So constantly our mind will be suffused with satisfaction, joy and bliss.

Let us look at a few of the common unwholesome states which too often pollute our minds:

Anger is a destructive vice which can be subdued with loving kindness or *mettā*.

Aggression is another vice that is responsible for much human suffering, errors and atrocities. Its antidote is compassion or *karuṇā*. Jealousy poisons one's system. It has a corroding effect on a person like rust on metal. It will destroy a person. Appreciative joy or *muditā* is the remedy.

There are other universal characteristics that upset the equilibrium of man. They are attachments to the pleasurable and aversion to the non-pleasurable. The opposite force is equanimity, or *upekkhā*, which alone can combat these two subtle but most prevalent defilements ever present in the mind.

Impregnated in the vices mentioned are the germs of a dreaded disease which seems to be taking its toll of many human lives today. Self-destruction, depression, a sense of hopelessness, despair, gloom, pessimism, meaninglessness of life, are some of the symptoms of this dreaded disease which leads to so much unhappiness. The disease is ignorance.

The cure for the disease is the substitution of the opposite virtues for each of the latent vices. This will lead to the recognition of the beauty of life, its worthwhileness, its purposefulness. The substitution of wholesome pleasant thoughts is a recognised form of mental therapy. These virtues tend to elevate man. If cultivated with diligence, man will realise that the earth is such a beautiful place, that human life is noble, and that it is still possible to gain peace for oneself and for others.

The Rebirth of Katsugoro

As reported by

Lafcadio Hearn

Bodhi Leaves No. 94

First published: 1983

The Rebirth of Katsugoro

I

The following is not a story—at least it is not one of my stories. It is only the translation of an old Japanese document—or rather a series of documents—very much signed and sealed, and dating back to the early part of the present (i.e. the 19th) century. Various authors appear to have made use of these documents, especially the compiler of the curious collection of Buddhist stories entitled Bukkyo-hiyakkwazensho, to whom they furnished the material of the twenty-sixth narrative in that work. The present translation, however, was made from a manuscript copy discovered in a private library in Tokyo. I am responsible for nothing beyond a few notes appended to the text.

Although the beginning will probably prove dry reading, I presume to advise the perusal of the whole translation from first to last, because it suggests many things besides the possibility of remembering former births. It will be found to reflect something of the feudal Japan that has passed away, and something of the oldtime faith—not the higher Buddhism, but what is incomparably more difficult for any Occidental to obtain a glimpse of: the common ideas of the people concerning pre-existence and rebirth. And in view of this fact, the exactness of the official investigations, and the credibility of the evidence accepted, necessarily become questions of minor importance.

II

1. *Copy of the Report of Tamon Dempachiro*

The case of Katsugoro, nine years old, second son of Genii, a farmer on my estate, dwelling in the Village called Nakano-mura in the District called Tamagori in the Province of Musashi.

Sometime during the autumn of last year, the above-mentioned Katsugoro, the son of Genzo, told to his elder sister the story of his previous existence and of his rebirth. But as it seemed to be only the fancy of a child, she gave little heed to it. Afterwards, however, when Katsugoro had told her the same story over and over again, she began to think that it was a strange thing, and she told her parents about it.

During the twelfth month of the past year, Genzo himself questioned Katsugoro about the matter, whereupon Katsugoro declared:

> That he had been in his former existence the son of a certain Kyūbei, a farmer of Hodokubos-mura, which is a village within the jurisdiction of the Lord Komiya, in the district called Tamagori, in the province of Musashi;
>
> That he, Katsugoro the son of Kyūbei, had died of smallpox at the age of six years, and that he had been reborn thereafter into the family of the Genzo before-mentioned.

Though this seemed unbelievable, the boy repeated all the circumstances of his story with so much exactness and apparent certainty, that the headman and the elders of the village made a formal investigation of the case. As the news of this event soon spread, it was heard by the family of a certain Hanshiro, living in the village called Hodokubo-mura; and Hanshiro then came to the house of the Genzo aforesaid, a farmer belonging to my estate, and found that everything was true which the boy had said about the personal appearance and the facial characteristics of his former parents, and about the aspect of the house which had been his home in his previous birth. Katsugoro was then taken to the house of Hanshiro in Hodokubo-mura; and the people there said that he looked very much like their Tozo, who had died a number of years before, at the age of six. Since then, the two families have been visiting each other at intervals. The people of other neighbouring villages seem to have heard of the matter, and now persons come daily from various places to see Katsugoro.

A deposition regarding the above facts having been made before me by persons dwelling on my estate, I summoned the man Genzo to my house, and there examined him. His answers to my questions did not contradict the statements before-mentioned made by other parties.

Occasionally in the world some rumour of such a matter as this spreads among the people. Indeed, it is hard to believe such things.

But I beg to make report of the present case, hoping the same will reach your august ear—so that I may not be charged with negligence.

[Signed] Tamon Dempachiro-5 The Fourth Month and the Sixth Year of Bunsei [1823]

2. *Copy of letter written by Kazunawo to Teikin, Priest of Sengakuji*

I have been favoured with the accompanying copy of the report of Tamon Dempachiro by Shiga Hyoemon Sama, who brought it to me, and I take great pleasure in sending it to you. I think that it might be well for you to preserve it, together with the writing from Kwanzan Sama, which you kindly showed me the other day.

[Signed] Kazunawo The twenty-first day of the Sixth Month

[No other date]

3. *Copy of the letter of Matsudaira Kwanzan [Daimyo] to the Priest Teikin of the Temple called Sengakuji*

I herewith enclose and send you the account of the rebirth of Katsugoro. I have written it in the popular style, thinking that it might have a good effect in helping to silence those who do not believe in the doctrines of the Buddha. As a literary work it is, of course, a wretched thing. I send it to you supposing that it could only amuse you from that point of view. But as for the relation itself, it is without mistake; for I myself heard it from the grandmother of Katsugoro. When you have read it, please return it to me.

[Signed] Kwanzan Twentieth day [No date]

4. *Relation of the Rebirth of Katsugoro: Introductory Note by the Priest Teikin*

This is the account of a true fact; for it has been written by Matsudaira Kwanzan Sama, who himself went [to Nakano-mura] on the twenty-second day of the third month of this year for the special purpose of inquiring about the matter. After having obtained a glimpse of Katsugoro, he questioned the boy's grandmother as to every particular; and he wrote down her answers exactly as they were given.

Afterwards, the said Kwanzan Sama condescended to honour this temple with a visit on the fourteenth day of this fourth month, and with his own august lips told me about his visit to the family of the aforesaid Katsugoro. Furthermore, he vouchsafed me the favour of permitting me to read the before-mentioned writing, on the twentieth day of this same month. And, availing myself of the privilege, I immediately made a copy of the writing.

[Signed] Teikin So [facsimile of the priest's kakihan, or private sign]

Sengaku-ji manual, made with the brush The twenty-first day of the Fourth Month of the Sixth Year of Bunsei [1823]

5. *Names of the Members of the Two Families Concerned*

Family of Genzo

Katsugoro—Born the 10th day of the 10th month of the twelfth year of Bunkwa [1815]. Nine years old this sixth year of Bunsei [1823].[8] Second son of Genzo, a farmer living in Tanit-suiri in Nakanomura, district of Tamagori, province of Musashi—Estate of Tamon Dempachiro, whose yashiki is in the street called Shichikencho, Nedzu, Yedo—Jurisdiction of Yusouki.

Genzo—Father of Katsugoro. Family name, Koyada. Fortynine years old this sixth year of Bunsei. Being poor, he occupies himself with the making of baskets, which he sells in Yedo. The name of the inn at which he lodges while in Yedo is Sagamiya, kept by one Kihel, in Bakuro-cho.

Sei—Wife of Genzo and mother of Katsugoro. Thirty-nine years old this sixth year of Bunsei. Daughter of Murata Kichitaro, samurai—once an archer in the service of the Lord of Owari. When Sei was twelve years old she was a maid-servant, it is said, to the house of Honda Dainoshin Dono. When she was thirteen years old, her father, Kichitaro was dismissed forever for a certain cause from the service of the Lord of Owari, and he became a ronin.[9] He died at the age

8 The Western reader is requested to bear in mind that the year in which a Japanese child is born is counted always as one year in the reckoning of age.

9 Lit: "A wave-man," a wandering samurai without a lord. The ronin were generally a desperate and very dangerous class, but there were some

of seventy-five, on the twenty-fifth day of the fourth month of the fourth year of Bunkwa [1807]. His grave is in the cemetery of the temple called Eirin-ji, of the Zen sect, in the village of Shimo-Yusuki.

Tsuya—Grandmother of Katsugoro. Seventy-two years old this sixth year of Bunsei. When young she served as maid in the household of Matsudaira Oki-no-Kami Dono [Daimyo].

Fusa—Elder sister of Katsugoro. Fifteen years old this year.

Otojiro—Elder brother of Katsugoro. Fourteen years old this year.

Tsune—Younger sister of Katsugoro. Four years old this year.

Family of Hanshiro

Tozo—Died at the age of six in Hodokube-mura, in the district called Tamagori in the province of Musashi. Estate of Nakane Uyemon, whose yashiki is in the street Atarashi-bashi-dori, Shitaya, Yedo. Jurisdiction of Komlya. [Tozo] was born in the second year of Bunkwa [1805], and died at about the fourth hour of the day [IV o'clock in the morning] on the fourth day of the second month of the seventh year of Bunkwa [1810]. The sickness of which he died was smallpox. Buried in the graveyard on the hill above the village before-mentioned—Hodokubo-mura—parochial temple: Iwoji in Misawa-mura. Sect: Zen-shū. Last year, the fifth year of Bunkwa [1822], the jiū-san kwaiki[10] was said for Tozo.

Hanshiro—Stepfather of Tozo. Family name, Suzaki. Fifty years old this sixth year of Bunsei.

Shidzu—Mother of Tozo. Forty-nine years old this sixth year of Bunsei.

Kyūbei (afterwards Togoro)—Real father of Tozo. Original name, Kyūbei, afterwards changed to Togoro. Died at the age of forty-eight,

---

fine characters among them.

10 The Buddhist services for the dead are celebrated at regular intervals, increasing successively in length, until the time of one hundred years after death. The jiū-san kwaiki is the service for the thirteenth year after death. By "thirteenth" in the context the reader must understand that the year in which the death took place is counted for one year.

in the sixth year of Bunkwa [1809], when Tozo was five years old. To replace him, Hanshiro became an iri-muko.[11]

Children—two boys and two girls. These are Hanshiro's children by the mother of Tozo.

6. *Copy of the Account written in Popular Style by Matsudaira Kwanzan Dono, Daimyo.*

Sometime in the eleventh month of the past year, when Katsugoro was playing in the rice-field with his elder sister, Fusa, he asked her—"Elder Sister, where did you come from before you were born into our household?"

Fusa answered him: "How can I know what happened to me before I was born?"

Katsugoro looked surprised and exclaimed: "Then you cannot remember anything that happened before you were born?"

"Do you remember?" asked Fusa.

"Indeed I do," replied Katsugoro. "I used to be the son of Kyūbei San of Hodokubo, and my name was then Tozo—do you not know all that?"

"Ah!" said Fusa, "I shall tell father and mother about it."

But Katsugoro at once began to cry, and said: "Please do not tell! It would not be good to tell father and mother."

Fusa made answer, after a little while: "Well, this time I shall not tell. But the next time that you do anything naughty, then I will tell."

After that day, whenever a dispute arose between the two, the sister would threaten the brother, saying, "Very well, then—I shall tell that thing to father and mother." At these words the boy would always yield to his sister. This happened many times; and the parents one day overheard Fusa making her threat. Thinking Katsugoro must have been doing something wrong, they desired to know what the matter was, and Fusa, being questioned, told them the truth. Then Genzo and his wife, and Tsuya, the grandmother of Katsugoro, thought it a very strange thing. They called Katsugoro, therefore

11 The second husband, by adoption, of a daughter who lives with her own parents.

and tried, first by coaxing, and then by threatening, to make him tell what he had meant by those words.

After hesitation, Katsugoro said: "I will tell you everything. I used to be the son of Kyūbei San of Hodokubo, and the name of my mother then was O-Shidzu San. When I was five years old, Kyūbei San died; and there came in his place a man called Hanshiro San, who loved me very much. But in the following year, when I was six years old, I died of smallpox. In the third year after that I entered mother's honourable womb, and was born again."

The parents and the grandmother of the boy wondered greatly at hearing this; and they decided to make all possible inquiry as to the man called Hanshiro of Hodokubo. But as they all had to work very hard every day to earn a living, and so could spare but little time for any other matter, they could not at once carry out their intention.

Now Sei, the mother of Katsugoro, had nightly to suckle her little daughter Tsune, who was four years old,[12] and Katsugoro therefore slept with his grandmother, Tsuya. Sometimes he used to talk to her in bed; and one night when he was in a very confiding mood, she persuaded him to tell her what happened at the time when he had died. Then he said: "Until I was four years old I used to remember everything; but since then I have become more and more forgetful; and now I forget many, many things. But I still remember that I died of smallpox; I remember that I was put into a jar;[13] I remember that I was buried on a hill. There was a hole made in the ground; and the people let the jar drop into that hole. It fell pon!—I remember that sound well. Then somehow I returned to the house, and I stopped on my own pillow there.[14] In a short time some old man—looking

---

12 Children in Japan, among the poorer classes, are not weaned until an age much later than what is considered the proper age for weaning children in Western countries. But "four years old" in this text may mean considerably less than three by Western reckoning.

13 From very ancient time in Japan it has been the custom to bury the dead in large jars, usually of red earthenware, called Kame. Such jars are still used, although a large proportion of the dead are buried in wooden coffins of a form unknown in the Occident.

14 The idea expressed is not that of lying down with the pillow under the bead, but of hovering about the pillow or resting upon it as an insect might do. The bodiless spirit is usually said to rest upon the roof of the home. The apparition of the aged man referred to in the next

like a grandfather—came and took me away. I do not know who or what he was. As I walked I went through empty air as if flying. I remember it was neither night nor day as we went: it was always like sunset-time. I did not feel either warm or cold or hungry. We went very far, I think; but still I could hear always, faintly, the voices of people talking at home; and the sound of the Nembutsu[15] being said for me. I remember also that when the people at home set offerings of hot botamochi[16] before the household shrine [butsudan], I inhaled the vapour of the offerings … Grandmother, never forget to offer warm food to the honourable dead [Hotoke Sama], and do not forget to give to priests—I am sure it is very good to do these things[17] … After that, I only remember that the old man led me by some roundabout way to this place—I remember we passed the road beyond the village. Then we came here, and he pointed to this house, and said to me: "Now you must be reborn—for it is three years since you died. You are to be reborn in that house. The person who will become your grandmother is very kind; so it will be well for you to be conceived and born there." After saying this, the old man went away. I remained a little time under the kaki-tree before the entrance of this house. Then I was going to enter when I heard talking inside; someone said that because father was now earning so little, mother would have to go to service in Yedo. I thought, "I will not go into that house," and I stopped three days in the garden. On the third day it was decided that, after all, mother would not have to go to Yedo. The same night I passed into the house through a knot-hole in the sliding-shutters; and after that I stayed for three days beside the kāmado.[18] Then I entered mother's honourable womb.[19] … I remember that I

---

sentence seems a thought of Shinto rather than of Buddhism.

15 The repetition of the Buddhist invocation Numu Amida Butsu is thus named. The *nembutsu* is repeated by many Buddhist sects besides the sect of Amida proper, the Shinshu.

16 *Botamochi*, a kind of sugared rice-cake.

17 Such advice is a commonplace in Japanese Buddhist literature. By Hotoke Sama here the boy meant, not the Buddhas proper, but the spirits of the dead, hopefully termed Buddhas by those who loved them, much as in the West we sometimes speak of our dead as angels.

18 The cooking-place in a Japanese kitchen. Sometimes the word is translated "kitchen-range," but the *kāmado* is something very different from a Western kitchen-range.

19 Here I think it better to omit a couple of sentences in the original rather too plain for Western taste, yet not without interest. The meaning

was born without any pain at all. Grandmother, you may tell this to father and mother, but please never tell it to anybody else."

The grandmother told Genzo and his wife what Katsugoro had related to her; and after that the boy was not afraid to speak freely with his parents on the subject of his former existence, and would often say to them: "I want to go to Hodokubo. Please let me make a visit to the tomb of Kyūbei San." Genzo thought that Katsugoro, being a strange child, would probably die before long, and that it might therefore be better to make inquiry at once as to whether there really was a man in Hodokubo called Hanshiro. But he did not wish to make the inquiry himself, because for a man to do so [under such circumstances!] would seem inconsiderate or forward. Therefore, instead of going himself to Hodokubo, he asked his mother Tsuya, on the twentieth day of the first month of this year, to take her grandson there.

Tsuya went with Katsugoro to Hodokubo; and when they entered the village she pointed to the nearer dwellings, and asked the boy, "Which house is it? Is it this house or that one?" "No," answered Katsugoro, "it is further on—much further," and he hurried before her. Reaching a certain dwelling at last, he cried, "This is the house!" and ran in, without waiting for his grandmother. Tsuya followed him in, and asked the people there what was the name of the owner of the house. "Hanshiro," one of them answered. She asked the name of Hanshiro's wife. "Shidzu," was the reply. Then she asked whether there had ever been a son called Tozo born in that house. "Yes," was the answer; "but that boy died thirteen years ago, when he was six years old."

Then for the first time Tsuya was convinced that Katsugoro had spoken the truth, and she could not help shedding tears. She related to the people of the house all that Katsugoro had told her about his remembrance of his former birth. Then Hanshiro and his wife wondered greatly. They caressed Katsugoro and wept; and they remarked that he was much handsomer now than he had been as Tozo before dying at the age of six. In the meantime, Katsugoro was looking all about; and seeing the roof of a tobacco shop opposite to the house of Hanshiro he pointed to it, and said, "That used not to

---

of the omitted passages is only that even in the womb the child acted with consideration, and according to the rules of filial piety

be there." And he also said, "The tree yonder used not to be there." All this was true. So from the minds of Hanshiro and his wife every doubt departed [ga wo orishi].

On the same day Tsuya and Katsugoro returned to Tanit-suiri, Nakano-mura. Afterwards Genzo sent his son seven times to Hanshiro's house, and allowed him to visit the tomb of Kyūbei, his real father in his previous existence.

Sometimes Katsugoro says: "I am a Nono-Sama:[20] therefore please be kind to me." Sometimes he also says to his grandmother: "I think I shall die when I am sixteen; but, as Ontake Sama[21] has

---

20 Nono-San (or Somali, the child-word for the spirits of the dead, for the Buddhas, and for the Shinto Gods, Kami.) Nono-San wo ogamu, "to pray to the Nono-San," is the child-phrase for praying to the gods. According to Shinto thought, the spirits of the ancestors become Nono-San-Kami.

21 The reference here to Ontake Sama is of particular interest, but will need some considerable explanation. Ontake, or Mitake, is the name of a celebrated holy peak in the province of Shinano—a great resort for pilgrims. During the Tokugawa Shogunate, a priest called Isshin, of the Risshū Buddhists, made a pilgrimage to that mountain. Returning to his native place (Sakamoto-cho, Shitaya, Yedo), he began to preach certain new doctrines and to make for himself a reputation as a miracle-worker, by virtue of powers said to have been gained during his pilgrimage to Ontake. The Shogunate considered him a dangerous person, and banished him to the island of Hachijo, where he remained for some years. Afterwards he was allowed to return to Yedo, and there to preach his new faith, to which be gave the name of Azuma-Kyo. It was Buddhist teaching in a Shinto disguise—the deities especially adored by its followers being Okuni-nushi and Sukuna-hikona as Buddhist avatars. In the prayer of the sect called Kaibyaku-Norito it is said: "The divine nature is immovable (fudo) yet it moves. It is formless, yet manifests itself in forms. This is the incomprehensible divine body. In heaven and earth it is called Kami: in all things it is called spirit, in man it is called mind. From this only reality came the heavens, the four oceans, the great whole of the three thousand universes; from the one mind emanate three thousands of great thousands of forms."

In the eleventh year of Bunkwa (1814) a man called Shimoyama Osuke, originally an oil-merchant in Heiy-emoncho, Asakusa, Yedo, organized, on the basis of Isshin's teaching, a religious association named Tomoye-Kyo. It flourished until it was overthrown by the Shogunate when a law was issued forbidding the teaching of mixed doctrines and the blending of Shinto with Buddhist religion. Shimoyama Osuke then applied for permission to establish a new Shinto sect, under the name of Mitake-Kyo, popularly called Ontake-Kyo, and the permission was given in the sixth year of Meiji [1873]. Osuke then remodeled the Buddhist sutra Fudo Kyo into a Shinto prayer-book, under the title, Shinto-Fudo Norito. The sect still flourishes

taught us, dying is not a matter to be afraid of." When his parents ask him, "Would you not like to become a priest?" he answers, "I would rather not be a priest."

The village people do not call him Katsugoro anymore; they have nicknamed him "Hodokubo-Kozo" (the Acolyte of Hodokubo).[22] When anyone visits the house to see him, he becomes shy at once, and runs to hide himself in the inner apartments. So it is not possible to have any direct conversation with him. I have written down this account exactly as his grandmother gave it to me.

I asked whether Genzo, his wife or Tsuya could remember having done any virtuous deeds. Genzo and his wife said that they had never done anything especially virtuous, but that Tsuya, the grandmother, had always been in the habit of repeating the Nembutsu every morning and evening, and that she never failed to give two mon[23] to any priest or pilgrim who came to the door. But excepting these small matters, she never had done anything which could be called a particularly virtuous act.

This is the End of the Relation of the Rebirth of Katsugoro

Note by the Translator

The foregoing is taken from a manuscript entitled Chin Setsu Shu Ki or "Manuscript-Collection of Uncommon Stories," made between the fourth month of the sixth year of Bunsei and the tenth month of the sixth year of Tempo [1823–1835]. At the end of

---

and one of its chief temples is situated about a mile from my present residence in Tokyo. "Ontake san" (or "Sama") is a popular name given to the deities adored by this sect. It really means the Deity dwelling on the peak Mitake, or Ontake. But the name is also sometimes applied to the high-priest of the sect, who is supposed to be oracularly inspired by the deity of Ontake and to make revelations of truth through the power of the divinity. In the mouth of the boy Katsugoro, "Ontake Sama" means the high-priest of that time [1823], almost certainly Osuke himself, then chief of the Tomoye-Kyo.

22 Kozo is the name given to a Buddhist acolyte, or a youth studying for the priesthood. But it is also given to errand-boys and little boy-servants sometimes—perhaps because in former days the heads of little boys were shaved. I think that the meaning in this text is "acolyte."

23 In that time the name of the smallest of coins = 1/10 of 1 cent. It was about the same as that now called rin, a copper with a square hole in the middle and bearing Chinese characters.

the manuscript is written—"From the years of Bunsei to the years of Tempo—Minamisempa, Owner. Kurumacho, Shiba, Yedo." Under this, again, is the following note: "Bought from Yamatoya Sakujiro Nishinokubo: twenty-first day [?], Second Year of Meiji [1869]." From this it would appear that the manuscript had been written by Minamisempa, who collected stories told to him, or copied them from manuscripts obtained by him, during the thirteen years from 1823 to 1835, inclusive.

Meditating on No-Self

A Dhamma Talk
Edited for Bodhi Leaves by

Ayyā Khemā

Bodhi Leaves No. 95

First published: 1983

Meditating on No-Self

In Buddhism we use the words "self" and "no-self," and so it is important to understand just what this "no-self," *anattā*, is all about, even if it is first just an idea, because the essence of the Buddha's teaching hinges on this concept. And in this teaching Buddhism is unique. No one, no other spiritual teacher, has formulated no-self in just this way. And because it has been formulated by him in this way, there is also the possibility of speaking about it. Much has been written about no-self, but in order to know it, one has to experience it. And that is what the teaching aims at, the experience of no-self.

Yet in order to experience no-self, one has first to fully know self. Actually know it. But unless we do know what this self is, this self called "me," it is impossible to know what is meant by "there is no self there." In order to give something away, we have to first fully have it in hand.

We are constantly trying to reaffirm self. Which already shows that this "self" is a very fragile and rather wispy sort of affair, because if it weren't why would we constantly have to reaffirm it? Why are we constantly afraid of the "self" being threatened of its being insecure, of its not getting what it needs for survival? If it were such a solid entity as we believe it to be, we would not feel threatened so often.

We affirm "self" again and again through identification. We identify with a certain name, an age, a sex, an ability, an occupation. "I am a lawyer, I am a doctor. I am an accountant, I am a student." And we identify with the people we are attached to. "I am a husband, I am a wife, I am a mother, I am a daughter, I am a son." Now, in the manner of speech, we have to use "self" in that way— but it isn't only in speech. We really think that that "self" is who we are. We really believe it. There is no doubt in our mind that that "self" is who we are. When any of these factors is threatened, if being a wife is threatened, if being a mother is threatened, if being a lawyer is threatened, if being a teacher is threatened—or if we lose the people who enable us to retain that "self"—what a tragedy!

The self-identification becomes insecure, and "me" finds it hard to say "look at me," "this is me." Praise and blame are included. Praise reaffirms "me." Blame threatens "me." So we like the praise and we dislike the blame. The ego is threatened. Fame and infamy—same thing. Loss and gain. If we gain, the ego gets bigger; if we lose, it gets a bit smaller. So we are constantly in a quandary, and in constant fear. The ego might lose a little bit of its grandeur. It might be made a bit smaller by someone. And it happens to all of us. Somebody is undoubtedly going to blame us for something eventually. Even the Buddha was blamed.

Now the blame that is levied at us is not the problem. The problem is our reaction. The problem is that we feel smaller. The ego has a hard time reasserting itself. So what we usually do is we blame back, making the other's ego a bit smaller too.

Identification with whatever it is that we do and whatever it is that we have, be it possessions or people, is, so we believe, needed for our survival. "Self" survival. If we don't identify with this or that, we feel as if we are in limbo. This is the reason why it is difficult to stop thinking in meditation. Because without thinking there would be no identification. If I don't think, what do I identify with? It is difficult to come to a stage in meditation in which there is actually nothing to identify with any more.

Happiness, too, may be an identification. "I am happy." "I am unhappy." Because we are so keen on survival, we have got to keep on identifying. When this identification becomes a matter of the life or death of the ego, which it usually is, then the fear of loss becomes so great that we can be in a constant state of fear. Constantly afraid to lose either the possessions that make us what we are, or the people that make us what we are. If we have no children, or if they all die, we are no longer a mother. So fear is paramount. The same goes for all other identifications. Not a very peaceful state of living and what is it due to? Only one thing: ego, the craving to be.

This identification results, of course, in craving for possessing. And this possessing results in attachment. What we have, what we identify with, we are attached to. That attachment, that clinging, makes it extremely difficult to have a free and open viewpoint. This kind of clinging, whatever it may be that we cling to—it may not be clinging to motor cars and houses, it may not even be clinging to people—but we certainly cling to views and opinions. We cling to our world view. We cling to the view of how we are going to be happy. Maybe we cling to a view of who created this universe. Whatever it is we cling to, even how the government should run the country, all of that makes it extremely difficult to see things as they really are. To be open-minded. And it is only an open mind which can take in new ideas and understanding.

Lord Buddha compared listeners to four different kinds of clay vessels. The first clay vessel is one that has holes at the bottom. If you pour water into it, it runs right out. In other words, whatever you teach that person is useless. The second clay vessel he compared to one that had cracks in it. If you pour water into it, the water seeps out. These people cannot remember. Cannot put two and two together. Cracks in the understanding. The third listener he compared to a vessel that was completely full. Water cannot be poured in for it's full to the brim. Such a person, so full of views he can't learn anything new! But hopefully, we are the fourth kind. The empty vessels without any holes or cracks. Completely empty.

I dare say we are not. But may be empty enough to take in enough. To be empty like that, of views and opinions, means a lack of clinging. Even a lack of clinging to what we think is reality. Whatever we think reality is, it surely is not, because if it were, we would never be unhappy for a single moment. We would never feel a lack of anything. We would never feel a lack of companionship, of ownership. We would never feel frustrated, bored. If we ever do, whatever we think is real, is not. What is truly reality is completely fulfilling. If we aren't completely fulfilled, we aren't seeing complete reality. So, any view that we may have is either wrong or it is partial.

Because it is wrong or partial, and bounded by the ego, we must look at it with suspicion. Anything we cling to keeps us bound to it. If I cling to a table-leg, I can't possibly get out the door. There is no way I can move. I am stuck. Not until I let go will I have the opportunity to get out. Any identification, any possession that is clung to, is what stops us from reaching transcendental reality. Now we can easily see this clinging when we cling to things and people, but we cannot easily see why the five *khandha*s are called the five clung-to aggregates. That is their name, and they are, in fact, what we cling to most. That is an entire clinging. We don't even stop to consider when we look at our body, and when we look at our mind, or when we look at feeling, perception, mental formations, and consciousness—*vedanā, saññā, saṅkhāra,* and *viññāṇa*. We look at this mind-and-body, *nāma-rūpa*, and we don't even doubt the fact that this is my feeling, my perception, my memory, my thoughts, and my awareness of my consciousness. And no one starts doubting until they start seeing. And for that seeing we need a fair bit of empty space apart from views and opinions.

Clinging is the greatest possessiveness and attachment we have. As long as we cling we cannot see reality. We cannot see reality because clinging is in the way. Clinging colours whatever we believe to be true. Now it is not possible to say "all right, I'll stop clinging." We can't do that. The process of taking the "me" apart, of not believing any more that this is one whole, is a gradual one. But if meditation has any benefit and success, it must show that first of all there is mind and there is body. There isn't one single thing acting in accord all the time. There is mind which is thinking and making the body act. Now that is the first step in knowing oneself a little clearer. And then we can note "this is a feeling" and "I am giving this feeling a name" which means memory and perception. "This is the thought that I am having about this feeling. The feeling has come about because the mind-consciousness has connected with the feeling that has arisen."

Take the four parts of the *khandha*s that belong to the mind apart. When we do that while it is happening—not now when we are thinking about it—but while it is happening, then we get an inkling that this isn't really me, that these are phenomena that are arising, which stay a moment, and then cease. How long does mind-consciousness stay on one object? And how long do thoughts last? And have we really invited them?

The clinging, the clung-to, are what make the ego arise. Because of clinging the notion of "me" arises and then there is me, and me having all the problems. Without me would there be problems? If there weren't anyone sitting inside me—as we think there is—who is called I or me or John, Claire, then who is having the problem? The *khandha*s do not have any problems. The *khandha*s are just processes. They are phenomena, and that is all. They are just going on and on and on. But because I am grasping at them, and trying to hold on to them, and saying: "it's me, it's me feeling, it's me wanting," then problems arise.

If we really want to get rid of suffering, completely and totally, then clinging has to go. The spiritual path is never one of achievement; it is always one of letting go. The more we let go, the more there is empty and open space for us to see reality. Because what we let go of is no longer there, there is the possibility of just moving without clinging to the results of the movement. As long as we cling to the results of what we do, as long as we cling to the results of what we think, we are bound, we are hemmed in.

Now there is a third thing that we do: we are interested in becoming something or somebody. Interested in becoming an excellent meditator. Interested in becoming a graduate. Interested in becoming something which we are not. And becoming something stops us from being. When we are stopped from being, we cannot pay attention to what there really is. All this becoming business is, of course, in the future. Since whatever there is in the future is conjecture, it is a dream world we live in. The only reality we can be sure of is this particular moment right now; and this particular moment as you must be able to be aware of—has already passed and this one has passed and the next one has also passed. See how they are all passing! That is the impermanence of it all. Each moment passes, but we cling, trying to hold on to them. Trying to make them a reality. Trying to make them a security. Trying to make them be something which they are not. See how they are all passing. We cannot even say it as quickly as they are doing it.

There is nothing that is secure. Nothing to hold on to, nothing that is stable. The whole universe is constantly falling apart and coming back together. And that includes the mind and the body which we call "I." You may believe it or not, it makes no difference. In order to know it, you must experience it; when you experience it, it's perfectly clear. What one experiences is totally clear. No one can say it is not. They may try, but their objections make no sense because you have experienced it. It's the same thing as biting into the mango to know its taste.

To experience it, one needs meditation. An ordinary mind can only know ordinary concepts and ideas. If one wants to understand and experience extraordinary experiences and ideas, one has to have an extraordinary mind. An extraordinary mind comes about through concentration. Most meditators have experienced some stage that is different than the one they are used to. So it is not ordinary any more. But we have to fortify that far more than just the beginning stage. To the point where the mind is truly extraordinary. Extraordinary in the sense that it can direct itself to where it wants to go. Extraordinary in the sense that it no longer gets perturbed by everyday events. And when the mind can concentrate, then it experiences states which it has never known before. To realise that your universe constantly falls apart and comes back together again is a meditative experience. It takes practise, perseverance and patience. And when the mind is unperturbed and still, equanimity, evenmindedness, peacefulness arise.

At that time the mind understands the idea of impermanence to such an extent that it sees itself as totally impermanent. And when one sees one's own mind as being totally impermanent, there is a shift in one's viewpoint. That shift I like to compare with a kaleidoscope that children play with. A slight touch and you get a different picture. The whole thing looks quite different with just a slight shift.

Non-self is experienced through the aspect of impermanence, through the aspect of unsatisfactoriness, and through the aspect of emptiness. Empty of what? The word "emptiness" is so often misunderstood because when one only thinks of it as a concept, one says "what do you mean by empty?" Everything is there: there are the people, and there are their insides, guts and their bones and blood and everything is full of stuff—and the mind is not empty either. It's got ideas, thoughts and feelings. And even when it doesn't have those, what do you mean by emptiness? The only thing that is empty is the emptiness of an entity.

There is no specific entity in anything. That is emptiness. That is the nothingness. That nothingness is also experienced in meditation. It is empty, it is devoid of a specific person, devoid of a specific thing, devoid of anything which makes it permanent, devoid of anything which even makes it important. The whole thing is in flux. So the emptiness is that. And the emptiness is to be seen everywhere; to be seen in oneself. And that is what is called *anattā*, non-self. Empty of an entity. There is nobody there. It is all imagination. At first that feels very insecure.

That person that I've been regarding with so much concern, that person trying to do this or that, that person who will be my security, will be my insurance for a happy life—once I find that person—that person does not really exist. What a frightening and insecure idea that is! What a feeling of fear arises! But as a matter of fact, it's just the reverse. If one accepts and bears that fright and goes through it, one comes to complete and utter relief and release. I'll give you a simile: Imagine you own a very valuable jewel which is so valuable that you place your trust in it so that should you fall upon hard times, it will look after you. It's so valuable that you can have it as your security. You don't trust anybody. So you have a safe inside your house and that is where you put your jewel. Now you have been working hard for a number of years and you think you deserve a holiday. So now, what to do with the jewel? Obviously you cannot take it with you on your seaside holiday. So you buy new locks for the doors to your house and you bar your windows and you alert your neighbours. You tell them about the proposed holiday and ask them to look after you house—and the safe in it. And they say they will, of course. You should be quite at ease and so you go off on your holiday.

You go to the beach, and it's wonderful. Marvellous. The palm trees are swaying in the wind, and the spot you've chosen on the beach is nice and clean. The waves are warm and it's all lovely. The first day you really enjoy yourself. But on the second day you begin to wonder; the neighbours are very nice people, but they do go and visit their children. They are not always at home, and lately there has been a rash of burglaries in the neighbourhood. And on the third day you've convinced yourself that something dreadful is going to happen, and you go back home. You walk in and open the safe. Everything is all right. You go over to the neighbours and they ask, "Why did you come back? We were looking after your place. You didn't have to come back. Everything is fine."

The next year, the same thing. Again you tell the neighbours, "Now this time I am really going to stay away for a month. I need this holiday as I've been working hard." So they say, "Absolutely no need to worry, just take off. Go to the beach." So once more you bar the windows, lock the doors, get everything shipshape, and take off for the beach. Again, it's wonderful, beautiful. This time you last for five days. On the fifth day you are convinced that something dreadful must have happened. And you go home. You go home, and by golly, it has. The jewel is gone. You are in a state of complete collapse. Total desperation. Depressed. So you go to the neighbours, but they have no idea what has happened. they've been around all the time. Then you sit and consider the matter and you realise that since the jewel is gone, you might as well go back to the beach and enjoy yourself!

That jewel is self. Once it is gone, all the burden of looking after it, all the fears about it, all the barring of doors and windows and heart and mind is no longer necessary. You can just go and enjoy yourself while you're still in this body. After proper investigation, the frightening aspect of losing this thing that seemed so precious turns out to be the only relief and release from worry that there is.

There are three doors to liberation: the signless, the desireless, and emptiness. If we understand impermanence, *anicca*, fully, it is called the signless liberation. If we understand suffering, *dukkha*, fully, it is the desireless liberation. If we understand no-self, *anattā*, fully, then it is the emptiness-liberation. Which means we can go through any of these three doors. And to be liberated means never to have to experience an unhappy moment again. It also means something else: it means we are no longer creating *kamma*. A person who has been completely liberated still acts, still thinks, still speaks and still looks to all intents and purposes like anybody else, but that person has lost the idea that I am thinking, I am speaking, I am acting. Kamma is no longer being made because there is just the thought, just the speech, just the action. There is the experience but no experiencer. And because no *kamma* is being made any longer, there is no rebirth. That is full enlightenment.

In this tradition, three stages of enlightenment have been classified before one comes to the fourth stage, full enlightenment. The first stage, the one we can concern ourselves with—at least theoretically—is called *sotāpanna,* stream-enterer. It means a person who has seen Nibbāna once and has thereby entered the stream. That person cannot be deterred from the Path any more. If the insight is strong, there may be only one more life-time. If the insight is weak, it can be seven more life-times. Having seen Nibbāna for oneself once, one loses some of the difficulties one had before. The most drastic hindrance that one loses is the idea that this person we call "I" is a separate entity. The wrong view of self is lost. But that doesn't mean that a *sotāpanna* is constantly aware of no-self. The wrong view is lost. But the right view has to be reinforced again and again and experienced again and again through that reinforcement.

Such a person no longer has any great interest, and certainly no belief, in rites and rituals. They may still be performed because they are traditional or that are customary, but such a person no longer believes they can bring about any kind of liberation (if they ever believed that before). And then a very interesting thing is lost: sceptical doubt. Sceptical doubt is lost because one has seen for oneself that what the Buddha taught was actually so. Until that time sceptical doubt will have to arise again and again because one can easily think: "Well, maybe. Maybe it's so, but how can I be sure?" One can only be sure through one's own experience. Then, of course, there is no sceptical doubt left because one has seen exactly that which has been described, and having seen it, one's own heart and mind gives an understanding which makes it possible to see everything else.

Dhamma must have as its base the understanding that there is no special entity. There is continuity, but there is no special entity. And that continuity is what makes it so difficult for us to see that there really isn't anybody inside the body making things happen. Things are happening anyway. So the first instance of having seen a glimpse of freedom, called stream-entry, makes changes within us. It certainly does not uproot greed and hate—in fact, they are not even mentioned. But through the greater understanding such a person has, the greed and the hate lessen. They are not as strong anymore, and they do not manifest in gross ways, but do remain in subtle ways.

The next stages are the once-returner, then the non-returner, then the *arahat*. Once-returner, one more life in the five-sense world. Non-returner, no human life necessary, and *arahat*, fully enlightened. Sensual desire and hate only go with non-returners, and complete conceit of self, only with *arahat*.

So we can be quite accepting of the fact that since we are not arahats, we still have greed and hate. It isn't a matter of blaming oneself for having them: it's a matter of understanding where these come from. They come from the delusion of me. I want to protect this jewel which is me. That is how they arise. But with the continued practise of meditation, the mind can become clearer and clearer. It finally understands. And when it does understand, it can see transcendental reality. Even if seen for one thought-moment, the experience is of great impact and makes a marked change in our lives.

To the Cemetery and Back

Leonard Price

Bodhi Leaves No. 96

First published: 1983

To the Cemetery and Back

In this city, as in all, the dead are granted a little space. Our business and pleasure take us past the old iron gates a hundred times on the way to seemingly more immediate destinations. But on this odd morning when time hangs lightly and pure chance finds us here gazing over these hills of stone and ivy, let us actually turn our steps into the cemetery and along its crooked paths. The day is fine (or certainly we'd never venture here), the flowers glisten with last evening's rain, and a fair fragrance rises with the first breeze. Just inside the gates, someone stands at an easel and paints flowers. Farther off, a caretaker trims a hedge. The signs are propitious—we shall have privacy but not solitude, and the morning's grace restrains the onslaught of gloom. We may even, carefully, allow ourselves to think thoughts appropriate to the place.

On these finely tended hillsides the music of birds mingles strangely with the numberless testimonies of death. The earth is half-paved with the stone remembrances and the middle air is full of obelisks and angels. Names and dates surround us, some sharp and raw, some worn nearly to oblivion, all crowding upon us with the particulars of spent lives—of this family, of this age, with these virtues, with this hope of heaven. What can this mean to us, especially if we have no family here? The wind flings a rag of shade across the bright grass: We too shall die. The birds sing on, the bees hum in the violets, and the thought is not so terrible. Not so terrible, we remind ourselves, if the fever of life ends here, swathed in honeysuckles and southern airs.

We stroll on, reading the chronicles of grief: beloved wife, infant aged three days, daughter, son, darling children. Generations are drawn from the world by the chain of mortality. Do these stones mark an ending or only a continuance? The deceased fare on according to their deeds while we living stay to grieve. Where is there an end? These picturesque stones only mark the limit of our knowledge. Dress them how you will, O gardener, they bespeak our helplessness.

The rumble of the city dwindles and fails in these granite acres until a somber stillness attends our steps. Despite our resolutions and the sparkling sun, we are troubled and would turn back to the gates, but unaccountably we are lost and the hills roll on with their bare legends. Nothing to do but keep walking. assuredly we still live, and while we live we can try our philosophies against enormous mortality around us. Look now, a butterfly flails at the air in what we hope is joy. Beneath that tomb lives a chipmunk—see him frisk about and vanish down his hole. We are briefly cheered and then plunged in doubt, for why should we lament the extinction of life and hail its repetition? We grow weary of sentiments careening back and forth and wish for equilibrium within the volatile universe. *saṃsāra*, we are told, is the terrible round of birth and death, but this disquiet, this resolution of doubt—is it not *saṃsāra* as well? Hardly can we set a foot down for fear of treading wrongly, so crowded is this cemetery. We walk narrowly, wobbling on over the beautiful, terrible hills. Here where the path straightens for a moment let us pause and experiment by closing our eyes. At once the world collapses into red darkness and the pressure of the wind and sun. Now we shall take a step, hesitantly, feeling the gravel underfoot, imagining boundaries and perils. We move further. Somewhere the ground drops off, but where? Anxiety throws its coils around us, and we are walking through our minds—with danger unseen but guessed on every side. Open eyes! The world blurs back to us, green and lovely, composing itself slowly and almost mockingly. Are we quite sure what is real? Are we quite sure we understand death?

Here's an iron bench in the shade where we can rest and consider our position. Eyes closed or open, it's mind that assembles our world. Mind stirs up fear, mind accommodates grief, mind moves thoughts and limbs according to its nature. What is this nature? To judge from our confusion and instability, it is restlessness. We are, it would seem, not firm in space or conviction, not fully in control of anything. If we watch closely, here in the semi-silence, we may discern the flutter, the whir, the unease of this shifting mind. It knows not itself, it knows not the world, it only wants and hates by turns. The odor of flowers heaves it momentarily to paradise. The chiseled history of dead children hurls it down to despair. A crow on a stone angel's head call forth a smile. A fresh name on an old monument chills us. Delight pulls us one way, grief another. Neither can bear us across doubt or fear.

The mind runs endlessly in moments that flare and fizzle. There is a being-born and a dying with every one of them—a birth and death of every thought and every breath happening right here while we worriedly scan the horizon for a supposed Great Death. Consider this dying that goes on all the time—fits of memory and feeling, spasms of cells, torrents of desire and aversion, all tumbling in birth and death, birth and death—the weary reiteration of *saṃsāra*. Each instant ends but gives no rest because it ignites its successor; and in this the physical death memorialized around us is no different—the troubled flame of being is passed on and on. What we fear out there, among the graven sorrows of the cemetery, is burning in here, in the mind, right now. Death has been our neighbor long before we came to ponder headstones. The Buddha understood this. We as yet do not, and tremble in the presence of innocent stone—wide-eyed toward the symbol, blind to the blazing fact.

Sitting here alone, while the shade splashes silently around us, we hold all the worlds in our lap and can study them as the Buddha taught us, not with hunger, but with the clean dispassion that lays bare truth and liberates the beholder. The Buddha called craving the source of suffering, and indeed, as we bend our attention closer, what do we find but craving nesting even in the fractured moment? Every little death, every wretch of disappointment, is preceded by a birth, an upsurge of craving founded on ignorance. Being blind to the true nature of things, we continually give rise to passion that veers this way and that, never satisfied, forging link by link in the moment the chain binds us over the years. Events in themselves are only events; the deluded mind invests them with horrors and delights and ties the mortal chain around itself.

This cemetery with its solid stones is only a mirror, into which the Buddha bids us look to find the funeral procession within ourselves. Say we look, then. Say we are able to observe the deplorable state of our mind. What can we do about it? If birth and death are whirling on so mechanically and inexorably all efforts would appear futile. Indeed, though we begin to notice the cascading instability of body and mind, our mere intellectual recognition does nothing to free us. Birth—that is, the uprising of craving—will of necessity be followed by death—that is, the pang of impermanence and loss. But craving itself is not an inevitable phenomenon; it springs up only in the soil of ignorance, and when ignorance is dispelled craving and its resultant miseries cease to exist. The whole teaching of the Buddha drives to this end. We are urged to strive diligently to see things as they are, to resist craving, to observe it unsparingly, to uproot it altogether. All the defilements and afflictions of mind exist, as it were, with our permission. Not knowing we have the power to end them, we go on muttering," Yes, go ahead, there's no help for it." But when we realize we do have the power to alter the painful course of life our excuses will no longer suffice. We must look closely, fix on a straight line, and sail by the three points of morality, concentration, and wisdom.

Spurred by these thoughts, we rise from the iron bench (how quickly it has become uncomfortable!) and continue walking through the endless field of graves. This business of being alive once seemed simple—either you were or you weren't—but even a brief contemplation reveals surprising complexities. It appears we have long considered death as a single grim monolith that will one day thump us on the head, while in reality death is subtle, manifold, and coexistent with the mind that fears it. Our steps drag slowly over the gravel, and around us the cemetery seems more empty than ever. There is nobody to be seen, even the birds have vanished, and our solitude is complete. The question must arise now; if we have misunderstood death, have we not misunderstood its corollary, life, as well? If what we have been calling death is not singular and unique but threaded throughout the living process, can we even draw a clear and meaningful distinction between the two? Here we must turn to the Buddha, who did not speak of "life" and "death" as independent realities but rather pointed out that experience is a continual becoming, a process of ceaseless change, a flux of arising and perishing—which is to say *saṃsāra*, the great wheel of cause and effect, on whose flashing rim no beginning and no end can be found.

As we examine mind and body we feel increasingly the inadequacy of conventional words such as "birth," and "death." We have taken definitions for granted and now find them useless when we need them. Experience upsets imagination. We are forced to ask ourselves, "Whatever these words mean, who is it that is born, who is it that lives, who is it that dies?" Having so grossly misunderstood events we reach desperately for the one who undergoes events, but can we even find such a one? The Buddha many times patiently explained that human beings are temporary compounds of five aggregates: form, feelings, perceptions, mental formations, and consciousness. These aggregates are constantly changing, but so swiftly that they appear to retain a distinctive identity—hence the conventional notions of "you" and "I." But such words and ideas are only conveniences which do not accord with ultimate reality. Life and death are only the continual becoming of the five aggregates, within which there can be found no indwelling core, no identity or permanent "self." Well, we may ask, does such-and-such a person live or not? Of course we may say that he or she or they or I live—it is true enough on a mundane level. We are all, in a sense, lost beings wandering through cycles of existence. But we must clearly understand that ultimately there are only the five aggregates spinning through birth-and-death, afflicted with pain and pleasure, weighted with ignorance and goaded by desire and fear. The question "Who?" becomes meaningless as we study mind and body. Here we find instability, misery, and doubt burning in rightful chain-reaction. Rather than searching futilely for an owner of the fire, hadn't we better put it out?

The Buddha did not proclaim the Dhamma in order to satisfy our curiosity about the origin or end of the universe, or to reveal startling secrets, or to stimulate worship. His purpose was to teach us to put an end to suffering—the same suffering we feel now as we contemplate these symbols and evidences of death. By investigating with dispassionate minds we come to see things as they really are, seeing them we turn away from the destructive habit of craving, turning away we are by degrees liberated from all suffering. We may be familiar with this idea and may even give it our intellectual assent, but until we make it work in our daily lives we must remain in doubt and under the sway of continual death. We shall be buried soon enough—shall we stay in the tomb till then? The light of insight can dispel the charnel darkness and free the suffering mind even in this present life. If the present is well attended to, the future will take care of itself.

We look up through sunlight and find that our steps have gone full circle: just beyond a bank of ivy and flowers stand the gaunt gates of this cemetery. The painter has gone; the caretaker is nowhere to be seen; nobody accompanies us on this quiet journey. We pause by a final marker, an old one, whose legend has been eaten by time. It lays flat, abject to the sky, speaking no longer any name of man but uttering the truth of impermanence. Its individuality has been effaced—it is scarcely more regular then random nature—but still it declares in the sounding-box of thought the ineluctable fate of all compounded things. It will bear our names as easily as any others, and indeed already does so—let the wise man read his own! The death of the body is real, as are the small convulsions of flesh and thought in the present moment. Let us drive to the end of all of these. No evasion shall avail us, no distraction blur the sight—this marker is our own. It shall not yield to the blows of hope or fear, but only to the long, cool gaze of wisdom.

We issue from the iron gates into the churning city once again, and the granite hills slip into distance and memory. Walking familiar pavements we find, strangely, that we carry still a mood or vision before which all objects fall into atoms and aspects of the Buddha's revelation. The city shows as many symbols as the graveyard. Around us life burns as profligately as gunpowder—in getting and spending, gaining and losing, craving and hating. We see buildings, avenues, hurrying people, but if we are careful we also see that we are really still walking among monuments in the mind. We make our fate right here. The cemetery and the city are one. Shall we continue to build upon our little insight? It's not so hard: the body moves, feelings spring up, mind comprehends, mental objects succeed one another—all these may be observed. In city or cemetery the process is the same—let us simply keep looking, noting with cool attention the flow of the phenomena. The defilements of mind cannot stand the scrutiny; they must perforce dissolve. Who shall oppress us then? Life, till now one long fatality, may unfold in understanding. When birth and death are understood they are overcome, and with them all manner of suffering.

Whoever realizes a little, should he not strive to realize more? Whoever would be free, should he not lay hands on his chains? Whoever would act rightly, should he not found his actions on knowledge? The Buddha has declared the nature of suffering, its origin, its end, and the means to its end. His words hang in the air—pregnant, epic, awesome—until we begin to move by their guidance. Then they become living truth. Then the dark and mortal way we tread brightens with direct experience. Final emancipation may be far or near. What matters is the going

Dark Ages, Golden Ages

Without quite intending it, we find ourselves over the years burdened by more and more responsibilities, difficulties, and doubts. It seems practically a consequence of growing older. Time passes like a river—so smooth to our puzzled eyes—but leaves, as if by magic, these boulders on our backs. All of us but the very young sense this weight and wonder why, since we asked for none of it, it settles on us and will not be shirked. Troubles old and new bear on us despite all the care we take to persevere ourselves and to build our castles against a turbulent world. We will all, of course, acknowledge the possibility of catastrophes which could plunge us into genuine grief at any moment, but why now, as we live in relative comfort and health, should we feel this weight on the heart, this strain of apprehension?

Little annoyances and thorns of worry are just part of life, we tell ourselves as we make our way between the twin imponderables of birth and death. If we are brave, determined, and optimistic, that should be enough, should it not? Yet even in our joys there falls the shadow—the menace of great forces around us, the obscure sadness looking back at us from the mirror, the occasional sense of overwhelming futility and frailty. We look around, wondering who is to blame? If no culprit is forthcoming, we may turn with suspicion to the great, grim world at large and wonder if its influence goes deeper than the indigestion occasioned by the evening news. Even if we are personally healthy and prosperous, perhaps malaise of the times has subtly infected us. If the age we live in is corrupt and decadent can we remain altogether uncontaminated? What sort of age is this, anyway?

Probably all but the most fanatical optimists have from time to time, while hearing of the latest crime or war or degradation of human decency, considered the proposition that the world has gone screaming mad. The iniquity of mankind these days seems to surpass the merely incidental and to approach willful dementia. Moral values retreat before the onslaught of hysterical cruelty and lust, and everywhere we see wicked fantasy enthroned—mankind and nations having lost faith in the god and the right. Science, once hailed as our deliverance, labors mightily and produces bombs and video games to pacify—in one way or another—the frenzied multitudes. But there is no peace. Drugs, alcohol, and insanity hang on the communal body like leeches, draining what life remains and imparting a fever of nihilism that burns fearfully bright with decadent delights. There is a murmur of woe but little resistance, for who can turn the trend of history? The honest man—never easy to find—fades from view as evildoers are first excused, then celebrated by the timid and the envious. Like a worn-out carousel, our society jangles, and wheezes toward collapse.

The instinct of most of us in times such as these is to keep our heads down and hang onto our pleasures and possessions and bear our pains as best we may. We wish to run no risks in a world with chance so badly skewed against us. The result is that we are trapped, closeted with our fears while the storm rages worse outside. Here in this tight space dread grows, and the possibilities for remedy are few. On television maniacally cheerful people contrive to sell us happiness. Buy! Enjoy! Experience! Out on the streets glowering zealots paste up posters urging struggle, war, confusion, and the death of their enemies—after which, presumably, mankind will enjoy bliss. Civilization appears to be spiralling down into awesome decadence, and the fall of Rome comes to the minds of those not altogether oblivious to history. It's an unpleasant thought, so we take shelter in our small delights or else in the blandishments of psychological and religious quacks who—for a fee to defray the costs of their own indulgences—will tell us anything we want to hear. Do we feel guilty? It's probably someone else's fault. Are we tempted by vice? Go ahead, fulfill yourselves! Will we have to give up anything to achieve happiness? Oh, never! Perish the thought! A golden age is dawning.

Most of us avoid the worst excesses of the age—not out of sturdy virtue so much as out of a trembling sense of self-preservation. But all of us, Buddhists included, feel the sickness in our surroundings and grow fearful, hiding where we can. In a dark age, who can blame our caution?

Yet the trouble with such caution is that it may mask mere cowardice or sloth. Let us examine the matter a little closer. Does this hobbling, failing century really qualify as a dark age? Without pressing evidence to the contrary, we are apt to regard our own woes as the worst ever endured by the race. (Self-aggrandizement comes in curious forms.) But if we read a bit of history we will be hard put to champion the depravity of our own age against the past. If we define dark age as a period when the light of understanding is eclipsed and evils multiply, what age of history may not be called dark? The perfidy and wretchedness of our ancestors must give us pause and take the edge of our own complaints. Wars, plagues, persecutions, and crimes abound in every era. There's plenty of horror to go around, and the special poignancy of the present version is only that it's happening to us.

However dark the world may appear to us, we are not justified in retreating to the extremes of hedonism or nihilism. There is a task to be done, and that task is not—as many people believe—to readjust self, society, or world to fit our blind desires. Rather it is to train ourselves to the point where we know reality for what it is and free ourselves of the burdens of passion that now oppress us. This task faces all Buddhists, though we are reluctant to admit it and tend to excuse ourselves on the grounds that the times are so bad and responsibilities so weighty that we cannot—most regrettably—take on the additional project of earnest Dhamma practice. The woes of nations and the afflictions of persons are thereby perversely made reasons for not doing anything, and the way of Dhamma is implicitly called a burden. As if it were not suffering that first impelled the Buddha toward liberation. As if the Dhamma were not the means to that liberation.

Some of us may even rationalize to the extent of believing that since the times are too difficult for us to make a genuine effort toward emancipation, they are probably too difficult for everybody. The days of high attainment are gone, and with them any reason to exert ourselves beyond a modicum of morality and ritual observance. With war, crime, and madness round about, we have enough trouble just saving our skins. Better to keep our heads down and (over another glass of wine) lament cruel fate.

Yet to look honestly at ourselves and the Dhamma must bring us to another conclusion. One era may be better or worse than another—as the world goes—but old age, sickness, and death come to all. Anxiety, depression and grief come to all. If we cannot overcome them now, how should we ever face them in heaven or a golden age when we are swimming in bliss? What motivation would we have then? A dark age will pass in five years or five hundred, the age of *dukkha* never. This pervasive suffering, coarse or fine, settles like dust on us—swiftly or slowly with the winds of circumstance. We can't outwait it, yearning for a golden age which, if it ever came, could only enervate us and leave us none the wiser. Let it rain champagne, the heart will still thirst.

No time is worthier than now, for we have no other time. The past expires at our feet; the future is being wrought for our present action. We need not pretend that the world is good or evolving toward an age of light, or deny the dangers that beset us in this savage century, but we should rouse ourselves with the knowledge that the serenity and happiness preached by the Buddha remain as accessible now as ever, transcending and abolishing the jungle of the years. A thorn in the mind is the father of all griefs. The Buddha teaches us to pull it out

—§§§—

Sayings and Parables

Various Authors

Bodhi Leaves No. 97

First published: 1983

FOREWORD

The Buddha often taught in concrete terms, and his discourses abound in images, similes, and parables which translate the profound truths of the Dhamma into the familiar facts of everyday life. These devices arouse interest and facilitate understanding. They make the principles to be taught strong and vivid in their impact on those to whom they are addressed and provide an impetus to apply them in practice. It is one of the marvels of the Buddha's method of exposition that there is hardly an aspect of human life which is not made to serve as a means for illustrating his teaching.

The present brief selection of Buddhist sayings and parables is intended to provide a sampling of the Buddha's concrete way of teaching. The selection is taken from the book "The Teaching of Buddha" (133rd rev. ed., 1980), published by the Bukkyo Dendo Kyokai (Buddhist Promoting Foundation) of Japan. This book was compiled for the purpose of promoting the practice of Buddhism through a compact anthology of Buddhist texts reflecting the spirit of Japanese Buddhism. Its numerous brief selections draw from the scriptures of various Buddhist traditions, both Theravada and Mahayana. Some of the sayings taken for the present booklet are from selections based on Mahayana sources, but the principles they teach can readily be understood in terms of the general Buddhist tradition.

The Buddhist Promoting Foundation, which publishes the original in a bilingual English-Japanese edition, distributes it in the noble hope of seeing "a day come soon when as many homes as possible will have this book and as many as possible of our fellow men will enjoy and bathe in the light of the Great Teacher." The BPS hopes to contribute to the fulfilment of this aim with the present small anthology. Copies of the original may be obtained by writing to Bukkyo Dendo Kyokai, 3–14 Shiba 4–Chome, Minato-ku Tokyo, Japan

Sayings and Parables

Human Life

There is an allegory that depicts human life.

> Once there was a man rowing a boat down a river. Someone on the shore warned him, "Stop rowing so gaily down the swift current; there are rapids ahead and a dangerous whirlpool and there are crocodiles and demons lying in wait in rocky caverns. You will perish if you continue."

In this allegory, "the swift current" is a life of lust; "rowing gaily" is giving rein to one's passions; "rapids ahead" means the ensuing suffering and pain; "whirlpool" means pleasure; "crocodiles and demons" refers to the decay and death that follow a life of lust and indulgence; "someone on the shore" who calls out is Buddha.

* * *

Here is another allegory.

> A man who has committed a crime is running away; the guards are following him, so he tries to hide himself by descending into a well by means of some vines growing down the sides. As he descends, he sees vipers at the bottom of the well, so he decides to cling to the vine for safety. After a time when his arms get tired, he notices two mice, one white and the other black, gnawing at the vine.
>
> If the vine breaks, he will fall to the vipers and perish. Suddenly, on looking upward, he notices just above his face a bee-hive from which occasionally falls a drop of honey. Forgetting all the dangers, the man tastes the honey with delight.

"A man" means the one who is born to suffer and to die alone. "Guards" and "vipers" refer to the body with all its desires. "Vines" means the continuity of life. "Two mice, one white and the other black" refer to the duration of time, days and nights, and the passing years.

"Honey" indicates the physical pleasures that beguile the suffering of the passing years.

* * *

Here is still another allegory.

> A king places four vipers in a box and gives the box into the keeping of a servant. He commands the servant to take good care of them and warns that if he angers even one of them, he will be punished with death. The servant, in fear, decides to throw away the box and escape.
>
> The king sends five guards to capture the servant. At first they approach the servant in a friendly manner, intending to take him back safely, but the servant does not trust their friendliness and escapes to another village.
>
> Then, in a vision, a voice tells him that in this village there is no safe shelter, and that there are six bandits who will attack him, so the servant runs away in fright until he comes to a wild river that blocks his way. Thinking of the dangers that are following him, he makes a raft and succeeds in crossing the turbulent current, beyond which he finally finds safety and peace.

"Four vipers in a box" indicate the four elements of earth, water, fire, and air that make up the body of flesh. The body is given into the charge of lust and is an enemy of the mind. Therefore he tries to run away from the body.

"Five guards who approach in a friendly manner" mean the five aggregates—form, feeling, perception, volition and consciousness—which frame body and mind.

"The safe shelter" is the six senses, which are no safe shelter at all, and "the six bandits" are the six objects of the six senses. Thus, seeing the dangers within the six senses, he runs away once more and comes to the wild current of worldly desires.

Then he makes himself a raft of the Buddha's good teachings and crosses the wild current safely.

* * *

In a thicket at the foot of the Himalayan Mountains there once lived a parrot together with many other animals and birds. One day a fire started in the thicket from the friction of bamboos in a strong wind, and the birds and animals were in frightened confusion. The parrot, feeling compassion for their fright and suffering, and wishing to repay the kindness he had received in the bamboo thicket where he could shelter himself, tried to do all he could to save them. He dipped himself in a pond nearby and flew over the fire and shook off the drops of water to extinguish the fire. He repeated this diligently with a heart of compassion out of gratitude to the thicket. This spirit of kindness and self-sacrifice was noticed by a heavenly god who came down from the sky and said to the parrot: "You have a gallant mind, but what good do you expect to accomplish by a few drops of water against this great fire?" The parrot answered: "There is nothing that cannot be accomplished by the spirit of gratitude and self-sacrifice. I will try over and over again and then over again in the next life." The great god was impressed by the parrot's spirit, and together they extinguished the fire.

* * *

At one time there lived in the Himalayas a bird with one body and two heads. Once one of the heads noticed the other head eating some sweet fruit and felt jealous and said to itself: "I will then eat poison fruit." So it ate the poisonous fruit, and the whole bird died.

* * *

Once there was a wealthy but foolish man. When he saw the beautiful three-storied house of another man, he envied it and made up his mind to have one built just like it, thinking he was himself just as wealthy. He called a carpenter and ordered him to build it. The carpenter consented and immediately began to construct the foundation, the first story, the second story, and then the third story. The wealthy man noticed this with irritation and said: "I don't want a foundation or a first story or a second story; I just want the beautiful third story. Build it quickly."

A foolish man always thinks only of the results, and is impatient without the effort that is necessary to get good results. No good can be attained without proper effort, just as there can be no third story without the foundation and the first and second stories.

* * *

A foolish man was once boiling honey. His friend suddenly appeared and the foolish man wanted to offer him some honey, but it was too hot, and so without removing it from the fire, he fanned it to cool it. In like manner, it is impossible to get the honey of cool wisdom without first removing the fire of worldly passions.

* * *

There is no one way to get free from the trap of worldly passions. Suppose you caught a snake, a crocodile, a bird, a dog, a fox and a monkey, six creatures of very different nature, and you tie them together with a strong rope and let them go. Each of these six creatures will try to go back to its own lair by its own method: the snake will seek a covering of grass, the crocodile will seek water, the bird will want to fly in the air, the dog will seek a village, the fox will seek the solitary ledges, and the monkey will seek the trees of a forest. In the attempt of each to go its own way there will be a struggle, but being tied together by a rope, the strongest at any one time will drag the rest. Like the six creatures in this parable, man is tempted in different ways by the desires of his six senses: eyes, ears, nose, tongue, touch and brain, and is controlled by the predominant desire.

If the six creatures are all tied to a post, they will try to get free until they are tired out, and then will lie down by the post. Just like this, if people will train and control the mind, there will be no further trouble from the other five senses. If the mind is under control, people will have happiness both now and in the future.

* * *

Here is another allegory.

> Once there were two demons who spent a whole day arguing and quarrelling about a box, a cane, and a pair of

> shoes. A man passing by inquired, "Why are you arguing about these things? What magical power have they that you should be quarrelling about possessing them?"
>
> The demons explained to him that from the box they could get anything they desired—food, clothing or treasure; with the cane they could subdue all their enemies; and with the pair of shoes they could travel through the air.
>
> Upon hearing this, the man said, "Why quarrel? If you will go away for a few minutes, I can think of a fair division of the things between you." So the two demons retired and as soon as they were gone, the man put on the shoes, seized the box and the cane and was off through the air.

The "demons" represent men of false beliefs. "A box" means the gifts that are made in charity; they do not realize how many treasures can be produced from charity. "A cane" means the practice of concentration of mind. Men do not realize that by the practice of spiritual concentration of mind, they can subdue all worldly desires "A pair of shoes" means the pure disciplines of thought and conduct that will carry them beyond all desires and arguments. Without knowing these, they quarrel and argue about a box, a cane, and a pair of shoes.

* * *

Once a beautiful and well-dressed women visited a house. The master of the house asked her who she was, and she replied that she was the goddess of wealth. The master of the house was delighted and so treated her nicely.

Soon after, another woman appeared who was ugly and poorly dressed. The master asked her who she was, and the woman replied that she was the goddess of poverty. The master was frightened and tried to drive her out of the house, but the woman refused to depart, saying, "The goddess of wealth is my sister. There is an agreement between us that we are never to live separately; if you chase me out, she is to go with me." Sure enough, as soon as the ugly woman left, the other woman disappeared.

Birth goes with death. Fortune goes with misfortune. Bad things follow good things. Men should realize this. Foolish people dread misfortune and strive after good fortune, but those who seek Enlightenment must transcend both of them and be free of worldly attachments.

Marriage

The relation of husband and wife is not designed merely for their convenience. It has a deeper significance than the mere association of two physical bodies in one house. Husband and wife should take advantage of the intimacies of their association to help each other in training their minds in the Buddha's teachings.

An old couple, an "ideal couple," as they were called, once came to the Buddha and said, "Lord, we were married after we had been acquainted in childhood, and there has never been a cloud in our happiness. Please tell us if we can be remarried in the next life."

The Buddha gave them this wise answer: "If you both have exactly the same faith, if you both received the teaching in exactly the same way, if you perform charity in the same way, and if you have the same wisdom, then you will have the same mind in the next birth."

Family Life

A family is a place where minds come in contact with one another. If these minds love one another, the home will be as beautiful as a flower garden. But if these minds get out of harmony with one another, it is like a storm that plays havoc with the garden.

If discord arises within one's family, one should not blame others but should examine one's own mind and follow a right path.

* * *

Discordant minds often bring disaster. A trifling misunderstanding may be followed by great misfortune. This is especially to be guarded against in family life.

The Life of Women

There are no distinctions of sex on the path to Enlightenment. If a woman makes up her mind to seek Enlightenment, she will become a heroine of the True Path.

Mallikā, the daughter of King Pasenadi and the Queen of King Ayodrya, was such a heroine. She had great faith in the teaching of the Blessed One and made the ten following vows in his presence:

"My Lord, until I gain Enlightenment, I will not violate the sacred precepts; I will not be arrogant before people who are older than myself; I will not become angry with anyone.

"I will not be jealous of others or envy their possessions; I will not be selfish either in mind or property; I will try to make poor people happy with the things I receive and will not hoard them for myself.

"I will receive all people courteously give them what they need, and speak kindly to them; consider their circumstances and not my convenience: and try to benefit them without partiality

"If I see others in solitude, in prison, or suffering from disease or other troubles, I will try to relieve them and make them happy by explaining the reasons and laws to them.

"If I see others catching living animals and being cruel to them or violating any such precept, I will punish them if they are to be punished, or teach them if they are to be taught, and then I will try to undo what they have done and correct their mistakes, to the best of my ability

"I will not forget to hear the right teaching, for I know that when one neglects the right teaching one quickly falls away from the truth that abides everywhere, and will fail to reach the shore of Enlightenment."

Then she made the following three wishes to save poor people:

"First, I will try to make everyone peaceful. This wish, I believe, in whatever life I may receive hereafter, will be the root of goodness that will grow into the wisdom of good teaching.

"Second, after I have received the wisdom of good teaching, I will untiringly teach all people.

"Third, I will protect the true teaching, even at the sacrifice of my own bodylife or property"

The true significance of family life is the opportunity it gives for mutual encouragement and aid on the path to Enlightenment. Even an ordinary woman, if she has the same mind to seek Enlightenment, and makes the same vows and wishes, may become as great a disciple of Buddha as Mallikā was.

The Harmony of Society

Let us imagine a desert country lying in absolute darkness with many living things swarming blindly about in it.

Naturally they will be frightened, and as they run about without recognizing one another during the night, there will be frequent squirming and loneliness. It is indeed a pitiable sight

Then let us imagine that suddenly a superior man with a torch appears, and everything around becomes bright and clear.

The living beings in the dark solitude suddenly air a great relief as they look about to recognize one another and happily share their companionship

By a "desert country" is meant a world of human life when it lies in the darkness of ignorance. Those who have no light of wisdom in their minds wander about in loneliness and fear. They were born alone and die alone; they do not know how to associate with their fellow men in peaceful harmony, and they are naturally despondent and fearful.

By "a superior man with a torch" is meant Buddha assuming a human form, and by his wisdom and companion he illumines the world.

In this light people find themselves as well as others and are glad to establish human fellowship and harmonious relations.

Thousands of people may live in a community, but it is not one of real fellowship until they know each other mutually and have sympathy for one another.

A true community has faith and wisdom that illuminate it. It is a place where the people know and trust one another and where there is social harmony.

In fact, harmony is the life and real purpose of a true community or an organization.

* * *

Blood stains cannot be removed by more blood; resentment cannot be removed by more resentment; resentment can be removed only by forgetting it.

* * *

A pure mind soon becomes a deep mind, a mind that is commensurate with the Noble Path, a mind that loves to give, a mind that loves to keep the precepts, an enduring mind, a zealous mind, a calm mind, a wise mind, a compassionate mind, a mind that leads people to Enlightenment by many and skilful means. Thus shall the Buddha's land be built.

* * *

Indeed, earnestness and faithfulness in spreading the teaching of the Dhamma are what build the Buddha Land.

* * *

As the light of a small candle will spread from one to another in succession, so the light of Buddha's compassion will pass on from one mind to another endlessly.

* * *

Lay followers should always remember that the reason they believe in the three treasures and keep the precepts is to enable themselves ultimately to attain Enlightenment, and for that reason they should, though living in the world of desires, avoid becoming attached to such desires.

Lay followers should always keep in mind that sooner or later they will be obliged to part with their parents and families and pass away from this life of birth and death; therefore, they should not become attached to things of this life but should set their minds on the world of Enlightenment, wherein nothing passes away.

* * *

The mind of faith is pure and gentle, always patient and enduring, never arguing, never causing suffering to others but always pondering the three treasures—the Buddha, the Dhamma, and the Sangha. Thus happiness spontaneously rises in their minds, and the light for Enlightenment can be found everywhere.

* * *

Those who follow the teaching of Buddha, because they understand that everything is characterized by "nonsubstantiality," do not treat lightly the things that enter into a man's life, but they receive them for what they are and then try to make them fit for Enlightenment.

They must not think that this world is meaningless and filled with confusion while the world of Enlightenment is full of meaning and peace. Rather, they should taste the way of Enlightenment in all affairs of this world.

* * *

Blossoms come about because of a series of conditions that lead up to their blooming; leaves are blown away because a series of conditions lead up to it. Blossoms do not appear unconditioned, nor does a leaf fall of itself. So everything has its coming forth and passing away; nothing can be independent without any change.

* * *

It is the everlasting and unchanging rule of this world that everything is created by a series of causes and conditions and disappears by the same rule: everything changes—nothing remains without change.

Suppose a log is floating in a river. If the log does not become grounded, or sinks, or is not taken out by man, or does not decay, ultimately it will reach the sea. Life is like this log caught in the current of a great river. If a person does not become attached to a life of self-indulgence, or, by renouncing life, does not become attached to a life of self-torture; if a person does not become proud of his virtues or does not become attached to his evil acts; if in his search for Enlightenment he does not become contemptuous of delusion or fear it; such a person is following the Middle Way,

The important thing in following the path to Enlightenment is to avoid being caught and entangled in any extreme—that is, always to follow the Middle Way.

Heedfulness

Bhikkhu Khantipālo

Bodhi Leaves No. 98

First published: 1984

Heedfulness

by Bhikkhu Khantipālo

Who are not heedless, they
Dig up the root of suffering
By day and night give up things dear,
Deathly, sensuous and very hard to cross.

Most people in this world fall among the class of persons known as "heedless"—and for most of their lives at that. What is this kind of person like? A heedless man, one who dwells sunk in this mud of heedlessness, does not care to develop in himself any of the virtues in this life, and instead drifts about controlled by the currents of his desires, which lead him to do all sorts of things which are evil. He does not care to develop wisdom, which in the beginning means the ability to distinguish what is skilful, profiting oneself and others, from what is evil, poisoning oneself and others. He does not call to mind that this life is a short span between birth and death and that within it lies the experience of many bitter and unwelcome things. He is lazy, making no effort towards self-control. He does not aspire to any high ideal and thinks only to get his sense-desires fulfilled. He is bogged down in the slough of materialism and selfishly grabs for himself whatever he can get out of this world. O this heedless man! How much of sufferings he makes for himself and others! He is, in other words, a man who does not know where his own good, or the good of others lies. He helps forward strife and dissension, and because he is firmly attached to possessions, relations, people and places; he can never find the happiness for which, so vainly, he looks. This heedless man is not some strange and abstract character but veritably in myself and in yourselves whenever we do not guard ourselves and make no efforts in the Dhamma-training. And we are the people who in proportion to our heedlessness suffer the thorny fruits of evil which ripen for us, and of which, though bitter, we must partake.

Therefore, this heedless man is the very opposite of the true Buddhist who is well described by the adjective "heedful". The quality of heedfulness has been praised many times by the Exalted Buddha, just as the opposite, heedlessness, has been condemned. In this Dhamma, there is much to be practised and there is practice suitable for every posture of the body and every minute of the day. There is practice to be done concerning the stream of thoughts racing in the mind, there is more practice connected with the thousands of words spoken every day, and there is Dhamma-practice for the body, whatever it is doing. Now none of this can be accomplished without heedfulness, without making effort, without employing mindful awareness, or without wisdom. Heedfulness implies the conscious cultivation of these three aspects of Dhamma: effort, mindfulness and wisdom. These three mark the true Buddhist, one who is really trying to practise what the Exalted One has taught. So then, by way of contrast with that heedless fellow who is our untrained and unrestrained selves, let us take a look at the heedful Dhamma-practiser, whom we may occasionally resemble. A heedful man does take care to develop in himself all the virtues according to his ability and his need, and he does not drift about from desire to desire but lays some restraint upon his mind, speech and body with regard to this. As he does so, he is able to distinguish the wholesome from the evil, and he knows clearly why certain actions are harmful while others are helpful to Dhamma training. He is aware of the short span of this life which may at any moment, and in countless million ways, come to an end. Therefore, he is not lazy and does put forth effort towards self-control. He knows of higher ideals than mere materialism, and he does aspire to attain them for himself, thus benefiting others as well. He knows full well that to be the prey of desires all the time is the most potent way of increasing all kinds of sufferings and unhappiness. So then, he is a man who knows the good of himself and the good of others whom he can help in various ways. From the store of goodness and wisdom cultivated by him, he becomes happy and can show the way of true happiness to others. This heedful man is also no abstraction but truly ourselves whenever we see the I in our own hearts, smeared with greed, aversion and delusion, disturbed by the boiling-up of so many desires, there is much to be done. So we stir up energy within ourselves to practise Dhamma, that is, to be generous, helpful and kindly, to keep pure the Precepts, to develop the heart in calm and concentration by appropriate ways, and to wield the sword of wisdom within our hearts for the purification which should be made there; and again, through this effort, we become mindful, we become aware of the body in all its aspects, we develop awareness of feelings as they arise and pass away, we become aware of what sort of state the mind is in, and finally we know clearly the different constituents or the mind as they arise and pass away; and with this mindfulness goes wisdom and cleansing. No one can claim to be truly a Buddhist unless he is heedful, that is, he is making effort in training himself in Dhamma, to the extent possible for him.

Now we can turn to the verse spoken by the Exalted Buddha and consider its meaning for ourselves. In the first line are mentioned those people "who are not heedless" and they form the subject of this instruction. Those who are heedless are not mentioned directly but it is clear from the verses that they, whether by day or by night, do not "give up things dear" and so make no efforts to dig up the root of suffering which, as we shall see, is called craving. So these heedless people are trapped in things bound up with death, things which appeal to the senses and desires and seem to increase pleasure, things which are as an ocean, very extensive and perilous, which are difficult to overcome. The sufferings of the heedless will become clearer by contrast with the happiness born of Dhamma practice by the heedful, of which this verse speaks.

This "root of suffering"—let us look into the meaning of it. Roots are commonly the tough and deeply penetrating underground parts of trees and plants. Towards their tips they are much divided and very fine, and they seek constantly for nutriment. But the root spoken of here, though it has these characteristics, is found in the heart of every unenlightened person. The root of suffering is tough, for craving and desire are not easy to pull up but strongly resist the efforts of those who try. And this craving root is certainly deeply penetrating. It has not only been planted and grown in this life but over innumerable existences before our present birth; it has established itself in the very depths of our hearts. And this root, like others, is underground, for it cannot easily be seen. Some people are not even aware that they have any craving at all, and most people have little idea of its extent. The network of fibres of this craving become very fine, very subtle towards their ends, and even those who have long been heedful and practised Dhamma with devotion, may find it hard to root out the finest threads. But if they are not removed like twitch, bindweed or dandelions, this wretched craving springs up again. So it is that the Exalted One has said: "So dig up craving by its root". This root of suffering called craving also seeks for nutriment of many kinds, as do the roots of plants. For instance, there is ordinary food which is craved for its pleasing appearance, its subtle aroma, its delicious taste, its delightful texture, its allaying of hunger-pain, and its way of increasing one's sense of well being by fullness. So, in this way, craving is expressed through eye, nose, tongue and bodily sensibility. Then there is craving in the mind by thinking about the desired nutriment. Now, people "who are not heedless" look upon this craving as a parasite which has a stranglehold but must be destroyed as quickly as possible. And why do they think like this? From the clear understanding born of their not being heedless, they see that craving is the root of suffering. All the kinds of sufferings are all born of craving, or suffered because of craving. Whether those sufferings are slightly disagreeable, or whether they are very grave; whether they are physical, or whether they are mental; all kinds of sufferings are born of desires. How can this be? When one desires and gets, one suffers from keeping, from maintaining; when one does not get what is craved, one also suffers. Desires are never fulfilled entirely and if you look into this, you will find that the thing desired never quite lives up to expectations. We expect stability in the desired people or things. But neither ourselves nor those desired things whatever they are—people, places, experiences—neither subject nor object has any stability. Instability marks this world and when we grab at something desired, thinking it stable, we heap up this suffering for ourselves. Nor does a heedless man understand that unstable things are unsatisfactory or *dukkha*. Not living up to expectations, they disappoint him. Not being permanent or remaining in the form desired, they cannot be but unsatisfactory. That heedless fellow also has no idea about the non-selfnature of things. The most important "things" to explain here are the physical and mental aspects of oneself. Though ordinarily thought of as self, as belonging to self, a little reflection will prove how far from being "owned" this mind and body are. The heedless man never thinks whether "my body", "my mind", 'myself' could really be true. But neither body nor mind obey a self, they just work governed by certain laws and conditions. There is no possibility of a self who is the owner of mind and body—such ideas are born of craving for security. And where there is craving, there is bound to be suffering. So this root of suffering spreads its battening rootlets both deep and wide.

Obviously, the heedful man, knowing the direction in which happiness should be sought, will readily try to "dig up the root of" suffering. Now, in digging, one has to have some tools and one has to know the method in which these should be used. The land, in this case, is one's own heart, which is a bit of rough ground if ever there was, hardly ever cultivated, and besides the odds and ends of rubbish tipped on the surface which can be seen, the whole plot is riddled with every sort of weed and pest lurking underneath. Not the sort of ground a gardener would choose perhaps? But then we are not in the position of being able to choose. Unlike worldly gardeners, we ourselves have dumped the surface-rubbish just recently, and in past times we have allowed the thistles, twitch and bindweed to grow luxuriantly. So we have only to blame our own heedlessness that in the past we allowed things to get in this state. For our cultivation in Dhamma, the Exalted Buddha has provided us with three principal tools with which to "dig up the root of suffering". These tools are called: Moral Conduct or *sīla;* Collectedness or *samādhi;* and Wisdom or *paññā*. They may be rusty from long neglect in which case "elbow-grease" will be needed for polishing them up. This elbow grease is called "effort" or *viriya* and we shall never be able to wield these tools successfully unless we can see to it that the mental factor of effort is always present. And effort, of course, is one aspect of this heedfulness praised by all the Buddhas and Arahants, praised by all wise men everywhere.

Now that we know what the tools are, we must get to know the method. Digging is something of an art and digging up craving is the very subtlest of all arts. The method to be used is called "practising Dhamma according to Dhamma". Here the word, Dhamma has two meanings. In the first case, it means the various methods and ways adopted while training oneself. These methods may be given one by a Teacher in this tradition but one still has to apply them for oneself. But "Dhamma" in the second case means both the Law and the Goal. The way is to practise whatever one knows of Dhamma in oneself. This is the work which the heedful man sets himself to do. He has the tools of Moral Conduct, Collectedness and Wisdom and he has the instructions on how these are to be applied. If he lives far from Buddhist lands, these instructions will be the recorded words of the Exalted Buddha as preserved in Pali and translated into various modern tongues. But if he stays in a Buddhist country, these ancient instructions can be supplemented with living example and teaching of those who partly or wholly, have dug up "the root of suffering".

This root of suffering, this craving, goes down very deep, and like a gardener, the heedful man will have to dig deep using the three tools provided. With each tool he can clear the ground to a certain depth. For clearing the surface of rubbish he will want to use Moral Conduct or *sīla*, for when this is used, the surface rubbish of bodily misconduct and verbal misconduct can be carted off. The Five Precepts or the Eight Precepts which are guides for the practice of Dhamma upon special days of training such as the *Uposatha*, or the Ten Precepts of a novice, or the many rules practised by monks, all these have as their function, the restraint of the body from evil acts and the restraint of the tongue from evil speech. This outward rubbish may be swept away by sincerely keeping the Precepts, whereby a certain gladness will be experienced born of making effort and from seeing the success of one's efforts. By digging deeper with the tool called Collectedness, which means all sorts of meditative practice, the fibres of this craving-root, called the five hindrances, may be removed. These five hindrances block the way to the experience of the states of concentration (*jhāna*) and must be removed before the concentrations can be experienced. These five are as follows: sensual desire, ill-will, sloth and torpor, distraction and worry, and lastly, scepticism. The heedful man is one who can suppress these at will and enter into the far-ranging concentrations. The tool of wisdom or *paññā*, is needed to dig out the finest and deepest of roots connected with this craving. These fine roots ranging very deeply are called the pollutions or *āsava*s. Three of them are usually listed: the pollution of sensuality, the pollution of becoming, and the pollution of unknowing. Craving here takes these three forms—that is, the attachment to even subtle sensuality, the attachment to more and more of life—more and more of and pollution of not knowing the truth about this mind-body, not knowing that they are unstable, unsatisfactory, and do not make up a selfhood. These pollutions are a stench in the hearts of all beings who have not experienced Enlightenment and they flow into and infect all the operations of the mind, giving rise to the polluted mind, unable to know correctly and certainly.

Very briefly here the range of "the root of suffering" has been outlined. Everyone can make a start with this digging, while if one has made a start already, then what about making greater effort? It is important though that this training in Dhamma must be undertaken in the right way, in the way according with Dhamma and this means not according to what one thinks and wishes to do for oneself. As this idea of "self" is born of unknowing and craving, it will be no good training in Dhamma according to one's own ideas. The whole training must be undertaken in the spirit of Dhamma which leads away from craving. Indeed, in the third line of the verse above we see this clearly: "By day and night give up things dear". This is the way of the heedful man who wishes to practise Dhamma according to Dhamma, for the overcoming of craving, for digging up that root of suffering. This is called "renunciation", the very opposite direction to the craving driving most people in this world. In starting to practise renunciation, charity and generosity should be cultivated, thereby freeing to some extent the heart from meanness. But here, more than this is implied, for it is said" By day and night give up ... "This does not refer to the beginning of renunciation but this teaching reaches up to Enlightenment, to the final goal of Buddhist endeavour, that is: "Who are not heedless, they dig up the root of suffering". These are the instructions to arouse one to do something about oneself and the method to be used follows in the next line: "By day and night give up things dear". Before we can do this, we must know what the Exalted Buddha means by "things dear". By this he means everything for which we have attachment, beginning with the six sense bases themselves: eye, ear, nose, tongue, body and mind; to the six sense objects; sights, sounds, smells, tastes, touches, and mental stimuli, and then on through the six impressions upon these senses, and so to the six kinds of thought about these sense impressions, and finally to the six sets of craving arising with respect to the six objects. All this and more, for it has been simplified here, and all the world known to us, including all of what is thought of as "self", all this inside and outside, is called "things".

If we would "dig up the root of suffering" then it is obvious that we must be able to renounce attachment to these senses and sense-object and so on. To the heedless man, indeed, this must seem like total annihilation but then he revels in this world and plants in himself "the root of suffering". He has no deeper view, he has no path to make progress on.

But for the heedful man who has Dhamma as his guide, Dhamma as the lamp which lights his life, this renunciation can be made since he views the things of self and of the world in the light of the last line of the verse: "Deathly, sensuous, and very hard to cross". Because of this the heedful man thinks that it is worthwhile to train in Moral Conduct, Collectedness and Wisdom and makes efforts with his own training accordingly. The instructions have now been given and the method also, and now to spur us onward, there is the warning: that "things dear" are "Deathly, sensuous and very hard to cross". We should understand what these terms mean so that we feel roused to practise Dhamma wholeheartedly. There are first, the dear things of death, meaning that wherever craving has its roots, with attachment and clinging, there death will also take its toll. For there is no birth and death if there is no craving, while the more that things are dear to us, whether internal or external, sentient or insentient, the more of birth and death with all its accompanying *dukkha* we make for ourselves. By clinging to people, places and experiences, even people near to the end of their lives ensure that they will be born again. But this process of craving goes on for most people day and night and they thus ensure for themselves an endless round of birth and death, that is, unless they take up this path of renunciation. To practise Moral Conduct, one must renounce the pleasures which some people seem to get from bodily misconduct such as killing sentient beings, and from verbal misconduct which means such words as lying and slandering. And more renunciation is necessary if one would cultivate one's mind. One cannot develop in mindfulness and concentration and at the same time indulge to the full in worldly pleasures. These have to be given up if the deep states of collected meditation are to be experienced. And the cultivation of wisdom means the renunciation of attachment to the various sorts of defilement which afflict the heart. The more one is able to renounce the influence of the passions and defiling tendencies of the mind, the more will wisdom grow in the heart. In this way, renunciation of "things dear" by the heedful man leads away from the snare of death and leads him towards the Deathless State of Nibbāna.

Then again, these dear things are described by the adjective "sensuous". This is an imperfect translation of the Pali: "*āmisa*".

This word cannot be rendered by any one word in English but could be defined as "material objects, internal and external to ourselves as perceived by our senses and stimulating various feeling." Thus the word covers both the external stimulus and the internal reaction to it. That heedless fellow is bogged down in a morass of *āmisa,* of all this enjoyment, of all this bewailing due to materialism. But the heedful man takes care not to be drawn into the bogs of attraction and repulsion and by his heedfulness, his heart need not be spattered by even a drop of mud. The heedful man, praised by the Buddhas and all wise men, well knows the dangers in *āmisa,* that entangled with it men's views are distorted and restricted, and that they are driven to birth and death as dry leaves driven along the ground by the wind.

Lastly, these dear things are called "very hard to cross". The heedless man has no hope of finding a way beyond those dear things of death and materialistic pleasure. Even if he wished to find some way beyond his restricted and petty existence bounded by these things, there would be no way for him to go until he abandoned heedlessness, and practising became vigorous, mindful and of increasing wisdom. But those who are heedful and practice whatever they can of Dhamma, their crossing over the ocean of this involvement with things and pleasures, their crossing-over the ocean of birth-and-death, becomes quite easy. As they cultivate renunciation so heedfulness grows in them with its three aspects of effort, mindfulness and wisdom, and they come through this to the Other Shore which is called the Secure or Nibbāna. Heedfulness is the way to Deathlessness, for

Nibbāna is the experience of no death, no birth and no *dukkha*. It is as the Exalted Buddha has said in another verse: "Those heedful ones they do not die, the heedless are like unto the dead". Now, concerning ourselves, in this matter we are free to choose whichever class we like. No one can compel us to be heedful, or to be heedless. The Exalted One has certainly never ordered people to be heedful rather than the opposite. His own life is the best example of this heedfulness. Let us look at it.

After He left the comforts and security of His palace and took up the ascetic life, he was an unrivalled example of heedfulness. No one has ever made such great efforts as He made in the six years during which He practised extreme austerity. And when He turned away from this course and attained Perfect Enlightenment, He became known as the Buddha. Effort, mindfulness and wisdom were among the qualities which He had brought to perfection. He had no need to make effort and so on for these were revealed as intrinsic characteristics of the Enlightened State. To the highest degree He displayed effort, mindfulness and wisdom for forty-five years—and why? Out of compassion for people that they might learn the path of happy Dhamma-practice for themselves and in time be able to bring help to others. He walked in stages all the length and breadth of Northern India helping people who wished to be helped with this wonderful Dhamma. His whole life was one displaying effort, teaching all people who wanted to learn until His body was exhausted at the age of eighty. But even upon His deathbed, He has taught those who want to know how to practise the Dhamma way and so find in themselves the Dhamma truth. What words are so stirring as those last phrases uttered by Him as He lay beneath the sweetly scented Sala-trees: "Listen well, O bhikkhus, I exhort you: Subject to decay are all compounded things: with heedfulness strive on!" Even when His body was near to death, He did not forget to exhort His followers to practise heedfulness. His last utterance impresses us that all the compounded things of this life, interior, and exteriors, our minds and bodies themselves are all running down, deteriorating, bound to scatter and fall apart, to be lost.

All things dear and beloved are like this—including ourselves. It is only by making an effort that we can escape from the slime of attachment to all this deterioration. We are deteriorating, our families and friends are deteriorating, our material possessions are deteriorating, nothing that is put together can hope to be permanent. All must fail, all must fall apart, wither and die. So we should not bask in a pleasurable lethargy in this life. There is much to be done. All the time, on every occasion, there is heedfulness to cultivate according to the words of the Exalted One: "By day and night ..." Not just sometimes, not just when we remember, not just on Buddhist Holy Days, not just in temples, not just in front of Buddha images, but by day and by night. Day and night we are slipping towards death. And we never know when it will be or how. "Tomorrow death may come—who knows?", as the Exalted One has said, and it may be only a matter of minutes or seconds away. One who has made efforts to grow in Dhamma, who has secured for himself the riches of heedfulness, the coin of effort, mindfulness and wisdom, has nothing to fear, whenever death may come. But the heedless man, what indeed will help him who has not helped himself? All the time, NOW, is the time for effort, mindfulness and wisdom. Only when Dhamma is practised all the time is there any chance to "dig up the root of suffering". All the time we can try to "give up things dear" and so cross over Death and materialistic pleasure, over the ocean of craving so "very hard to cross".

Let us then, call to mind frequently this precious instruction of the Awakened One, that it may be the Dhamma to guide our lives, In Pāli the inspired words of the Awakened One are:

> *Ye ve divā ca ratto ca*
> *Appamattā jahanti piyarūpaṃ*
> *Te ve khaṇanti aghamūlaṃ*
> *Maccuno āmisaṃ durativattaṃ.*

And in English they have been translated:

> Who are not heedless, they
> Dig up the root of suffering
> By day and night give up things dear,
> Deathly sensuous and very hard to cross.

May we, through heedfulness, all cross over to the Further Shore.

—§§§—

The Middle Way and Other Essays

M. O'C. Walshe

Bodhi Leaves No. 99

First published: 1984

The Middle Way

It is always a good idea to seek the middle way, or the golden mean, between extremes whether in politics, in one's personal view and behaviour, or in fact in any walk of life. The difficulty arises when we attempt to discover what, in practice, is the middle way. It is not, as some appear to suppose, the mid-point between truth and falsehood, or between right and wrong! In fact the middle way itself is true, and is right: the difficulty lies merely in finding it. Here are some examples: it is the mean between (as the Buddha said) self-indulgence and self-mortification, or (the same thing as applied to other persons and animals) between pampering and cruelty.

These two cases, of course, raise the whole question of discipline, of oneself and others—a particularly knotty problem today. It is also the mean between excessive scepticism and credulity, which involves our religious or quasi-religious views and beliefs: also not easy today. But it is also, and positively, that calm and wakeful state of mind that lies between the extremes of slothful indulgence and restless agitation and tension, a state which, when truly achieved, will help us greatly to solve all our problems by seeing their nature dispassionately; and this in turn means having a vastly greater degree of insight than most people have into our own emotions—which again leads to greater insight into those of others.

The middle way, even at a fairly modest, mundane level, is not very popular in the world today. Probably it never was. But in these restless times it is perhaps especially needed, and at the same time especially hard to achieve. It is fatally easy to indulge in nostalgia, to conjure up a false and idealised picture of earlier times which in fact, whatever period of history we may envisage, all had their grave disadvantages of one kind or another. All the same, until recent times it may be said that, in general, life usually had a kind of placidity that has now been lost, and which is hard to recapture, except in the atmosphere of some temple, church, meditation centre or the like. This, however, may simply mean that in earlier times the tendency towards sloth and indolence was, on the whole, greater than that towards worry and flurry.

We can't go back and live in the past. But at least we can try to see the faults of the present age, and thereby equip ourselves to face it and do what we can to counter its disadvantages. One thing that is extremely obvious is that we are, as never before, sitting targets for propaganda of all kinds. First the newspapers, then the radio and now television, which penetrate into the intimacy of our homes, have exposed us as never before to the full flood of all the wickedness and folly of the entire world.

Violence is one thing, and there are probably few today (except interested parties) who would seriously maintain that constant exposure to a diet of violence has no harmful effects on the impressionable. It must be remembered, too, that the impressionable are not confined to the ranks of the very young. Sex, in a rich variety of forms, is another. But the effects of plain, ordinary commercial advertising are less widely recognised; this, being a shade less obviously harmful, is thereby all the more insidious.

Apart, then, from violence of all kinds, and from sex in its direct, now very direct manifestations, advertising is in fact one of the major harmful factors in our present situation. This may sound like an extreme statement, and of course as long as we have any sort of a commercial civilisation at all, it must be admitted that advertising has some legitimate place. But in a better organised state, I submit, this would be a much more modest one than it is at present.

The naked appeal to human greed is an ugly thing, and a dangerous thing. It conditions us to equate the good life with material gadgets and comforts, many of which incidentally, such as alcohol and tobacco, are thoroughly bad for us. By urging us to a continually rising 'standard of living', it leads us more and more into a state of mind where we consider mere luxuries as 'necessities'; and it is a potent factor in stimulating, or at least aggravating, the constant demands for increased wages which beset us. Much more could be said on this score.

For instance, the proliferation of cars, which most people don't really need, clutters up our roads intolerably, causes a monstrous number of accidents, ruins the landscape, creates pollution and is on the verge of wrecking our once excellent public transport system. The indefinite expansion of hire-purchase undermines the old-fashioned virtue of thrift and tempts people to take on more and more burdensome commitments. And, not least, preoccupation with our own 'higher' standards of living tends to make us callously indifferent to the state of other people still battling with desperate poverty.

Thus, be it noted, the evils of violence are at least generally recognised, even if it sometimes seems there is little we can do to curb it; the dangers of excessive 'permissiveness' in sexual matters are at least constantly before us, even if there is rather less consensus on how to cope with this problem; but the evils of sheer instigated acquisitiveness are far less clearly seen, though they too make their potent and dangerous contribution to the general scene.

Until recently it was widely held, at least in 'progressive' circles, that poverty was the principal cause of crime. This may in fact be so, but only if we understand something rather different by the word 'poverty', i.e. poverty of mind and spirit and not mere material deprivation. By this poverty of mind and spirit I do not, of course, mean that true 'spiritual poverty' (in Christian terminology) which is blessed, but its very opposite, which is born of blindness and emotional inadequacy. True 'spiritual poverty' means, among other things, being satisfied with little; its opposite is being dissatisfied with whatever one has, much or little; and this is as much manifested in the big property tycoon with his multi-million takeover bids as it is in the genuinely hard up back-street burglar. And it is also manifested, in a slightly different form, by a lot of clever propagandists for trendy causes with their incessant demands, usually for things of, at best, doubtful worth.

So, in seeking the middle way, let us beware, for one thing, of the demanders. What they seek may, at least in part, be justified, but their methods are wrong and their motives are at the very least mixed, when they are not in fact almost wholly bad. By the same token, we should of course, and especially as Buddhists, be always alert to the demanding voices within ourselves, and at least make some effort to distinguish clearly between our needs and our greeds. On inspection, our true needs may turn out to be surprisingly modest.

In fact the middle way is hard to find, and those who have found at least an approximation to it are liable to be shot at from both sides. If we stand up for people's genuine rights we are 'subversive', but if we suggest that besides rights people may also have duties, we are reactionaries or even 'fascists'. Let us learn to ignore all such foolish abuse, from whatever quarter, and follow our chosen path.

SANGHA, November-December 1972

The Middle Way

Recently in my reading I came across a truly inspired misprint: Hahayana. There is a lot that is laughable in Western (and occasionally even some Eastern) forms of Buddhism. "My cat's got Zen," a lady once said to me. "Really," I replied, "has he got rid of greed, hatred and delusion?"

More excusable, perhaps, was the mistake of a very distinguished Anglican divine who takes a deep and sincere interest in Buddhism. I heard him say that Buddhist mindfulness consisted of concentrating the mind on one point, till subject and object become one. Perhaps he didn't mean mindfulness but *samādhi* which at any rate is what he described.

Concentration is a very fine thing, and Buddhists should certainly practise it. It brings great calm and peace of mind, but unless mindfulness is present as well, it will never bring one to Enlightenment. The lady's cat is perhaps a case in point. Cats are very graceful animals, with a magnificent economy of movement. They often seem to be in a very happy state of mind, purring away with obvious contentment. This may not be unconnected with their considerable power of concentration, which may be readily observed, for instance, when they are watching birds. It would be difficult to suppose, however, that they were watching these with detachment. If a cat could watch itself with the same degree of intensity, it might well be on the way to Enlightenment. Probably we can learn something from cats, or other animals, but we should not overestimate them.

It is time Western Buddhists got to know a bit more about the various possible states of consciousness which are 'available' to us. Much can be learnt from the valuable book Altered States of Consciousness edited by Charles T. Tart. Such knowledge would save many people from making mistakes and, in particular, from supposing that through some possibly quite interesting and even valuable 'experience' they have had, they have attained or nearly attained Enlightenment. There is, in fact, in Vipassanā practice, a kind of zone in which peculiar things can happen (though they don't always), which one has to learn to pass through.

This zone marks, not the end of the road, but merely the culmination of a certain preliminary stage. In it, feelings of great joy, great faith, visions of light, and so on, can occur. One can feel that one has no body, or no head, The thing is, in such cases, simply to press on regardless—being clearly aware but as far as possible not involved. It is probably mainly at this stage that Zen masters get tough with their pupils—for their own good. The great thing is not to dwell in such states, and above all not to get conceited about one's 'progress'. In point of fact, serious progress only begins when one is safely over this particular 'hump'.

There is much serious interest in meditation nowadays. This an excellent thing—and a most important development. And for this very reason, it is important that as many people as possible should be aware of what can happen in the fairly early stages, and what it means—and what it doesn't mean! Meditation can bring, as one proceeds, both joyful and painful feelings. We must learn to pass through both—mindfully and clearly aware.

'Meditation' today is a kind of collective label for a wide range of activities indulged in by all sorts of people. There are of course various kinds of traditional Christian meditation, especially in the Roman Catholic and Greek Orthodox Churches. Various systems of genuine and alleged Hindu and yogic practices have been introduced, often by people with few, if any, qualifications—though of course serious teachers and practitioners also exist. Even so, what they teach may differ considerably from what is taught by any genuine school of Buddhism. Nowadays there are hippy-cults and the like, involving the use of hallucinogenic (so-called 'psychedelic') drugs. Some of the experiences produced by any of these methods may equate with the phenomena mentioned above. Thus, in fact, it is not even necessary to risk the grave dangers of an LSD 'trip' or the like in order to have such experiences. Drugs apart, it is easy for some to fall victim to the hypnotic sway of some charlatan or 'Earl's Court guru', or to the group-hypnosis of some possibly half-baked 'community'. The critical faculty is one of the first victims, especially in an atmosphere where anti-intellectualism is positively encouraged.

It is true the intellect can be overrated, and that in a very real sense it has to be 'transcended'. But a little critical common-sense is no bad safeguard all the same. And above all, right motive is very important. The purpose of serious meditation is not ego-boosting but the very opposite. It may be nice to feel one is 'enlightened' but it is not healthy. And if the motive is to gain power over others, it is even worse ... The true aim is to overcome *dukkha,* which is rather misleadingly rendered 'suffering'. By concentration alone we can certainly gain very happy states—sometimes. But they won't last, and so they are no real cure for 'suffering', though they may help. Their true function is as a basis for penetrating deeper.

Some people would say the true motive should be compassion. This is fair enough, if properly understood. According to Mahāyāna doctrine, which such people usually invoke, compassion is inseparable from wisdom. Only the wise can practise true compassion, through their understanding. This understanding, however, is only gained by self-knowledge—i.e. by developing increased awareness of this mysterious thing called 'self'.

As a matter of fact, we can cure neither our own suffering nor that of others without wisdom. This is common ground to all schools of Buddhism. When we have seen into the nature of our own troubles—and only then— we shall have the necessary skill to practise true compassion towards others. We won't, in fact even have to bother very much about trying to do this, it will just happen of its own accord. So don't bother overmuch about 'Theravāda' or 'Mahāyāna' but just press on with the good work in your own mind.

If you do feel over-concerned with developing 'universal compassion' rather than solving your own problems, beware! It is a symptom of an unhealthy state in you. It is always easier to 'solve' (at least in theory) others' problems than one's own, because they don't hurt so much. Think of the definition of a minor operation: 'one performed on somebody else.'

If, in the course of Vipassanā meditation or otherwise, you have attained to the 'happy zone', just carry on, regarding it with detachment and not getting too excited about it. This may prove difficult, but by even trying you will at once become more and more aware of the strength of your attachment to happiness.

Continuing, you will shortly afterwards come to see a bit more clearly than before the true nature of all things including your 'self': impermanence. Frustration and impersonality will present themselves to you, not yet with the final clarity of Enlightenment, but quite sharply. You will still not have got rid of 'self', but you will have at least a distinct inkling of what *anattā* or 'non-self' really means. If you care to call it *sunyata* or 'voidness' it doesn't matter. There is no real difference. But you will also begin to find that this seemingly negative thing is in reality, somehow, positive after all.

There are many subtle traps along the Path. That is why most people need a teacher, not only to start them off but to give them continuing guidance, at least until a certain point is reached. But above all things else—awareness is always required. There should be no let-up in this. Whatever state you may have attained or think you have attained, it must be seen with awareness. And we should always be aware in advance that conceit can only too easily be aroused—and what is still more difficult, we should be able to recognise it when it has arisen. It is one of the most vital functions of a teacher to point this out at times—and the information is not always very well received ... But if we can catch this on the wing the rest will probably follow in due course. Then the Middle Way will reveal itself instead of the Muddle Way too many people are following.

The Obstacle-Race

Life may be thought of as an obstacle-race. Many people have to cope with appalling obstacles, even in the heart of 'Western civilization': poverty, ill-health, lack of housing, lack of privacy (or too much of it, in the form of desperate loneliness), noise, squalor, ill-treatment—the list is almost endless. And in places like London, or New York, or Tokyo, the obstacle-race is a real rat-race in which great masses of people quite literally struggle and fight to get in and out of town, to get and keep a job, to keep up with the neighbors, to preserve their 'self-respect' (which may be something foolish but it means a lot to them). Add to this the continual threat of disaster impending: nuclear war, even a nice little 'conventional' war; race-riots and general hooliganism, chemical poisoning of food and atmosphere; regimentation, computerisation and general depersonalization; personal conflicts with wives or husbands, children or parents, bosses or employees; emotional appeals for doubtful causes; advertising with its incessant appeal to greed and pandering to our lower natures. All this in a relatively 'fortunate' community—the depths of suffering, degradation and despair to be found in places like the Sahel or Vietnam, or in many police-states and impoverished countries, go far beyond this. Nor does this take into account the manifold sufferings endured by animals at man's hands, which those who are at all sensitive cannot fail to see.

Some of us may be spared a good deal of the personal suffering implied by this by no means exhaustive list, but we are aware of it if we stop to think, and even in our own lives we are harried and badgered from pillar to post by the sheer pace and pressure of modern life. This is indeed a rat-race and an obstacle-race!

What can we do about it? Let us face the situation squarely to begin with. For one thing, it confirms the Buddha's description of the nature of life as *dukkha* or suffering. As a matter of fact, we don't hear quite so many objections raised to this statement nowadays as used to be the case. *Dukkha* has become a bit too obvious to most people by now.

It is sometimes claimed that Buddhism is selfish. Both Christians and Humanists are heard to say that they do more to relieve suffering in the world than the Buddhists do. There may even, in some ways, be some truth in this. Certainly we should do everything in our power to relieve starvation, to stop or prevent wars (if we can!), and so on. But we might as well recognise two things: we can never clear away all the *dukkha* in the world, however hard we try; and secondly, our efforts will anyway be largely in vain unless there is a good measure of understanding.

By science and technology man has gained an increased control over many aspects of nature. But even highly-skilled scientists, with the best of intentions, have made and are making terrible mistakes, the results of which may well prove disastrous. Let us take just one example: DDT. This at first seemed to be a practically unmixed blessing. We may note that even so it must have caused suffering: how many animals had to suffer during the experiments necessary for its development? And do we even stop to think of the possible sufferings of insects killed by it? We don't even know whether it causes them an agonising death or not, and perhaps few people care. But now we have good reason to believe that the widespread use of DDT is a threat to man himself. Perhaps the world would after all have been better off—or no worse off—without it ...

Also, efforts to help others—wisely—do not exclude the necessity to help ourselves. In fact, we cannot do the one without the other.

So far we have considered only those problems which man has to face without. What about the problems within? We all have in our make-up, as the Buddha declared, the three unhealthy roots of greed, hatred and delusion. This is one of those truths proclaimed by the Buddha, which surely no sane person of any religion or none could deny. How many of our problems including so-called 'external' ones—can be traced back to these? Why are we so vulnerable to advertisements for whiskey, to pornographic films, to gambling, and all the rest ? Because of the root of greed within us. Why do we fall for incitements to violence, whether directed against those of another nation or 'race', or whatever? Obviously because of the root of hatred within us. Why do we constantly commit acts of plain stupidity? Because of ignorance—within us!

We can generally see these things operating, clearly enough, in other people, especially when their actions are directed, against us or our supposed 'interests'. But somehow we don't always seem to notice them in ourselves.

Let us look within—not in the first place to find the 'Buddhanature' or some such thing (though we might eventually come to that)—but to detect the stirrings of greed, hatred and delusion inside our own minds. These are the real obstacles, not those outside. 'External' troubles like sickness, poverty and so on may be the product of past *kamma* and possibly have to be borne with as much cheerfulness and resolution as we can manage. They can also provide the spur to look within and see what is wrong with ourselves. If, because I'm ill or too poor, or merely too old, I can't go out and have a 'gay old time', then maybe that gives me all the more chance to meditate instead. It might even be better that way …

Yes, life is an obstacle-race, but where are the real obstacles—without, or within?

Is There Free-Will in Buddhism?

"Is there free-will in Buddhism?" is one of those hardy perennial questions that crop up at meetings. And I have heard it answered, by different speakers, both positively and negatively. Now strictly speaking, this is not a Buddhist concept at all: it is a Christian one (and the Christians, too, have come up with different answers to it!). Still, we needn't quibble about terms too much. Though the question could be differently put from a Buddhist point of view, it is a problem which worries some people (though I don't think it has, somehow, ever particularly worried me!), and so we must try to answer it. Before attempting a re-formulation in Buddhist terms, let me say at once that the short answer is "Yes". This needs explanation and qualification, but it is as well to note that, broadly speaking, such is the case.

We ought, probably, to consider briefly what the idea of freewill means in Christian theology. True, most professing Christians today are not, to put it mildly, very strong on theology, but all the same their thinking on such subjects is conditioned, however remotely, by what the Church Fathers had to say, many centuries ago. Broadly, free-will in a Christian sense means that man is permitted by God to choose between good and evil, with the corollary that his choice of the one or the other will determine his place of residence in the Hereafter. While most Christians accept that man has free-will, some (notably the Calvinists) declare that God has fixed each individual's destiny in advance, so that he really cannot help himself and will automatically go to Heaven or Hell as the case may be. But the matter can also be argued out on a secular basis, in which case Predestination (by God) is replaced by Determinism (by genetics, etc.). In the latter case it is normally thought that the consequences do not extend beyond this life, since this is all we have.

All views such as the above were, in essence, to be found in ancient India in the Buddha's time. With others, they are included among the 62 types of wrong view enumerated in the Brahmajāla Sutta, the very first discourse in the Pali scriptures. Another type of view there mentioned has recently been dug up, with a great air of triumphant originality, by a French scholar, Prof. Monod, to the effect that everything there is, including man and all his works, is the result of pure chance. This, too, is refuted in the Brahmajāla Sutta (a text which is well worth reading, for those who hanker after such philosophising).

From a Buddhist point of view, the whole thing is, of course, a question of *kamma*. I use the Pali form of the word karma, for a variety of reasons. Karma is used by Mahāyāna Buddhists, it is true, and many of them use it precisely and correctly. But it is also used by Hindus, Theosophists, and nowadays by all sorts of people, with a variety of different meanings which may or may not be legitimate but which certainly are not applicable in correct Buddhist usage. The literal meaning of *kamma* is "action". But the Buddha defined it with another Pali word, *cetanā*, "volition". It therefore means "volitional action". Whatever I will to do, good or bad (in Pali *kusala* "skilled" or *akusala* "unskilled"), constitutes my *kamma*. This is a "deed", but it also is a "seed" which I have planted, and in due course that seed will ripen as *vipāka* or result, nice or nasty as the case may be. As a man sows, so shall he reap—in this life or some other. This looks in a way very like the Christian idea, so that a Christian formulation could even be applied to it. The difference is, of course, that *kamma-vipāka* is an impersonal process, whereas in the Christian view it is God who rewards or punishes us, Of course, too, the rewards and penalties of *kamma* are not eternal but temporal and commensurate.

Now we go through life committing acts of *kamma* of various kinds all the time. We are therefore continually sowing seeds which in due course will ripen, with nice or nasty results for us. Obviously also, we are now reaping the results from the past, including previous lives.

There is therefore no doubt whatsoever that, in the Buddhist view there is an element, at least, of what we may call free-will. In a given situation, I can at least to some extent choose to do the "right" thing or to do the "wrong" thing. The fact that I may not always know clearly which is the "right" choice is neither here nor there. If I want to go to Upper Popple I may come to an unmarked crossroads and guess that I should turn left. If I end up at Nether Wallop instead, it is because I guessed wrong. I should have studied the map. It is in fact just not true, though some would argue for it, that my choice of path was predetermined either by God or by some mysterious force such as genetics. Nevertheless, the odds may have been weighted in favour of my choosing the path I did. It may have looked more attractive. It may in fact have been something like "the primrose path to the eternal bonfire". I may, like Macbeth, have listened to bad advice and false prophecies (of which there are plenty about nowadays). But still I could have chosen to go the other way.

So far so good. Probably most people would really agree with what has been said so far, by and large. After all, many a man must have got up early on a winter's morning, reluctantly, because he knew he would lose his job if he didn't. We all know that we can choose to do, or not to do, certain things only if we are prepared to take the consequences. And we generally accept that we have to pay for our pleasures whether in cash or otherwise. At this level, *kamma* is only glorified common-sense. "You pay your money and you take your choice," though it may rather be a case of "live (or love) now—pay later".

Now come the clever objections. There are at least two of these. One is: "If all things are the result of previous conditions, then there is no room for freedom of choice, it's all predetermined." The other is: "If the self is not real, then there is no 'I' to choose," the argument then probably proceeding further as Objection 1.

Conditions are not immutable "causes". They are always multiple—in fact extremely complex—and changing. We can prepare the soil and plant the seed. If all the necessary factors are favourable, that seed will grow. If any one necessary condition is absent, that seed will not grow. The conditions are both external to the seed, and internal to it. If we are talking literally of a plant-seed, the concept of *kamma* does not apply. But if by the seed we mean the mind of man, it does. This brings us to Objection 2, and involves some discussion of the nature of that which we call "self".

Of course it is a basic Buddhist tenet that what we call "self" is not real. But at a certain level, that of conventional truth, it exists. And it is in this sphere of conventional truth that *kamma* actually operates. Remember that *kamma* is a volitional act which is going to have results, nice or nasty, for that being which I think of as

"me", even if it may be "me" in a future life. Therefore, Arahants create no *kamma*, because they don't think of themselves as "me" any more. What then is the true situation concerning this — whatever it is—that I call "me" and that I love so much? Perhaps we can find out something about this by meditation. But we can also read up a bit about it in the books, which is not as good in the long run, but can still be quite helpful.

To put it briefly, "I" am a process. Every bit of "my" mind and body is changing the whole time with inconceivable rapidity. The mental process consists of a continuous series of ever-changing (but not arbitrarily changing) constellations of factors. These are listed under various headings in the first book of the Abhidhamma, the Dhammasaṅgaṇī translated by Mrs. Rhys Davids as A Buddhist Manual of Psychological Ethics. Each such infinitesimally brief constellation is of one of 89 different types. Some of the higher of these types of consciousness are never experienced by the ordinary person. Of the 89, twenty are karmic, i.e. they involve *kamma* or volition, whether skilled ("good") or unskilled ("bad"). A wonderfully vivid account of the interplay of these factors in (by way of example) just one type of consciousness is given in Abhidhamma Studies by the Ven. Nyanaponika: a little book every Buddhist should have at his bedside.

It is the factor "volition" which operates to produce *kamma*. It is the persistence of this factor through a series of consciousnessmoments which, above all else, produces the illusion of "I". Normally, in the ordinary person, it manifests as *taṇhā* or craving. And here we can get at it.

In the formula of *Paṭicca-samuppāda* or Dependent Origination we find it stated that contact (of sense-base and sense-object, e.g. eye and that which is seen) conditions feeling (pleasant, unpleasant or neutral), and that feeling conditions craving. In other words if, (conventionally speaking), I see a desirable object, I have a pleasant feeling, and then I react by wanting that thing. It is possible, however, by Mindfulness to inhibit the arising of that wanting, simply by observing the feeling with detachment.

These turn out, on closer inspection, to be deep matters which, as the Buddha has said, cannot be fully comprehended by the ignorant. Nevertheless by the practice of awareness (or mindfulness) we can increasingly learn about them. The point really is that theoretical debates about "free-will" and the like are arid. But by practice we can find out the truth, and the truth shall make you free.

The Doctrine of Rebirth in Eastern and Western Thought

Karel Werner

Bodhi Leaves No. 100

First published: 1985

The Doctrine of Rebirth in Eastern and Western Thought

There is one essential difference between a modern European or American who approaches the study of Buddhism today and a citizen of Ancient India who, amazed and fascinated, listened to the message of final release offered to him in the words of the Buddha. This difference lies in the fact that in the minds of the Buddha's listeners at his time—as in most Orientals even today—there was a deep-rooted intuition of what we call the doctrine of rebirth which formed a solid basis for the acceptance of the new teaching.

The Buddha, in fact, nowhere in his discourses explains this doctrine in extenso; we can clearly see from his words that it was quite current among his contemporaries, not exactly as a doctrine, but as a living belief of nearly everybody, except an unimportant number of followers of the sceptical or materialistic schools such as the Charvakas. The Buddha only formulated more precisely the already known doctrine, rejected its old mythical and ritualistic connotations, and set it upon firm rational and ethical foundations. The doctrine of rebirth in union with the law of cause and effect in the moral sphere received thus a similar validity as, in Western thought today, the so-called laws of nature.

For an average Westerner today, however, the teaching of rebirth is a more or less new doctrine, quite different from the Christian, agnostic or materialistic outlook he is already familiar with. When he now comes to study Buddhism, it is certainly of advantage if he becomes acquainted with this belief in the various forms it has taken outside the sphere of Buddhist thought. He can then perceive more clearly the fundamental change the Buddha introduced into the formulation of the doctrine and the importance of this new formulation.

It is difficult to settle with definiteness the question when and how the idea of rebirth emerged in Indian thought. The first allusions to it are found in the Rig Vedic hymns. The pious Aryan poet believed, according to some of his songs, that as a reward for good deeds he would gain a long, though not eternal, life among the gods. It is not yet clear, however, what his lot would be at the end of this long life among the gods. Later texts often mention that a repeated death will then follow, and this death is something to be dreaded.

From this notion it was only a small step to the idea of a series of deaths occurring in an endless sequence. Such series seems to be implied in the Satapatha Brāhmaṇa (10:4:3:10) where departed fathers are mentioned as falling prey to death again and again. Though a rebirth on earth is not yet explicitly mentioned; this last step is taken in the oldest Upanishads, where a clear formulation of the concept of rebirth can be found several times.

Among the factors which may have contributed to the emergence of the idea of rebirth in Aryan thought, the influence of the original subjugated inhabitants of India has often been mentioned. It must certainly be admitted that in the course of more than a millennium's co-existence, the aborigines must have considerably influenced their conquerors racially and culturally. It is quite possible that, in some form, the idea of rebirth may have been current among them.

It has been proved, in fact, that various forms of the rebirth doctrine as "reincarnation" or "transmigration of souls" were held by almost all ancient peoples of the world, including African Negroes, Polynesians, Indians of all three Americas, etc. But if the Ariyans acquired this notion from the previous inhabitants of the country, it certainly was readily assimilated in terms of the previous Aryan notions. It then received a new and higher elaboration, especially with respect to ethical formulation.

In the period of the Brāhmaṇa texts the course of cosmic and human events became closely linked with priestly sacrifices and ritualistic practice. The idea of evil consequences of bad deeds, however, was not extinguished entirely, and as soon as the idea of rebirth became explicit in the oldest Upanishads, the concept of moral retribution was linked with it.

Though still coupled with many naive features, these texts present a very high conception of rebirth which is not to be found in other ancient cultures in which primitive notions of transmigration do not imply moral criteria. Rather the fate to which the departed individual is destined is usually determined by his social rank in this life and sometimes by heroism in battles, the most rightly estimated quality of man in those times.

In a few passages of the Brhadaranyaka Upanisad we find allusions to a still higher conception of rebirth, as for example when Yajnavalkya says that the departed person is accompanied by knowledge and deed and by previous experience.

This conception comes very near to that of the Buddha. It must have prevailed among the educated classes of his time just prior to his renunciation. An average educated Indian of those times evidently believed in the existence of an endless chain of successive lives. Some people tried to influence the quality of their future lives by religious practices such as rituals and sacrifices, hoping thereby to achieve final salvation sometime in the distant future. More refined thinkers, particularly of the higher classes, appear to have believed that moral conduct could improve their lot in future lives. But they did not believe such religious practices led to final freedom, which now seemed to them the only desirable aim. They could no more find satisfaction in the hope of a happy rebirth as a reward for a righteous life, but felt the endless round of rebirths as itself a heavy burden.

Seeking an escape from the repetitive patterns of life and death, eager to find a solution, many earnest thinkers left their homes. One among them was Siddhattha Gotama, the future Buddha. His story is known sufficiently well; so it need not be repeated here. After he gained final knowledge, he also formulated anew the old doctrine of rebirth according to his experience and insight. His formulation appears even in this modem age as rational and logical. Even without previous verification, it can be accepted by educated people today as the only plausible explanation of the inequality in the fates of men.

The idea of rebirth coming to the modern West from the East, however, is not altogether new to the European mind. European thought has deep roots in ancient Greece and there the doctrine of rebirth was not only known but also endorsed by a number of eminent thinkers. The oldest mention of the idea can be found in Herodotus, who held that it came to Greece from Egypt. The Greeks may have borrowed it from the Egyptians and pretended it was their own theory. However, this doctrine has not yet been proven to have existed in Egypt. Some scientists such as Schroder and Grabe held the opinion that it came to Greece from India. Whether or not this be so, in Greece itself there were quite favourable conditions for the doctrine to evolve without foreign importation. In other parts of ancient Europe, too, the idea of rebirth must have been known. The beliefs of ancient European tribes are not known sufficiently well, but Caesar mentions that in Britain the Druids held the belief in rebirth (De Bella Galileo VI, 14).

Earlier than in Greece, this idea can be found among Thracian tribes, particularly the Gaels. Herodotus tells us that they believed their god Zalmoxis lives in a hollow mountain. Departed men come to him, but after three years return to the earth.

In Orphism the doctrine of rebirth is formulated still more clearly. Orphism was a mystery religion which taught that the human soul was of divine origin, but had fallen into sin. As a consequence it was obliged to transmigrate through various forms of life, human and animal. The soul can liberate itself through purification, renunciation and non-killing. At a certain period between two lives on earth, soul was tortured in hell or lived in bliss among the gods, according to its deeds and endeavours during its life on earth. The next life was also influenced thereby. This, we can see, is the highest formulation of this doctrine to be found outside India.

The official Greek religion based on the epic poetry of Homer does not teach this doctrine, but it seems to have been quite well known by the people. It also formed a part of the teachings of some philosophers. According to Cicero it was Pherekydus who first taught this doctrine, but the first clear formulation comes from Phythagoras (570–500 B.C.). Phythagoras was a practical philosopher, teaching not only theoretical knowledge, but also a way of life. He took over the whole Orphic doctrine and therefore attached the greatest importance to the right way of living. He founded an Order with a discipline based on renunciation, aimed at gaining liberation from the wheel of lives.

The same doctrine was further taught by Empedocles (ca. 490–430 B.C.). In early years a politician, he later felt a higher calling in himself and refused even the crown. In his poems we find the following verses:

> "For I have been here now a boy and
> a girl, a bush and a bird and a
> dumb fish in the sea!
> From what honour, from what height
> of bliss have I fallen to go about
> among mortals here on earth!"

His poems are full of compassion for suffering beings. He reprimands the killing of animals for food and sacrifices. During his life as a philosopher he wandered from place to place preaching his doctrine. He was admired and venerated.

Of interest to us also is the poet Pindarus who wrote poems about popular heroes. He held these heroes to be souls of those who had purified themselves in the course of previous lives and were then born on earth for the last time as kings, heroes and sages, no more to return hereafter.

Among philosophers, we find the rebirth doctrine again taught by Plato (ca. 428–347 B.C.), who took it over from the general body of knowledge and expounded it in the form of myths or parables in his famous philosophical dialogues. Contrary to Empedocles, who claimed to remember his previous lives, Plato admits he has no exact knowledge of the facts but holds the doctrine plausible. Plato's myth on rebirth is as follows:

The soul was cherishing once the state of divine being, but in the course of time became unable to maintain the inner balance of its qualities and due to this lack of mindfulness fell into matter and according to its level took birth in some position among men. After death the soul of a bad man suffers in Tartarus and that of a good man rejoices in a heavenly abode. After a thousand years every soul takes birth on earth again, possibly also in some animals. The soul chooses its own rebirth and during the next life it can acquire merits for better insight and choice when further rebirth is to take place. After ten lives on earth soul becomes purified and regains the state of a divine being, but a new fall is again possible.

Plato's notion of the rebirth doctrine is apparently inferior to that of Empedocles and other former teachers, including the Orphics. The thought of post-Platonic philosophers took another course, away from belief in rebirth, particularly due to Aristotle. Only in Neoplatonism do we again find the rebirth doctrine. It was Philo of Alexandria (15–10 B.C.–50 A.D.) who first taught that souls attached to the body and earthly life must again and again take birth on earth until, no longer deceived by this life, they realise that the body is a prison of the soul.

The rebirth doctrine reached its full height again with Plotinus (205–270 A.D.), whose system of philosophy was the last great fruit of the declining spirit of the Attic age. This system holds that souls were once in unity with the universal principle called the "One." As a consequence of some inexplicable course of necessity and, at a time, due to their own fault, the souls fell from their blissful state into empirical, temporal exigency. There they have to transmigrate, according to the strength of their sensual attachments, through successive lives in celestial, human, animal and even vegetable forms. Their fate exactly corresponds to their previous deeds. If they succeed in purifying themselves from sensuality and attachment to matter, they will become re-unified with the One and thus gain liberation.

The doctrine of rebirth was taught by later Neo-Platonists such as Porphyry (ca. 234–330 A.D.) and Iamblichus (died 330). These, however, restricted its validity to the realm of humans.

We have seen that the doctrine of rebirths was embodied in Greek thought during the entire period of its evolution. Its ethical aspect was well elaborated and corresponds to the Indian conception of karma. However, as the doctrine never became widespread and did not prevail, it could not withstand the influence of the new Christian faith and only survived for some time in a few Gnostic communities.

Gnosticism was no unitary movement or teaching. The name applies to a variety of Hellenistic and early Christian doctrines with mystical tendencies, some showing a deep desire to penetrate to the final truth through inner experience. The doctrine of rebirth found in some Gnostic schools may have been taken over from Greek sources, but Jewish influence cannot be excluded.

The best formulation of the doctrine can be found in Basileides (2nd century) of Alexandria. He taught that all suffering is in fact deserved, being the outcome of sins committed either consciously or unknowingly. In the course of rebirth, salvation may be gained through purification and knowledge. The same doctrine was held by Carpocrates who thought it found support even in Jesus Christ's words (Matt. 5, 25–26; Luke 12, 58–59). In the parables of Jesus, Carpocrates maintained the jail stands for the body and the paying of the last farthing for expiation of all wrong doings.

Among Christians, we find the famous Clement of Alexandria (died 216) and his pupil Origen (185–254) whose thoughts were influenced by Gnosticism. According to Origen, souls were created by God and they all will come back to him again. Lower worlds, including hell, are not eternal (as taught by the Church even today) and serve only the purpose of purifying the soul.

Neoplatonic thoughts were awakened within Christianity itself by Pseudo-Dionysius Areopagita (ca. 500). His description of the soul's final goal—which he, of course, calls God—resembles quite closely the conception of the Buddhist Nirvana. His system tacitly implies rebirth.

As European thought evolved, the idea of rebirth disappeared from the surface, although below the surface it must have been preserved in certain strains of heretical thought. Explicitly, however, we find it as late as the Renaissance in the works of Giordano Bruno (1548–1600), a keen philosopher who was burned to death by the Catholic Inquisition for teaching things contrary to official dogma.

One of his teachings was a kind of pantheism: the soul (which he calls the "monad") penetrates as the world soul the entire universe, but at the same time is present in every man, animal and even plant, transmigrating from one being to another.

The repressive atmosphere of ecclesiastical dogmatism, however, prevented European thought from grasping the revolutionary idea of rebirth alluded to in Bruno's philosophy. The dogma of

God's creation of the soul and its single existence on earth was so deep-rooted in the minds of even philosophers and scientists (and is so, in fact, up to this day in those who resorted to materialism) that only a genius or open-minded artist like Lessing or Goethe could break through this narrow-mindedness and grasp the universal validity and rationality of the doctrine of rebirth. At the same time that it satisfied such thinkers emotionally, it fulfilled their logical demands and their reasoned reflections concerning themselves and the evolution of mankind. Thus it was the German poets, and later on philosophers as well, who clearly accepted this idea, sometimes with great enthusiasm. This is particularly conspicuous in Lessing's book The Education of Humankind (Erziehung des Menschengeschlechtes, 1780). Goethe confessed several times that he believed in rebirth—in his poems as well as in a letter to Wieland (April 1776), who showed great understanding of it. Friedrich Schiller gave expression to his feeling concerning his previous lives on earth in his poem "The Mystery of the Reminiscence" (Das Geheimnis der Reminiszenz), dedicated to his Laura.

Goethe's brother-in-law, J.G. Schlosser, even started an open literary discussion on this theme with his book on the transmigration of the souls (Über die Seelenwanderung, 1781). His opponent J.G. Herder later changed his mind and only rejected the return of the soul to earth, assuming an evolution of it in higher worlds. Less known believers in this doctrine were J.C. Edelmann and P. Hebel.

Then the pure philosophers came on the scene again. In his work The Critique of Pure Reason (1788), Kant tries to prove the immortality of the soul. He argues that the soul must gain perfection. As we seldom see this accomplished in this life, it is possible only in the course of an unending process. In his early work Natural History and Theory of the Heavens (1755), he formulates a hypothesis on rebirth on other celestial bodies. In his academic lectures he criticized the teaching of the Church concerning the eternal punishments and rewards for temporary deeds on earth.

Some post-Kantian philosophers were more open. F.N.J. Schelling in his Philosophy and Religion (1804) shows an inclination to a conception similar to that of Plotinus: the souls, having departed before "the beginning of time" from the "eternal One," must now pass through a course of rebirth in order to become purified from their "selfhood" (selbstheit) and come back to their home.

Arthur Schopenhauer (1788–1860) was the one philosopher who was influenced directly by the Upanishads and Buddhism. The basic principle of his philosophy is the conception of the will to live. Where the will to live exists, there is, of necessity, life which exists only in its presence. The eternal presence of the will to live cannot be lost and so the will to live manifests itself successively in new forms.

Despite these cases of wider insights, modern European thought, on the whole, remained bound to the presuppositions of natural science. Its sphere of examination was very narrow, lying within the five senses. Contemporary philosophy has accepted this as its starting point, but is unable to go beyond it. The philosopher today does not possess the experience of extrasensory perception, so he takes refuge in abstract or metaphysical speculations without any intuition.

Thus philosophy has withdrawn into isolation, losing contact with the ways of thinking and living of most people. It has become academic. It does not, consequently, satisfy the spiritual needs of people. Meanwhile the old religions have lost their influence and significance. The gap thus arisen has brought forth several new movements trying to fill it. They overcame new scientific conceptions, but were themselves inspired chiefly by old religions, particularly the Oriental ones.

The most important of these movements has been Theosophy, as represented by the Theosophical Society founded in 1875. Its teaching is syncretic, being based on Hinduistic ideas and penetrated by the spirit of some Mahayana doctrines. The influence of Christianity can be traced too, particularly in the ideas of the Anthroposophic Society, which arose in Germany and broke away from Theosophy in 1913.

The doctrine of rebirth became merged in Theosophical theory with the modern idea of evolution. The picture of individuals, evolving towards perfection in an ever-ascending line, proved to be very attractive; but it abolishes, in fact, the notion of the round of rebirths, the ever-revolving wheel of life which is so essential to the Buddhist teaching of rebirth. According to the Theosophical theory, evolution is God's plan and man cannot but follow it. The place on the scale of evolution once acquired cannot be lost again. In consequence, some European Buddhists influenced by Theosophy also assume that it is impossible to fall back to lower forms of life, such as the animal state.

In the light of the Buddha's exposition of the doctrine, however, this seems to be a very dangerous mistake which may undermine the feeling of an urgent need to strive for the goal. According to the Buddha's description there is no invariable evolution in a continuously upward direction. In the beginningless and endless *saṃsāra*, except for those who enter the definite path to deliverance, there are only ever repeated ups and downs. An unenlightened being who reaches even the highest celestial sphere cannot maintain it. After exhausting his store of accumulated merits, he falls back to this world of uncertainty, and again finds himself at a crossroads. If such a being, who for long periods enjoyed heavenly bliss, cannot maintain mindfulness, he must sooner or later fall as a result of wrong-doings performed in pursuit of pleasures. The pains of lower states of life may bring better insights so that he gradually rises to higher states again. Thus the story goes on, endlessly.

According to the Buddha, only the high degree of mindfulness which comes from the practice of his teaching can bring man to certainty, to the assurance of reaching the goal. This assurance comes when the first stage of sanctity, "stream-entry," (*sotāpatti*) has been reached. This is so according to the Theravada tradition, but other schools have their own, slightly different, stages of assurance.

Most people in the West, upon first hearing about the doctrine of rebirth, experience a kind of agreeable satisfaction. Previously they had feared death as final extinction or as eternal damnation except perhaps the few who dare to feel assured they will gain eternal salvation in heaven. Now they perceive a new hope for further lives on this earth, which they love. Unlike truth-seekers in the Buddha's time, they do not dread the "miseries of *saṃsāra*," but feel relief and joy.

I think we need not despise this attitude. If the majority of people truly believed in rebirth in this way, and lived so as to secure a happy rebirth, the sad picture of the present world torn by hatred and selfish recklessness would change considerably. The Buddha, too, taught the way to a happy rebirth to those who were not yet prepared to accept the more profound doctrine. This should, perhaps, be borne in mind by Buddhists. For sometimes, in their haste to explain to fresh inquirers the fundamental truths of suffering etc., they do not allow them time to cherish the new outlook for the future. In the Orient, too, this prospect of joy in repeated lives is quite common, the idea of gaining liberation being very often postponed to an indefinite future.

The doctrine of rebirth, as we have seen, is not unfamiliar to the European mind. If it were really grasped and incorporated in life, it would form an excellent basis for a conscious unfolding of moral qualities in the individual's self-education, qualities which today are so often neglected. Thus it could help heighten the general level of morality.

The doctrine is also perfectly logical. If thought over, it could satisfy in its rationality every scientific-minded person. In contrast the conceptions of human destiny after death taught by Christianity, as well as by modern "scientific" materialism, are quite irrational, or even anti-rational and arbitrary. The doctrine of rebirth, however, besides being rational and logical, can also give the believer a great amount of emotional satisfaction. Moreover, it is testified to by the words of the Buddha, a man second to none in human history.

The doctrine of rebirth should, therefore, be widely propagated wherever possible. We can only look with hope and encouragement at the efforts of the few psychologists and other modern scientists who are trying to find a method of verifying this theory. Again, we can only look with great pity at the sad fact that an increasing number of Orientals are taking over fallacious and inferior materialistic views from the West.

Appendix: Eminent Western Thinkers on Rebirth

Note: All selections are from Reincarnation, an East-West Anthology, compiled and edited by Joseph Head and S.I. Cranston (New York: The Julian Press, 1961). It should be emphasized that the passages cited here have been included solely because they illustrate or affirm a belief in rebirth. Inclusion does not imply that they agree with Buddhism in their understanding of rebirth. One significant respect in which the Buddhist conception of rebirth differs from that of speculative thought in the West is its denial of transmigrating self or soul. According to Buddhism, rebirth occurs through the continuation of the mental process in causal sequence from life to life, not through a reincarnating soul. For a fuller account, see Wheel No. 9: Nyanatiloka, Karma and Rebirth, and Wheel No. 167/169: V. P. Gunaratna, Rebirth Explained.

Editor

Pythagoras (582–507 B.C.), Greek philosopher

[Pythagoras] was accustomed to speak of himself in this manner: that he had formerly been Aethalides ... At a subsequent period, he was reborn as Euphorbus, and was wounded by Menelaus at the siege of Troy, and so died. In that life he used to say that he had formerly been Aethalides; and that he had received as a gift from Mercury (god of wisdom) the memory of his soul's transmigrations ... also the gift of recollecting what his own soul and the souls of others had experienced between death and rebirth.

Life of Pythagoras, Diogenes Laertius

What Pythagoras wished to indicate by all these particulars was that he knew the former lives he had lived, which enabled him to begin providential attention to others and remind them of their former existences.

Life of Pythagoras, Iamblichus

Plato (427–347 B.C.), Greek philosopher

The soul of the true philosopher ... abstains as much as possible from pleasures and desires, griefs and fears ... because each pleasure and pain, having a nail, as it were, nails the soul to the body, and fastens it to it, and causes it to become corporeal, deeming those things to be true whatever the body asserts to be so. For, in consequence of its forming the same opinions with the body, and delighting in the same things … it can never pass into Hades in a pure state, but must ever depart polluted by the body, and so quickly falls into another body … and consequently is deprived of all association with that which is divine, and pure, and uniform.

Phaedo

Virgil (70–19 B.C.), Roman poet

All these souls, after they have passed away a thousand years, are summoned by the divine ones in great array, to the Lethean river … In this way they become forgetful of their former earth life, and revisit the vaulted realms of the world, willing to return again into living bodies.

The Aeneid

Ovid (43 B.C.-17 A.D.), Roman poet

Then death, so call'd, is but old matter dress'd
In some new figure, and a varied vest.
Thus all things are but alter'd, nothing dies
And here and there the unbodied spirit flies …
From tenement to tenement though toss'd,
The soul is still the same, the figure only lost
And, as the soften'd wax new seals receives.
This face assumes, and that impression leaves;
New call'd by yore, now by another name.
The form is only changed, the wax is still the same.
So death, so call'd, can but the form deface;
The immortal soul flies out in empty space
To seek her fortune in some other place.

Metamorphoses

Origen (185–254 A.D.), early Church father

Is it not more in conformity with reason that every soul for certain mysterious reasons (I speak now according to the opinion of Pythagoras and Plato and Erapedocles, whom Celsus frequently names) is introduced into a body, and introduced according to its deserts and former actions? …

Is it not rational that souls should be introduced into bodies in accordance with their merits and previous deeds, and that those who have used their bodies in doing the utmost possible good should have a right to bodies endowed with qualities superior to the bodies of others? …

The soul, which is immaterial and invisible in its nature, exists in no material place without having a body suited to the nature of that place. Accordingly, it at one time puts off one body, which was necessary before, but which is no longer adequate in its changed state, and it exchanges it for a second.

Contra Celsum

The soul has neither beginning nor end … Every soul … comes into this world strengthened by the victories or weakened by the defeats of its previous life. Its place in this world as a vessel appointed to honour or dishonour is determined by its previous merits or demerits. Its work in this world determines its place in the world which is to follow this …

De Principiis

David Hume (1711–1776), British philosopher

Reasoning from the common course of nature, and without supposing any new interposition of the supreme cause, which ought always to be excluded from philosophy, what is incorruptible must also be ungenerable. The soul, therefore, if immortal, existed before our birth, and if the former existence in no ways concerns us, neither will the latter … The metempsychosis is, therefore, the only system of this kind that philosophy can hearken to.

The Immortality of the Soul

J.G. von Herder (1744–1803), German thinker

Have you never had remembrances of a former state, which you could find no place for in this life? … Have you not seen persons, been in places, of which you were ready to swear that you had seen those persons, or had been in those places before? … And such are we, who, from a hundred causes, have sunk so deep and are so wedded to matter, that but few reminiscences of so pure character remain to us. The noble class of men who, separated from wine and meat, lived in perfect simplicity according to the order of nature, carried it further, no doubt, than others, as we learn from the example of Pythagoras, Iarchas, Apollonius and others, who remembered distinctly what and how many times they had been in the world before.

If we are blind, or can see but two steps beyond our noses, ought we therefore to deny that others may see a hundred or a thousand degrees farther, even to the bottom of time, into the deep, cool well of the foreworld, and there discern everything, plain and bright and clear?

Dialogues on Metempsychosis

J. W. von Goethe (1749–1832), German poet

I am certain that I have been here as I am now a thousand times before, and I hope to return a thousand times.

Letter to I. Folk

Arthur Schopenhauer (1783–1860), German philosopher

Were an Asiatic to ask me for a definition of Europe, I should be forced to answer him: it is that part of the world which is haunted by the incredible delusion that man was created out of nothing, and that his present birth is his first entrance into life.

Parerga and Paralipomena

What sleep is for the individual, death is for the will ... It would not endure to continue the same actions and sufferings throughout an eternity without true gain, if memory and individuality remained to it. It flings them off, and this is Lethe; and through the sleep of death, it reappears refreshed and fitted out with another intellect, as a new being—"a day tempts to new shores."

These constant new births, then, constitute the succession of the life-dreams of a will which in itself is indestructible ... Every new-born being comes fresh and blithe into the new existence, and enjoys it as a free gift; but there can be nothing freely given. Its fresh existence is paid for by the old age and death of a worn-out existence which has perished, but which contained the indestructible seed out of which this new existence has arisen: they are one being. To show the bridge between the two would certainly be the solution of a great riddle.

The World as Will and Idea

Victor Hugo (1802–1885), French writer

For half a century I have been writing my thoughts in prose and in verse. History, philosophy, drama, romance, tradition, satire, ode and song, I have tried all. But I feel I have not said a thousandth part of what is in me. When I go to the grave I can say like many others, "I have finished my day's work," but I cannot say, "I have finished my life." My day's work will begin again the next morning. The tomb is not a blind alley; it is a thoroughfare. It closes on the twilight. It opens on the dawn.

From The Philosophy of Life, by A.M. Baten

Gustav Mahler (1860–1911), German composer

We all return; it is this certainty that gives meaning to life and it does not make the slightest difference whether or not in a later incarnation we remember the former life. What counts is not the individual and his comfort, but the great aspiration to the perfect and the pure which goes on in each incarnation.

From his biography by R. Specht

G. Lowes Dickinson (1862–1932), British philosopher

The whole series of (man's) actions and feelings in one life are determined by those of a previous, and determine those of a subsequent, life ... It is, I think, a really consoling idea that our present capacities are determined by our previous actions, and that our present actions again will determine our future character. It seems to liberate us from the bonds of an external fate and make us the captains of our own destinies. If we have formed here a beautiful relation, it will not perish at death, but be perpetuated, albeit unconsciously, in some future life. If we have developed a faculty here it will not be destroyed, but will be the starting-point of later developments.

Is Immortality Desirable? Ingersoll Lecture, Harvard University, 1909

John M. Ellis McTaggart (1866–1925), British philosopher

Even the best men are not, when they die, in such a state of intellectual and moral perfection as would fit them to enter heaven immediately ... This is generally recognised, and one of two alternatives is commonly adopted to meet it. The first is that some tremendous improvement—an improvement out of all proportion to any which can ever be observed in life—takes place at the moment of death ... The other and more probable alternative is that the process of gradual improvement can go on in each of us after the death of our present bodies ...

Would it not be worth much to be able to hope that what we missed in one life might come to us in another? And would it not be worth much to be able to hope that we might have a chance to succeed hereafter in the tasks which we failed in here?

Some Dogmas of Religion

C. D. Bread (1887–1977), British philosopher

We shall behave all the better if we act on the assumption that we may survive; that actions which tend to strengthen and enrich our characters in this life will probably have a favourable influence on the dispositions with which we begin our next lives; and that actions which tend to disintegrate our characters in this life will probably cause us to enter on our next life "halt and maimed." If we suppose that our future lives will be of the same general nature as our present lives, this postulate, which is in itself intelligible and not unreasonable, gains enormously in concreteness and therefore in practical effect on our conduct.

Examination of McTaggart's Philosophy

Henry Ford (1863–1947), American industrialist

I adopted the theory of reincarnation when I was twenty-six ... Religion offered nothing to the point ... Even work could not give me complete satisfaction. Work is futile if we cannot utilize the experience we collect in one life in the next. When I discovered reincarnation it was as if I had found a universal plan. I realized that there was a chance to work out my ideas. Time was no longer limited. I was no longer a slave to the hands of the clock ...

The discovery of reincarnation put my mind at ease ... If you preserve a record of this conversation, write it so that it puts men's minds at ease. I would like to communicate to others the calmness that the long view of life gives to us.

Genius is experience. Some seem to think that it is a gift or talent, but it is the fruit of long experience in many lives. Some are older souls than others, and so they know more.

San Francisco Examiner

J. Ducasse (1881–1969), philosopher

Whether or not survival as plurality of lives on earth is a fact, it is at least coherently thinkable and not incompatible with any facts known to us today. Of all the conceptions of significance of human life on earth the reincarnation hypothesis, which regards each life of a person as being like a day in school, is the only one that makes any sense.

How come one person is born a genius and another a boob; one is born beautiful and another ugly; one is born healthy and another crippled? The concept of rebirth on earth, perhaps after an interval occupied by the individual in distilling out of memories of a life just ended such wisdom as his reflective powers enabled him to extract, would enable us to believe there is justice in the universe.

Providence Evening Bulletin

The relation between the man who sows in one life and man who reaps in a later one is essentially the same kind as that between the child and the adult. The two are the "same" person not in the sense that any item, physical or mental, in the infant's makeup has persisted unchanged and is identically present in the mature man, but only in the sense that the former has changed into the latter by a gradual transformation from hour to hour, day to day, year to year. The sameness of the two is thus in the sense only of continuousness of becoming.

A Philosophical Scrutiny of Religion

—§§§—

Mind Training in Buddhism

and Other Essays

Natasha Jackson
and
Hilda M. Edwards

Bodhi Leaves No. 101

First published: 1985

Mind Training in Buddhism

Natasha Jackson

> "Man is only a reed, the feeblest in nature, but he is a thinking reed. The whole universe must not rise in arms to crush him. A vapour, a drop of water, suffices to kill him. But, if the entire universe were to crush him, man would still be more noble than that which slays him, because he knows that he is dying, and of the advantage which the universe possesses over him the universe knows nothing. Thus all our dignity consists in thought. It is that upon which we must take our stand, not upon space and duration. Let us, then, labour to think well; that is the principle of morals."
>
> Pascal

> "All that we are is the result of what we have thought:
> it is founded on our thoughts, it is made up of our thoughts.
> If a man speaks or acts with an evil thought, pain follows him,
> as the wheel follows the foot of the ox that draws the carriage.
> If a man speaks or acts with a pure thought, happiness
> follows him, like a shadow that never leaves him."
>
> Dhammapada (trans. Max Muller)

Buddhism is a jewel of many facets, the lights of which attract all sorts and conditions of men and women, to each of whom it has its own special and particular appeal. This is certainly very pertinent to the West where no one finds himself a Buddhist as a matter of routine following the religion of his parents, but by deliberate choice.

Assuming that the interest is real and not a passing phase of romantic hankering for a taste of 'the mystic East', the attraction may lie in its rationality, its cogency as a system, its philosophy, its way of life, the character of the Buddha himself as guide and exemplar, or all of these factors combined. Nevertheless, for anyone who takes Buddhism at all seriously, it is essentially a system of mind training. To speak of 'taking Buddhism seriously' means making an earnest effort of trying to apply it by keeping its precepts which are negative and by amplifying them through the Noble Eightfold Way which is dynamically positive.

Many people never get around to taking this step. They like to come, listen to a lecture, read a few books and have a talk about Buddhism—especially about the intriguing indeterminates, like the origins of everything and 'what is reborn'. That, for many, is as far as it goes. The interest often peters out when they learn that the Buddha was not concerned with trying to solve the baffling riddles of the universe, but confined himself strictly to life in the here-and-now, in which these questions are irrelevant. Reasoning and speculation not bound together by a common aim of all the arguments is foolish and a futile pastime, no matter how logical it may appear to be.

The question that directly concerns all of us here-and-now and throughout our whole lifetime is the consciousness of suffering and of happiness—how to avoid the one and to attain the other. All the great religions and all the great teachers of mankind have stated very definitely in various ways that a fundamental and abiding happiness is not to be achieved by seeking to possess, to hoard and not to share, to woo promotion and superiority by trampling down others; that the man who is prepared for his own petty welfare, or for the narrow sectional interests of the group to which he happens to belong, to deprive other beings of greater happiness and even of life, deprives himself, in the long run, as much, if not more, as others. They all agree that the spirit in which life should be lived should be creative, rather than possessive; that the man who tries to give something, however little, who tries to make the world less cruel, less hard for others, has his own reward in his own inner joy that the vicissitudes of time and circumstance cannot take away from him.

Most people would agree, in principle at least, that honesty, kindness and unselfishness are highly desirable as counsels of perfection but would be dubious about the practicability of trying to attain such high standards in this wicked, wicked world. Others are convinced that these and most of the other virtues are theirs already but that their present unhappiness, boredom or frustration is due, not to their own inadequacies, but to the machinations of evil men, to the blindness of other people who do not appreciate their sterling qualities, or to other similar causes external to themselves.

In regard to this aspect, that shrewd old philosopher of our century, Bertrand Russell, with shattering insight observes that almost everybody suffers in a greater or lesser degree from elements of persecution mania which he declares to be always rooted in a too exaggerated conception of our own merits.

Spiritual aspiration does not consist of the desire to feel cosy and comfortable. Rather, its most notable characteristic is an earnest desire for self-improvement, which in turn means self-mastery. To make any headway in self-improvement one must first learn to know oneself. To see the mote in our brother's eye is very easy but extremely difficult to recognize the beam in our own. For this complicated project Buddhism offers mindfulness, the most original technique in the history of religions. Buddhism is the only religion that not only shows us that we suffer mainly from ourselves, but also provides a practical and down-to-earth method by which we can re-educate and remake ourselves into the type of being we would like to be. It is not sufficient to tell or advise people what they should do. Many of us want to lead the good life and make it even better, but how? The Buddhist way is the way of mindfulness. The Buddha maintained that the only way we can remake ourselves is by understanding ourselves, by self-observation and analysis, to see ourselves 'as we really are'. There is no other way to correct defects of character, for how can anyone correct a fault if he is unaware of its existence?

The practice of mindfulness involves becoming fully and constantly aware of four things:

1. the body and its state, functions and activities;
2. the feelings as pleasant, painful or neutral (not emotions);
3. states of mind (these include the emotions and moods);
4. contents of the mind (what we actually think about).

These should be undertaken and practised in that order. Mindfulness applied consistently and over a sufficient period of time enables the practitioner to learn exactly how his body works, and what is even more important, how his mind works.

Using these techniques, the aspirant for self-mastery becomes increasingly aware of all that he thinks, says and does and of all that happens to him and within him.

What is vitally necessary is that we should be absolutely honest with ourselves. The slightest self-deception defeats the object. If this sounds simple, just try it. Actually, it is difficult though not impossible. It involves constant effort until it becomes habitual. The result is that gradually the mind learns how to control the body and the senses.

This is where our mind training should begin—not directly with attempts at meditation in the formal manner. With the popularization of hatha yoga in the West, reinforced by an awakening of interest in the Eastern religions generally due to the resurgence of Asia in the international field of affairs, people are curious and intrigued with the subject of meditation.

However, it should be understood that meditation, which can be extremely beneficial, requires considerable preparation. Most important and vital is the question of motive in undertaking it. The motives should be right; the aspirant should be well established in morality (*sīla*) and should lead a life consistent with his aims. Drugs and alcohol do not go with meditation, nor is Enlightenment to be gained by LSD.

Unfortunately, there is, in some instances, a great deal of misrepresentation on the question of meditation. One writer starts off with:

> "Do you desire success in life? Will you take the means that infallibly secure it? Will you choose, and say to yourself, 'I will have wealth; I will have fame; I will have virtue; I will have power?' Let your imagination play upon the thought and watch the dim clouds of hope shape themselves into heavenly possibilities."
>
> *Concentration*, E. Wood

The motives inspiring this kind of advance publicity, blatantly calculated to get people in by appealing to their latent greed, are more than merely questionable—they are highly suspect. The author either knows no better—in which case he is not competent to write on meditation or on any other form of yoga—or if he does know better, then he is writing with his tongue in his cheek. The insinuation of the preposterous promises is obviously designed to catch the unwary. Unfortunately, there are still many people in the world who are gullible, a fact that makes the cynic say: "There's a mug born every minute."

Mind training in Buddhism should not be pursued with any object of personal aggrandisement or 'to win friends and influence people'. Meditation is not a gimmick for self-promotion and mindfulness is not a purely mechanistic exercise resembling those taught by specialized organisations. These have no pretensions at aiming at something spiritual or transcendental.

Undertaken with wrong motives, meditation can become dangerous, strengthening, not weakening, delusion. Meditation itself is a means to an end, not an end in itself. Its aim is to develop insight and wisdom and the desirable states of mind like universal love (*mettā*), compassion (*karuṇā*), sympathy (*muditā*), and serenity (*upekkhā*). It is a technique for the cultivation of non-greed, non-hatred, non-delusion.

We should know not only why we meditate, its value and its objective, but we also require to know how to go about it, what to do. Ideally, it should be practised under the surveillance of a meditation master. However, competent meditation masters are very few indeed.

When we get down to meditation proper, it is amazing how uncritically people allow themselves to be swept up by a fashion or a cult. (Yes, there are fashions in everything—not only in clothes but in art, hobbies and religion). At long last, the West has discovered meditation! That is all to the good but what is less understandable is the unquestioned acceptance of the craze for instituted meditation centres sponsoring marathon sessions of practice of up to 18 or 20 hours a day and lasting for weeks!

When the Buddha advocated the practice of meditation, he was speaking to his monks, who were leading a life entirely dedicated to the attainment of Nibbāna under his own matchless guidance and supervision. It is a very far cry from those conditions to the environment of a Western layman, living for the most part in one of the large cities and subject to all the distractions, worries and temptations of a householder's life. Under such circumstances, meditation cannot be recommended indiscriminately to everyone, let alone crash meditation programs. If a layman can manage to devote half-an-hour to one-hour a day to meditation, he is doing as much as it is wise to attempt at this stage of our development. For those who are ready, and who set about it in a sane and rational way, it can indeed prove of great benefit. A verse in the Dhammapada says:

> Without knowledge there is no meditation;
> Without meditation there is no knowledge.
> He who practises knowledge and meditation
> Is near unto Nibbāna.

We can note that knowledge is mentioned first.

The follower of the Buddha has always to bear in mind that his prime duty is to work on himself. This work that he does on himself does not mean that he should not engage in any kind of collective welfare work for the common good by means of social and economic reform, in order to bring about a more equitable system of society. However, good legislation alone will not bring about the regeneration of the world. Society is composed of individuals and the question of regeneration inevitably reverts to the individual. If a sufficient number of individuals could jack themselves up to making the effort to overcome their spiritual ignorance, even if they succeeded in achieving partial insight, reform of social and economic injustices and anomalies would come automatically, because there would not be any significant opposition, owing to that moral regeneration of individuals. Thus, whenever a man succeeds in overcoming a fault, a prejudice or a blemish within himself, he also changes the world to some extent, because after his victory over himself, even in his own small circle things will happen differently.

And because the Buddhist methods of mind training enable people to see their weaknesses and to overcome them, they are invaluable. Incidentally, the methods are very much in line with modern psychology which the Buddha anticipated over 2500 years ago.

Freedom Of Mind

Natasha Jackson

"So it is, monks, that the holy life is not lived for advantage in gains, honours, fame; it is not for advantage in moral habit; it is not for advantage in concentration; it is not for advantage in knowledge and vision.

That, monks, which is unshakable freedom of the mind, this is the goal, monks, of holy life, this is the pith, this is the culmination."

Greater Discourse on Simile of the Pith, Majjhima Nikāya 29

Throughout the march of time, man has won through to many freedoms: freedom to work, freedom to move about as he wishes, freedom of speech and assembly, freedom of worship ... and to many other freedoms. However, the most important freedom—freedom of mind from all illusion—that he has still to achieve. It still eludes him. The blame is not entirely his own, because every culture has tried and still tries to impose on him its own dominant image as the ideal to be followed and perpetuated.

However, today the battle for freedom of the mind is at a much more subtle level than in the days of struggle against absolute rulers, oligarchies, theocracies, or any other form of naked power. The highly technical age of the present aims at the standardisation of increasingly large masses of men and women within a rigidly mechanical framework, and conditions them without the use of direct force into becoming men who think alike, who feel alike, and who are amenable to conformity with the vast bureaucratic structures, content to be cogs in the ever expanding industrial machine of bureaucratic 'bumbledom'. But though the iron hand of authority is now encased within a velvet glove, and operates in the much more rarefied atmosphere of the mass media (especially TV and radio), the social pressures and coercion are still with us—perhaps even in greater force.

It can hardly be otherwise within a purely materialistic society, geared for maximum profit and one in which the emphasis is on man as a producer—and above all, as a consumer—of more and more goods. Within such a framework the image of the archetype which emerges is that of the tycoon, the man of extreme wealth as the model and pace-setter to be admired and emulated. But as most of the nations of the world are concerned in the scramble for wealth, and power, the conflicts are sharpened, wars are being fought, and the stockpiling of nuclear warheads continues.

It is hardly surprising that today, in such an atmosphere dominated by greed, fear, and hatred, an increasing number of people should feel estranged, disorientated, unable to see any meaning in life, helpless in coping with its tensions and to serve as their own monitors. The general malaise within our society is reflected in the wave of protest movements and demonstrations throughout the world (hardly an unnatural development under the circumstances), in the loss of moral standards, in the disintegration of family life, the decay and impotence of organized religion, the prevalence of drug-addiction and delinquency, in the intrusion of numerous psychotic cults in art, music and fashion.

It is in the present situation, perhaps more than at any other time, that Buddhism, were it to become widely known and appreciated, could have much to offer.

The Buddha's conclusion that life is *dukkha* (suffering) is not original per se, seeing that it is shared to some extent by other religions and freely admitted by all thinking people. What is strikingly original is his solution of the problem of suffering which he made his chief concern. The Buddha analysed suffering as arising, not by reason of man looking for welfare and happiness (a built-in aspiration of the human organism), but by seeking welfare and happiness in the wrong places, and by using wrong methods to attain these; by wanting the wrong things; by pursuing goals that do not lead to any abiding welfare and happiness but only to further misery; by pandering to an illusory ego and giving way to greed and hatred in the course of its promotion, thus paving the way for other manifestations of suffering: disappointment, frustration, dejection, apathy, despair; by yielding to the pleasure principle in sensuality, lust, gluttony, drunkenness, which inevitably culminate in guilt, worry, self-hatred, restlessness, and doubt. He taught that people suffer until they learn the true reason for their behaviour and that they must stop doing things—even good things—for the wrong reasons.

Thus, the crucial point of the Buddha's message is the question of motive. It is quite possible to keep the Five Precepts (or, for that matter, the Ten Commandments), be a generous dispenser of largesse to various charities, all with the purpose of gaining social approval and prestige, obtaining civic honours, or assuring for oneself a place in heaven, or at least a favourable rebirth—all of which, strictly from a Buddhist point of view are wrong motives, all being more or less subtle forms of self-seeking. The Buddha did not aim at a partial repair of a disordered personality. His objective was a radical cure.

The Buddha did not speak of the subconscious mind as such (that clarification had to wait 2500 years to be revealed by the genius of Freud) though the methods and techniques of his system of mind-training bear witness that he fully recognised the existence of vast subterranean forces within the deep layers of the human consciousness. He also penetrated to the compulsive nature of the dark underground which he called *avijjā* (ignorance). What Freud called the 'id', the Buddha called *taṇhā*, best translated as thirst or craving. The equation is: A + T = CB, or: *avijjā* (ignorance) plus *taṇhā* (craving) equals Compulsive Behaviour. Like Freud, he, too, maintained that once the negative, unhealthy motives are exposed to the light and seen clearly for what they are, they cannot flourish or persist to grow. The whole of the Buddhist discipline, the Noble Eightfold Way and more particularly the section directly covering mental training (Right Effort, Right Mindfulness and Right Meditation), is calculated to illumine the darkness of ignorance, and so to liberate man from the tyranny of his unconscious compulsive drives, and make him master in his own house.

That too, is ostensibly the objective of modern psychiatry, which, like everything else on this planet, can be used and abused. The present trend in America is for everybody who is anybody, to have a psychiatrist in tow, not only for the usual therapeutic interviews, but also on-call for consultation on every conceivable subject demanding a decision. Apparently, the psychiatrist is to the well-to-do American of today what the court astrologer was to the Eastern potentate of the Middle Ages. It would be difficult indeed, to think up a more imaginative procedure to ensure a rich harvest of psychological cripples.

The Buddha, on the other hand, insisted that a man should do his own striving and experimentation.

Naturally, such an ambitious and important project requires a considerable measure of preparation. Experience has taught us the inadvisability of taking raw recruits and introducing them prematurely to the practice of meditation. It is necessary, first of all, to gain some knowledge of fundamental Buddhist teachings— which, though admittedly is surface knowledge, is nevertheless vital.

Secondly, there should be some semblance of order established in the life pattern of the individual through the practice of morality (*sīla*), or Right Speech, Right Action and Right Livelihood. To plunge headlong into meditation, all practices without attaining a reasonably moral life is to court disaster. The reason is simple. How, for example, can a man, drinking heavily, or one who is mainly preoccupied with planning acts of seduction, or recovering from such forays, venture to delve into the deep layers of his mind without setting up further inner conflicts? Indeed, it would not be safe for him to attempt meditation. However, such is the perverseness of human nature that we have had people interested in meditation which they were prepared to practise, hoping it would cure them of alcoholism (or of some other equally devastating character defect), not realizing that if they did not have the will-power to halt the defect even temporarily, meditation for them was out of the question. A person with a groundwork in the fundamental teachings of the Buddha would know that meditation is not something in the nature of a magic wand, but only one step (though a very important one) of the Buddhist training and discipline, the Noble Eightfold Way. All eight steps are interrelated and should be practised concurrently.

Moreover, experience has also taught us that the safest and surest way of beginning is by way of mindfulness. Just noticing what happens to us, in us, and around us (that is, 'bare attention') can be practised by everyone, irrespective of whatever imperfections of character may exist. The Four Stations of Mindfulness include mindfulness of the body, of the feelings (as pleasant, painful or neutral), of the thoughts and ideas, and of the mental contents (the nature of what we think about).

Formal meditation begins by exercises in concentration on a single object to achieve one-pointedness of mind, commencing with observation of the breath (*ānāpānasati*), and progressing onwards towards realizing the four Noble Truths.

Such is a very brief and cursory survey of the Buddha's system of mind-training. Needless to say, it is inadequate and needs a great deal more amplification and study. Its range and scope establishes the Buddha among the greatest liberators of mankind. As one modern writer has summarized the value of the Buddha's method:

> "In his insight on taṇhā, the Buddha won his greatest penetration into his major problem, the problem of suffering. It is particularly unfortunate for the understanding of this penetration that his observations have been obscured by the mistaken notion that the annihilation of the individual was his objective, rather than the release of the person from unconscious controls ...
>
> In its unenlightened state, human behaviour is driven and rigidly constrained by unconscious motives, not just among psychoneurotics, but among us all, and this is the central diagnosis of our predicament. The mentally disturbed represent only extreme and sharply defined cases of the obsessions that afflict us all. In the sense we use it here, as applying to all people, behaviour is compulsive so long as it is motivated, i.e. aroused, driven and controlled, by forces of whose identity a person is unaware ...
>
> Buddhism may restore to Western people the rich qualities of inner experience which, in the last resort, are the individual's only defence against tides that seem to be sweeping him weakly if not helplessly along ...
>
> Man can purify and free himself from all evil propensities without going to a psychiatrist. This is the message of Buddhism to modern man."

Buddhism, the Religion of Analysis,
by Nolan Pliny Jacobson

—§§§—

THE UNGUARDED MIND

Hilda M. Edwards.

The mind, which is the essence of man, is probably the least understood although the most important feature in the whole complicated mechanism of the human being. As everything we think, say or do is coloured by the mind, it is far better to understand how the wrong states of mind arise, than to try and curb them once they are in operation, without knowing the reasons for their existence.

The first stage is contact, which is physical—sights, sounds, smells, tastes, touch, and organic sensations—and arising out of these basic elements and dependent on them are emotions, desires, concepts, and volitions. It is at this stage that our future conduct is determined, and by a variety of wrong thoughts we are prone to fall into error, even at times by lack of thought, that is, the following of thought patterns formed originally by the acceptance of wrong concepts to which we keep returning.

The Buddha himself said, "I know not of any other single thing so intractable as the untamed mind," and it seems that this intractability of mind is more prevalent at the present time than one would imagine, despite the opportunities for education and constructive thought. But although education is no longer the monopoly of a fortunate few, we must not fall into the assumption that it has necessarily helped man to think more clearly, or to understand himself, as most education tends to present facts and help people to memorise them.

How many people, for example, are content to accept the persuasive propaganda that is included in the mass media of radio, TV, and the press? It is possible, indeed probable, that public opinion is quite often influenced by partial truths and distortions, particularly in times of wars and conflicts when appeals to the emotions are more likely to be accepted than those based on objective reasoning.

> "Emotion has nothing whatsoever to do with the attainment of truth. That which we prize under the name of 'emotion' is an elaborate activity of the brain, which consists of like

and dislike, motions of assent and dissent, impulses of desire and aversion. It may be influenced by the most diverse parts of the organism—by the craving of the senses, the muscles, the stomach, etc. The interests of truth are far from being promoted by these conditions and vacillations of emotions; on the contrary such circumstances often disturb that reason which is adapted to the pursuit of truth, and frequently mar its perceptive power. No problem is ever solved or even advanced by the cerebral function we call emotion."

The Riddle of the Universe, by Ernst Haeckel

There is also the something-for-nothing school of thought—or perhaps we should say 'substitute for thought'—which seems to be a feature of the age. Otherwise how can one explain the prevalence of lotteries, poker-machines, and betting on sporting events, to mention only a few of the popular forms of gambling, the existence of which is founded upon human credulity and optimism and greed, carried to absurdity.

The modern layman has many more distractions to confuse his mind than had his earlier counterpart. Not the least of these is noise, which pervades all sections of city life and includes an over-abundance of the spoken word. From the immense surface of the globe at this and every moment there arises a great clamour of words in hundreds of languages. In any one moment of the day or night, millions of words are whispered, spoken aloud, shouted, muttered or otherwise uttered, and most of these serve absolutely no purpose whatsoever. It may be, of course, that to some people quietness is a vacuum that must be filled with sound, even if it is only the cacophony that often goes under the name of popular music. Speech as a means of communication and music as a form of relaxation and inspiration are both a necessary part of life, but used to excess they become like a drug that stupefies the mind.

Man is a gregarious creature, but in so many ways of life he carries 'togetherness' to extremes, so that it becomes a form of escapism. When part of the crowd, he does not have time to think about his problems; they can be postponed while he passes the time. But time does not pass. It stays with us, and we live the present and the past together. If we have not yet learnt this then we are indeed backward scholars.

Love of power has always been a part of man and is stronger and more corrupting than any material or economic motive. At the present time the widespread conflicts can only be described as struggles for power in most cases. U Thant, the former Secretary General of UN, believes that the root cause of the troubles is moral, and in a recent interview he said, "International morals have degenerated in the last few years, if I may say so, and like other human emotions it is contagious. If morals are debased in one region, then it catches on. Moral development has not kept pace with the scientific and material development of many nations. I am thinking of general morals like good behaviour and live-and-let-live. As far as those things are concerned, we are still in the Middle Ages."

There are those who profit from wars, both nations and individuals; others who are pawns in the game of kill or be killed, and in a country participating in the conflict, everyone is involved, willy-nilly, if only by taxation, direct or indirect, a part of which is allocated for 'defence'. But although this cannot be avoided, it is no reason why we should tacitly approve of the futility and waste of life.

In a computerised age when things are presented to us ready-made or 'instant', it is more that ever necessary to be alert, self-reliant, and to question everything. "Man is a reed", said Pascal, "but a thinking reed", and as the reed is swayed by every wind, so man is swayed by desires, emotions, and illusions, and instead of being master of his mind he is enslaved by it.

There are some misconceptions which are quite as real today as they were when Cicero drew up his list in the first century BC:

- The delusion that individual advancement is made by crushing others.
- The tendency to worry about things that cannot be altered.
- Insisting that a thing is impossible because we cannot personally accomplish it.
- Neglecting refinement and development of the mind.
- Attempting to compel persons to believe and live as we do.

—§§§—

Bhikkhu Tissa Dispels Some Doubts

Leonard Price

Bodhi Leaves No. 102

First published: 1985

Bhikkhu Tissa Dispels Some Doubts

It is near sunset on a hot summer afternoon. Outside a temple a Buddhist monk named Bhikkhu Tissa sits quietly on a mat in the shade of a tree. Mr Prentice, a layman, comes hiking up the road, wiping his perspiring face with a handkerchief. He sees the monk and approaches him.

Mr Prentice: Oh, Bhikkhu Tissa, I was hoping I'd find you here.

Bhikkhu Tissa: Good afternoon, Mr Prentice.

Prentice: You remember my name. I wasn't sure if you would. I've come around the temple every now and then—just out of curiosity, mainly.

Bhikkhu Tissa: Is it curiosity that brings you here now?

Prentice: I guess you could say that. Isn't this heat awful?

Bhikkhu Tissa: Sit down, Mr Prentice. There's plenty of lawn.

Prentice: Ah, so there is. Thank you.

(He looks around doubtfully, then he settles in the shade at a respectful distance from the monk.)

I'm a bit worn out. It's kind of a long walk from my house to here. I wonder if you might have time to answer a couple of questions?

Bhikkhu Tissa: I'll try. What's on your mind?

Prentice: In a word, Buddhism.

Bhikkhu Tissa: All of it?

Prentice: Ha, ha. No, it's just that I've been doing some reading—plus hearing an occasional lecture here—and I must say I find Buddhism very attractive, at least in theory. It's very cool, rational, and scientific in its explanations of reality. I can appreciate that. I like to think I'm a man of science. The Buddhist analysis of mind and matter appears to me almost like a scientific investigation. But the other part, the religious part, gives me trouble.

Bhikkhu Tissa: You're a great admirer of science, are you, Mr Prentice?

Prentice: Oh yes, no question.

Bhikkhu Tissa: Could it be that you appreciate Buddhism in proportion as it resembles science?

Prentice: Uh, well, possibly.

Bhikkhu Tissa: If that's so, why not stay with the real article? Why bother with Buddhism?

Prentice: Well, of course, science lacks a … it lacks …

Bhikkhu Tissa: The religious part?

Prentice: Exactly. You see, venerable sir, the problem is this. Much as I like what I know of Buddhism, much as I approve of it intellectually, I find it difficult to actually commit myself to it as a religious discipline. I have too many doubts. I admire the philosophy, but I suppose I just can't take it seriously.

Bhikkhu Tissa: Seriousness is precisely the difference between philosophy and religion. The philosopher deals in expendable theories; the religious man puts his life on the line.

Prentice: And that's exactly what I'm not prepared to do.

Bhikkhu Tissa: Many people feel that way.

Prentice: And yet—it's what I'd like to do. To be serious. To put my life on the line. The trouble is I don't have any motivation.

Bhikkhu Tissa: Hmm. How far is it from your house to here?

Prentice: What? Oh, eight or ten blocks, I guess.

Bhikkhu Tissa: And you walked eight or ten blocks on a hot afternoon to tell me you don't have any motivation?

Prentice: Ah! Good point.

Bhikkhu Tissa: Buddhist discipline begins and ends with selfexamination. Buddhist philosophy or theory, if you will, instructs us how to carry out that examination and the efforts that follow. We can read the philosophy all we want but if we don't practise it—if we don't take the medicine, so to speak—it won't do anything for us. Now, you tell me that you've been reading Buddhist literature, and you say you have doubts. What specifically is troubling you?

Prentice: Nothing specific, I think. Just general doubts keep me from taking the medicine. To put it bluntly, why should I undertake what promises to be a horrendously hard discipline of meditation and religious observances and so on? What will I get out of it?

Bhikkhu Tissa: First of all, a "horrendously hard discipline" will by itself accomplish nothing.

Prentice: Nothing!

Bhikkhu Tissa: You should get rid of the notion of investing an effort in order to get something in return.

Prentice: I don't understand.

Bhikkhu Tissa: We've already 'got' more than we can handle—namely, suffering. We follow the teachings of the Buddha in order to get rid of suffering. Most people don't understand this important point. They think that they have to try to acquire something— wisdom or knowledge or freedom.

Prentice: But the Buddha does speak of wisdom and knowledge and freedom and so on. Aren't these things worthwhile?

Bhikkhu Tissa: Certainly. But they are not objects to be grasped at as we habitually grasp at things we desire. The highest truth is not a prize to be seized. It is here all the time. Buddhist discipline aims at removing the obstructions that prevent our seeing the truth. The practitioner must certainly make an effort, but he should not try to "get" anything by his effort.

Prentice: It seems paradoxical to me.

Bhikkhu Tissa: Only because you are accustomed to the ordinary way of doing things—a way which, I might guess, has not brought you the happiness you seek.

Prentice: Perhaps you're right about that. Let me re-phrase my question. I mean, even though I appreciate Buddhist thought, I don't feel motivated to actually commit myself to it. Why should I just … leap into the dark, so to speak?

Bhikkhu Tissa: You should not leap into the dark under any circumstances.

Prentice: But isn't that what Buddhism demands? A leap of faith, anyway.

Bhikkhu Tissa: Absolutely not. Blind hope of faith won't help you in the least.

Prentice: Then what reason do I have to …

Bhikkhu Tissa: Ah, there's the word—reason. You see, Mr Prentice, the practising Buddhist needs reason founded on direct insight. The two go together. Don't believe out of mere hope. Don't believe from abstract logic. Don't believe what you can't see clearly for yourself.

Prentice: There's very little I can see. I certainly can't see enlightenment ahead, I can't see Nibbāna.

Bhikkhu Tissa: And what can you see, Mr Prentice?

Prentice (after a troubled pause)**:** My own confusion. My uncertainty. My unhappiness.

Bhikkhu Tissa: Yes?

Prentice: I don't want to sound grandiose, but I see, well, suffering—at least my own suffering.

(Bhikkhu Tissa is silent. Mr Prentice continues haltingly)

I don't mean to say I have any kind of penetrating vision. I just have this recognition that things aren't the way they ought to be, that I'm getting older but not any wiser, that something is wrong in the world or in me. I'd like to do something about it. I'd like to get free from this confusion, this … well, what word can I use but 'suffering'? I suppose that's why I got interested in Buddhism— because it talks about suffering and the way to the end of suffering. If some kind of deliverance is really possible, I'd like to achieve it.

Bhikkhu Tissa: I think you've found your own reason, Mr Prentice.

Prentice: Yes, I suppose so! Then maybe it's just doubt or fear that holds me back. You mentioned self-examination a moment ago. Maybe that's what I have to do.

Bhikkhu Tissa: It sounds like you've already begun. Please understand that the traveller on the Buddhist path proceeds step by step. He doesn't leap into darkness. He keeps his eye on the present moment—on the present step—observing and analysing what is right before him, not troubling himself with what is past or what yet may come. He examines himself constantly as the Buddha taught, learning what is true and false and what is beneficial and harmful. As he learns these things he must act accordingly—by resisting unwholesome influences, by striving to cultivate wholesome thought, speech, and action, and by gradually deepening and purifying his understanding.

Prentice: It sounds terrifically difficult.

Bhikkhu Tissa: It needn't be so. The way of the Buddha is not an ascetic discipline, not some extraordinary programme of penances. It is simply right living—the easiest and best way to live. We are so used to living the wrong way—stumbling blindly through pain and confusion—that we find it hard to believe there is any other way to live.

Prentice: You call it the Middle Way ...

Bhikkhu Tissa: Yes. The Dhamma, the Buddha's teaching, is the Middle Way between the extremes of self mortification and selfindulgence. We shouldn't torment our bodies and minds in the belief that this will purge us of evil and make us wise. Nor should we rush to gratify all our desires for pleasure. The Middle Way of the Buddha is a balanced and sensible life that avoids foolish extremes.

Prentice: Yes, that was clear to me even from my first reading. As I said, on an intellectual level I find it eminently satisfying. Still the actual practice of it is somehow—I don't know—daunting. I wonder if I'm the only one who feels this way.

Bhikkhu Tissa: The Buddha teaches that the mind of a *puthujjana*, an ordinary, worldly person, is dominated by defilements which distorts his view of reality. Such a mind is wild, tormented, deluded. It ranges here and there with the ebb and flow of passion. Obsessed with greed and aversion, it doesn't want to be restrained and tamed. You might say that the defilements fear the power of Dhamma and do everything they can to turn us away from it, to keep us enslaved. For a very long time we have rushed about according to whims and fears, and the idea of even attempting to resist the defilements seems preposterous at first.

Prentice: Well, why are we loaded with defilements?

Bhikkhu Tissa: In a word, because of our ignorance. Because of not knowing, not understanding things as they really are. In our ignorance we are easy prey to defilements, and our minds rush foolishly this way and that, not knowing the harm in such actions. Ignorance is the terrible burden we bear that makes it so difficult to act wisely and happily. Remember, I said that one practises Dhamma not to "get" wisdom but to get rid of suffering. Insight wisdom appears as one studies the world and oneself according to Dhamma. As this wisdom grows, ignorance is gradually destroyed. When ignorance is gone, craving is conquered and suffering vanishes. This is enlightenment.

Prentice: You talk as though these things happen automatically.

Bhikkhu Tissa: In a sense they do. We should not attempt to throw suffering out of our lives by brute force. Instead we should go to the source, to pull out the roots of suffering and let it wither by itself.

It's a matter of cause and effect.

Prentice: I'm beginning to see that there is a certain impersonality about the whole process. But surely one has to make a definite effort to accomplish anything.

Bhikkhu Tissa: Of course. Let me explain in this way: when you bring a lamp into a dark room, darkness is dispelled and the room is filled with light. The lamp is Dhamma. What before was obscured is illuminated. What before was unknown is made manifest. We have to carry that lamp of Dhamma into the darkness of our own minds. That's our task, that's what the Buddha shows us how to do.

Prentice: And that means meditation, right?

Bhikkhu Tissa: Not just meditation.

Prentice: But that's the essence, isn't it? That's what is most important.

Bhikkhu Tissa: No. You shouldn't single out any one aspect of the Buddha's teaching and ignore the rest. The Buddha taught the Noble Eightfold Path as the way to the end of suffering. All the factors of the path are necessary for complete deliverance. Just to understand this in itself is one aspect of Right Views. There are of course many others.

Prentice: I presume the factor of Right Views has to be perfected, to be developed fully?

Bhikkhu Tissa: All the factors have to be developed fully.

Prentice: I see. So after perfecting Right Views, one moves on to Right Intentions, Right Speech, Right Action, Right Livelihood, Right Effort, Right Mindfulness, and Right Concentration. Am I correct?

Bhikkhu Tissa: No, you're not. The path is not a staircase.

Prentice: You mean you don't climb up from steps one to eight?

Bhikkhu Tissa: Not at all. The eight factors of the path are to be practised together. They do not exist in isolation, but reinforce one another and thereby sustain the practitioner. The traditional sequence of the list has nothing to do with the actual cultivation of the factors.

Prentice: Well, this is somewhat of a relief. I was wondering how I could even get past the first factor, much less all the others!

Bhikkhu Tissa: Oh, you still have to 'get past them', as you put it, but there is no fixed order to worry about. The path is a programme of practice—an eightfold programme—which attends to all the important aspects of one's development. At the outset we should be correctly informed of the nature of the world and our duties in it. Then it is up to us to gradually purify ourselves through practice of these factors. Another way of looking at the path is in terms of three categories of training: *sīla*, *samādhi* and *paññā*—or morality, concentration, and wisdom. Morality is the foundation of the whole practice; it supports concentration, which in turn supports wisdom. Without morality, we can achieve nothing of value. Please understand that this does not mean that you should devote yourself exclusively to the perfection of morality before turning your attention to concentration and wisdom. These three aspects of training are intimately related and must be practised together so that you can develop yourself completely and advance toward liberation.

Prentice: Perhaps it's just my ignorance, but it does seem that wisdom is the most important part, and I confess I can't get too excited about morality and concentration.

Bhikkhu Tissa: You are quite mistaken. First, wisdom is a tool, not an end in itself. Wisdom is the power by which we come to discern the true nature of reality and cut off harmful tendencies. Second, there is no value in regarding wisdom as a more important factor than the others when all of them are essential.

Prentice: I must be confusing wisdom with the enlightenment that follows its application. Well then, it still seems to me that Buddhist discipline involves some kind of a leap of intuition to the higher plane.

Bhikkhu Tissa: There's that leap again. Tell me, Mr Prentice, on your way here didn't you pass an apple orchard?

Prentice: An orchard? Well, yes, I did.

Bhikkhu Tissa: And have you ever seen the apples being harvested in the fall?

Prentice: Certainly.

Bhikkhu Tissa: When people want to pick apples do they stand beneath the trees and leap mightily into the air and snatch the fruit off the boughs?

Prentice: No, of course not. Oh, I see where this is heading …

Bhikkhu Tissa: How do they pick apples?

Prentice: They get a ladder and prop it up against the trunk and climb up—yes, I see your point—step by step. And of course you're right, the bottom rung is no less important than the top rung. Well, Bhikkhu Tissa, I'll have to re-think my views on spiritual accomplishment.

Bhikkhu Tissa: It would be ridiculous, wouldn't it—dozens of earnest apple-pickers grunting and leaping and crashing back down on the ground? And yet, believe it or not, this is how many people pursue religion. They very much want some kind of sublime deliverance, but they go about it in the wrong way, without preparing themselves for what must necessarily be a gradual process.

Prentice: I have an uncomfortable feeling that I might be one of those people.

Bhikkhu Tissa: Are you? What do you think?

Prentice: Certainly I'm not the most patient fellow in the world, and I admit that your comments make me feel a bit foolish. But, in the hope of improving myself, let me question you further about morality and concentration. Concentration seems to be selfevident—steadiness or stability in meditation. Is that wrong?

Bhikkhu Tissa: Not so much wrong as incomplete. Concentration is one-pointed attention to an object. It is that power by which the mind is fixed unwaveringly on whatever we wish to know and understand. We all possess this power to one degree or another, or else we could never write a letter or ride a bicycle or perform any simple task. The training in concentration that Buddhism speaks of is a systematic strengthening and development of this ordinary faculty until it becomes a powerful tool for uncovering truth. It is, in fact, indispensable for the development of wisdom, which like everything else in the world does not arise out of nothing, but from causes and conditions. Ordinarily our minds are scattered and weak, without focus or purpose, and unable to hold still long enough to examine anything in depth. We lack the necessary stillness and steadiness for the arising of wisdom. Without these conditions wisdom simply will not appear to us. When we develop concentration we do not create wisdom, but we make it possible for wisdom to occur, just as a gardener does not create fruit but tends the plant so that fruit will result out of the workings of its own nature.

Now you seem to subscribe to the common notion that concentration is confined to the practice of meditation, which you further presume to belong to a single compartment in Buddhist practice. On the contrary, concentration is appropriate and necessary in all our activities.

Prentice: I suppose I hadn't thought of concentration being useful outside of specific mental exercises, but now I must say that it does appear logically necessary for the attainment of wisdom. The solution to any problem certainly requires some amount of concentration and reflection, and when the problem is as profound as that of human suffering, I can see that concentration must be very intense indeed! All right, so far this fits together. But as for morality, I'm still rather confused. Why should morality be as indispensable as concentration and wisdom? It seems, if you'll pardon my saying so, that morality is somehow peripheral to the main issue. Why should the Buddha consider morality so important in what is otherwise a rather scientific process of investigation and development?

Bhikkhu Tissa: What makes you think that morality is not scientific?

Prentice: Well … it's just not, surely! I don't mean to denigrate it— it's certainly praiseworthy—but I don't see how it possibly fits into the dispassionate process you have described.

Bhikkhu Tissa: Mr Prentice, the Buddha extolled moral behaviour not because it provides some agreeable sauce for the main meal of wisdom but because it is indispensable—indeed a prerequisite—for any progress on the path. Interested newcomers like you are often struck by the rational or "scientific" nature of Buddhist philosophy but fail to grasp that Buddhist morality is equally rational. We try to follow the moral precepts not out of sentimental attachment or deference to convention, but simply because they are conducive to our own spiritual development and to the well-being of others. Remember, to get anywhere we have to overcome obstructions to our understanding, namely, greed, hatred, delusion, and all other defilements that spring from them. What do you think—if we cannot control our overt behaviour, can we ever claim to control our own minds?

Prentice: No, certainly not.

Bhikkhu Tissa: There are a great many actions we can perform by thought, word, or deed. Some we call good, some evil, some neutral. For instance, to give charity is good; to harm another person is evil; to wash a frying pan is probably neutral.

Prentice: This is common sense.

Bhikkhu Tissa: Common sense, but not only common sense. What are good and evil after all? Just conventional distinctions. And why do we recognise these distinctions? Because one kind of action leads to pain, woe, misery, and another kind of action leads to happiness, well-being, and peace. 'Good' rebounds to the benefit of oneself and others. 'Evil' causes suffering for the evil-doer and his victims. Am I wrong?

Prentice: No. It's abundantly clear what kinds of actions cause woe or welfare in the world.

Bhikkhu Tissa: Morality, Mr Prentice, is not just helpful for the practitioner of the path—it is essential, being the foundation of concentration. An immoral, unrestrained person can never develop the power of concentration because his mind is constantly swarming with passions. He is distracted, deluded, restless, unable to settle down and examine himself in any systematic way. On the other hand, a person who does his best to follow the moral precepts enjoys a free conscience, self-respect, and a weakening of the defilements which obstruct the inquiring mind. Moreover, by acting morally he begins to discover the spaciousness of a life not devoted to the gratification of selfish craving. Though he restrains himself he becomes freer; though he denies himself he becomes richer. The Buddha's teaching of non-self begins to appear in his own experience—not merely as some remote theory—and thus he is prepared for the work of concentration.

Prentice: I confess I hadn't considered these matters as much as I should have before talking to you.

Bhikkhu Tissa: No, don't say that. It's right and proper for you to read, to inquire, to listen, to gather all the useful information you can. Nobody starts out with a comprehensive understanding of what Buddhism teaches. It would be a mistake to keep entirely to yourself and proceed on what might be false assumptions.

Prentice: One thing that strikes me particularly about what you've told me is the definitive nature of Buddhism. I mean, for a time I had the idea that Buddhism was sort of esoteric and other-worldly, full of rhapsodies about cranes flying across the autumn moon and life being an unreal dream and so on. I'm beginning to understand that Buddhism is not at all vague, but precise and specific. Where is the mysticism I've heard so much about?

Bhikkhu Tissa (laughing)**:** Where indeed? Find it if you can!

Prentice: Of course, I understood that Buddhism has a specific body of doctrine, but your explanation seems more down-to-earth than I had expected. You don't leave much room for dilettantes and dabblers! It makes me a bit uncomfortable with my own approach.

Bhikkhu Tissa: Everybody with a serious interest must inquire and consider carefully. That doesn't make you a dilettante. Also, some people will feel inclined to devote themselves to the path more intensively than others. But you are right that vague dabbling has no place in Buddhism. The Buddha did not teach a doctrine consisting of so many theories. He taught Dhamma, which is to say truth, reality, the actual nature of things. Now, in an ordinary philosophical system, a person might browse about sampling this or that idea, amusing himself with this or that hypothesis as much as he pleases. But in Buddhism such an approach is totally unprofitable and foolish. For one thing, the Dhamma of the Buddha is not to be admired but practised. It has no value as a museum piece. For another, Dhamma is Dhamma regardless of whether we believe it or not. That is, reality doesn't need our stamp of approval; it doesn't accommodate itself to our petty preferences. We can't divide it up and take only the parts we like. Even the Buddha, you may remember, did not invent the Dhamma but discovered it and made it known to mankind. Someone who hears about Dhamma, who learns something of the teaching, may accept this or reject that or approve of this or disapprove of that, and may even try to fit the teaching, in whole or in part, into his own galaxy of beliefs. This is mere dabbling, and it indicates that the individual is only leaping about, looking for amusement or confirmation of his prejudices, and can't hold still long enough to learn. To jump toward something or to jump away from something—it's all the same. Blind doubt is as bad as blind faith. Anyone who wants to make progress must proceed with an open and alert mind, going step by step, quickly or slowly, but going, not making qualifications or excuses, not making a hobby out of religious practice. Insincerity is a great obstacle.

Prentice: I'm a little nervous wondering about my motives in interesting myself in Buddhism. I'm not as open-minded as perhaps I should be. But at least I can say that I'm sincere. I have no interest in being a mere dabbler!

Bhikkhu Tissa: Good. By all means examine Buddhist teaching and try it for yourself.

Prentice: And Buddhist teaching, I believe you said, begins with examining oneself.

Bhikkhu Tissa: Yes, but in order to get anywhere, that examination must be systematic. Since you were a child you've been wondering about yourself, who you are, why you act the way you do, where you are going, and so forth—but such examination is only preliminary; it's incomplete and likely to remain so until you begin to practise in a disciplined way. Once you have come to certain tentative conclusions about your situation in the world and about the possibility of freeing yourself, it is up to you to take the necessary steps. Nobody is going to do it for you. It's very important to understand this. Nobody can do your work for you. You can't simply declare yourself a believer in Buddhism and wait for enlightenment to sweep you up.

Prentice: As I told you earlier, Venerable Tissa, I've examined myself to the point where I feel the need for the kind of path the Buddha points out, and I'm favourably disposed toward undertaking it. I've even been doing some meditation on my own, but I'm not sure I'm following the books correctly. Oh, well, to be frank, I'm just stumbling in the dark at the moment, and I'd appreciate any advice you have on the correct meditation method to follow and what to watch out for and so on.

Bhikkhu Tissa: Let's not put the cart before the horse, Mr Prentice. You are, I think, talking about formal sitting practice. But I'm not sure you understand what meditation really means. Can you define it for me?

Prentice: I could. But I strongly suspect I'd be wrong!

Bhikkhu Tissa: In that case, let's talk basics. The Pali word usually translated as meditation is *bhāvanā*, which really means mental cultivation or self-development. It actually encompasses a great deal more than the English word. Without any instruction in the matter a person is likely to think that Buddhist meditation means sitting in a dark place with crossed legs and contemplating infinity or something like that.

Prentice: I did entertain a similar idea.

Bhikkhu Tissa: Out of such ideas comes a host of mystical notions that have nothing to do with Buddhism. Correct meditation is never dreamy or romantic, nor is it confined to one particular bodily position or place or time of day. The key to the practice is mindfulness—in Pali *sati*. Mindfulness means presence of mind, attentiveness, awareness, observation, bare attention. It is an attitude of impartial watchfulness and alertness. To 'meditate' means to set up mindfulness and maintain it by the power of concentration—in whatever position or circumstance you find yourself.

Prentice: It sounds like you're saying that meditation can be practised along with any human activity.

Bhikkhu Tissa: Not 'along with', Mr Prentice. Meditation is not something separate from ordinary life; it is not an exercise we impose on top of something else. Rightly speaking, meditation is the mindful practice of daily life itself.

Prentice: Do you mean there really is no difference between meditation and daily life? That's extraordinary.

Bhikkhu Tissa: There should be no difference, no distinction. Unfortunately, many people cling tenaciously to the notion that there is a time for meditation and a time for comfortable carelessness. They think that sitting for an hour or two a day on a cushion is sufficient.

Prentice: And it isn't?

Bhikkhu Tissa: One hour, two hours—the time is irrelevant. This is an example of putting the cart before the horse. First you have to understand what the practice is all about. If you look at meditation in the same way as, say, practising the piano, you are already off on the wrong path. Since it is the whole man or woman we want to develop, what use is there in confining our attention to one brief activity or period of time? If we are going to understand the world in its entirety we have to look at that world. We have to develop and apply mindfulness at all times.

Prentice: Yes, I see, but how can we remember to be mindful at all times in the bustle of daily life? We can only think of one thing at a time.

Bhikkhu Tissa: The original meaning of the Pali word *sati* is just 'memory,' and that meaning is still present within the idea of mindfulness. We have to have presence of mind, alertness, readiness, recollection of our duty to observe. You are right that we can only think of one thing at a time, but this does not mean that mindfulness is impossible except when we are idle. To be mindful is to be established in the present moment. If you are working, then your attention should be fully on that work, not wandering hither, and you. If you are eating, you should be mindful of eating. If you are taking a shower, you should be mindful of showering. The objects that present themselves to your senses are the objects of your meditation. You should merely look at them, acknowledge them, and let them go.

Prentice: I don't understand. How does this differ from an ordinary state of mind?

Bhikkhu Tissa: People ordinarily have only a little bit of mindfulness. They are usually not attentive to the present moment. Their minds are scattered, constantly wandering here and there, thinking about the past, thinking about the future, thrashing about with desire and aversion—just as we spoke of earlier. They are always in a hurry to be some place other than where they are, and as a consequence they pay as little attention as possible to what is going on right before them. If you stop and think about it you will realise that most of the time the ordinary mind is without mindfulness and far away from matters at hand. By consciously practising mindfulness we counteract the wasteful agitation of the mind and return it to the present moment, which is, after all, the only place we can really live and work.

Prentice: So meditation is really a kind of training for the mind?

Bhikkhu Tissa: Yes. Just as we train our overt behaviour by observing the moral precepts, we train or minds with the practice of meditation.

Prentice: Is paying attention to the present moment all there is to meditation?

Bhikkhu Tissa: No. Bare mindfulness must be linked with concentration—*samādhi*. Mindfulness is the observing, the investigating, the attention to phenomena. Concentration is the focusing power that holds our attention continuously to any object. Then we must have a further development of mindfulness called *sampajañña*—clear comprehension. Having fixed our attention on an object, having held it there and acknowledged the object dispassionately, we need this factor of clear comprehension to know what the object is, to fully comprehend it, to know what, if any, action is required of us and what benefit or danger the object represents. If we have clear comprehension of all acts we perform, we will be able to distinguish the true from the false and the noble from the ignoble. Carried to the highest level, such a practice can dissolve the difference between daily life and meditation.

Prentice: You refer to 'objects'. Are there special objects recommended for meditation?

Bhikkhu Tissa: Any material thing or mental phenomenon can be an object of meditation. Whatever we can cognize by means of eye, ear, nose, tongue, body, or mind can be scrutinised as the Buddha teaches.

Prentice: That covers just about everything. I can see you really mean it when you say that daily life itself should be meditation! But, tell me, do teachers recommend specific objects or exercises to their students?

Bhikkhu Tissa: In your reading have you come across something called the Four Foundations of Mindfulness?

Prentice: Yes, I think so, but to tell the truth my memory is a bit weak.

Bhikkhu Tissa: In the Mahā-Satipaṭṭhāna Sutta, the Buddha's great discourse on mindfulness, four categories or foundations of mindfulness are explained. First, there is contemplation of the body, *kāyānupassanā*. This concerns everything of a physical nature that arises in our own bodies. The Buddha has declared that "in this very fathom-long body with its perceptions and thoughts there are the world's origin, the world's ending, and the path to the world's ending." In other words, everything we need to discover and understand to reach liberation can be found right here in the body. So mindfulness applied to the body and its processes is especially fruitful. The second foundation of mindfulness is called *vedanānupassanā*—contemplation of feelings.

Prentice: What do you mean by feelings—emotions?

Bhikkhu Tissa: No. 'Feelings' here refers specifically to pleasant feelings, unpleasant feelings, and neutral feelings. Every object which appears to us arouses feelings which may be pleasant, unpleasant, or simply neutral. To practise *vedanānupassanā* is to notice mindfully the nature of these feelings—without, I might add, clinging to pleasant feelings or trying to avoid unpleasant feelings. For any meditation to be effective it must be without partiality or grasping.

Prentice: Now that sounds difficult! Not to prefer pleasant feelings to unpleasant feelings! But, please, go on.

Bhikkhu Tissa: The third foundation of mindfulness is *cittānupassanā*—contemplation of mental states. This means observing the character of the mind at any given moment. For instance, is the mind happy, unhappy, troubled, elated, slothful, energetic, concentrated, unconcentrated? And so on.

Prentice: But how can the mind observe itself? It's a paradox.

Bhikkhu Tissa: Not really. The problem is only one of language. We use words like 'mind' as mere conventions. Actually, what happens is that mindfulness observes or contemplates the mind—which is nothing but a collection of processes—and notes what its character is at any given moment.

Prentice: I see. So contemplation of mental states concerns everything that is going on in the mind?

Bhikkhu Tissa: No. Contemplation of mental states concerns only the character or state of the mind at a particular time. For the contents of the mind, or the specific phenomena that engage our attention, we refer to the fourth foundation—*dhammānupassanā*, or the contemplation of mental objects. In this practice, mindfulness is directed toward the mental objects that the mind deals with. These may be ideas, memories, concepts, hopes, fears, thoughts of all kinds.

Prentice: Why are these called 'foundations' of mindfulness?

Bhikkhu Tissa: Mindfulness is the same thing no matter what its object. But as a practical matter we need to be directed to specific objects or classes of objects in order to learn what mindfulness is and how it operates. The Four Foundations of Mindfulness are specific aspects of experience on which we can set up or establish our practice. For instance, in contemplation of the body, *kāyānupassanā*, we direct our attention to the body and note the experiences that rise to our attention out of the body. In formal sitting practice a teacher will likely advise a student to concentrate on a single bodily object, such as the breathing or the rising and falling of the abdomen. Mindfulness is founded on the body and built up by repeated effort and exertion. The procedure is exactly the same with regard to feelings, mental states, and mental objects.

Prentice: Are the four foundations then purely arbitrary categories?

Bhikkhu Tissa: Not at all. The four foundations concern distinct aspects of human experience which we usually confuse. Remember that Buddhism emphasises the necessity of self-examination. In practising the Four Foundations of Mindfulness we gradually learn the useful lesson that what we take to be the self is in fact a collection of quite impersonal processes. The body is, we discover, just a body, not a self. Feelings are just feelings. Mental states are just mental states. Mental objects are just mental objects.

Prentice: Yes, I understand that.

Bhikkhu Tissa: Excuse me, Mr Prentice. You may understand my words. You may agree with what I am saying. But let me impress upon you that you have to reach these conclusions for yourself, in your own direct experience. Real understanding depends on seeing for yourself.

Prentice: I hope I can do that. But what you said a moment ago troubles me. In connection with contemplation of feelings you said that we should not prefer pleasant feelings to unpleasant feelings. How is such a thing possible?

Bhikkhu Tissa: In practising any of these contemplations, the meditator aims only to be mindful of the rising and passing away of phenomena. When he experiences a certain kind of feeling, for instance, he merely acknowledges it for what it is. If it is pleasant, he notes it as pleasant. If it is unpleasant, he notes it as unpleasant. If it is neutral, he notes it as neutral.

Prentice: But, Bhikkhu Tissa, surely nobody can help preferring the pleasant to the unpleasant.

Bhikkhu Tissa: The Buddha doesn't expect us to like what is unpleasant or to dislike what is pleasant. These feelings are what they are—agreeable or disagreeable or neither. What the Buddha does expect us to do is to set aside desire and aversion and simply observe what is. Desire and aversion cloud our understanding. When practising any of the contemplations I have mentioned, don't hanker after something you don't have, and don't run away from something you do have. You should stay exactly where you are and note with equanimity whatever appears.

Prentice: Are you saying that we should endure any kind of unpleasantness without trying to do anything about it?

Bhikkhu Tissa: Not at all. The Buddhist path aims at the total elimination of suffering, remember. One who starts along the path does indeed diminish the suffering or unpleasantness in his life. Even a highly experienced practitioner will experience unpleasantness, yet this need not be a problem because he will understand the unstable nature of all phenomena and will not indulge in vain clinging or aversion. By developing equanimity in the face of changing circumstances he frees himself from the jungle of likes and dislikes and their attendant miseries. He refrains from grasping. Mental and physical events occur—he knows them for what they are, only knows them, and does not take the further step of celebrating or lamenting them.

Prentice: That must require a highly developed mind.

Bhikkhu Tissa: Every highly developed mind was once a wild and ignorant mind. If you practise the Buddhist path earnestly, you will begin to train your mind and make it less dependent on changing conditions. By practising mindfulness you recognise impermanence within and without you. All phenomena are changing with incredible speed, arising and perishing, flowing on and on. If you see this truly, you will no longer wish to cling to anything.

Prentice: It all comes back to craving, doesn't it?

Bhikkhu Tissa: Craving lies deep in the mind, deeper than we can imagine. By practising the Dhamma we come to know ourselves better and better, and gradually we see where craving hides. If we are attentive we will understand that craving continues as long as it is nourished by ignorance. If we fall back into our old, slothful habits of mind, we may be sure that craving will go on generating suffering in our lives. The wheel of cause and effect just keeps on turning. If, on the other hand, we develop morality, concentration, and wisdom, we will be able to diminish and ultimately destroy craving and the suffering that follows it. There is a task to be done; we can do it or not, as we choose.

Prentice: And ... if we choose not to do it, what happens? (He pauses with a troubled look.)

More of same?

Bhikkhu Tissa (nodding slowly)**:** More of same.

Prentice: So it's my responsibility. I'm feeling this more and more. Happiness just will not happen to me by accident, will it?

Bhikkhu Tissa: The joys of the world come and go, Mr Prentice. Certainly permanent happiness will not come to you by accident.

Prentice: Is it possible to grasp real, permanent happiness?

Bhikkhu Tissa: No, it is not possible.

Prentice (startled)**:** No?

(He thinks a moment, then brightens).

But … is it possible by not grasping to attain such happiness?

Bhikkhu Tissa (with a smile)**:** Yes, it is possible.

Prentice: Oh, I see—excuse me, I begin to see!

Bhikkhu Tissa: Words of Dhamma are written down in books. Words come out of the mouths of monks and laymen. It is worthwhile to listen and remember. But it is not enough.

Prentice (blurting out)**:** Bhikkhu Tissa, if a person were to—if I were to start on the Buddhist path, could I be sure of—I mean, do you think I would—succeed?

(Bhikkhu Tissa says nothing. Mr Prentice waits nervously. It is twilight now, the air heavy and fragrant and still. The darkness thickens moment by moment. Bhikkhu Tissa makes no answer at all. Mr Prentice fidgets uncomfortably in the silence. At last he realises that the monk is not going to reply. Eventually, in some embarrassment, he breaks the silence himself.)

Prentice: Oh, yes. Yes, of course. A foolish question. It only came to my mind because I feel I should do something—do this. What you've told me makes me think that—I mean, I want to be free, I do!

(After a moment, Bhikkhu Tissa's voice floats out of the shadow.)

Bhikkhu Tissa: Go easy, Mr Prentice. Keep your mind in the present moment. Look at your own hand there, clutching the grass so tightly and nervously. Just release it, that's it. Let go easy.

Prentice: All right.

Bhikkhu Tissa: Now keep on letting go.

Prentice: Keep on? Oh! Yes venerable sir.

(A moment passes, then he straightens up)

It's getting late. If you'll excuse me, I'll be going now.

Bhikkhu Tissa: Good night, Mr Prentice.

Prentice: Thank you for your advice, Bhikkhu Tissa. You've cleared up a number of doubts I had. I think I … well, enough said. (He gets stiffly to his feet.)

Good night, venerable sir. (He starts off across the lawn.)

Bhikkhu Tissa: Mr Prentice.

Prentice: Sir?

Bhikkhu Tissa: Stay mindful.

Prentice: Yes. I'll try.

(Mr Prentice goes. Bhikkhu Tissa remains where he is as the evening descends. Grass, tree, and monk are lost to view. Time goes on passing.)

—§§§—

Religious Convention and Sīla Practice

Ajahn Sumedho

Bodhi Leaves No. 103

First published: 1985

Religious Convention and Sīla Practice

> He who with trusting heart takes a
> Buddha as his guide, and the Truth,
> and the Order ... When a man with trusting heart takes
> upon himself the precepts ... that is a
> sacrifice better than open largesse, better
> than giving perpetual alms, better than the
> gift of dwelling places, better than accepting guidance.
> (Dīgha Nikāya V—145, 146)

I would like to say a few words about the uses of conventional religion. Of course, I am only speaking from my own experience as a Buddhist monk, although I would say that in this respect one can recognise the values of religious convention in whatever form.

Nowadays there is a tendency to think that religious convention and form are no longer necessary. There is a kind of hope that, if you can just be mindful and know yourself, then that is all you need to do. Anyhow, that is how we would like it, isn't it? Just be mindful throughout the day, throughout the night, whatever you are doing; drinking your whisky, smoking your marijuana cigarette, picking a safe open, mugging someone you met in Soho—as long as it's done mindfully, it's all right.

There is a brilliant Buddhist philosopher in Thailand who is quite old now, but I went to stay at his monastery a few years ago. I was coming from Ajahn Chah's monastery, so I asked him about the Vinaya—the rules of the monastic order—and how important these were in the practice of meditation and enlightenment.

'Well,' he said, 'only mindfulness—that's all you need. Just be mindful, and everything is all right, you know. Don't worry about those other things.'

And I thought: 'That sounds great, but I wonder why Ajahn Chah emphasises all these rules?'

I had great respect for Ajahn Chah, so when I went back I told him what the philosopher-bhikkhu had told me. Ajahn Chah said, "That's *true*, but it's not *right*."[24]

Now we are prone to having blind attachments, aren't we? For example, say you're locked up in a foul, stinking prison cell and the Buddha comes and says, 'Here's the key. All you have to do is take it and put it in the hole there underneath the door handle, turn it to the right, turn the handle, open the door, walk out, and you're free.'... But you might be so used to being locked up in prison that you didn't quite understand the directions and you say, 'Oh, the Lord has given me this key'—and you hang it on the wall and pray to it every day. It might make your stay in prison a little more happy; you might be able to endure all the hardships and the stench of your foul-smelling cell a little better, but you're still in the cell because you haven't understood that it wasn't the key in itself that was going to save you. Due to lack of intelligence and understanding, you just grasped the key blindly. That's what happens in all religion: we just grasp the key, to worship it, pray to it ... but we don't actually learn to use it.

So then the next time the Buddha comes and says, 'Here's the key', you might be disillusioned and say, 'I don't believe any of this. I've been praying for years to that key and not a thing has happened! That Buddha is a liar!' And you take the key and throw it out of the window. That's the other extreme, isn't it? But you're still in the prison cell—so that hasn't solved the problem either.

Anyway, a few years later the Buddha comes again and says, 'Here's the key,' and this time you're a little more wise and you recognise the possibility of using it effectively, so you listen a little more closely, do the right thing and get out.

The key is like religious convention, like Theravada Buddhism: it's only a key, only a form—it's not an end in itself. We have to consider, to contemplate how to use it. What is it for? We also have to expend the energy to get up, walk over to the door, insert the

---

24 That is to say although the statement is quite correct, taken out of context it could be used—as this talk points out—to justify any action. Similarly the meticulous 'mindfulness practice' described later can also be used unskilfully Ajahn Sumedho is not criticising these views, but pointing to the danger of attaching to any view.

key into the lock, turn it in the right direction, turn the knob, open the door and walk out. The key is not going to do that for us; it's something we have to comprehend for ourselves. The convention itself cannot do it because it's not capable of making the effort; it doesn't have the vigour or anything of its own other than that which you put into it—just like the key can't do anything for itself. Its usefulness depends on your efforts and wisdom.

Some modern day religious leaders tend to say, 'Don't have anything to do with any religious convention. They're all like the walls of prison cells'—and they seem to think that maybe the way is to just get rid of the key. Now if you're already outside the cell, of course you don't need the key. But if you're still inside, then it does help a bit!

So I think you have to know whether you're in or out; then you'll know what to do. If you still find you're full of doubt, uncertainty, fear, confusion—mainly doubt is the real sign—if you're unsure of where you are, what to do or how to do anything; if you're unsure of how to get out of the prison cell then the wisest thing to do, rather than throwing away keys, or just collecting them, is to take one key and figure out how to use it. That's what we mean by meditation practice. The practice of the Dhamma is learning to take a particular key and use it to open the door and walk out. Once you're out, then you know. There's no more doubt.

Now, we can start from the high kind of attitude that mindfulness is enough—but then what do we mean by that? What is mindfulness, really? Is it actually what we believe it to be? We see people who say, 'I'm being very mindful,' and they're doing something in a very methodical, meticulous way. They're taking in each bite of food and they're lifting, lifting, lifting; chewing, chewing, chewing; swallowing, swallowing, swallowing …

So you think, 'He eats very mindfully, doesn't he?', but he may not be mindful at all, actually. He's just doing it in a very concentrated way: he's concentrating on lifting, on touching, on chewing and on swallowing. We confuse mindfulness with concentration.

Like robbing a bank: we think, 'Well, if you rob a bank mindfully, it's all right. I'm very mindful when I rob banks, so there's no *kamma.*[25] You have to have good powers of concentration to be a good bank robber. You have to have mindfulness in the sense of fear conditions, of being aware of dangers and possibilities—a mind that's on the alert for any kind of movement or sign of danger or threat … and then concentrating your mind on breaking the safe open and so forth.

But in the Buddhist sense, mindfulness—*sati*—is always combined with wisdom—*paññā*. *Sati-sampajañña* and *sati-paññā*: they use those two words together in Thailand. They mean, 'mindfulness and clear comprehension' and 'mindfulness-wisdom'. So I might have an impulse to rob a bank—'I need some money so I'll go rob the National Westminster Bank'—but the *sati-paññā* says, 'No, don't act on that impulse!' *Paññā* recognises the bad result if I acted on such an impulse, the kammic result; it confers the understanding that such a thing is wrong, not right to do.

So there's full comprehension of that impulse, knowing it as just an impulse and not-self, so that even though I might have the desire to rob a bank, I'm not going to make neurotic problems for myself out of worrying about those criminal tendencies. One recognises that there is just an impulse in the mind that one refrains from acting upon. Then one has a standard of virtue—*sīla*—always as a conventional foundation for living in the human form in this society, with other beings, within this material world—a standard or guideline for both action and non-action.

The Five Precepts consist of not killing; not stealing; refraining from wrong kinds of sexual activities; not lying or indulging in false speech; and not taking drink or drugs that change consciousness. These are the guidelines for *sīla*.

Now, *sīla* in Buddhism isn't a rigid, inflexible kind of standard in which you're condemned to hell if you in any way modify anything whatsoever—as you have in that rigid, hard morality we all associate with Victorian times. We all fear the prudish, puritanical morality that used to exist, so that sometimes when you say the word 'morality' now everybody shudders and thinks, 'Ugh, Victorian prude! He's probably some terrible moralistic

25 *Kamma*: action which comes from habitual impulse, volitions, or natural energies, leading to an inevitable reaction.

person who's afraid of life. We have to go out and experience life. We don't want morality—we want experience!'

So you see people going out and doing all kinds of things, thinking that experience in itself is all that's necessary. But there are some experiences which it's actually better not to have—especially if they're against the ordinary interpretation of the Five Precepts.

For example, you might say, 'I really want to experience murdering someone because my education in life won't be complete until I have. My freedom to act spontaneously will be inhibited until I actually experience murder.'

Some people might believe that … well perhaps not so much for murder, because that's a really heavy one—but they do for other things. They do everything they desire to do and have no standard for saying 'No'.

'Don't ever say "no" to anything,' they say. 'Just say "yes"—go out and do it and be mindful of it, learn from it … Experience everything!'

If you do that, you'll find yourself rather jaded, worn out, confused, miserable, and wretched, even at a very young age. When you see some of the pathetic cases I've seen—young people who went out and 'experienced everything'—and you say, 'How old are you? Forty?' And they say, 'No, actually, I'm twenty-one.'

It sounds good, doesn't it? 'Do everything you desire'—that's what we'd like to hear. I would. It would be nice to do everything I desire, never have to say 'No'. But then in a few years you also begin to reflect that desires have no end. What you desire now, you want something more than that next time, and there's no end to it. You might be temporarily gratified, like when you eat too much food and can't stand to eat another bite; then you look at the most delicious gourmet preparations and you say, 'Oh, disgusting!' But it's only momentary revulsion and it doesn't take long before they start looking all right again.

In Thailand, Buddhism is an extremely tolerant kind of religion; moralistic attitudes have never really developed there. This is why people are sometimes upset when they go to Bangkok and hear horrendous stories of child prostitution and corruption and so on. Bangkok is the Sin City of the world these days. You say 'Bangkok', and everybody's eyes either light up or else they look terribly upset and say: 'How can a Buddhist country allow such terrible things to go on?'

But then, knowing Thailand, one recognises that, although they may be a bit lax and loose on some levels, at least there isn't the kind of militant cruelty there that you find in some other countries where they line all the prostitutes up and shoot them, and kill all the criminals in the name of their religion. In Thailand one begins to appreciate that morality really has to come from wisdom, not from fear.

So some Thai monks will teach morality on a less strict basis than others. In the matter of the first precept, non-killing, I know a monk who lives on the coast of the gulf of Thailand in an area where there are a lot of pirates and fishermen, who are a very rough, crude kind of people. Murder is quite common among them. So this monk just tries to encourage them not to kill each other. When these people come to the monastery, he doesn't go round raising non-killing to the level of 'You shouldn't kill anything—not even a mosquito larva' because they couldn't accept that. Their livelihood depends very much on fishing and the killing of animals.

What I'm presenting isn't morality on a rigid standard or that's too difficult to keep, but rather for you to reflect upon and use so that you begin to understand it, and understand how to live in a better way. If you start out taking too strict a position, you either become very moralistic, puritanical, and attached, or else you think you can't do it, so you don't bother—you have no standard at all.

Now the second precept is refraining from stealing. On the coarsest level, say, you just refrain from robbing banks, shoplifting, and things like that. But then if you refine your *sīla* more, you refrain from taking things which have not been given to you. As monks, we refrain even from touching things that are not given to us. If we go into your home, we're not supposed to go around picking up and looking at things, even though we have no intention of taking them away with us. Even food has to be offered directly to us: if you set it down and say, 'This is for you,' if we stick to our rules, we're not supposed to eat it until you offer it directly to us. That's a refinement of the precept to not take anything that's not been given.

So there's the coarse aspect of just refraining from the grosser things, like theft or burglary; and a more refined training—a way of training yourself.

I find this a very helpful monastic rule, because I was quite heedless as a layman. Somebody would invite me to their home, and I'd be looking at this, looking at that, touching this; going into shops, I'd pick up this and that—I didn't even know that it was wrong or might annoy anybody. It was a habit. And then when I was ordained as a monk, I couldn't do that any more, and I'd sit there and feel this impulse to look at this and pick that up—but I'd have these precepts saying I couldn't do that … And with food: somebody would put food down and I'd just grab it and start eating.

But through the monastic training you develop a much more graceful way of behaving. Then you sit down, and after a while you don't feel the urge to pick up things or grab hold of them. You can wait. And then people can offer, which is much more beautiful way of relating to things around you and to other people than habitually grabbing, touching, eating and so on.

Then there's the third precept, about sexuality. The idea at the present time is that any kind of sexuality is experience, so it's all right to do—just so long as you're mindful! And somehow, not having sexual relations is seen as some kind of terrible perversity.

On the coarsest level, this precept means refraining from adultery: from being unfaithful to your spouse. But then you can refine that within marriage to where you are becoming more considerate, less exploitive, less obsessed with sexuality, so you're no longer using it merely for bodily pleasure.

You can in fact, refine it right down to celibacy, to where you are living like a Buddhist monk and no kind of sexual activity is allowed. This is the range, you see, within the precepts.

A lot of people think that the celibate monastic life must be a terrible repression. But it's not, because sexual urges are fully accepted and understood as being natural urges, only they're not acted upon. You can't help having sexual desires. You can't say, 'I wont have any more of that kind of desire ...' Well you can say it, but you still do! If you're a monk and you think you shouldn't have anything like that then you become a very frightened and repressed kind of monk.

I've heard some monks say: 'I'm just not worthy of the robe. People shouldn't give me alms food. I'll have to disrobe because I've got so many bad thoughts going through my mind.' The robe doesn't care about your thoughts! Don't make a problem out of it. We all have nasty thoughts going through our minds when we're in these robes just like everybody else. But we train ourselves not to speak or act upon them. When we've taken the Pātimokkha discipline, we accept those things, recognise them, are fully conscious of them, and let them go—and they cease. Then, after a while, one finds a great peacefulness in one's mind as a result of the celibate life.

Sexual life, on the other hand, is very exciting. If you're really upset, frightened, bored or restless, then your mind very easily goes into sexual fantasies. Violence is very exciting, too, so often sex and violence are put together, as in rape and things of that nature. People like to look at those things at the cinema. If they made a film about a celibate monk keeping the discipline, very few people would appreciate that! It would be a very boring film. But if they made a film about a monk who breaks all the precepts, they'd make a fortune!

The fourth precept is on speech. On the coarsest level, if you're a big liar, say, just keep this precept by refraining from telling big lies. If you take that precept, then at least every time you tell a big lie you'd know it, wouldn't you? But if you don't take any precept, sometimes you can tell big lies and not even know you're doing it. It becomes a habit.

If you refine this from the coarse position, you learn to speak and use communication in a very careful and responsible way. You're not just chattering, babbling, gossiping, exaggerating; you're not being terribly clever or using speech to hurt or insult or disparage other people in any intentional way. You begin to recognise how very deeply we do affect one another with the things we say. We can ruin whole days for each other by saying unkind things.

The fifth precept is refraining from alcoholic drinks and drugs which change consciousness. Now that can be on the level of just refraining from drunkenness—that's what everybody likes to think it means! But then the sober side of you says maybe you shouldn't have a drink of any kind; not even a glass of wine with your dinner. It's a standard to reflect upon and use.

If you've committed yourself to these precepts, then you know when you've broken them. So they're guidelines to being a little more alert, a little more awake and also more responsible about how you live. If we don't have standards, then we just tend to do what we feel like doing, or what someone else feels like doing.

I have a very natural kind of moral nature. I've never really liked being immoral. But when I lived in Berkeley, California, because the more clever, intelligent and experienced beings around me that I greatly admired seemed to fully commend immoralities, I thought: 'Well, maybe I should do that too!' Certainly, when you're looking up to somebody, you want to be like them. I got myself into a terrible mess, because people can be very convincing. They can make murder sound like a sacred act!

So *sīla* is a guide, a way of anchoring yourself in refraining from unskillful actions with your body and speech, both in regard to yourself and to the other beings around you. It's not a kind of absolute standard. I'm not telling you that if you kill a worm in your garden you'll be reborn in the next 10,000 lifetimes as a worm in order to frighten you into not killing. There's no wisdom in that. If you're just conditioned, then you're just doing it because you're afraid you'll go to hell. You wouldn't really understand; you've not reflected and watched and really used your wisdom to observe how things are.

If you're frightened of action and speech then you'll just become neurotic; but, on the other hand, if you're not frightened enough and think you can do anything, then you'll also become confused and neurotic!

Sigmund Freud had all kinds of people coming to him with terrible hang-ups and, as sexual repression was the ordinary thing in Europe and America at the time, he thought: 'Well, if we just stop repressing, then we won't have these problems any more. We'll become free, happy, well-integrated personalities.' But nowadays there's no restriction—and you still get hysterical, miserable, neurotic people! So it's obvious that these are two extremes springing from a lack of mindfulness in regard to the natural condition of sexuality.

We have to recognise both what's exciting and what's calming. Buddhist meditation—why is this so boring? Repetitions and chanting … why don't we sing arias? I could do it! I've always wanted to be an opera singer. But on the conventional level of propriety, or when I'm sitting on the teacher's high seat doing my duty, then I chant in monotone as best I can. If you really concentrate on monotone chanting, it's tranquillising.

One night, we were sitting in our forest monastery in Thailand meditating, when I heard an American pop song that I really hated when I was a layman. It was being blasted out by one of those medicine sellers who go to all the villages in big vans with loudspeakers that play this kind of music in order to attract the villagers to come and buy their quacky medicines. The wind was blowing in the right direction and the sound of 'Tell Laura I Love Her' seemed right here in the meditation hall itself. I hadn't heard American pop music for so many years, so while this smarmy sentimental song was playing I was actually beginning to cry! And I began to recognise the tremendous emotional pull of that kind of music. If you don't really understand it, it grabs your heart and you get caught up in the excitement and emotion of it. This is the effect of music when you're not mindful.

So our chanting is in monotone, because if you concentrate on it it's not going to carry you away into sentimental feelings, into tears or ecstasy. Instead, you feel tranquil, peaceful, serene. *Ānāpānasati*[26] also tranquillises, because it has a gentle rhythm—subtle, not exciting. And though the monastic life itself is boring in the sense of lacking romance, adventure and excitement, it is tranquillising, peaceful, calming …

---

26 *Ānāpānasati*: a widely used meditation technique. One composes the mind by focussing attention on the inhalation and exhalation of breath.

Therefore, reflect in your life upon what excites and what calms, so that you begin to understand how to use *paññā*: your wisdom faculty. As Buddhists, we do this so that we know what's affecting us. We understand the forces of nature with which we have to co-exist. We can't control everything so that nothing violent or exciting ever happens around us—but we can understand it. We can put forward some effort towards understanding and learning from our lives as we live them.

Walking Dhutaṅga in Britain

Bowing to Conventions

Bhikkhu Sucitto

Bodhi Leaves No. 104

First published: 1985

Walking Dhutaṅga in Britain

The first three years of my life as a *bhikkhu* were spent largely in one monastery, or more accurately, in a hut (*kuti*) in one section of a monastery on the outskirts of a town in central Thailand. I had travelled widely, almost frantically, as a layman, and this had resulted in the kind of disenchantment with experiences that was a perfect incentive to get to the root of discontent: to meditate. I had no inclination to go anywhere even though I could come up with all kinds of grievances about the weather, the food, the noise, the insects, the teacher, and my mind. It was clear that there was no point in going anywhere carrying that discontent. Without its customary means of distraction, the mind dissolved into a flux of moods, memories and anguish at its own vacuousness, and the dumb-founding effect of confronting that left me with little interest in doing anything other than establishing some firm base and equilibrium. It was time to sit still.

One thing did come through the haze—occasionally on *piṇḍapāta* I would see *bhikkhu*s wearing robes of a dull brown, robes that looked patched and heavy, strikingly different from the immaculate bright yellow of the town *bhikkhu*s. While the yellow-robed *bhikkhu*s darted through the streets looking for almsfood, these strange *bhikkhu*s walked slowly, with patient, downcast eyes, apparently indifferent to the fact that the alms offerings were running out. They seemed to have nowhere special to go and yet nowhere worth lingering either. They evoked in me a feeling of nobility, and a mixture of sadness that there was no refuge in the world, and joy that men could walk with such gentle composure, clearly conscious of that raw truth. When I asked my teacher about them, he said they were tudong monks.

Tudong is the Thai form of *dhutaṅga*, meaning literally "means of shaking off," i.e. the practises that emphasise renunciation, and it can refer to the thirteen *dhutaṅga* austerities, or to the forest *bhikkhu*s who live observing all or some of these and other renunciate practises, or more narrowly, to the custom of walking for weeks, months, or even years on end with just a bowl containing spare robes and essentials such as a razor, sewing equipment, matches, a water kettle, and a glot—a large umbrella with mosquito-net which acts as a tent. Mostly *dhutaṅga* walks are undertaken by *bhikkhus* of the forest monasteries when they are considered stable enough and well grounded in the Vinaya discipline. You have to learn to live simply to go tudong, and to handle yourself with skill in the face of such difficulties as not finding almsfood, disease, and bad weather. Moreover, for a foreigner there are the problems of language and custom, and as a meditator outside the shelter of the teacher, doubts about one's practise and one's purity. I could see quite clearly that it would be enormously strengthening to walk through that lot and keep on going, and its flavour and appearance very much fitted those ideals of homelessness and simplicity that had led me to take ordination. However, my basic practise was attendance on the teacher, and giving up to the situation of the monastery seemed to give me enough to work on, so I stayed put and let things take their natural course.

A few years later at Chithurst in England the subject of tudong would occasionally crop up again. Sometimes, when we were sitting around Ajahn Sumedho in his room in a convivial mood, someone's conviviality would overflow into fantasies of tudong in Britain, walking along the Downs … and when could we go? … all of which was given short shrift by the Ajahn. This was not the time for restless *bhikkhus* to go off fulfilling personal ambitions; needless to say, we all gladly surrendered to that wisdom.

But times change. When it is no longer an overflow of fantasy and restlessness; when it is appropriate to the Sangha and the Buddhist community; when, like many things in the training, what needs to be done and what you want to do merge, best, perhaps, when it doesn't matter any more—then you can go.

In spring of '82 we received a terse postcard from Ven. Vīradhammo, then resident at Harnham Vihara. It was posted from Lindisfarne, where he was on part of a brief *dhutaṅga* tour. Accompanied by a lay supporter, he had walked for eight days over fell and moor, sleeping in lambing sheds and receiving food in the homes of various of the layman's friends en route. It was a small but significant beginning—you can keep warm enough, you can sleep rough, you can get fed. When Ajahn Sumedho subsequently invited me to spend the Vassa at Golden Square (near Honiton) in Devon, and consented to my returning on foot for the Kaṭhina in October, I got more advice from Ven. Vīradhammo on footwear, rainwear, and eating: "Try to get some breakfast before you begin to walk, otherwise you turn to jelly after a couple of hours." ... To which he added, "But don't just do it the way I did; I'd like to see how you do it."

By the end of the Vassa, making my intentions known, I had accumulated three tents, three backpacks, a series of Ordinance Survey maps of the 140 mile route, a camping stove and cooking pot, canteens, foot lotions, and invitations to stop in several houses on the way. I had about two weeks to get back to the Kaṭhina, a beautiful stretch of country ahead, the experience of a few longdistance walks to measure things by, and the company of an *anāgārika* who made excellent tea. It couldn't go wrong; there was nothing perilous or even arduous about it, and witnessing the way that it had all come together—with invitations and loans of equipment that involved many people—it seemed that the practise that the walk was about was not a personal trial but the opportunity to share merit. It was a way to bring an example of the spiritual life to those who don't live near a monastery. I dedicated the walk to all practitioners of the Dhamma, especially to Ajahn Chah, who had given so much of himself and now lay seriously ill in a Bangkok hospital. The dedication fitted very well. I noticed on long walks how one would feel compelled to get to where one was going, walk too fast, be insensitive to and overtax the body. This is typical of all self-conscious endeavour. Putting the walk into the perspective of fulfilling a religious function for other people's wellbeing, "for the benefit of the many-folk" as it says in the Canon, gave me the space to not have to prove myself, to resist the temptation to turn it into a personal epic, and to be content to take one step at a time.

Rather than having the convenience of a backpack, I decided to carry my equipment in two bowl bags, one over each shoulder, which was more awkward but did allow me to wear the *bhikkhu*'s outer robe, an important sign. I also decided to go on a route that allowed contact with people, and to keep equipment and supplies minimal so that people could offer help and take part in that way. After some ascetic longings, I finally succumbed to carrying a one man tent, a sleeping bag, a pair of treck shoes and my bowl, a change of undergarments, a toothbrush and some first aid; also a rain poncho and groundsheet (which doubled as a waterproof lower robe). I eventually walked most of the way in a pair of lightweight wellies I'd brought with me, preferring to use everyday equipment to specialised gear.

Anāgārika Tony carried his clothing, sleeping bag and blanket, the small stove and pot, things for hot drinks and an old ice-cream container filled with about 4lbs of muesli. The final touch was a small *rūpa* (statuette) from the shrine at Golden Square that Douglas, our host, had given us with some incense.

We set out at 10 a.m. on October 2nd as we did on every subsequent morning after chanting the names and virtues of the Twenty-Eight Buddhas as a protection and blessing for our hosts. We walked in silent single file about ten metres apart, along the river valley through Axminster and on the back lanes around the lower rim of Marshwood Vale to Charmouth, where Richard and Anne Bancroft had invited us for the night. It took about seven hours, but we rested in a couple of breaks for two and a half hours. We were wet, my feet were blistered and the heel was coming off my boot, but there was ease in the heart from a day of being attuned to silent mindful walking. Whatever the changes in the next two weeks, that pattern remained the same.

And of course, the royal welcome. The lovely thing about the mendicant life is that your presence is a mirror that allows people to recognise their own goodness with a charity that is joyous and caring rather than burdensome. Throughout the journey, people we stayed with ushered us into hot baths, offered to wash clothes, gave us a meal and often gave Tony some food to take with us. Sometimes we would meditate together or talk Dhamma, but it was always clear that it was all right to sit quietly or rest.

The second day we turned back inland from the cliffs of the Dorset coast through twisting lanes and deep mud slopes on a hot morning. With the changeable English weather, choice of clothing had a skill to it. My basic clothing was light summer wear—a t-shirt, lower robe, and aṅgsa (a light shirt), with a blanket thick saṅghāti, or upper robe, to be used when the weather was chilly, as a blanket or pillow and for proper appearance in towns. The initial feeling one has on wearing a robe is that it is a hindrance to free movement, but in this situation it came into its own as I watched Tony continually changing sweaters, jackets, thin and thick trousers and having to carry all his spare clothing. We passed through Bridport with scarcely a catcall, before we went up onto the downs to the north and east, and stopped to ask for water in the one-street stone village of Loders. This met with an invitation to drink tea, pull our boots off and sit for a while. Meeting people, the relationship is so clean. They know what your life means and that you're not hiding or expecting something from them. That gives people the chance to be honest without fear of reproach or the need to impress. You share in someone else's life for an hour, say goodbye and nothing is left but a genuine smile and that openness—"Oh, yes, go up on to Eggardon Hill, the view is really beautiful"—and it certainly was, looking back west over Marshwood Vale and the hills lounging into Devon.

The wind was cold up on that ridge: a lone Roman road and open land. We found a spinney and spent our first night in the tent. Two men in a one-man tent makes for mindfulness of small movements. You have to operate the body like a complex machine, one joint of a limb at a time—roll on left side, draw up right arm, uncurl fingers, reach gently for matches. You don't sleep very much, and in the darkness of early morning, getting up and getting dressed is an exercise in concentration. We would begin about 3 a.m. and be drinking black tea by 4 a.m. A small night-light, the *rūpa* set on top of my alms bowl and a stick of incense made the shrine for the morning's sitting practise, or if it was too wet outside, reclining in the lion posture. There would be a couple of hours before dawn, and as the mind composed, I would reflect *mettā* to everyone who had helped me on the spiritual path—it was a colossal list. When the night receded, we would chant the "Twenty Eight Buddhas", eat breakfast, pack up and move on.

Jane Browne was driving Sisters Sundara and Candasiri back from Cornwall on the next day: they had said that they'd look out for us on the road into Dorchester. Sure enough, late in the morning, an aged Volvo steamed past with a flash of smiles and flapping white robes, and ploughed to a halt on the verge. There were a few moments in which everyone adjusted their joy to the appropriate greetings and set to the practicalities of finding the right place to eat Sundara's birthday picnic. Tony and I bundled into the back and the car settled down on its springs and obediently rolled off to the north—Cerne Abbas, Minterne Magna, and a manor house where Candasiri's uncle and aunt lived. It was strange for them, but they were good-hearted and took our oddness well; in fact Candasiri's cousin invited the two of us to stay at his farm for the night while he went out. "Make yourselves at home," he said and left us his house. In the morning he waved Tony into the kitchen "Help yourself to food"—and went off to chase a runaway cow. He said he knew all about monks, as the friars of Hillfield lived only a mile away.

It was a long walk from there across Dorset, south-east to Bere Regis and Waltham Forest, with just one short break in a country churchyard. It was sunny and the leaves were turning red and rattled in the breeze. The Hardy monument stood over to the west, dwindling as the day went by, and a rainstorm swept over just catching us in a peripheral shower. In the evening we nestled in some pine woods, built a fire, sat and stretched out, feet throbbing, and allowed the rhythm of walking to fade out into meditation and sleep. We spent the next day walking across the forest and camped early to rest and restore physical energy.

Despite the physical effort and fatigue, the walking was very energising for the mind. Most nights, I would sleep lightly for about four hours, whereas Tony dozed rather than slept because of feeling cold. The rhythm of the day had no stress, no tension that needed to be resolved, and although we hardly spoke, it was a very easy and natural silence, as we applied ourselves to walking, sitting, eating, and putting up and packing the tent. Watching the mind in the day within the framework of the walking, ancient memories would unravel and dissolve—a sure sign that there was nothing much getting stuck in the mind by the day's activities.

About halfway home, on the sixth and seventh days, we stayed with Mary, a friend of the Sangha living in Poole. Walking through the town, our "mirror" picked up the usual reflections— shouts of "Hare Krishna", "Skinhead!", and genuine inquiries and offers of help from complete strangers. In the centre of town a policeman pulled up in his van, looked me in the eye and asked— "Had we come far? Where had we been at ten o'clock that morning?" He explained in a level manner that someone had been shoplifting in the Arndale Centre and the description exactly fitted me! Tony and I looked at each other and laughed—alms bowl, tent, robes and shaven bead—what are shoplifters getting up to these days? He didn't pursue the investigation, asked a few polite questions about the monastery and let us go on our way.

Spending that evening and all the next day in Poole allowed time for some interesting Dhamma discussion with a few Buddhists and like-minded people whom Mary had invited around. Spiritual company is a blessing, and with all our best wishes we left the little *rūpa*—a plump and smiling Chinese figure-squatting on the mantelpiece among spiritual paintings and statuettes bowed in prayer, as a reminder of the companionship of the Refuge. The next morning we left for the New Forest, and as a concession to preference, took a ride in Mary's car through Bournemouth and its urban districts for about eight miles to allow more time for walking in the open country. This made possible an unhurried tour from southwest to northeast, and we spent the night in the Forest with plenty of time and energy to sit in meditation. The weather was clear, my body had got used to carrying extra weight, my feet had hardened, and walking seemed as natural an effort as breathing— things felt very balanced. Forests are places where the harmony of nature can leave its impression on an open mind, and the Buddha, recognising how we are conditioned by our environment, recommended his disciples to seek out "roots of trees and lonely places." Ironically enough, on entering the forest we had passed a fox hunt, where the humans were charging around chaotically, tooting horns, and the nonchalant fox ambling close by where we stood was the only being in clear control of his faculties. Our route went via Minstead Lodge—the other side of the human coin, where a community founded on Christian principles directs itself towards exemplifying working in harmony with each other and with Nature. The choice is up to us—we may have to live within restrictions and conventional roles; but we do have the freedom to choose those that lead out of pain and delusion.

Rain began in earnest as we left Minstead Lodge, and persisted for the next three days on our walk through the urban back garden of Southampton—Totton, Chilworth. Chandlers Ford—past Eastleigh and up onto the South Downs at Droxford. By the time we got to Eastleigh my boots were worn out. The heels had come off, the soles split, and my feet were always wet. Tony had some money given by a thoughtful lay supporter against just such a contingency, and bought me a new pair. They didn't leak, but … the effect of wearing a rain poncho and a waterproof lower robe was to channel rainwater into my boots as efficiently as having drainpipes installed. When it came down to it, I finally recognised that wet feet weren't so bad after all.

We crossed the river Meon at Droxford in a thunderstorm, hid in a disused railway station until it spent itself, and as the sun beamed down from a clean sky, walked up onto the open Downs that presided over the Meon Valley. The fields and copper woodlands glowed: it was marvellous to walk under such a sky with the land stretched out on either side. A line of oak and beech trees conveniently appeared as a pleasant spot to eat our meal of leftover fruit and some pies that Tony had bought on the way. As we chanted the Anumodana, fluffy clouds came bobbing towards us, magnificent at first but then revealing dark grey bellies that signified only one thing. "Don't worry," I said to Tony, "think positive." The sun disappeared and a sense of urgency entered our eating as I glanced around—not a shelter in sight. Silently praying, "Please don't rain, or at least not on us, or at least not now," I suddenly recalled the power of asseveration of truth, and began: "If I have been mindful …" thought I'd better make it easy, and rephrased it as: "If, at least during this Vassa, I have done the best I can, please don't rain!" The response was as swift and adroit as that of a Zen Master. Lightning flashed and it poured down. You don't stop rainstorms with anything less than a "Lion's Roar!" Tony instinctively threw a sheet over his pack and headed for the trees, but actually there was nowhere to go. I slipped my poncho over my head, and, with the rain pinging into the lid of my bowl and turning my pies soggy, munched on peacefully. I might as well be wet and full as wet and hungry. As the rainwater began to flow under my poncho, Tony, catching the mood, reappeared with hands in *añjali* and a courteous smile: "May I offer you some coffee, *bhante*?" I declined, finished the meal and stood bowed under a tree while the rain did the washing up.

Storms don't last long but we did need to dry out. About four miles down the road we stopped in some woods by the trunk of a felled beech and a huge pile of branches. Tony had discovered that, no matter if it rains, if the wood is dead and not in contact with the ground, it doesn't become waterlogged. We were always able to start fires with twigs and use the heat to dry out larger branches and build up that way. As this fire matured, the rain poured down again, but I lashed the tent to the tree trunk, made an awning over us and the fire, and crawled under the giant leg. In a dry period we erected the tent and finally stood around the fire getting alternately roasted and rained on, which seemed better than lying down cramped and damp.

The next morning, we went over Butser Hill and surveyed Petersfield and the valley of the Rother where Chithurst Monastery lies. Colin and Jane, who live about six miles from the monastery, had said that they would like to drive out to meet us and offer us alms-food at Buriton. After the meal, it was only another four muddy miles along the South Downs Way to their house where we could get cleaned up and rest before returning to the busy monastery. Looking at Tony's mud caked white clothing, I recognised another blessing of the ochre robe, yes it would he best to get cleaned up. We came into Buriton like those *dhutaṅga bhikkhus* I had been inspired by years before. Living with attention focused on the body, you didn't waste its energy. Walking, and other movements were steady and composed, and although you spoke little, the mind remained turned towards other people's wellbeing, a lot of the self-concern had died. It was all right to have sore feet, getting wet didn't send you into a panic, there wasn't the need to impress yourself or others, and when there wasn't anywhere to go, it was all right to sit by the church in Buriton watching the ducks on the pond and not thinking of anything much. We waited a while, received alms food, and after the meal walked on to Colin and Jane's house. When we arrived everything felt so balanced and peaceful amongst us that there wasn't a lot to say.

When you keep your personal achievements at the level of putting one foot in front of the other and being mindful, you listen to what the world has to say. In that listening, the mind is fresh and alert to the mystery of life, and being unable to express that mystery only purifies the aspiration to live in harmony with it. When the walk came to an end, thirteen mornings after leaving Golden Square, the practise-path that it symbolises continued; the monastic life is about non-abiding, it is a giving up of personal possessions, desires, concerns and opinions. You listen and live close to the heart of life, and the only refuge from the rawness of our nature is to do good and be mindful. Sometimes that seems to leave you completely alone with nothing to hold on to, but the path evokes a compassion in us that fills the heart, and a respect for our way of life that gives us many friends. Before we reached the monastery, we stopped to say hello to Sam, the woodsman who works in the barn at the top of Chithurst Lane. "You've just got back, have you?" he said. "Please, just wait a moment." He walked to the back of his workshop and returned with half of his packed lunch. "Can I put this into your bowl?"

Bowing to Conventions

In the monastic life, if it is well-lived, you have to give up a lot, you have to surrender a lot. More than just the renunciation implied by the precepts, there comes about a giving up of oneself through living the life of an alms-mendicant. This rather bleak prospect is in reality joyous—the mind becomes open and peaceful with the realisation that there wasn't a self to give up anyway. Rather than being a substantive entity, self is only a notion, a view and a conventional way of coming to terms with sensory experience. Although selfhood is a useful convention for most purposes, clinging to it gives rise to the feeling of being the owner of the senses who is then beset by the birth and death process that the senses experience. We become helpless if we can't get beyond the sensory movement of attraction towards objects that we can't keep, or repulsion from things that cause us pain. And this volitional tide creates the notion of a being who is moved by it, trapped in it, the creator of it. With the practise of Dhamma, a clear understanding replaces the compulsion of that volition and we can use the conventional notion of self wisely. For this purpose, not for the extinction of any real self the Buddha gave instructions on selflessness and established a monastic order that would enable ordinary people to let go of personal volition and learn to respond to life at it happened:

> They do not lament over the past,
> They do not hanker for things in the future,
> They maintain themselves on whatever comes:
> Therefore they are serene.
>
> (Saṃyutta Nikāya 1, 3)

The practise of bowing is a meaningful sign for the practise of giving oneself up. When I first entered a monastery in Thailand, eager to meditate, I was introduced to the Abbot, who indicated that I should bow to him. This seemed to be a polite social gesture that I had no objection to carrying out, so I went down onto my knees and bowed forehead, hands and elbows to the floor at his feet, three times. It seemed to be just a custom, but when carried out in a life of mindful reflection, it takes on a more profound spiritual significance: the self has to be made to serve rather than govern the spiritual life.

I had quite a clear picture of what I was doing when I turned up at the monastery after an introductory lecture in Chiang Mai: a few days of meditation to learn how to get clarity and calm, and then off to Malaysia and Indonesia. After a few days, it became clear that things weren't going according to plan. I certainly witnessed a lot more of the movements of my mind, but the more I looked, the more intrinsic the mental flux appeared, and the more elusive the clear being that I had expected to become. After leaving the country to get a new visa, I returned determined to live for three months as a *samanera* and sort things out.

Apart from the giving up denoted by the ten *samanera* precepts—entailing chastity, poverty, sobriety and a daily fast of 20 hours—life as a *samanera* also meant giving up one's personal habits, dress, and hair. Strangely enough, this seemed peripheral to the major surrender that I was adjusting to in the practise of meditation: the surrender to the Dhamma, the way things are. For one who has lived his life on a series of false premises and become accustomed to following his desires, the way things are seems rather tough. Restlessness, boredom, agitated memories, longing, and the struggle to get rid of these are common experiences. I could see plenty of reasons not to continue: but what was mystifying was the deepening resolve to persevere. After three months, I half realised that my life was motivated by deeper instincts than the plans of my conscious mind, and I began to give up the desire to become something, and instead, to observe the way things are. That was a bow to the Buddha, that in us which observes and reflects, and it was a bow to the Dhamma, the way that one's life actually is, beyond conceptions and self consciousness.

As a *samanera,* one is on the fringes of the Bhikkhu Sangha, and, at least as a privileged Westerner, not really involved with the running of the monastery or the duties to the lay community. However, I was a mendicant, living dependent on a supportive lay community who had unquestioningly provided a hut (*kuti*) and robes, and continued to offer alms-food daily. Every day, just after dawn, I would walk into town for alms, and people who didn't know me would be waiting by the side of the road to put food into my alms-bowl. The whole procedure was carried out in silence, without even an exchange of glances. Generosity uncluttered by the desire to evoke a response is a very touching thing. Far from making me feel complacent, it brought up a silent exhortation from my own mind to practise the life of purity and to make myself worthy of offerings. After years of trying to fit into small and large communities, or find one that matched my ideals, I found myself taking part in a community action that centred around the attitude of kindness to others. People weren't making judgments, they weren't making demands: they were giving. No matter what the purity of the rest of their day, or my own, might have been, there was that gesture of selflessness. It was practical and something that we could all take part in without having to be more than human. Moreover, people weren't giving to me because I was a particularly praiseworthy or fascinating person, but because of what I represented in human terms—the potential for enlightenment.

Finding one's life gradually taking the form of a symbol can have its disquieting moments. It threatens one's personal identity. I started to think of places to go and other things to do, without really knowing why. After all, I had food, shelter and a tremendous amount of support from the teacher and the people around me … but there was still the residual desire to go somewhere else where I could live life on my own terms, get up when I wanted, eat when I wanted: in short, reinforce my personal identity. Yet having followed that impulse for several years and recognised its fruitlessness, I realised that the only place to go was away from personal volition. Letting go of choices opened up a path of learning to respond skilfully to whatever came up. Uncertain at first, it proved more fruitful than my attempts to attain profound mental states. There was something gladdening about being part of the world rather than trying to find something in it.

Taking higher ordination as a *bhikkhu* was more of a surrender than a promotion: commitment was something that I had always shied away from. The occasion was brought about by some 700 ladies visiting the monastery and taking on temporary ordination there as eight-precept nuns. I had been a *samanera* for about six months by then, and had always side-stepped the issue of higher ordination: my mind still wanted to play with the idea of an imaginary future when I wouldn't have to do all this monastic stuff. But when I was told how much they would like to provide a bowl and robes for my *bhikkhu* ordination, something in me gave up. Despite the seeming impossibility of sorting myself out, I could see that my life could provide some uplift for others, and really there was nothing else to do.

Perhaps I might have had second thoughts had I known what the ceremony entailed. Disrobed from being a *samanera*, I was dolled up in a lacy white gown and placed at the head of a procession, clutching flowers and incense in my "praying" hands (*añjali*). Followed by the more able-bodied of the 700, I proceeded at a snail's pace for the mile or so to the ordination monastery clicked at by cameras along the way. After a triple circumambulation of the ordination hall, the ladies seemed keen to have a last "lucky" touch of the monk-to-be, who would in future be untouchable. It was getting a little scary when a large fat man picked me up and carried me over the threshold of the ordination hall to prevent an "unlucky" trip. The impression in my mind, however, was of suddenly being tendered completely helpless and dependent on others, with vestiges of personal identity falling away. I was even given a new name without having any say in the matter. (My name, Sucitto, meaning "good mind" or "good heart" seemed tame compared with other possibilities such as Noble Wisdom or Enlightenment Bliss, It has, however, been enough to try to live up to.)

Obviously, in becoming a *bhikkhu,* one did more than join the Bhikkhu Sangha as a recluse. One joined the larger Buddhist community in a unique and dynamic way, as a symbol and reminder of the path, irrespective of one's personal attainments. Although I had little confidence in my own "attainments," having a conventional identity did take some of the pressure off. I didn't have to have an opinion about myself, and because I didn't have to think about myself in order to justify myself, I didn't keep creating myself. I realised that my life was not my own, but it was better that way: I could have a little more dispassion, a little more tolerance of myself and a little more patience.

At first, integration into the monastic community as a junior *bhikkhu* was slow. I helped my teacher to the best of my ability, and gave up more of my time to look after the newly-arrived meditators. But it wasn't until a death in my family took me back to England that I became an integral part of a monastic community. In England I didn't have the privilege of being a foreigner anymore, so I had to learn to use my "Englishness" to help the Dhamma and the Sangha in the very mundane matters of running a *vihara* and relating to visitors. In our small London community, we were all very accessible; nobody could take refuge in being serene or anonymous. And it was another kind of surrender to relate to lay people who didn't understand the conventions of a *bhikkhu* and wanted to know what you would like for dinner and why you had to wear those "funny robes." After all, this is England. Nobody seemed to understand that it was not about becoming something, but about giving oneself up.

In a monastic community, a junior monk lives in dependence on a teacher (or "Ajahn" in the Thai tradition). This means that you follow his guidance, and offer service to him. It is another bow, and one that is reflected frequently by physically bowing to him on formal occasions such as after the twice-daily period of group meditation. A junior monk also defers to monks who have spent more years in the Order than himself: he walks behind them, sits lower than them, and eats after them. This can be frustrating if you take deference and respect as something that you have to give to others because they are better than you. In fact, paying respect enables you to establish a cool and kindly presence of mind with another person, rather than bring up feelings of comparison, or attach to any opinions that you may have about them. Bowing to others according to conventional hierarchy eliminates the need to compete or form judgments; it is an act of giving, and as in all true giving, it opens the heart and composes the mind. Because of this training in showing respect, a Sangha can maintain its unity and harmony, without dividing into cliques of bosom friends who cut themselves off from others; and it can abide without its members holding onto grudges that may form around differences of opinion. One can use bowing as a means to bring some sensitivity into a situation; it is also away of letting go of the mind that makes permanent personalities out of transitory perceptions. Rather than idolising someone, respect gives them space. I found that if I idolised the teacher, I eventually became disappointed when he no longer fitted into my perception of what he should be; or one would want a more personal relationship or one would want to prove him better than any other teacher. But if I didn't carry around an idea of him, there was always something instructive and joyous in his company. With a teacher that one respects, there is the opportunity to develop this letting go of views until one knows that action in the mind, trusts it, and brings it to bear on a wider scale.

The detailed training in care and attention towards our simple requisites of bowl, robes and lodgings is also helpful for personal mindfulness and a peaceful atmosphere in a community. Rather than rushing around, mind filled by a train of thought, one has to let go of personal obsessions in order to be mindful of whether one is carrying the bowl correctly, or whether the awkward robes are falling off, or whether one's deportment is correct. These are some of the minor rules that people challenge: "Why be hide-bound?

Why be attached to traditions? Why not be more practical?" Actually I found these conventions, although occasionally irritating, enormously practical. Being aware of a robe and deportment continually brings the mind back to the body, one of the basic foundations of mindfulness. You have to be clear in the moment rather than concerned with getting anywhere fast; and you also have to be able to let go of the variety of opinions that it can bring up. Of course people do in time recognise the robe as belonging to someone they can trust, someone who is living in faith. This is very helpful in an age dominated by materialistic images that encourage people to be greedy and feel discontent with what is simple and unexciting.

With more minor matters of etiquette, one also had to learn when not to apply them. In a non-Buddhist country, the attitude of respect can easily be misunderstood as subservience: not everyone is able to appreciate its purpose at first. Unfamiliar customs can create comparisons in people's minds whereby they feel compelled to justify themselves or criticise monasticism. For its part, the Sangha has to be aware of the desire to have everything established in its traditional way without any challenge. There is something in all of us which yearns for security in the world; so we have to be mindful of that instinct. And in order to be mindful, it is necessary to examine our instinctual relationship with the world through reflecting on the conventions that establish that relationship. For the most part, our social conventions are habitual and lead to inattention or false motivation, and we take our personal quirks and customs as being what we are. For me there was a tremendous amount of clinging to being a non-conformist, or to political views, or to personal "rights." And for all of us unawakened beings there is the clinging to self, which is just another convention and view. Dhamma training allows us, as mendicants or as householders, to take on a role and responsibility, not for becoming, not for comparison, not for reputation, but for wise reflection. This training can shift the mind beyond the perspective of self to that realm where there is freedom from convention, and the compassion to use conventions for the welfare of others.

—§§§—

An Exhortation

Self-Image or Self-Knowledge?

Two Dhamma Talks

Ayyā Khemā

Bodhi Leaves No. 105

First published: 1986

An Exhortation

Every evening we chant, *"Pamādamūlako lobho … doso … moho." Lobha, dosa, moha,* the three roots of evil: greed, hate and delusion. We are born with these roots, We wouldn't be born at all if we didn't have them. But there are also the three opposite roots: non-greed, non-hate, and non-delusion. It is these roots of good which we must cultivate.

Non-greed is generosity, generosity shown in giving one's things away, giving one's money away, giving one's understanding away, giving one's love away. That is generosity. And the more one gives away, the richer one is. But unless one can give freely, one is caught by greed, by *lobha*.

The opposite of *dosa* is the root of non-hate, loving kindness, *mettā*. The more we can generate *mettā* in our hearts, the less we will suffer. But we have to work consciously at abiding in loving kindness. There is no hoping, wishing or praying that brings *mettā*. There is no creator to grant *mettā* to us. There is no grace which will bestow *mettā* on us. It is we who must create *mettā*.

There must be deliberate action, a deliberate action of the heart which opens towards love. Loving kindness must not be directed only towards what is lovable. To love that which is lovable is possible for anyone. It's easy. To love that which is lovable is not even interesting. That is what all the romances, the movies, the novels are about. To love that which is lovable is not the spiritual path, but a worldly endeavour. The reason for loving kindness is because the heart has the ability to give; its purpose is for purification.

But trying to understand loving kindness with the mind can never succeed. It's got to be felt with one's heart. The heart has to be involved "wholeheartedly," for unless loving kindness is felt in the heart, the root of hate, *dosa*, will remain.

There is no intellectual understanding that will make *mettā* possible because the mind is caught up in delusion, *moha*. The mind can take a stand on either side of any debate. It can say "pro" or "con" on anything. The heart cannot. The heart opens up and feels love, or it shrinks and feels hate. The mind can judge very easily, "This is lovable." Or the negative mind can say, "Oh no, it's not. It's detestable!" The mind can do that. But the heart cannot. Rely on the heart and not on the judgments of the mind. Work on the purification of one's heart. See within. Become fully aware when there is greed. Become aware when there is hate. Then substitute the roots of good, generosity, and loving kindness, for the evil roots. The more often we look within, the more often we substitute the good for the evil, the sooner the ego-delusion will diminish.

Moha is the delusion of a self. Its opposite, non-delusion, is the knowledge that the idea of self is the cause of suffering, that our mind and body are coreless. It is because of the delusion of self that the other two roots, greed and hate, beset us. Without delusion, there would be no greed or hate, it is the self-delusion, saying "This is me, this is the way I see things, this is the way I want it, this is the wav I'm separating myself," that is the cause of hatred, separation, isolation, resistance, and rejection.

The more deluded one is, the more greed and hate one generates. And how deluded one is depends on how much one identifies with what and who one thinks one is, and what one wants to get out of life for oneself. The more self-identification there is, the more delusion; the more greed, the more hate; the more hate, the more unhappiness.

Even the views we hold are stained with ego-discolouration. They cannot be absolutely true. But they are true from the standpoint of the ego. The ego says and the ego thinks and therefore the ego wants. This is the root of *moha*.

It is not possible to work on eliminating ego-delusion alone. It is done through awareness of the three roots: greed, hate and delusion. For this is the path of purification. This is the path of self-inquiry. This is the path of self-discipline. And there is nothing else on this path as important as mindfulness—watching the mind. This is a simple formula, but just sitting and waiting for enlightenment is not going to bring enlightenment. Nothing happens by itself. What matters is action. Take the action of following the Noble Eightfold Path. With awareness, with no fixed views, but only the knowledge of something to be done: the elimination of *lobha, dosa, moha*. Without that deliberation to remove the three roots of evil, meditation is a total waste of time.

So, we watch the mind. A mental state arises. Don't believe it! Check it out. Which part of the ego-delusion is talking—greed or hate? Or both? And then—watch. The thought arises and it ceases. If the thought doesn't cease, there is clinging, hanging on for "dear life," keeping the thought. There are even people who are enormously attached to their own dissatisfaction, to their own *dukkha*. This is one of the greatest absurdities: being attached to one's own suffering.

Remembering to be aware is another problem because our minds get caught up in our own thinking processes. Drop the thinking processes. They aren't worth having. Look instead at the greed and the hate and the delusion, the things worth seeing.

Our ego-delusion has at its roots the identification of ourselves with the five aggregates, the *khandha*s: the body, feelings, perceptions, mental formations, and consciousness. Yet we know that our problems, our suffering, our unhappiness, stem from that identification. And we know we must abandon this wrong view. For we are not the aggregates.

But there is no way of getting at the root of delusion as long as one strongly identifies with one's thoughts, and with who one thinks one is. The identification takes away the possibility of stepping back and watching, of stepping back and watching mindfully. Mindfulness is what we learn through meditation, and mindfully we learn to watch every moment of our daily life. Mindfulness means being fully aware, "the miracle of being awake," which is not the opposite of being sleepy, but the opposite of being foggy. Not thinking foggily and woozily, but being fully aware—fully awake to what is going on within oneself.

Self-identification with one's state of being is the great trap. So we must first become aware of the props we use to maintain who we think we are. It begins with: "I'm a woman" or "I'm a man."

There's strong identification. There's strong support for the ego, for that "I am" is the ego itself talking. Next we identify with our abilities and our knowledge. "This is what I can do" and "This is what I know." Two further strong supports for the ego.

Ask yourself: "Who do I think I am? Why do I think I am like that? What makes me think like this? Is it because I'm identifying with the body? … the feelings? … the perceptions? … the thoughts?

… the consciousness?" If you identify with any or all of these, what misery! What a miserable situation owning all those aggregates. Drop the identification and you get nearer the truth. This is just a body, prone to *dukkha*. These are just feelings. These are just perceptions. These are just mental formations. This is just consciousness.

So greed, hatred and delusion, *lobha, dosa* and *moha,* are everybody's lot. The work on the spiritual path is eliminating these roots. For unless something is done about them, they'll be with us—life after life after life.

The three roots of evil, with delusion as the base, make the world go round, "Love makes the world go round," it is said. But if love really did make the world go round, this would be a very different world! No, it is greed that makes the world go round; it is hate that makes the world go round; it is delusion that makes the world go round. Because of these, relationships don't work, friendships deteriorate, people have personal difficulties with one another. That is why love is lacking. That is why people steal, kill, wage wars.

But the only world we need be concerned with is the world we have inside of ourselves. And doesn't that world look different for each one of us? And different each time we look? And one does have to look to see for oneself what one is really like. Do you know that the whole of the universe lies within this mind and body? Each one of us has an entire universe within him. Let's get to know the universe by getting to know ourselves. And we get to know ourselves through meditation.

Meditation is about purification. Meditation is about finding the Dhamma within oneself. The Buddha said: "Whoever sees me, sees the Dhamma. Whoever sees the Dhamma, sees me." And the

Dhamma can be seen with an inner vision—but only if one does the work. One can't get an inner vision by merely thinking about wanting one. There's work to be done. Nothing can replace the work each of us must do. But with the joy of the path there is energy. And when the joy of the path arises, there is confidence. Have that confidence in your experiences.

The Buddha said that we are like children playing in a house on fire and are too foolish to jump out. We don't realise that the fire of our passions, of our wanting, of our rejections, of our views and opinions, of our self-centred assertions is the fire that is burning us, and we are too foolish to let go. Like little children we want to keep on playing. That's childish, not childlike. And if we keep on playing we're going to get burned by our passions over and over again.

Each day has a limited number of hours, each week a limited number of days. Knowing that time grows shorter each day, a state of mind called urgency, *saṃvega*, arises. See that urgency. Jump out of the house which is on fire. This work is the seeking of enlightenment. Get on with it.

Self-Image or Self-Knowledge

The question arises: What is the difference between having a self-image and knowing oneself? This is an important question, and one well-worth discussing, because it does seem at first that they are one and the same. But they are not.

First of all, a self-image is a burden to carry. Yet, unfortunately, everyone does carry around a self-image, and some people carry around a heavier burden than others. And carrying around a self-image is not only a burden, but a danger. For a self-image is fragile. At any time it is likely to be broken, smashed, shattered. And when one's self-image is broken—or even just jarred a bit—then there is pain, grief, and lamentation, *dukkha*, suffering, When one's self-image is shattered, for that precise moment it is seen to be untrue, unstable. *Dukkha* arises because self-identification has been momentarily lost.

Yet one carries around with oneself that self-image because that identity is supposed to bring security. This security, of course, is imaginary, it has no basis in fact: In fact, it creates insecurity because a self-image is imaginary, and I has to be protected all the time: So one runs around with an illusory self-image as if one were carrying a porcelain figure made out of the finest porcelain on one's head and trying to protect it from being smashed!

It's not a very viable situation, is it? Yet everybody does it. This self-image, in most cases, is built upon the best one hopes to offer. In some cases, though, it is built upon the worst one has to offer. Those who develop a negative self-image are the people who have created a poor image of themselves, those who think they can never do anything right. Now people in the other lot have created images of themselves as worthy persons, preferably kind, sweet, good-natured balanced, always understanding, in perfect command of every situation, never upset, never angry.

But having any kind of self-image cannot possibly bring security. On the contrary, it invariably brings worry and fear. Just below the surface lie the underlying tendencies, which indicate clearly that one may not be quite the way one thinks one is. But if one doesn't look too closely, maybe one can sustain the image. Or if nobody pokes enough. Of course there's no guarantee for that—everyone gets poked and pushed. But people who don't practise meditation and don't train themselves will shift blame to the one that's poking and pushing. By blaming an outside agency, they are able to keep their self-image intact or they tell themselves: That's only momentary anger and fury, which is excusable.

A person who has gained some insight may feel bereaved. He has lost something he thought he owned. Maybe he thought he owned kindness—or maybe he thought he owned equanimity. Or love towards all beings. Or any of the lofty qualities that everybody praises. All of a sudden what he thought he had disappears and cannot be restored. Because he has already trained himself a little, such a person does not blame another, but he can become extremely unhappy. Some people react by crying, some by sulking: Some become so upset about the loss of their self-created image of themselves that they cannot handle it and run away.

The only useful response is understanding: to know that this self-created idea about oneself has absolutely no genuine basis in real fact. With the seven underlying tendencies, the *anusaya*—sensuality, irritation, doubt, wrong view, conceit, clinging to existence, and ignorance—constantly rearing their ugly heads, how could there be a person who is always perfectly kind, always perfectly loving, always sweet, always pliable, always giving? Where is such a person? Where can it be found?

Obviously it stands to reason that one has made up nothing but a self-protection—a shield—so that one doesn't have to see the qualities which really exist and which are based on the three roots of evil and the three roots of good: greed, hate and delusion, and greedlessness, hatelessness and undeludedness. All six are there. And if one doesn't see the three negative ones, how is one ever going to get rid of them? As long as one imagines one is free of the roots of evil, there is no way of getting rid of them.

A self-image is a created figure—a persona—which is supposed to be the same all the time. One carries around that image of an ideal person wherever one goes. Whatever image is desirable. And that image is intended to be a permanent vision of oneself. "That's the way I am. That's my true self. Let no one dare change it."

That way of thinking certainly prevents self-knowledge. For nothing is permanent—least of all one's own reactions, one's own feelings, one's own thoughts, one's own emotions. Nothing of the kind exists which is permanent. If one has this image of an ideal person being carried around—this porcelain figure of oneself that one has made up—then that view prevents knowledge of the change in oneself, that prevents a true understanding of oneself. For every time the defilements rear up, the mind says: "Oh, no! That couldn't be me. I'm the other kind. I'm the good kind."

It often takes a trauma for one to wake up from this dream, a trauma with enough impact to make one fully aware that what one has thought about oneself is a total myth. Only then will one start investigating oneself. Before that everything one does has a veil around it. It's foggy and unclear. And whatever one does cannot have any truth within it. Because all that one does must comply with one's image, and whatever cannot comply is not accepted. One actually tries to fit reality to the self-image instead of seeing oneself according to reality.

Knowing oneself means knowing whatever happens. Whether one approves of it or disapproves of it doesn't matter. It's happening, isn't it? And anyone who is not an *Arahant* has to deal constantly with the defilements of the mind in all their subtlety and variety. Deny them—either totally or partially—and we deny the truth. And if we deny the truth within us, we cannot find the truth anywhere. The truth is within us. We don't have to be resigned to the fact that we have defilements in our minds. But we do have to recognise them when they arise. We have to know them with direct knowledge. Direct knowledge does not mean that we know lists of names and categories; it means that we recognise and identify the defilements when they arise within us. Only then can one acquire self-knowledge.

A self-image is hard and brittle. Because it is hard, it does not easily change; because it is brittle, it is easily broken. And after it's broken, we pick up the pieces and put it back together again saying: "I've got to have that self-image! I need to believe I'm a good person!" What's the good in believing in that? Believing in something which cannot possibly be true. What one needs to do is practise and make the image conform to reality.

Some people need a self-image more than others because they feel more insecure. When one feels insecure, one needs to grab hold of something and if there's nothing external to grab hold of, then one grabs hold of the self-image. One can create a self-image based on anything. Being a woman, a nun, a nun in-training, a lay person—being tall or short, fat or thin, beautiful—anything. And every self-image is something self-created. It denotes a collection of physical characteristics and personal traits, but surely it does not denote an "I." If one has an idea that "I" am a certain person, obviously that idea cannot be true because that certain person is always changing.

It is our need for inner security that makes it imperative for us to find something which seems secure, solid, unchanging. So we make up a self-image and try to maintain that it is secure, solid, unchanging. But there is nothing in the universe which is solid and unchanging. Not only do we make up this self-image of ours, but we create a certain kind of a self. One that we find pleasing, one that we can approve of.

If we repeatedly insist that our self-image is real, we are distorting reality, trying to make it fit our self-image instead of abandoning the self-image in order to see reality. It's a difficult habit to overcome, and the less insight we have, the harder it is to overcome. Usually one needs a real push to be woken up. Sometimes that push can come from "losing one's cool," from being the exact opposite of one's self—image. Then one suddenly sees that there is something wrong with the self-image, and one actually starts to recognise what one has created—a false picture of oneself—and then one really sees the suffering to which it gives rise.

The introspection which is necessary on the path in order to know with mindfulness one's feelings, thoughts, and the content of the mind can only start when one knows each facet of one's mental make-up—how each facet changes, how it operates, how it arises and ceases, how one reacts to these aspects of the mind. This self-knowledge is extremely valuable and cannot be dispensed with. But a self-image will block the way. Self-image and self-knowledge are diametrically opposed to each other. One is imaginary, the other real. With self-knowledge comes the ability to work with one's own difficulties, and from that arises wisdom, which is the third aspect of the threefold path: moral conduct or *sīla*, concentration or *samādhi*, and wisdom or *paññā*. The only knowledge really worth gaining is self-knowledge. Each one of us is no different from the rest of humanity. What is happening inside of oneself is happening inside of everybody. But most people are totally unaware of what is going on inside. If wisdom is to arise, it has to come through self-knowledge.

The wisdom that the Buddha gained and passed on to us is based on the direct knowledge of the Four Noble Truths. Direct knowledge is the inner-seeing, the inner-vision.

The impermanence of all states of being has to be reflected upon, contemplated, and directly experienced. If we only know about impermanence, unsatisfactoriness and non-self—*annica*, *dukkha*, and *anattā*—without experiencing them, we know something interesting and true, but the mere knowing doesn't help us to progress on the path. We do not gain insight just by knowing. And so we look within. And what better way is there to experience these truths than to see them in oneself, to see how one's own mental states are constantly changing? One then knows when one responds with love and kindness, and one knows when one reacts with negativity. And one clearly knows that it is utter foolishness to create a self-image from such responses and reactions, constantly changing, very often not even predictable.

The sooner we can drop our self-image and become aware of the here and now, the moment to moment, the sooner we're starting to practise, We are not practising if we cling to a cherished idea about ourselves and then try to impress that idea on others. A self-image is a mask. Sometimes we can actually feel it as bodily armour, and sometimes it shows through as body language. There is a way of feeling this armour: by becoming attentive, completely attentive to oneself.

Since there is nothing else really worth attending to, let us attend to our own body and mind. "The whole of the universe, O monks, lies in this body and mind." If that is where it lies, we might as well fix our attention right there.

And that person we've been trying to portray, the person we'd like to be, is the terrible burden, the bearer of *dukkha,* which must be seen for what it really is—an imagined self-image. Then it must be dispensed with, the quicker the better. A real impact comes when we can see ourselves as we really are, and see that we are not the same from one thought-moment to the next.

Think back over only today—just one day. Were you the same person all day long? Happy, smiling, loving and kind? All day, from morning to night? Always the same? Having the same kind of thoughts? The same kind of feelings? Were there feelings and thoughts of resistance, of worry, of hope, of planning? Or were they strictly in the moment and constantly the same? Just look at one day—today. Or one hour, or ten minutes, or five minutes. If there is total attention, you can be aware of the constant changes within yourself even within seconds.

Get in touch with your self-created image and let go of it. The whole of the practise is letting go, for this is where security lies. That image was supposed to bring you security, which is why it was created in the first place: to give you something solid and unchanging to hang on to. But if you really examine it, you will find that security is gained by letting go, by having absolutely nothing. If there's nothing, there's no threat, no fear of losing anything. There is just each moment.

Let go of all self-images, of all ideations, of all hopes and plans. Then you can dwell in this particular moment—and no one can take that away from you. It can't disappear, or be broken, or get lost. It just is. Security lies in the simple fact that in essence one has nothing and one is nothing.

The Ups and Downs of Rebirth

Stories from the Buddhist Texts as told by

The Venerable Mahāsi Sayādaw of Burma

Bodhi Leaves No. 106

First published: 1986

The Story of Queen Uparī

Queen Uparī was the chief queen of King Assaka who once ruled over the country of Kāsi at its capital Pāṭali. She was said to be of great beauty, Ancient kings used to select the most attractive maidens of their kingdom to become their queens. Consequently all their queens were noted for their charm and loveliness. Queen Uparī was outstanding amongst them because of her raving beauty and enchantment. Bewitched by her alluring comeliness King Assaka, had lost his heart on her.

Much adored by the monarch and while still in the prime of her beauty and charm, Queen Uparī went to the gods' abode. Now "to go to the abode of the celestial being" is a Burmese cultural usage to denote the death of a royal personage. Likewise, "flying back" means the passing away of a Buddhist monk, a mere cultural usage. A dead person finds rebirth in an existence as conditioned by *kamma* the previous volitional activities. As it happened, Queen Uparī, in spite of the saying according to the cultural usage that "she had gone to the god's abode," actually made her rebirth in the abode of the lowly beetles.

With the passing away of his adored queen, King Assaka was consumed by fiercely burning fires of sorrow and lamentation, He caused the corpse of the queen embalmed in oil, to be placed in a glass coffin and kept it underneath his bedstead. Overwhelmed by grief, the king lay on the bed without food or sleep, wailing and moaning over the loss of his beloved queen. The royal relatives and his wise ministers tried to console him and give solace by reminding him of the nature of impermanence and conditionality of existence, all to no avail. The corpse in the coffin, being embalmed in oil, would remain well preserved just like those treated with chemical preservatives of modern times. The queen would therefore appear to the king as if she were lying, sleeping in the coffin. The sight of the corpse acted like fuel to his burning sorrows and lamentations which continued to consume him for seven days. At that time, the *Bodhisatta* was a hermit, endowed with *abhiññā* supernormal jhānic powers, living in the forest of the Himalayas. He happened to scan the whole world using his *abhiññā*, and saw King Assaka in the throes of intense sorrow. He knew also that no one but himself could save the king from his misery. He therefore made his way to the royal garden of King Assaka by means of his jhānic powers.

There a young Brahmin came to see the hermit, who enquired him about King Assaka. The young man told him how the king was being overwhelmed by grief and requested him to save the king. "We do not know the king. But if he came and asked us, we could tell him about his wife's present existence," replied the hermit. Thereupon the young man went to the king and said to him. "Great Sir, a hermit endowed with celestial eye and celestial ear has arrived in the royal garden. He said he knew and could show the present existence of the departed queen. It would be worthwhile to go and see him."

Upon hearing that the hermit could show him the queen in her present existence, the king immediately took off for the royal gardens in a carriage. Arriving there, he paid respectful homage to the hermit and addressed him. "Reverend Sir, is it true that you claim to know the present existence of the queen Uparī?" On the hermit admitting his claim, the king wanted to know where she was reborn now.

"Oh, great King, Queen Uparī took delight in her beauteous appearance and was very vain about it. She had spent her time engaged only in beautifying herself to make herself more alluringly attractive, forgetting all the while to perform meritorious deeds, to give alms and observe moral precepts. In consequence, she has passed over to a lowly existence. She is presently reborn as a female cow-dung-beetle in this very garden," the hermit told the whole story very frankly.

Persons favoured by fortune enjoying privileges of wealth, family, education, rank, physical beauty etc., are prone to exhibit haughtiness in their dealings with others. Shrouded in their own vanity and self-esteem, they become neglectful in their performance of meritorious deeds. Humility plays no part in their make-up. The Blessed One had taught in the Cūlakamma-vibhaṅga Sutta that such vainglorious, haughty persons are liable to land up in lowly inferior rebirths. On the other hand, unpretentious persons who show humility and pay reverential respect to those deserving homage will be reborn in noble families.

Queen Uparī of our story was extremely beautiful, and, being the chief queen of the ruling monarch, was of very high status in life. She had her head turned by these pre-eminent qualities and looked down with contempt on those to whom she should have shown her respect. For such unwholesome attitudes and actions, it may be presumed she was reborn a lowly female cow dung-beetle. On hearing this account of the rebirth of his beloved queen as a female beetle, King Assaka promptly rejected it, saying, "I don't believe it."

The hermit replied, "I can show you the female beetle and make her talk too." The king said, "All right. Please do so and make her talk too." The hermit, using his supernatural powers of *abhiññā*, made a vow for both the male and female beetles to make their appearance before the king.

When the male and female beetles emerged from the heap of cow dung into the presence of the king the hermit said, "O King, the female beetle which is following from behind was your chief queen Uparī. Having abandoned you, she is now trailing the male cow dung-beetle wherever it goes. O king, have a good look at the female beetle who was lately your chief queen Uparī."

The king refused to believe the hermit. "I can't believe that such an intelligent being as my queen Uparī was reborn as this female beetle," said the king.

True, for those who do not quite believe in the laws of *kamma* and its resultant effect, who do not understand the principles of conditionality or casual relationship, as explained in *paṭiccasamuppāda*, it would be difficult to accept that a being of the human world should have gone down as low as to become a mere beetle. Even in these days when Buddha's teachings are widely prevalent, there are some people holding the view that "when man dies, he cannot descend into an existence inferior to that of a human being." So it is not surprising that during the dark ages when Buddha's dispensations were yet unheard of, such stories of incarnation were received with scepticism.

Nevertheless, according to the teachings of the Buddha, for as long as one has not yet attained the status of an Ariya, one can descend from the human world or the celestial realm into the four lower states of existence; conditioned by the bad *kamma* and the mental reflex just before death, rebirth may take place in the lower order of beings. On the other hand, conditioned by good *kamma* and wholesome mental attitude on the threshold of death, ascent may be made from an inferior sphere of existence into the higher realm of human and celestial beings.

There is the story of a *bhikkhu* named Venerable Tissa who developed attachment to his saffron robes when he was about to die. As a consequence, he was reborn a body louse making his home on those very robes. There is another story of a frog who met its death while listening to a discourse by the Buddha. He became a celestial being in Tavatimsa celestial abode. These are examples which serve as evidences of various transformations at the time of rebirths.

But King Assaka, not having heard of such discourses, could not accept that his queen had become a female beetle. Accordingly he refused to believe it. The hermit therefore proposed that he would make the female beetle talk. The king accepted the proposal. Thereupon the hermit made the vow, using his supernatural powers, to have the conversation between him and the female beetle comprehensible to the king and his audience.

"Who were you in your past life?" the hermit asked.

"I was the chief queen Uparī of King Assaka," replied the female beetle.

"What now, female beetle, do you still love King Assaka or do you love only this cow dung-beetle?"

To which the female beetle gave the reply: "True, King Assaka was my husband in my past life. At that time, I used to roam about in this garden, in the company of King Assaka, enjoying the five sense pleasures of sight, sound, smell, taste, and touch. But, now that I am in the new existence, I have nothing to do with King Assaka."

The King Assaka was greatly distressed to hear the harsh, unfeeling words of estrangement from the lips of the female beetle. He thought to himself: "I had loved and adored her so much. I could not betake myself to throw away her dead body. But she had become so antipathetic and nasty to me."

He felt so disgusted with his old queen Uparī that he ordered even while sitting there: "Go and have that woman's body removed." Then having bathed and washed himself, the king went back to the palace. He made another court-lady his chief queen and carried on ruling over his country wisely. The hermit *Bodhisatta*, after giving good advice to the king, went back to the Himalayan sanctuary.

The moral from this story is that Queen Uparī, while in the human world, had taken delight in being a human person, and a queen at that. She would never have even dreamed of being reborn a female beetle. But in accordance with her past *kamma*, when she happened to be reborn a female beetle, she at once took to the life and delight in the physical body of a beetle. She esteemed and adored the physical body of the male beetle a hundred times, a thousand times more than that of King Assaka.

That she felt quite at home in her lowly existence as a cow dung beetle is due to *taṇhā*, craving, which finds delight everywhere; that is why the Buddha had said, "craving has the tendency to delight wherever it finds rebirth."

Reborn as a dog, it takes delight in a dog's existence; reborn as pig, as a fowl, there is always delight in each existence. Even having been born as children of affluent parents of upper social class, there are cases of them sinking down to poverty-stricken existences and yet enjoying their lives therein. Some of them even resisted the efforts of their parents to take them back into the fold of family, since they are finding their new life quite enjoyable. It is craving again which is giving them pleasure wherever they are, delighting in whatever sense object presents itself.

From Brahmā Land to Pigpen

At one time the Blessed One went into Rājagiri for alms round. On seeing a young female pig, the Blessed One smiled. Noticing the white radiations which shone forth from the teeth of the Buddha, the Venerable Ānanda knew that the Buddha was smiling. Accordingly he asked; "What has caused Sire to smile?"

The Blessed One pointed out the young female pig to Ānanda and said, "See that young female pig? She was a young woman in human existence during the dispensation of Kakusandha Buddha. When she died, she was reborn a hen in the neighbourhood of a monastic feeding-hall. The small hen fell victim to an eagle. But earlier she happened to have heard the recitation by a Buddhist monk of a meditation subject which aroused wholesome thoughts in her. By virtue of these merits, the small hen was reborn as a princess named Ubbarī in a royal family. The princess Ubbarī later left the household life and became a wandering mendicant. Residing in the mendicants' residence she happened one day to gaze at the maggots in the latrine. The worms served as an object for meditation (contemplation of ugliness of worm-infested corpse or contemplation of a white object) by which she attained the first *jhāna*. When she passed away, she was reborn a Brahmā in the first jhānic Brahmā world. On expiry from the Brahma world, she became the daughter of a rich man in the human world, which she left again only to be born a pig now. I saw all these events which made me smile."

On hearing this story of repeated births in various existences, Venerable Ānanda and other monks became greatly alarmed and agitated with religious emotion. The Blessed One stepped going on the alms-round, and while still standing on the roadway, stated teaching the Dhamma in six verses the first one of which stated:

"If the main roots of a tree remain undamaged and in good condition, even when the upper branches are cut off, that tree will grow again developing new buds and shoots. Likewise, if there remain defilements (lying dormant) which are not yet eradicated by the noble path, this suffering of rebirth will arise time and again successively."

What is conveyed by this verse is this: "During her existence as princess Ubbarī, she renounced the world to become a wanderer. By practising meditation, she attained the first *jhāna* which could dispel or cut away only the defilements of craving for sensual pleasure which appear as sensuous thoughts at the mind's door. By means of suppression *jhāna* can put away the defilements only to a certain distance for a certain period of time. Thus she was able to dispel the craving for sensual pleasure when she attained the first *jhāna* and later in the Brahmā world. But when she was born again in the human world as the daughter of a wealthy man, the craving for sensual pleasure re-appeared because it had not been rooted out by the noble path. The craving for existence, of course, persisted even when she had attained the *jhāna*. Thus, because the latent defilements had not been completely uprooted, she had to descend from the Brahma world, through the human world, into a pig's existence. As long as craving persists, repeated rebirths will take place in this way in various existences."

In reference to this story of descent from the Brahmā World to a pig's existence, ancient Sayādaws had left an aphorism: "in Brahma land, she shines bright; in pig's pen, too, she finds delight." But it is not possible to be reborn as a pig, straight from the Brahmā world, nor as any other animal, nor in the realms of petas, starving ghosts, nor in the states of misery. By virtue of access concentration, proximate to the *jhāna* previously attained, rebirth can take place only as a human being or in a celestial abode. The young female pig of the above story also passed through human life where she was born as the daughter of a wealthy man. It is quite possible that she landed in a pig's existence after being the daughter of a wealthy man because of the bad *kamma* she had committed then in being haughty and insolent to those to whom she should have shown respect.

When the young female pig died, she was reborn in a royal family of Suvaṇṇabhūmi which is generally taken to be the country of Thaton. From being a princess of Suvaṇṇabhūmi, she passed over to Varaṇasi, India, as a woman. She then became a woman in Vanavasi, southeast of Bombay. From there, she was reborn the daughter of a horse-merchant in the seaport town of Supparaka, northwest of Bombay. Next she became the daughter of a shipowner at the port of Kavira in the south-eastern most part of the Indian peninsular. This is the coastal district inhabited by the Tamil people. After that life, she was reborn in the family of a government official at Anuradhapura of present day Sri Lanka. Her next life was as a daughter of a rich man, named Sumana from Bhokanta, a village south of Anuradhapura. She took the same name, Sumana as her father. Later her father left that village and settled down in the Mahāmuni village of the Dīghavapi District. One day a minister of the king Duṭṭhagāmini, named Lakundaka Atimbara, happened to visit the Mahāmuni village on a certain business. Upon seeing the young lady Sumana, he fell madly in love with her. He married her with great pomp and ceremony and carried her off to his village Mahāpunna.

The Venerable Mahā Anuruddha who resided at the monastery of Taungsun happened to visit her village for alms round. While waiting for offer of alms food at the gate of Sumana's house, he saw Sumana and said to his monk. followers: "Bhikkhus, how wonderful, what a marvel! The young female pig of the Blessed One's time is now the wife of the minister Lakundaka Atimbara."

On hearing this exclamation, Sumana, the wife of the minister, developed jātissara ñāṇa, knowledge of previous existences. With the help of this faculty, she recalled to her mind the previous existences she had passed through. In consequence, she became agitated with fear at the prospect of repeated births in the cycle of existences. Asking permission from her minister husband, she went to a *bhikkhunī* monastery and got herself ordained. After ordination, she listened to the discourse on Satipaṭṭhāna Sutta at Tissa Mahā Vihara monastery. Practising mindfulness meditation in accordance with the *sutta*, she became a *sotāpanna*, well established as a stream-winner in the first stage of the path and fruition. Then when king Dutthagamini came on the throne, she went back to her native village, Bhokkanta, where at the Kalla Mahā Vihara monastery she heard a discourse on Asivisopama Sutta which enabled her to attain the fourth stage of the fruition and become an Arahat, completely free from influxes, passions.

The Story of Samana Deva

Even if one were engaged in meditation practise to dispel craving until one became fully developed in the knowledge of the path, craving could still give rise to rebirth. This fact is borne out by the story of a *deva* (god) named Samana.

During the lifetime of the Buddha, a certain young man, having established faith in the dispensation of the Buddha, got himself ordained and stayed with his preceptor for five years. He performed all the major and minor incumbent duties and learnt thoroughly the *pātimokkha* discipline for the *bhikkhus*. He also mastered the procedure for purifying himself from serious as well as trifling offences. Then, taking a meditation object of his choice, he repaired to a solitary abode in the forest and devoted himself incessantly to the practise of meditation.

His efforts at meditation were very strenuous. Even at midnight, which the Blessed One had allowed as the time for rest and sleep, he continued on with the practise. Thus striving day and night and getting enervated by lack of sufficient nourishing food, he was suddenly seized with a cutting pain, a paralytic stroke, which ruptured the spinal nerve causing him instant death. He was meditating while walking and thus is said to have passed away in the course of performing the duties of a *bhikkhu*.

According to the commentary, if any *bhikkhu*, while engaged in walking up and down the cloister walk or standing, leaning against the leaning post, or sitting or lying down at the head of the cloister walk with the double robe on his head, passes away, he is said to die in harness. So also a *bhikkhu* dies in harness if he passes away in the course of preaching a sermon, particularly on liberation from the chain of existences.

As the *bhikkhu* of our story was engaged in meditating while walking up and down the cloister walk, we could take it that he passed away while he was contemplating the nāmarūpa of the body postures in accordance with the teaching in the Satipaṭṭhāna Sutta. Although he had put in a great deal of effort in the practise of meditation, he passed away without attaining the Arahat path, because he was not yet fully endowed with supporting acts of perfections (pāramis) necessary for such attainments.

Complete eradication of craving is not possible unless the Arahat path has been attained. That this *bhikkhu* had not yet developed even up to the stage of the stream-winner will become clear later. Therefore, because of craving which can cause rebirth, he was reborn in the celestial abode of Tāvatiṃsa. A magnificent celestial palace awaited him in consequence of the merit he had acquired in the practise of meditation. By spontaneous rebirth, he appeared as if just awakened from sleep, at the entrance of the palace, a celestial being resplendent in full celestial attire.

At that moment about one thousand celestial princesses who had been awaiting the arrival of the master of the palace, saying, "Our Lord has arrived, let us entertain him," came gathering round him, holding musical instruments in their hands to welcome him joyously. The *deva* lord of the palace, however, did not even realise that he had taken a new existence in a new world. He was under the impression that he was still a *bhikkhu* of the human world. On the sight of the celestial damsels, he took them to be female visitors to his monastery. He covered up his bare left shoulder with the upper garment and remained seated, his eyes lowered and assuming a very dignified and reserved pose.

Realising at once that the new being must have been a *bhikkhu* in his previous existence, the celestial ladies addressed him, "My lord, this is the abode of the celestial beings. It is not the time to be observing the code of *bhikkhu* discipline It is the occasion for enjoyment of celestial pleasures." But he continued on maintaining solemn reserve and dignity. "This *deva* has not realised that he has become a celestial being in the realm of the *deva*'s. Let us drive home this fact to him, by our welcoming revelries." So saying, the celestial damsels started playing the musical instruments accompanied by songs. The *deva* all the more tightened his retiring disposition, maintaining his dignified solemnity, thinking that the female visitors had come to his forest abode to abandon themselves to frivolous merriment.

Whereupon the celestial ladies brought out a body-length mirror and placed it in front of the *deva*. On seeing his reflection in the mirror, he finally realised that he had left the *bhikkhu*'s existence and taken rebirth in the celestial land. The Samana *deva* was greatly perturbed then. He reflected: "I did not take up meditation to be reborn in this celestial land. My object was to attain the most profitable goal of Arahat fruition. But I am now like a boxer who entered the boxing competition aiming at the championship gold medal but was awarded only a bundle of turnips." Extremely agitated in mind, he thought: "The celestial pleasures are easily attainable. The lifetime of an Enlightened One is a rare occasion. To hear the teaching of the Buddha and to attain the noble path is of utmost importance. By wallowing in the celestial pleasures, there is the danger of losing the opportunity of meeting the Buddha." So without taking the trouble of entering the palatial building, he repaired hastily to the presence of the Buddha while the restraint he had observed as a *bhikkhu* still remained intact. His celestial damsels also accompanied him as if they were anxious not to lose sight of him. On reaching the presence of the Buddha, he addressed him:

"Most Venerable Blessed One, in what manner will it be possible to avoid and proceed along past the Nandavana garden otherwise known as the Mohana garden, the grove of stupidity, because it serves to encourage foolish behaviour in the celestial beings who visit it; where thousands of female celestial beings indulge in singing and yodelling; where numerous demons, goblins and spirits haunt."

Here the *deva* referred to the celestial females as demons and goblins and to the Nandavana gardens as the grove of stupidity because he was still in a repulsive mood towards sensual pleasures as a consequence of his intense efforts at *vipassanā* meditation. The commentary explanation of the *deva*'s query as to "how to proceed along" was that he was requesting the Blessed One for guidance on *vipassanā* which provides access to the Arahat fruition. The Buddha reflected on all the circumstances concerning the *deva* and taught him the Noble Eightfold Path.

The *deva* Samana, while listening to the discourse, reflected on the meditation practises of his former existence. Although he had not been able to attain to higher knowledge as a *bhikkhu* in spite of strenuous efforts at meditation, in the existence of a *deva* whose physical body was free from impurities, he was able to develop, in no time, successive stages of insight until he attained the path and fruition of the first stage and realised Nibbāna thus becoming a *sotāpanna*, a stream-winner.

The main point which this story of Samana *deva* has brought home is that, although the *bhikkhu* had been engaged ardently in *vipassanā* meditation, as the Ariya path which could cut off craving had not yet been attained, this craving had, after death, caused rebirth in the new existence as a celestial being. The story also pointed out how the Ariya path could be developed and how, as a *deva*, higher knowledge could be attained with ease.

A Story from Sri Lanka

There lived in a village in Sri Lanka, a man who was misbehaving with the wife of his elder brother. The woman was more passionately attached to her paramour than to her legitimate husband. She therefore instigated her lover to get rid of his elder brother. The man remonstrated, "Woman! Don't ever talk like that." But after she had repeated her evil suggestion three times, the lover asked, "How would I go about it?" She replied, "You go with an axe and wait for him at the riverside near the big caper tree. I'll send him there." Thereupon, the man proceeded there and lay in wait for his elder brother, hiding amongst the branches of the tree.

When the husband came back from his work in the forest, the wife made a show of loving affection for him, and fondly brushing his hair she said, "Your hair needs cleaning, it is too dirty. Why not go and shampoo it at the riverside near the big caper tree?" Happy with the thought, "My wife is very tender with her affections for me," he went accordingly to the bathing place at the riverside. He was preparing to wash his hair, bending his head down, when his young brother came out from the hiding place and cruelly chopped his head off with an axe.

Because of the clinging attachment to his wife, he was reborn a green snake (a rat snake according to Ceylonese scholars). Still attached to his wife, the snake took to dropping himself down from the roof of the house upon the woman. Realising that the snake must have been her former husband, she caused it to be killed and removed. Even after passing away from the snake's existence, his attachment for his former wife still remained strong and he was reborn a dog in his old house. As a dog it was still clinging to his former wife, following her everywhere even she went out to the forest. People made derisive remarks, "The hunter woman with the dog is going out. Wonder where she is headed for!" The woman asked her lover again to kill the dog.

His attachment still intense and persisting, the dog was reborn a calf in the same house. The young calf also went following her everywhere, drawing laughter and ridicule from the people again, "Look, the cowherd has come out. Wonder which pasture her cattle are going to graze in!" Again the woman asked her man to kill off the young calf. Again his tenacious attachment to his wife caused rebirth, this time in her womb.

In the human world which he regained, he was born endowed with the faculty of recalling previous existences. Exercising this faculty, he went over the past four existences and was greatly distressed when he came to know that they were all terminated at the instance of his former wife. "What an irony to have taken rebirth in the womb of such an enemy" he lamented.

He would not let his mother, the enemy, touch him. Whenever the mother tried to hold him, the baby cried out vociferously. So the grandfather had to take over the task of bringing up the child. When the child reached the age when he could speak, the grandfather asked him, "My dear child, why do you cry out when your mother tries to hold you?" "This woman is no mother to me. She is my enemy who killed me off for four successive existences." So saying, he recounted to his grandfather the story of his previous lives. On hearing this sad tale, the old man wept, embracing the child and said, "Come, my poor grandchild, let us get away. I see no gain in staying here." They went away and stayed in a monastery where both of them received ordination and in time, through practise of meditation, were able to attain Arahatta path and fruition and gained Arahatship.

The moral to be drawn from this episode is that attachment gives rise to repeated existence at the very location of that attachment. This story clearly bears out the truth of the teaching, "attachment brings about fresh existences." But after the existences of a snake, a dog and a calf, meeting violent death in each, in the last life as a human being, when he attained Arahatship, the craving was completely extinguished. There would be no more rebirth for him, and he would be free from all forms of suffering. It would be well to take to heart the moral of this story and strive for freedom from all suffering through the practise of *vipassanā*.

The Training of the Heart

A talk given to a group of Western Monks from Wat Bovornives, Bangkok, March 1977

Ajahn Chah

Bodhi Leaves No. 107

First published: 1986

The Training of the Heart

In the time of Ajahn Mun and Ajahn Sao[27] life was a lot simpler, a lot less complicated than it is today. In those days monks had few duties and ceremonies to perform. They lived in the forests without permanent resting places. There they could devote themselves entirely to the practise of meditation.

In those times one rarely encountered the luxuries that are so commonplace today, there simply weren't any. One had to make drinking cups and spittoons out of bamboo and lay people seldom came to visit. One didn't want or expect much and was content with what one had. One could live and breathe meditation!

The monks suffered many privations living like this. If someone caught malaria and went to ask for medicine, the teacher would say, "You don't need medicine! Keep practicing". Besides, there simply weren't all the drugs that are available now. All one had were the herbs and roots that grew in the forest. The environment was such that monks had to have a great deal of patience and endurance; they didn't bother over minor ailments. Nowadays you get a bit of an ache and you're off to the hospital!

Sometimes one had to walk ten to twelve kilometres on almsround. You would leave as soon as it was light and maybe return around ten or eleven o'clock. One didn't get very much either, perhaps some glutinous rice, salt or a few chillies. Whether you got anything to eat with the rice or not didn't matter. That's the way it was.

---

27 Ajahn Mun was probably the most respected and most influential meditation master of the 20th century in Thailand. Under his guidance the ascetic forest tradition (*dhutaṅga kammaṭṭhāna*) became a very important tradition in the revival of Buddhist meditation practise. The vast majority of recently deceased and presently living great meditation masters of Thailand are either direct disciples of the Venerable Ajahn or were substantially influenced by his teachings. Ajahn Mun passed away in November 1949. Ajahn Sao was Ajahn Mun's teacher.

No one dared complain of hunger or fatigue; they were just not inclined to complain but learned to take care of themselves. They practised in the forest with patience and endurance alongside the many dangers that lurked in the surroundings. There were many wild and fierce animals living in the jungles and there were many hardships for body and mind in the ascetic practise of the *dhutaṅga* or forest-dwelling monk. Indeed, the patience and endurance of the monks in those days was excellent because the circumstances compelled them to be so.

In the present day, circumstances compel us in the opposite direction. In ancient times, one had to travel by foot; then came the oxcart and then the automobile. Aspiration and ambition increased, so that now, if the car is not air-conditioned, one will not even sit in it; impossible to go if there is no air-conditioning! The virtues of patience and endurance are becoming weaker and weaker. The standards for meditation and practise are lax and getting laxer, until we find that meditators these days like to follow their own opinions and desires. When the old folks talk about the old days, it's like listening to a myth or a legend. You just listen indifferently, but you don't understand. It just doesn't reach you!

As far as we should be concerned about the ancient monks' tradition, a monk should spend at least five years with his teacher. Some days you should avoid speaking to anyone. Don't allow yourself to speak or talk very much. Don't read books! Read your own heart[28] instead. Take Wat Pah Pong for example. These days many university graduates are coming to ordain. I try to stop them from spending their time reading books about Dhamma,[29] because these people are always reading books. They have so many opportunities for reading books, but opportunities for reading their own hearts are rare. So, when they come to ordain for three months following the Thai custom, we try to get them to close their books and manuals. While they are ordained they have this splendid opportunity to read their own hearts.

---

28 In this translation heart is used where mind, *citta*, is normally used in other translations.

29 Dhamma and *dhamma*: please note the various meanings of the words "Dhamma" (the liberating law discovered and proclaimed by the Buddha), and "*dhamma*" (any quality thing, object of mind and/or any conditioned or unconditioned phenomena).

Listening to your own heart is really very interesting. This untrained heart races around following its own untrained habits. It jumps about excitedly, randomly, because it has never been trained. Therefore train your heart! Buddhist meditation is about the heart; to develop the heart or mind, to develop your own heart. This is very, very important. This training of the heart is the main emphasis. Buddhism is the religion of the heart. Only this! One who practises to develop the heart is one who practises Buddhism.

This heart of ours lives in a cage, and what's more, there's a raging tiger in that cage. If this maverick heart of ours doesn't get what it wants, it makes trouble. You must discipline it with meditation, with *samādhi*. This is called "Training the Heart". At the very beginning, the foundation of practise is the establishment of moral discipline (sîla). Sîla is the training of the body and speech. From this arises conflict and confusion. When you don't let yourself do what you want to do, there is conflict.

Eat little! Sleep little! Speak little! Whatever it may be of worldly habit, lessen them, go against their power. Don't just do as you like, don't indulge in your thought. Stop this slavish following. You must constantly go against the stream of ignorance. This is called "discipline". When you discipline your heart, it becomes very dissatisfied and begins to struggle. It becomes restricted and oppressed. When the heart is prevented from doing what it wants to do, it starts wandering and struggling. Suffering (*dukkha*)[30] becomes apparent to us.

This *dukkha*, this suffering, is the first of the four noble truths. Most people want to get away from it. They don't want to have any kind of suffering at all. Actually, this suffering is what brings us wisdom; it makes us contemplate *dukkha*. Happiness (*sukha*) tends to make us close our eyes and ears. It never allows us to develop patience. Comfort and happiness make us careless. Of

30 *Dukkha*: refers to the implicit unsatisfactoriness, incompleteness, imperfection, insecurity of all conditioned phenomena, which, because they are always changing, are always liable to cause suffering. *Dukkha* refers to all forms of unpleasantness from gross bodily pains and the suffering implicit in old age, sickness and death, to subtle feelings such as being parted from what we like or associated with what we dislike, to refined mental states such as dullness, boredom, restlessness, agitation, etc. This is one of the most important concepts for spiritual development.

these two defilements, Dukkha is the easiest to see. Therefore we must bring up suffering in order to put an end to our suffering. We must first know what *dukkha* is before we can know how to practise meditation.

In the beginning you have to train your heart like this. You may not understand what is happening or what the point of it is, but when the teacher tells you to do something, then you must do it. You will develop the virtues of patience and endurance. Whatever happens, you endure, because that is the way it is. For example, when you begin to practise *samādhi* you want peace and tranquillity. But you don't get any. You don't get any because you have never practised this way. Your heart says, "I'll sit until I attain tranquillity". But when tranquillity doesn't arise, you suffer. And when there is suffering, you get up and run away! To practise like this can not be called "developing the heart". It's called "desertion".

Instead of indulging in your moods, you train yourself with the Dhamma of the Buddha. Lazy or diligent, you just keep on practicing. Don't you think that this is a better way? The other way, the way of following your moods, will never reach the Dhamma. If you practise the Dhamma, then whatever the mood may be, you keep on practicing, constantly practicing. The other way of selfindulgence is not the way of the Buddha. When we follow our own views on practise, our own opinions about the Dhamma, we can never see clearly what is right and what is wrong. We don't know our own heart. We don't know ourselves.

Therefore, to practise following your own teachings is the slowest way. To practise following the Dhamma is the direct way. Lazy you practise; diligent you practise. You are aware of time and place. This is called "developing the heart".

If you indulge in following your own views and try to practise accordingly, then you will start thinking and doubting a lot. You think to yourself, "I don't have very much merit. I don't have any luck. I've been practising meditation for years now and I'm still unenlightened. I still haven't seen the Dhamma". To practise with this kind of attitude can not be called "developing the heart". It is called "developing disaster".

If, at this time, you are like this, if you are a meditator who still doesn't know, who doesn't see, if you haven't renewed yourself yet, it's because you've been practising wrongly. You haven't been following the teachings of the Buddha. The Buddha taught like this: "Ānanda, practise a lot! Develop your practise constantly! Then all your doubts, all your uncertainties, will vanish". These doubts will never vanish through thinking, nor through theorising, nor through speculation, nor through discussion. Nor will doubts disappear by not doing anything. All defilements will vanish through developing the heart, through right practise only.

The way of developing the heart as taught by the Buddha is the exact opposite of the way of the world, because his teachings come from a pure heart. A pure heart, unattached to defilements, is the Way of the Buddha and his disciples.

If you practise the Dhamma, you must bow your heart to the Dhamma. You must not make the Dhamma bow to you. When you practise this way suffering arises. There isn't a single person who can escape this suffering. So when you commence your practise suffering is right there.

The duties of meditators are mindfulness, collectedness and contentment. These things stop us. They stop the habits of the hearts of those who have never trained. And why should we bother to do this? If you don't bother to train your heart, then it remains wild, following the ways of nature. It's possible to train that nature so that it can be used to advantage. This is comparable to the example of trees. If we just left trees in their natural state, then we would never be able to build a house with them. We couldn't make planks or anything of use in building a house. However, if a carpenter came along wanting to build a house, he would go looking for trees such as these. He would take this raw material and use it to advantage. In a short time he could have a house built.

Meditation and developing the heart are similar to this. You must take this untrained heart, the same as you would take a tree in its natural state in the forest, and train this natural heart so that it is more refined, so that it's more aware of itself and is more sensitive. Everything is in its natural state. When we understand nature, then we can change it, we can detach from it, we can let go of it. Then we won't suffer anymore.

The nature of our heart is such that whenever it clings and grasps there is agitation and confusion. First it might wander over there, then it might wander over here. When we come to observe this agitation, we might think that it's impossible to train the heart and so we suffer accordingly. We don't understand that this is the way the heart is. There will be thought and feelings moving about like this even though we are practicing, trying to attain peace. That's the way it is.

When we have contemplated many times the nature of the heart, then we will come to understand that this heart is just as it is and can't be otherwise. We will know that the heart's ways are just as they are. That's its nature. If we see this clearly, then we can detach from thoughts and feelings. And we don't have to add on anything more by constantly having to tell ourselves that "that's just the way it is". When the heart truly understands, it lets go of everything. Thinking and feeling will still be there, but that very thinking and feeling will be deprived of power.

This is similar to a child who likes to play and frolic in ways that annoy us, to the extent that we scold or spank him. We should understand that it's natural for a child to act that way. Then we could let go and leave him to play in his own way. So our troubles are over. How are they over? Because we accept the ways of children. Our outlook changes and we accept the true nature of things. We let go and our heart becomes more peaceful. We have "right understanding".

If we have wrong understanding, then even living in a deep, dark cave would be chaos, or living high up in the air would be chaos. The heart can only be at peace when there is "right understanding". Then there are no more riddles to solve and no more problems to arise.

This is the way it is. You detach. You let go. Whenever there is any feeling of clinging, we detach from it, because we know that that very feeling is just as it is. It didn't come along especially to annoy us. We might think that it did, but in truth it is just that way. If we start to think and consider it further, that too, is just as it is. If we let go, then form is merely form, sound is merely sound, odour is merely odour, taste is merely taste, touch is merely touch and the heart is merely the heart. It's similar to oil and water. If you put the two together in a bottle, they won't mix because of the difference in their nature.

Oil and water are different in the same way that a wise man and an ignorant man are different. The Buddha lived with form, sound, odour, taste, touch and thought. He was an *arahat* (enlightened one), so He turned away from rather than toward these things. He turned away and detached little by little since He understood that the heart is just the heart and thought is just thought. He didn't confuse and mix them together.

The heart is just the heart; thoughts and feelings are just thoughts and feelings. Let things be just as they are! Let form be just form, let sound be just sound, let thought be just thought. Why should we bother to attach to them? If we think and feel in this way, then there is detachment and separateness. Our thoughts and feelings will be on one side and our heart will be on the other. Just like oil and water—they are in the same bottle but they are separate.

The Buddha and his enlightened disciples lived with ordinary, unenlightened people. They not only lived with these people, but they taught these ordinary, unenlightened, ignorant ones how to be noble, enlightened, wise ones. They could do this because they knew how to practise. They knew that it's a matter of the heart, just as I have explained.

So, as far as your practise of meditation goes, don't bother to doubt it. If we run away from home to ordain, it's not running away to get lost in delusion. Nor out of cowardice or fear. It's running away in order to train ourselves, in order to master ourselves. If we have understanding like this, then we can follow the Dhamma. The Dhamma will become clearer and clearer. The one who understands the Dhamma, understands himself; and the one who understands himself, understands the Dhamma. Nowadays, only the sterile remains of the Dhamma have become the accepted order. In reality, the Dhamma is everywhere. There is no need to escape to somewhere else. Instead escape through wisdom. Escape through intelligence. Escape through skill don't escape through ignorance. If you want peace, then let it be the peace of wisdom. That's enough!

Whenever we see the Dhamma, then there is the right way, the right path. Defilements are just defilements, the heart is just the heart. Whenever we detach and separate so that there are just these things as they really are, then they are merely objects to us. When we are on the right path, then we are impeccable. When we are impeccable, there is openness and freedom all the time.

The Buddha said, "Listen to me, Monks. You must not cling to any dhammas". What are these dhammas? They are everything; there isn't anything which is not dhamma. Love and hate are dhammas, happiness and suffering are dhammas, like and dislike are dhammas; all of these things, no matter how insignificant, are dhammas. When we practise the Dhamma, when we understand, then we can let go. And thus we can comply with the Buddha's teaching of not clinging to any dhammas.

All conditions that are born in our heart, all conditions of our mind, all conditions of our body, are always in a state of change. The Buddha taught not to cling to any of them. He taught his disciples to practise in order to detach from all conditions and not to practise in order to attain to any more.

If we follow the teachings of the Buddha, then we are right. We are right but it is also troublesome. It's not that the teachings are troublesome, but it's our defilements which are troublesome. The defilements wrongly comprehended obstruct us and cause us trouble. There isn't really anything troublesome with following the Buddha's teaching. In fact we can say that clinging to the path of the Buddha doesn't bring suffering, because the path is simply "let go" of every single dhamma!

For the ultimate in the practise of Buddhist meditation, the Buddha taught the practise of "letting go". Don't carry anything around! Detach! If you see goodness, let it go. If you see rightness, let it go. These words, "let go", do not mean that we don't have to practise. It means that we have to practise following the method of "letting go" itself. The Buddha taught us to contemplate all dhammas, to develop the path through contemplating our own body and heart.

The Dhamma isn't anywhere else. It's right here! Not someplace far away. It's right here in this very body and heart of ours.

Therefore a meditator must practise with energy. Make the heart grander and brighter. Make it free and independent. Having done a good deed, don't carry it around in your heart, let it go. Having refrained from doing an evil deed, let it go. The Buddha taught us to live in the immediacy of the present, in the here and now. Don't lose yourself in the past or the future.

The teaching that people least understand and which conflicts the most with their own opinions, is this teaching of "letting go" or "working with an empty mind". This way of talking is called "Dhamma language". When we conceive this in worldly terms, we become confused and think that we can do anything we want. It can be interpreted this way, but its real meaning is closer to this: It's as if we are carrying a heavy rock. After a while we begin to feel its weight but we don't know how to let it go. So we endure this heavy burden all the time. If someone tells us to throw it away, we say, "If I throw it away, I won't have anything left!" If told of all the benefits to be gained from throwing it away, we wouldn't believe them but would keep thinking, "If I throw it away, I will have nothing!" So we keep on carrying this heavy rock until we become so weak and exhausted that we can no longer endure, then we drop it.

Having dropped it, we suddenly experience the benefits of letting go. We immediately feel better and lighter and we know for ourselves how much of a burden carrying a rock can be. Before we let go of the rock, we couldn't possibly know the benefits of letting go. So if someone tells us to let go, an unenlightened man wouldn't see the purpose of it. He would just blindly clutch at the rock and refuse to let go until it became so unbearably heavy that he just had to let go. Then he can feel for himself the lightness and relief and thus know for himself the benefits of letting go. Later on we may start carrying burdens again, but now we know what the results will be, so we can now let go more easily. This understanding that it's useless to carry burdens around and that letting go brings ease and lightness is an example of knowing ourselves.

Our pride, our sense of self that we depend on, is the same as that heavy rock. Like that rock, if we think about letting go of selfconceit, we are afraid that without it, there would be nothing left. But when we can finally let it go, we realise for ourselves the ease and comfort of not clinging.

In the training of the heart, you mustn't cling to either praise or blame. To just want praise and not to want blame is the way of the world. The Way of the Buddha is to accept praise when it is appropriate and to accept blame when it is appropriate. For example, in raising a child it's very good not to just scold all the time. Some people scold too much. A wise person knows the proper time to scold and the proper time to praise. Our heart is the same. Use intelligence to know the heart. Use skill in taking care of your heart. Then you will be one who is clever in the training of the heart. And when the heart is skilled, it can rid us of our suffering. Suffering exists right here in our hearts. It's always complicating things, creating and making the heart heavy. It's born here. It also dies here.

The way of the heart is like this. Sometimes there are good thoughts, sometimes there are bad thoughts. The heart is deceitful. Don't trust it! Instead look straight at the conditions of the heart itself. Accept them as they are. They're just as they are. Whether it's good or evil or whatever, that's the way it is. If you don't grab hold of these conditions, then they don't become anything more or less than what they already are. If we grab hold we'll get bitten and will then suffer.

With "right view" there's only peace. Samādhi is born and wisdom takes over. Wherever you may sit or lie down, there is peace. There is peace everywhere, no matter where you may go.

So today you have brought your disciples here to listen to the Dhamma. You may understand some of it, some of it you may not. In order for you to understand more easily, I've talked about the practise of meditation. Whether you think it is right or not, you should take and contemplate it.

As a teacher myself, I've been in a similar predicament. I, too, have longed to listen to Dhamma talks because, wherever I went, I was giving talks to others but never had a chance to listen. So, at this time, you really appreciate listening to a talk from a teacher. Time passes by so quickly when you're sitting and listening quietly.

You're hungry for Dhamma so you really want to listen. At first, giving talks to others is a pleasure, but after awhile, the pleasure is gone. You feel bored and tired. Then you want to listen. So when you listen to a talk from a teacher, you feel much inspiration and you understand easily. When you are getting old and there's hunger for Dhamma, its flavour is especially delicious.

Being a teacher of others you are an example to them, you're a model for other *bhikkhus*. You're an example to your disciples. You're an example to everybody, so don't forget yourself. But don't think about yourself either. If such thoughts do arise, get rid of them. If you do this then you will be one who knows himself.

There are a million ways to practise Dhamma. There's no end to the things that can be said about meditation. There are so many things that can make us doubt. Just keep sweeping them out, then there's no more doubt! When we have right understanding like this, no matter where we sit or walk, there is peace and ease. Wherever we may meditate, that's the place you bring your awareness. Don't hold that one only meditates while sitting or walking. Everything and everywhere is our practise. There's awareness all the time. There is mindfulness all the time. We can see birth and death of mind and body all the time and we don't let it clutter our hearts. Let it go constantly. If love comes, let it go back to its home. If greed comes, let it go home. If anger comes, let it go home. Follow them! Where do they live? Then escort them there. Don't keep anything. If you practise like this then you are like an empty house. Or, explained another way, this is an empty heart, a heart empty and free of all evil. We call it an "empty heart", but it isn't empty as if there was nothing, it's empty of evil but filled with wisdom. Then whatever you do, you'll do with wisdom. You'll think with wisdom. You'll eat with wisdom. There will only be wisdom.

This is the teaching for today and I offer it to you. I've recorded it on tape. If listening to Dhamma makes your heart at peace, that's good enough. You don't need to remember anything. Some may not believe this. If we make our heart peaceful and just listen, letting it pass by but contemplating continuously like this, then we're like a tape recorder. After some time when we turn on, everything is there. Have no fear that there won't be anything. As soon as you turn on your tape recorder, everything is there.

I wish to offer this to every *bhikkhu* and to everyone. Some of you probably know only a little Thai, but that doesn't matter. May you learn the language of the Dhamma. That's good enough!

Aggression, War, and Conflict

Three Essays

Bhikkhu Khantipālo

Bodhi Leaves No. 108

First published: 1986

Dealing with Aggression

Aggression is rampant almost everywhere nowadays, sometimes in its legal and approved form and increasingly in illegal activities. Where it is approved, it may be called "getting on in the world," that is, stepping on others' heads so that you can get to the top. This is success in a worldly sense, but not in a Buddhist one. It is also approved of for men (though not by them for women!) as being a mark of mastery and virility, yet it will never bring happiness. For if people are mastered forcibly, then how will happiness follow for the one who inflicts suffering? The rationale is that "progress," that materialistic god so widely worshipped, will not come about unless force and power are used. But this argument does not take into account the fact that, sooner or later, what is won by aggression will surely be lost through conflict.

When has aggression ever achieved any permanent results? The empires of the world have all been built on aggression. Their founders and rulers were all sure that they would last till the end of time, but all are now like the ruins of Ozymandias. Where is the Thousand-Year Reich of the Nazis now? On the other hand, the non-violent teaching of the Buddha, the king of Dhamma, has outlasted them all. Force leads to counter-force and violence to more violence, but the practise of Dhamma has no harmful backlash. Dhamma well-practised leads only to more peace, contentment and happiness.

What does the Buddha say about aggression?

Here are some verses from the Dhammapada:

> Though a thousand times a thousand
> in battle one may conquer,
> yet should one conquer just oneself
> one is the greatest conqueror.

Greater the conquest of oneself
than subjugating others,
that one who's tamed of self
whose conduct is ever well-restrained.

Neither deva nor minstrel divine,
nor Māra together with Brahma,
can overthrow the victory
of such a one as this.

Victory gives birth to hate,
in misery the defeated dwell: happily the peaceful dwell
having abandoned victory and defeat.

(103–105, 201)

Let us consider these verses and see how we can train our aggressive impulses into the way of peace. "A thousand times a thousand (men)" the Buddha says. That is a large number to conquer, but he did not think it at all worthwhile. They may be prisoners and conquered by us, but we are still the prisoners of our own greed, hate, and delusion. When there is conflict in the mind, an internal battle between what I know I should do and what, guided by those unwholesome motives, I actually do, then the unwholesome motives are the conquerors! If they conquer us, then what have we achieved by mastering so many others when we are not even our own masters?

Of course the battlefield is only one place of conflict, only one arena where aggression is let loose. Our "battlefield" may be in the home or at work. We do not have to go as far as slaying others, but even if the slaying is confined to verbal attack's, that is bad enough: we still create unwholesome karma. Our aggression may be limited in its range to one or two people, or it may affect thousands or even millions, but either way we still have to master ourselves.

The Buddha says:

Oneself is master of oneself,
who else indeed could master be?
By the good training of oneself
one gains a master hard to gain.

Dhammapada 160

No one else, human or divine, can be the master of oneself: each person has to train his own aggression into peacefulness. Even if one has a meditation master to guide one, it is still necessary to do the work oneself. He cannot do it for you!

There must be a change in direction: the conquest of self instead of conquering others. It is a change that involves looking closely at oneself and one's motivations. We should first see clearly the dangers in the conquest of others. Several dangers are mentioned by the Buddha in these verses. The victor has his false "glory" to indulge in, but what is this except food for pride and conceit? Intoxicated by conquest and drunk with pride, such people are surely heading for a fall. This is the most obvious danger for the victor. The dangers for the conquered are different. "In misery the defeated dwell" and because of this they will develop strong resentment. Nourishing that resentment by mentally and verbally reviewing the past defeats, they plan revenge. Then, with the combination of resentment and revenge, hatred will never cease.

Examples of this cycle of hatred are all too common in human society. In the sphere of international relations there are many glaring cases, particularly of hatreds kept alive through many generations among people of opposing religions and racial groups: the enmity that breaks out from time to time among Hindus and Muslims in India, the hostility of Protestants and Catholics in Northern Ireland, the power struggles between Christians and Muslims on Cyprus and in Lebanon. Buddhists would say that by storing up such hatred and keeping it alive, there will be a strong tendency to be reborn in that same aggressive situation, life after life. Some people do learn, but so many learn very slowly.

In smaller units of society, particularly where the Dhamma is practised, there ought to be no victors and no defeated. Such communities would be governed by consensus rather than by the vote of a majority. No one has cause to feel defeated when decisions are arrived at after patiently talking them over, discussing them thoroughly, and deciding to take action only when everyone agrees. This procedure involves letting go of self, an amiable spirit of compromise, and a willingness not to force one's own viewpoint. This accord is possible where people practise Dhamma, but it would be difficult for it to work elsewhere. Those in the majority have to compromise with the minority, and the minority in turn have to agree to modify their ideas in keeping with the majority. Consensus is, in fact, the way the Sangha (the Order of Buddhist monks and nuns) conducts its formal affairs. It is known that a consensus has been reached by the silence of all who are present.

The individual who tries only to conquer himself should not suffer because of that change in direction. He will not suffer if he acts skilfully in accordance with the Dhamma, but when the methods of the Dhamma are not known, there may be self-inflicted wounds. This is sure to happen if one takes "the conquest of oneself" to be an internal battle. The mind will be the battlefield, but who will be the combatants? There is only one person, not two. It is not "me fighting my mind" although that is the way many people go about it. When they act in such a way, much suffering must result from the internal battle. The conquest of oneself comes about naturally, first by using mindfulness and second, loving kindness. No force is used with mindfulness so no suppression is involved, while the practise of loving kindness dissolves the accumulated aggression and resentment.

There are various methods for arriving at peace. The worst way of attempting to bring about peace is by aggression or force, for a peace maintained by fear will not endure. Only slightly better is the peace that results from trickery, but that too collapses as soon as the fraud is revealed. Then there is the kind of peace established by negotiation, treaty, rule and law. This has some chance of enduring while the different people involved agree to keep their own parts in it. However, since in any society many people do not practise the Dhamma very much, various penalties must be imposed for breaking this peace.

The peace that exists on the basis of Dhamma-practice is much more secure because Dhamma upholds the principle of nonharming. This is how peace comes about. The more that the Dhamma is practised, the more peace there will be. For when could virtue, meditation, and penetrative wisdom ever lead to war or conflict?

But there is a higher peace even than this, which depends for its existence on continual practise. When that practise has reached the point where all the defilements of greed, hatred, and delusion have disappeared, what cause for conflict will remain? It is such people the Buddha calls "the Peaceful." The peace won through freedom from defilements is called Enlightenment or Nibbāna. It is the only secure way of having peace within oneself as there is nothing to cause war. It was of a person who has reached this peace that the Buddha said:

> Abandoning likes and dislikes too,
> become quite cool and assetless,
> hero, the all-worlds-conqueror
> that one I call a Brāhmaṇa.

Dhammapada 418

War and Peace

The Sutta:

King Ajātasattu of Magadha, son of Princess Vedehī, mustered a fourfold army[31] against King Pasenadi of Kosala and attacked Kāsi. When King Pasenadi heard that King Ajātasattu had mustered an army and had attacked Kāsi, he mustered a fourfold army against King Ajātasattu and marched to Kāsi. The two kings battled and King Ajātasattu was the victor. Defeated, King Pasenadi retreated to his royal capital, Sāvatthī.

At that time, in the morning, many *bhikkhus* took their bowls and robes and went into Sāvatthī on alms round. Having walked for alms there, after their meal they returned and approached the Lord. Having done so, they respectfully saluted him and sat down, and told the Lord about this matter.

(He said to them:) "King Ajātasattu of Magadha is one who has evil friendships, evil companionship, evil comrades, while King Pasenadi of Kosala is one who has good friendships, good companionship, and good comrades. But today King Pasenadi will pass this night in misery (*dukkha*) because he has been defeated.

> "Victory gives birth to hate,
> in misery the defeated dwell
> happily the peaceful dwell
> having abandoned victory and defeat."

31 Elephants, cavalry chariots and infantry

Again King Ajātasattu mustered a fourfold army against King Pasenadi and attacked Kāsi. This time though, King Pasenadi was the victor and he captured King Ajātasattu.

King Pasenadi then thought: "How is it that although this King Ajātasattu is my nephew, he is treacherous to me while I am not treacherous to him? Suppose I take away all his elephants, cavalry, chariots and infantry, and leave him only his life?" So that is what he did.

The *bhikkhus* on alms round learned about this and later informed the Lord about it all.

Then the Lord, knowing the meaning of it at that time, spoke these verses:

"A person may plunder
so long as it serves his ends,
but when by others he is plundered
he plunders them in turn.
'Now's the hour' thinks the fool
so long as the evil is unripe,
but when the evil ripens up,
then to the fool comes suffering.[32]

One who kills, a killer gets,
the victor, one who conquers him,
the insulter is insulted,
the angry one gets one angrier still.
So by the turn of *kamma*'s wheel
the plunderer is plundered."

Related (Saṃyutta) Collection 3, 14–15

Comments:

The Buddha could not dissuade King Ajātasattu from his campaigns against old King Pasenadi because the former had allied himself with Devadatta, the Buddha's cousin. Devadatta had advised his royal supporter to kill his own father, King Bimbisara, while he in turn was aided by the king in his plot to

32 Very strong words to speak about a king! The Buddha could do so because the king was a devoted supporter and his words are obviously true.

murder the Buddha. Ajātasattu did not dare approach the Buddha until the last few years of the Teacher's life, and thus the Buddha had no influence upon him. Because of the king's friendship with Devadatta, he is spoken of in the discourse as "one with evil friendships, evil companionship, evil comrades;" he had no influence of the Dhamma to lighten the dark burden of his crimes. Even when Ajātasattu did pluck up courage and go to see the Buddha, he was so tortured by remorse that he could not fully comprehend the Buddha's discourse. It should be noted, in view of the Buddha's words, "So by the turn of *kamma*'s wheel the plunderer is plundered," that Ajātasattu, the parricide, was murdered by his own son, Udayibhadda.

The uselessness of war as a way of solving conflicts is summed up in the last two lines of the verse. The Buddha saw how fruitless would be Pasenadi's action in confiscating the army of his troublesome nephew. The effect that it had was to harden Ajātasattu's resolve to conquer Kosala, which he did eventually do. In our times the huge reparations demanded of Germany after the First World War is another good example—our revenge is followed by their revenge as seen in Hitler and the Second World War. Patterns of wars and revenge for wars, as seen in the past with England and Scotland, or between the former with France—and more recently between Greece and Turkey, Arabs and Israel, Pakistan and India—never solve anything, but only exacerbate the bias and tension to provoke new trouble.

The Buddha says that it is not only in the sphere of international politics that these troubles are found, and he might actually have had Ajātasattu in mind when he said, "One who kills, a killer gets," but that is the principle followed by gangsters through the ages. As to victory, that need not involve troops, just the feuding and fighting that goes on in homes and workplaces everywhere; for if one rejoices in victory over a rival, then sooner or later one is sure to be depressed by defeat. And is it not always the case that insulters are insulted? If, of course, they are powerful, the counter-insult takes place only behind their backs, but insults always come back to the one who mouthed them. Anger does not succeed either, because the bully who is accustomed to get his way by anger will surely meet up with someone angrier who can bully him into submission. So wars, of whatever extent and duration, never bear good fruit.

How is it then that they still go on? This is because wars are the exteriorization of the greed, hatred, and delusion in our hearts. If these three defilements were absent, war would cease. But since not many people are willing to lessen the power these three unwholesome roots hold over their own hearts, the wars continue.

Greed has its part in wars, as when there is the desire to plunder and pillage or when territorial gain is the motive. How foolish all this appears when we compare the evanescent states and empires of this world with the Reign of Dhamma which has lasted now for more than 2,500 years. What is gained by greedy grabbing is lost quite quickly too—this is the way of all the world's countries and their "possessions." But the Reign of Dhamma does not depend upon greed: it teaches people to give up, let go, renounce and not be aggressive, so it lasts for a long time.

As for hatred, its part in war is also well known: the enemy is always evil and there can hardly be any higher good than in killing him. This attitude takes no account of the fact that most enemies are both as good and as evil as we are ourselves—in fact, as ordinary as we are. Still they have to be hated, otherwise a "successful" war could not be waged. The actual killing, of course, usually involves hatred, particularly when it is hand-to-hand combat. Modern pushbutton warfare, where the target may not even be visible, involves less manifest hate, though some aversion must be present for without hatred the buttons are not going to be pressed.

Delusion is not usually thought of as a factor in war, though it is a powerful cause. Delusion appears as the assumption that war will be the way to end some unpleasant situation. We have all heard of the "war to end all wars" or even of "fighting for peace," but all such notions are heavily deluded. Wars bring more wars and peace cannot be attained by fighting for it, nor even by threatening others. For through fear and threats only a rough and unstable peace can be achieved, and that not for long. In our days the idea that peace (what sort of peace indeed?) can be maintained by keeping up with the other side, balancing our nuclear weapons with theirs, is truly a delusion. Force won't keep peace! Notice also how the nuclear powers are unwilling to do the very thing that would lead to peace: to start dismantling these terrible weapons.

Though humanity has had a long and bloody history of wars, we do not learn from the past at all, it seems, but keep repeating those mistakes in ever more disastrous ways. The wise words of the Buddha and other great teachers of peace have been around for a long time, but the thick delusion of so many people still stirs them to "right" wrongs by means of war.

The Buddha himself prevented one war between his relatives the Sakyas and the Koliyas over the waters of the river Rohini. He managed twice to stop his relatives, the Sakyas, from being massacred though even he was not able to prevent the fruition of the evil *kamma* that they had made for themselves. Apart from this, he tirelessly taught people the way to live in peace—in their homes, at work, in society in general and within their own hearts. He had no trace of anger or resentment and taught others how they could also rid themselves of these destructive tendencies. His Dhamma was wholly one of peacefulness of body, speech and mind, and was directed towards finding the great Peace of Nibbāna:

> Of peaceful body peaceful speech,
> peaceful, well-composed of heart,
> having spewed out the world's desires,
> "truly peaceful" that *bhikkhu* is called.
> Peaceful his mind and peaceful
> his speech and action too,
> perfect in knowledge of freedom,
> one "Thus" is of utmost peace.

Dhammapada 378, 96

As the Sangha of *bhikkhu*s has always been the guiding light for Buddhists and for those who want to know about the Dhamma, and as that Sangha in its laws and discipline was instituted as an example of peacefulness, so the history of Buddhism has not been blotted by "religious wars." Actually, this phrase is a contradiction in terms for Buddhists, for the Dhamma as a religious path means peace and loving kindness. For Buddhists, no war can be religious, and if others see that such a thing is possible then there must be very great failings in that religion which allows or condones such a thing. There have been, of course, Buddhist kings in Asia who were greedy for power and fame, and cruel in their territorial ambitions, but they could not claim even one word of support from either the Buddha's words or from good members of the Sangha. No *bhikkhu* would ever praise the virtues of war; he might see the inevitability of conflict and the need to protect his country against aggression, but he would never praise war. He would not count as a good *bhikkhu* if he did so. The Sangha in Buddhist countries is in fact the refuge for pacifists of the best kind, for *bhikkhu*-life involves not harming oneself or others with body, speech and mind. The renunciation of the *bhikkhu* makes such pacifism both practical to one who undertakes it and impressive to others. You really profess peace? All right then, give up the causes of war within yourself! Live a disciplined and compassionate life: this is the best way to bringabout peace.

Settling Conflicts

The Sutta

This happened at Sāvatthī. (The Buddha said:)

"Long ago, monks, a battle was raging between the gods and the demons. Then Vepacitti, lord of the demons, said to Sakka, lord of the gods, 'Let victory be according to the wisdom of speech, O lord of the gods!'

'Let it be so, Vepacitti.'

So the god and the demon arranged their companies, thinking, 'They will judge what is wisely or unwisely spoken.'

Then Vepacitti, lord of the demons, said to Sakka, lord of the gods: 'Chant a verse, O lord of the gods.'

When this was said Sakka replied to Vepacitti, 'You are the older god, Vepacitti. Therefore you should chant a verse.'

At this, Vepacitti spoke as follows:

'Fools become more violent
 if none are there to stop them,

so by heavy punishment
the wise restrain the fool.'

When this was said the demons approved but the gods were silent.

Then Vepacitti said to Sakka: 'Chant a verse, O lord of the gods.' Sakka then spoke as follows:

'But here's the way that I conceive the foolish person
should be stopped: that other's anger having known,
the mindful one is quite allayed.'[33]

When this was said the gods approved but the demons were silent.

Then Sakka said to Vepacitti: "Chant a verse, Vepacitti."

"An error I see, *Vāsava*,[34]
in your forbearance, for the fool
who knows of that then understands
that you forbear from fear of him,
then the idiot will overwhelm you,
as a bull goes faster as you flee."

When this was said the demons approved but the gods were silent.

Then Vepacitti said to Sakka: "Chant a verse, O lord of the gods." Sakka then spoke as follows:

"Let him think as he likes—or not,
that you forbear from fear of him,
It's the means of one's highest good—
what's better than patience is not found.

That one who, being strong indeed,
forbearing always with the weak,
is ever patient with those who're weak:
the highest patience that is called.

Who says the strength of fools is strength[35]
will say the strong one is not strong;

33 "Allayed:" Laid down his own anger, become peaceful.

34 Another name for Sakka.

35 There is punning here, which cannot be reproduced in English, between "*bāla*" strength, strong person; and "*bala*" a fool.

that a strong one, Dhamma-guarded,
is overturned-cannot be!

With one who's angry one is worse
who angered is in turn
but one who pays not back in kind
wins a battle hard to win.

For benefit of both he lives—
for himself and the other one,
knowing the other's anger,
mindful he is, allayed.

He is indeed healer of both—
himself and of the other one
yet people who know not Dhamma
think he is a fool."

When this was said the gods approved but the demons were silent. Then the companies of gods and demons spoke as follows: "The verses spoken by Vepacitti, lord of the demons, are words about force, words about weapons, quarrelling, strife and contention. But the verses spoken by Sakka, lord of the gods, are words about persuasion, words about gentleness, concord, amity and harmony. Sakka, lord of the gods, is by wise speech the victor."

In this way, monks, did Sakka, lord of the gods, by wise speech become the victor."

Related (Saṃyutta) Collection, 11, 5.

Comment:

This discourse is called, "Victory by Speech" and perhaps its message should be introduced to the international conference scene, for by means of it no wars occur and no cannon-fodder is needed, besides which it is perfectly non-violent. However, in the present political climate neither of the major powers would win and there might even be some difficulty in finding a set of suitable judges. How good to win a "war" by such non-violent means! There are some who would say that it is not practical, for the big brass will not be pleased, the weapons contractors will have no work, and thousands will lose their jobs. Moreover, they would argue, powerful enemies will just not agree to such a contest, or if they do, they would not be sincere and would not follow up their words with the appropriate actions.

In fact, these people would probably agree with Vepacitti that the only way to stop fools from becoming more violent is to make it really hard for them, as the threat of vast arms-piling does among countries, or as the prison system does for criminals.

Whether international conflicts are being considered or lawbreakers within one's country, Vepacitti's prescription is "deterrence," rule by fear of punishment. Such a violent method is not consistent with the Buddha's Teachings.

Sakka's reply to Vepaciti points to non-violence as the one effective method to cure aggression. This seems to be most practical in the field of personal relations, where restraint towards an angry person can calm him down, while replying with more anger will only exacerbate the trouble.

Vepacitti's second verse puts the worldly point of view across very well. He is sure that non-violence will only make things worse, not better. As he says, the fools who want to make trouble will be delighted if you take no action against them. They are sure to think that you do nothing because you fear them, and thus they will make matters much worse for you. There is some truth in this, for this is the way that a defiled mind thinks. And it seems to be true that some can only be induced to behave themselves by threats and punishments, though this is usually because better methods have not been tried. Threats on one side produce fear on the other, so the fearful think it right to protect themselves with their own strong-arm tactics. The result is the continuing—indeed, neverending—violence which makes up human history.

Sakka's reply, again couched in terms of personal Dhammapractice, praises patience as a quality that cannot be excelled. Patience is especially characteristic of a person who is both strong and wise, for he will always be patient with those who are weaker— such is the strength of those who practise Dhamma and cannot be overwhelmed. A fool's strength is only his anger and he cannot be called really strong as the Dhamma-practitioner can overcome him.

Sakka notes that if one does not become angry in the presence of an angry person, then it is as though one wins a war. He goes on to point out that such a person is truly compassionate, living both for his own and others' benefit, a healer of both sides. Still, those who do not know Dhamma think that such a non-violent person is a fool. Well, times have changed but not defilements!

The question has been raised whether it is compassionate to allow others to do acts of violence, and whether force or punishment should be employed and then to what extent. Can it not be said that sometimes this is the only thing that fools will take notice of? So compassion, it is argued, should include forceful action. But no such doctrine is included anywhere in the original collections of the Buddha's discourses. Such a doctrine is obviously dangerous, as it can become a useful cover for all sorts of violence. After all, many violent acts can be dressed up as compassion. When violence is deemed necessary, it must not be disguised. Even though apparently necessary, it cannot be called Dhamma-practice, which does not recognise such means.

Means are important if ends are to be attained, but only Dhamma-means will lead to Dhamma-ends. Violent means can never lead there; on the contrary, they only make for more conflict. The idea that the "end justifies the means" can never be held by Buddhists: the means, Dhamma-practice, must be in line with the end, the good results of Dhamma. So if one would have peace—at home, at work, between groups and parties, states and countries— then the means of loving kindness and compassion must be employed.

—§§§—

Positive Response: How to Meet Evil with Good

Acharya Buddharakkhita

Bodhi Leaves No. 109

First published: 1987

Positive Response: How to Meet Evil with Good

Introduction

This essay looks at one of the *sutta*s spoken by the Buddha, preceded by a brief introduction by the translator. The theme of the *sutta*, The Parable of the Saw Kakacūpama Sutta (Majjhima Nikāya 21), may be called a positive response in dealing with provocative people and situations. It sets forth practical techniques for overcoming resentment, hatred and other such pollutants, and for cultivating such elevating mental qualities as good will, amity and compassion. For anyone intent on spiritual development these practical instructions will help to cleanse the mind and to unfold its great hidden potentials.

In the realm of spirituality, 'tit for tat,' very much a norm in the world, never works. It is only by a positive response that spiritual progress is possible. If one is reproached, even manhandled, and one reacts with resentment, one would certainly fail either to achieve a purposive result for oneself or to win over the opponent. But if one endures the reproach and responds with good will, then one can win over the offending person as well as effect a significant triumph over oneself, making progress on the onward path to spiritual liberation. An outlook that fosters a positive response to every negative move thus becomes imperative to any serious seeker of truth. It is essential, therefore, that a meditator should assiduously strive to cultivate a positive attitude leading to the conquest of evil by good.

In the masterly discourse entitled The Parable of the Saw, the Buddha makes this point amply clear. The Buddha exhorts the monk Phagguṇa: "Phagguṇa, if anyone were to reproach you right to your face … give you a blow with the hand, or hit you with a clod of earth, or with a stick, or with a sword, even then you should abandon those urges and thoughts which are worldly [i.e., the normal way of the world—tit for tat]. There, Phagguṇa, you should train yourself thus: 'Neither shall my mind be affected by this, nor shall I give vent to evil words; but I shall remain full of concern and pity, with a mind of love, and I shall not give in to hatred.'"

So that the point will go straight home, the Buddha recounts a delightful story of the mistress Vedehikā, which is again supported by several analogies: the great earth, empty space, the river Ganges, and the cat-skin bag.

To emphasise this philosophy of positive approach, the Buddha further tells the monks that even if bandits were to sever them limb by limb with a double-handled saw, they should not give way to hatred but must develop thoughts of boundless love towards the bandits as well as the entire world.

The monks, it is said, were greatly inspired as they heard this philosophy of positive response.

The Parable of the Saw, *Kakacūpama Sutta*

Thus have I heard.

…"Phagguṇa, if anyone were to reproach you right to your face, even then you should abandon those urges and thoughts which are worldly. There, Phagguṇa, you should train yourself thus: 'Neither shall my mind be affected by this, nor shall I give vent to evil words; but I shall remain full of concern and pity, with a mind of love, and I shall not give in to hatred.' This is how, Phagguṇa, you should train yourself.

"Phagguṇa, if anyone were to give you a blow with the hand, or hit you with a clod of earth, or with a stick, or with a sword, even then you should abandon those urges and thoughts which are worldly. There, Phagguṇa, you should train yourself thus: 'Neither shall my mind be affected by this, nor shall I give vent to evil words; but I shall remain full of concern and pity, with a mind of love, and I shall not give in to hatred.' This is how, Phagguṇa, you should train yourself.

The Story of the Mistress Vedehiká

"In the past, monks, in this very Sāvatthī there was a mistress, Vedehikā by name. And, monks, this good reputation had spread about the mistress Vedehikā: 'The mistress Vedehikā is gentle, the mistress Vedehikā is meek, the mistress Vedehikā is calm.' Now, monks, the mistress Vedehikā had a maid-servant, Kālī by name, who was able, energetic and very methodical in her work. Then, monks, it occurred to Kālī the maid-servant: 'This good reputation has spread about my lady: "The mistress Vedehikā is gentle, the mistress Vedehikā is meek, the mistress Vedehikā is calm." Could it be that my lady does have anger within her which she does not show, or could it be that she does not have anger? Or is it because I am methodical in my job that my lady, though she does have anger within, does not show it, and not because she does not have anger? Why don't I test my lady?'

"Thus, monks, the maid-servant Kālī got up late the next morning. And, monks, the mistress Vedehikā told this to the maidservant Kāli: 'Hey, you Kālī!'—'What is it, lady?'—'Why did you get up so late?'—'Oh, that is nothing, lady.'—'What! That is nothing, indeed! You bad maid-servant, you got up late!' Angry and displeased, she frowned.

"Then, monks, it occurred to Kālī the maid-servant: 'Though she does have anger within, my lady does not show it; it is not that she does not have anger. It is because I am methodical in my job that, though she does have anger within, my lady does not show it, and not because she does not have anger. Why don't I test my lady further?'

"Now, monks, Kālī the maid-servant got up even later than before. Then, monks, the mistress Vedehikā told the maid-servant Kāli: 'Hey, you Kālī!'—'What is it, lady?'—'Why did you get up even later than before?'—'Oh, that is nothing, lady.'—'What! That is nothing, indeed! You bad maid-servant, you got up even later than before!' Angry and displeased, she gave vent to her displeasure.

"Then, monks, it occurred to the maid-servant Kālī: 'Though she does have anger within, my lady does not show it; it is not that she does not have anger. It is because I am methodical in my job that, though she does have anger within, my lady does not show it, and not because she does not have anger. Why don't I test my lady further?'

"And, monks, the maid-servant Kālī got up even later than before. Then, monks, the mistress Vedehikā told the maid-servant Kālī: 'Hey, you Kālī!'—'What is it, lady?'—'Why did you get up so late?'—'Oh, that is nothing, lady.'—'What! That is nothing, indeed! You bad maid-servant, you got up so late!' And angry and displeased, she hit her on the head with the door-bar. And this injured her head.

"Now, monks, the maid-servant Kālī with her head injured and blood oozing, went about among the neighbours, shouting: 'Look, sirs, at the deed of the gentle one! Look, sirs, at the deed of the meek one! Look, sirs, at the deed of the calm one! How can she, saying to her own maid-servant, "You got up late today," angry and displeased, having taken a door-bar, give me a blow on the head and injure my head?'

"And then, monks, this ill-repute spread thereafter about the mistress Vedehikā: 'The mistress Vedehikā is violent, the mistress Vedehikā is arrogant, the mistress Vedehikā is not calm.'

"In the same way, monks, some monk here is very gentle, very meek, and very calm, so long as disagreeable ways of speech do not assail him; but when disagreeable ways of speech do assail the monk, it is then that the monk is to be judged whether he is 'gentle,' 'meek,' or 'calm.' Monks, I do not call that monk 'dutiful' who is dutiful on account of the requisites he gets, i.e., the robe, alms-food, lodging and medicaments, whereby he falls into pseudodutifulness. And why? For, monks, when that monk fails to get the requisites of the robe, alms-food, lodging and medicaments, he ceases to be dutiful, and is not in keeping with the norms of dutifulness. But, monks, whichever monk out of reverence for the Teaching, out of respect for the Teaching, out of dedication to the Teaching, showing honour to the Teaching, and giving regard to the Teaching, comes to be dutiful and is in keeping with the norms of dutifulness, him do I consider as dutiful. Therefore, monks, you should consider: 'Only out of reverence for the Teaching, out of respect for the Teaching, out of dedication to the Teaching, showing honour to the Teaching, and giving regard to the Teaching, shall we become dutiful, shall we be in keeping with the norms of dutifulness.' Thus, indeed, monks, you should train yourselves.

Positive Response of Love

"Monks, there are these five modes of speech which people might use when speaking to you: speech that is timely or untimely, true or false, gentle or harsh, with a good or a harmful motive, and with a loving heart or hostility.

"Monks, some might speak to you using speech that is timely or untimely; monks, some might speak to you according to truth or falsely; monks, some might speak to you gently or harshly; monks, some might speak to you with a good motive or with a harmful motive; monks, some might speak to you with a loving heart or with hostility. On all occasions, monks, you should train yourselves thus: 'Neither shall our minds be affected by this, nor for this matter shall we give vent to evil words, but we shall remain full of concern and pity, with a mind of love, and we shall not give in to hatred. On the contrary, we shall live projecting thoughts of universal love to that very person, making him as well as the whole world the object of our thoughts of universal love—thoughts that have grown great, exalted and measureless. We shall dwell radiating these thoughts which are void of hostility and ill will.' It is in this way, monks, that you should train yourselves.

The Great Earth

"Suppose, monks, a person were to come to you, holding a hoe and a basket and he were to say: 'I shall make this great earth earthless.' Then he would strew the earth here and there, spit here and there, and urinate here and there, and would say:' 'Be earthless, be earthless.' What do you think, monks, would this person render this great earth earthless?"

"No, indeed not, most venerable sir."

"And why?"

"Because this great earth, most venerable sir, is deep and without measure. It cannot possibly be turned earthless. On the contrary, that person would only reap weariness and frustration."

"In the same way, monks, others may use these five modes of speech when speaking to you—speech that is timely or untimely, true or false, gentle or harsh, with a good or a harmful motive, and with a loving heart or hostility. In this way, monks, you should train yourselves: 'Neither shall our minds be affected by this, nor for this matter shall we give vent to evil words, but we shall remain full of concern and pity, with a mind of love, and we shall not give in to hatred. On the contrary, we shall live projecting thoughts of universal love to that very person, making him as well as the whole world the object of our thoughts of universal love—thoughts that have grown great, exalted and measureless. We shall dwell radiating these thoughts which are void of hostility and ill will.' It is in this way, monks, that you should train yourselves.

Empty Space

"Suppose, monks, a person were to approach you, carrying paints of lacquer, turmeric, indigo or carmine, and he were to say: 'I will draw this picture, I will make this painting appear on this empty space.' What do you think, monks, could he make this painting appear on empty space?"

"No, indeed not, most venerable sir."

"And why not?"

"Because this empty space, most venerable sir, is formless and invisible. He cannot possibly draw a picture or make a painting appear on this empty space. On the contrary, that person will only reap weariness and frustration."

"In the same way, monks, others may use these five modes of speech when speaking to you—speech that is timely or untimely, true or false, gentle or harsh, with a good or a harmful motive, and with a loving heart or hostility. In this way, monks, you should train yourselves: 'Neither shall our minds be affected by this, nor for this matter shall we give vent to evil words, but we shall remain full of concern and pity, with a mind of love, and we shall not give in to hatred. On the contrary, we shall live projecting thoughts of universal love to that very person, making him as well as the whole world the object of our thoughts of universal love—thoughts that have grown great, exalted and measureless. We shall dwell radiating these thoughts which are void of hostility and ill will.' It is in this way, monks, that you should train yourselves.

The River Ganges

"Suppose, monks, a person were to come holding a burning grasstorch, and he were to say: 'With this burning grass-torch I shall set fire to and scorch this river Ganges.' What do you think, monks, could that person set fire to and scorch the river Ganges with a grass-torch?"

"No, indeed not, most venerable sir."

"And why not?"

"Because, most venerable sir, the river Ganges is deep and without measure. It is not possible to set fire to and scorch the river Ganges with a burning grass-torch. On the contrary, that person will only reap weariness and frustration."

"In the same way, monks, others may use these five modes of speech when speaking to you—speech that is timely or untimely, true or false, gentle or harsh, with a good or a harmful motive, and with a loving heart or hostility. In this way, monks, you should train yourselves: 'Neither shall our minds be affected by this, nor for this matter shall we give vent to evil words, but we shall remain full of concern and pity, with a mind of love, and we shall not give in to hatred. On the contrary, we shall live projecting thoughts of universal love to that very person, making him as well as the whole world the object of our thoughts of universal love—thoughts that have grown great, exalted and measureless. We shall dwell radiating these thoughts which are void of hostility and ill will.' It is in this way, monks, that you should train yourselves.

The Catskin Bag

"Suppose, monks, there was a supple and silky leather bag made of catskin that had been beaten, tanned, cured and fully processed, and made completely free of all creases and wrinkles. Then a man were to come with a stick or mallet and say, 'With this stick or mallet I shall make creases and wrinkles in this supple and silky catskin bag which has been beaten, tanned, cured and fully processed, and made free of creases and wrinkles.' What do you think, monks, could that person with a stick or mallet make creases and wrinkles in that supple and silky catskin bag which has been beaten, tanned, cured and fully processed, and made free of creases and wrinkles?"

"No, indeed not, most venerable sir."

"And why not?"

"Because, most venerable sir, that supple and silky leather bag made of catskin has been beaten, tanned, cured and fully processed, and made free of creases and wrinkles. It is not possible to make creases and wrinkles in it with a stick or mallet. On the contrary, he will only reap weariness and frustration."

"In the same way, monks, others may use these five modes of speech when speaking to you—speech that is timely or untimely, true or false, gentle or harsh, with a good or a harmful motive, and with a loving heart or hostility. In this way, monks, you should train yourselves: 'Neither shall our minds be affected by this, nor for this matter shall we give vent to evil words, but we shall remain full of concern and pity, with a mind of love, and we shall not give in to hatred. On the contrary, we shall live projecting thoughts of universal love to that very person, making him as well as the whole world the object of our thoughts of universal love—thoughts that have grown great, exalted and measureless. We shall dwell radiating these thoughts which are void of hostility and ill will.' It is in this way, monks, that you should train yourselves.

The Parable of the Saw

"Monks, even if bandits were to savagely sever you, limb by limb, with a double-handled saw, even then, whoever of you harbours ill-will at heart would not be upholding my Teaching. Monks, even in such a situation you should train yourselves thus: 'Neither shall our minds be affected by this, nor for this matter shall we give vent to evil words, but we shall remain full of concern and pity, with a mind of love, and we shall not give in to hatred. On the contrary, we shall live projecting thoughts of universal love to those very persons, making them as well as the whole world the object of our thoughts of universal love—thoughts that have grown great, exalted and measureless. We shall dwell radiating these thoughts which are void of hostility and ill-will.' It is in this way, monks, that you should train yourselves.

"Monks, if you should keep this instruction on the Parable of the Saw constantly in mind, do you see any mode of speech, subtle or gross, that you could not endure?"

"No, Lord."

"Therefore, monks, you should keep this instruction on the Parable of the Saw constantly in mind. That will conduce to your well-being and happiness for long indeed."

That is what the Blessed One said. Delighted, those monks acclaimed the Teaching of the Blessed One.

The Buddha and Catch-22

Sāmaṇera Bodhesako

Bodhi Leaves No. 110

First published: 1987

The Buddha and Catch-22

It is now twenty-five years since the publication, in 1961, of Joseph Heller's astonishing novel, Catch-22 (New York: Simon and Schuster; London: Jonathan Cape Ltd.); yet so far, it seems, there has been no public comment on certain striking parallels between the Buddha's Teaching and some of the content of that novel. Perhaps it would be as well to discuss those affinities now, before another quarter century elapses.

The most immediately obvious (though hardly the most profound) similarity between the Teaching and the novel is that both are deeply concerned with man's mortality. "Old age, sickness, and death" is a phrase that occurs repeatedly in the Buddha's Teaching, as recorded in the Pali Suttas (and, indeed, throughout the later Sanskrit, Chinese, and Tibetan texts as well). A citation of even a small portion of such textual references[36] would be far beyond the scope of this brief discussion: the fact of man's mortality—a constant peril in an inconstant world—is a perception absolutely fundamental to the perspective of life presented by the Buddha's Teaching.

And in Catch-22 the protagonist, Yossarian (a bombardier in World War II), is no less deeply concerned about old age, sickness, and death. The spectre of their imminence is his constant dread. As his friend Dunbar puts it,

"Do you know how long a year takes when it's going away? This long." He snapped his fingers. "A second ago you were stepping into college with your lungs full of fresh air. Today you're an old man."

"Old?" asked Clevinger with surprise. "What are you talking about?"

36 For example: As the herdsman drives his kine with a stick to pasture land, thus decay and health's decline drive out the life of man.—Dhp v 135.

…"You're inches away from death every time you go on a mission. How much older can you be at your age?" (pp. 38–9)

As for sickness, Yossarian had so many ailments to be afraid of that he was sometimes tempted to turn himself in to the hospital for good and spend the rest of his life stretched out there inside an oxygen tent with a battery of specialists and nurses seated at one side of his bed twenty-four hours a day waiting for something to go wrong … Aneurisms, for instance; how else could they ever defend him in time against an aneurism of the aorta? … He wondered often how he would ever recognise the first chill, flush, twinge, ache, belch, sneeze, stain, lethargy, vocal slip, lose of balance or lapse of memory that would signal the inevitable beginning of the inevitable end. (pp. 171–2)

But even more than old age and sickness, it is the spectre of death itself that haunts both Yossarian and the novel: "At night when he was trying to sleep, Yossarian would call the roll of all the men, women and children he had ever known who were now dead. He tried to remember all the soldiers, and he resurrected images of all the elderly people he had known when a child …" (p. 339). Yossarian is enmeshed in a killing war which is (as the novel's disclaimer makes clear) representative of a larger framework,[37] a war to which "there was no end in sight. The only end in sight was Yossarian's own" (p. 16). Nevertheless, Yossarian "had decided to live forever or die in the attempt, and his only mission each time he went up was to come down alive" (p. 29). Yossarian feels death hovering about him—indeed, even living with him, in the form of a dead man named Mudd, who was not easy to live with.

However, old age, sickness, and death are not apprehended merely as things, as objects in a world of objects, in themselves neutral. The fact of death changes Yossarian's world, as it does ours, radically, and Heller's insistence upon this point is the beginning of the novel's profundity.

---

37 Perhaps it would be going too far to discover in this larger framework a reference to the Buddha's recognition of *samsāra*, the round of deaths and rebirths; but it cannot be excessive to relate the facts of birth and death to the minute and Learical apocalypse achieved in the vision of Snowden's death: "Man was matter, that was Snowden's secret. … Ripeness was all" (pp. 429–30).

In a world in which death is an unavoidable presence, "it made sense to cry out in pain every night" (p. 54). Indeed, the disorder that the awareness of death introduces into a world which, throughout our lives, we are forever trying to order, leaves us with neither simple order nor simple disorder, but rather with "a world boiling in chaos in which everything was in proper orders" (p. 143). Death, the great modifier, alters everything, so that for Yossarian

"nothing warped seemed any more in his strange, distorted surroundings" (p. 402).

It is this strange distortion that is the keystone of the novel's humour—not merely that of its many throwaway jokes but also of the tragicomic perception which circles round and round the death of Snowden ("Where are the Snowdens of yesteryear?" (p. 35): what a poignant joker), drawing ever closer, while at the same time mockingly inverting that trivial sensibility which ordinary men use to deny the disorder of death: "the Texan turned out to be goodnatured, generous and likable. In three days no one could stand him" (p. 9); "Nately had a bad start. He came from a good family" (p. 12); "Yossarian couldn't be happy, even though the Texan didn't want him to be" (p. 16); "strangers he didn't know shot at him with cannons every time he flew up into the air to drop bombs on them, and it wasn't funny at all. And if that wasn't funny, there were lots of things that weren't even funnier" (p. 17). But it is not merely the one-liners that are inversions of everyday logic: that everyday sensibility is twisted into various shapes, so that each character is seen to exist in his own uniquely topsy-turvy world, a world whose shape hovers somewhere between a wry smile and a teardrop.

And of all the characters who live in their separate worlds of twisted logic (and the names, often as twisted as the logic, seem nearly endless: Hungry Joe, Chief White Half-oat, Doc Daneeka, Major de Coverly, Milo Minderbinder, Major Major Major Major ...) perhaps the most logically insane character of all is the soldier in white, who "was encased from head to toe in plaster and gauze. He had two useless legs and two useless arms" (p. 9). Sewn into the bandages over the insides of both elbows were zippered lips through which he was fed clear fluid from a clear jar. A silent zinc pipe rose from the cement on his groin and was coupled to a slim rubber hose that carried waste from his kidneys and dripped it efficiently into a clear, stoppered jar on the floor. When the jar on the floor was full, the jar feeding his elbow was empty and the two were simply switched quickly so that the stuff could drip back into him (p. 10).

Changing the jars was no trouble to anyone but the men who watched them changed every hour or so and were baffled by the procedure. "Why can't they hook the two jars up to each other and eliminate the middleman?" (p. 168). The other patients in the ward

... shrank from him with a tenderhearted aversion from the moment they set eyes on him ... They gathered in the farthest recess of the ward and gossiped about him in malicious, offended undertones, rebelling against his presence as a ghastly imposition and resenting him malevolently for the nauseating truth of which he was a bright reminder (p. 166).

Although Yossarian too is mystified by the soldier in white, yet he "would recognise him anywhere. He wondered who he was" (p. 358). And if we need an image of samsāra we would have to look far to find a better one, or one more universal. The message of the soldier in white (who keeps turning up again)[38] is as universal as that of the letters in black (p. 8)—the letters which Yossarian, as bored censoring officer, blacks out completely or nearly so (and endorses them "Washington Irving" or, sometimes, "Irving Washington," thus unwittingly endangering the chaplain's life), "thereby leaving a message far more universal."

This tragicomic perception of man's condition (in which lots of things aren't even funnier) leads naturally to the question of the purpose of such a life, or of any life at all. (On the soldier in

38 The circular nature of *saṃsāra* finds its parallel in Catch-22 (if circles can have parallels), not only in the re-appearance of the soldier in white, but also in the circling round the death of Snowden, going around twice over Ferrara, the soldier who saw everything twice, and many other recurrent events and phrases. Each time Yossarian gets close to having completed his missions Headquarters raises the number required: there is always another tour of duty Like Rohitassa (see S II 26 = A IV 45), and like us, Yossarian cannot reach an end by going.

white: "It wasn't much of a life, but it was all the life he had …") Dr. Stubbs, in conversation with Dunbar, raises this point but fails to answer it:

"I used to get a big kick out of saving people's lives. Now I wonder what the hell's the point, since they all have to die anyway."

…"The point is to keep them from dying for as long as you can."

"Yeah, but what's the point, since they all have to die anyway?"

"The trick is not to think about that."

"Never mind the trick. What the hell's the point?"

Dunbar pondered in silence for a few moments. "Who the hell knows?" (p. 108).

But if the point of life is not known, and if life is nevertheless perceived as both tragic and comic, then from another perspective it could as well be seen as both sane and insane: and this leads naturally to the novel's comic inversion of the notions of sanity and insanity, an inversion which is an underpinning of the book's logic (or, as some would have it, illogic). Continuing their conversation, Dr. Stubbs and Dunbar discuss Yossarian and the dreaded approach of a particularly dangerous mission:

"That crazy bastard."

"He's not so crazy," Dunbar said. "He swears he's not going to fly to Bologna."

"That's just what I mean," Dr. Stubbs answered. "That crazy bastard may be the only sane one left." (p. 109)

Indeed, in a world in which "men went mad and were rewarded with medals" (p. 16), who is sane, save he who would escape from that world? This is Yossarian's dilemma, the "vile, excruciating dilemma of duty and damnation" (p. 136): he doesn't want to be in the war. He doesn't want to die. "He thirsted for life" (p. 331). For Yossarian the enemy is not the Germans, or at least not only the Germans. "'The enemy,' retorted Yossarian with weighted precision, 'is anybody who's going to get you killed …'" And because of this "morbid aversion to dying" (p. 297), men shrink from him and regard him as crazy. Clevinger is such a one. "You're crazy!" Clevinger shrieks at Yossarian on p. 16; but later (p. 75) we are told that the patriotic and idealistic Clevinger was a dope "who would rather be a corpse than bury one"; and finally (p. 103): "Clevinger was dead. That was the basic flaw in his philosophy." And yet, by the very fact of being part of such a world one cannot be completely sane; and to be not completely sane is to be not sane at all. But if one tries to escape, is that not then evidence of a spark of sanity? Perhaps so; but the problem is that when we try to escape we discover that we can't: every effort to free oneself from (in Buddhist terms) involvement with craving, aversion, and delusion—or in the novel's terms, the war—every effort apparently brings one back to the same dilemma, and results only in making the problem more urgent (and perhaps also more evident), as will be recognised by anyone who has ever tried to extirpate the root of craving, and failed. Is it not madness, then, to try to escape?

And yet, if to do nothing is regarded as less insane, still that too does not lead to disengagement from a mad world. This is the very crux of Yossarian's dilemma, and ours as well: a dilemma illuminated in experience by the effort to practise the Buddha's Teaching and in fiction by Yossarian's effort to escape from the war. Heller puts it this way:

"Can't you ground someone who's crazy?" [Yossarian asks the flight surgeon, Doc Daneeka.]

"Oh, sure. I have to. There's a rule saying I have to ground anyone who's crazy. "

"Then why don't you ground me? I'm crazy … Ask any of the others. They'll tell you how crazy I am."

"They're crazy."

"Then why don't you ground them?" "Why don't they ask me to ground them?" "Because they're crazy, that's why."

"Of course they're crazy," Doc Daneeka replied. "I just told you they're crazy, didn't I? And you can't let crazy people decide whether you're crazy or not, can you?"

Yossarian looked at him soberly and tried another approach. "Is Orr crazy?"

"He sure is," Doc Daneeka said … "I can ground Orr. But first he has to ask me to."

"That's all he has to do to be grounded?" "That's all. Let him ask me."

"And then you can ground him?" Yossarian asked. "No. Then I can't ground him."

"You mean there's a catch?"

"Sure there's a catch," Doc Daneeka replied. "Catch-22. Anyone who wants to get out of combat duty isn't really crazy" (p. 45).

Thus Yossarian's efforts to establish a rational basis for being grounded must fail. Logic is an inadequate tool to deal with the human situation, for whenever we apply logic there is always a catch. This is not to suggest that logic is not necessary, but rather that it is not adequate. In this computer age we could hardly manage without logic, let alone computers. Without logic we could make neither mathematics nor music nor marmalade. But whenever we try to deal with the fundamentals of existence, with the forever unanswerable question, "Who am I?" (or any other question concerned with "me"), we find that logic neither answers that question nor shows us the way to stop asking it.[39] ("'Why me?' was his constant lament, and the question was a good one" (p. 34).) And the reason for this, the Buddha informs us, is because of *avijjā*, or ignorance. But *avijjā* is not a mere absence of information; it is a refusal to see what is at all times there to be seen. It is not failure to see one particular thing among other particular things, but a radical refusal to see the way all particular things are, and in this respect it is as great a modifier as death—indeed, the two are (so the Buddha tells us) inseparable. The dependent arising formulation says, in summary, "With ignorance as condition,

---

39 It is for this reason that the Buddha's Teaching is said to be *atakkāvacara*, not in the sphere of reason or logic. (Catch-22 is not the only well-known book which asserts the insanity implicit in being in a situation. In *Alice in Wonderland* the Cheshire Cat tells Alice, "We're all mad here. I'm mad. You're mad. You must be or you wouldn't have come." Indeed, Catch-22 contains a number of very specific allusions to the Alice books.)

ageing and death, sorrow, lamentation, pain, grief, and despair come into being."

The deluded person, in refusing to see the nature of all things, refuses also to see the nature of his refusal to see (which is also a thing). That is, he refuses to see delusion. Thus, by denying itself delusion sustains itself. This is stated in the *sutta*s (e.g. Sammādiṭṭhi Sutta, MN 9) as follows:

"Friends, that which is non-knowledge of suffering, nonknowledge of the arising of suffering, non-knowledge of the ceasing of suffering, non-knowledge of the way leading to the ceasing of suffering, this, friends, is called ignorance."

For after all, what is "the way leading to the ceasing of suffering"? It is (the *sutta*s tell us) the Noble Eightfold Path. And what is the first factor of this path? Right View. Ignorance, then, involves non-knowledge of Right View. And Right View is knowledge of the arising of suffering; that is to say, knowledge of ignorance. Right View is knowledge of Right View, and also knowledge of wrong view, whereas wrong view is non-knowledge of wrong view, and also non-knowledge of Right View. And this structure of ignorance is, in fact, Catch-22 at its most fundamental level. As Heller describes it (p. 46):

There was only one catch and that was Catch-22, which specified that a concern for one's own safety in the face of dangers that were real and immediate was the process of a rational mind. Orr was crazy and could be grounded. All he had to do was ask; and as soon as he did, he would no longer be crazy and would have to fly more missions. Orr would be crazy to fly more missions and sane if he didn't, but if he was sane he had to fly them. If he flew them he was crazy and didn't have to; but if he didn't want to he was sane and had to. Yossarian was moved very deeply by the absolute simplicity of this clause of Catch-22 and let out a respectful whistle.

"That's some catch, that Catch-22," he observed.

"It's the best there is," Doc Daneeka agreed.

Thus, with absolute simplicity, we are condemned to madness. And if this is not convincing, Heller presses his point home by telling us (on the same page) that Catch-22 is like the flies that Orr sees in Appleby's eyes.

"Oh, they're there, all right," Orr had assured [Yossarian] … "although he probably doesn't even know it. That's why he can't see things as they really are."

"How come he doesn't know it?" inquired Yossarian. "Because he's got flies in his eyes," Orr with exaggerated patience. "How can he see he's got flies in his eyes if he's got flies in his eyes?"

It made as much sense as anything else …

Yathābhūtaṃ na pajānāti: he does not see things as they really are: the phrase—so typical a *sutta* description of the *puthujjana,* the unenlightened commoner—is used here by Heller to illuminate precisely the characteristic of being entrapped in a situation. Not only does the *puthujjana* have flies in his eyes, he does not see that he has them, and he does not see this because he has them. His dilemma is that though he must find a way to see, yet he cannot find that way precisely because he cannot see. Indeed, he cannot even see for himself that this is his problem. And this is the dilemma which, at its most fundamental level, is the specific concern of the Buddha's Teaching. The structure of *avijjā,* the structure of Catch-22, the structure of "having flies in one's eyes": they are one and the same. Catch-22 is *avijjā.* The title character in both the novel and in our lives never appears and yet is omnipresent.

All of this does not oblige us to conclude that Heller is enlightened, or that he is even a Buddhist. Describing something and seeing it directly are two different things; and even in direct perception there are different levels of profundity. "At the field a heavy silence prevailed, overpowering motion like a ruthless, insensate spell holding in thrall the only beings who might break it. The chaplain was in awe" (p. 371). This, it is clear enough, is of the same nature as having flies in one's eyes; and yet it is also clear enough that this sort of spell is of a much less fundamental grade. Not only can we on the outside see it, it is conceivable that the men at the field could be aware of the spell at the same time they were (for the time being) powerless to break it. Appleby, on the other hand, must be entirely unaware of the flies in his eyes.

On an even less fundamental level is the situation of the men while they await the dreaded mission to Bologna. The mission cannot be flown until the rain stops and the landing strips dry out. But the rain-forced delay in the mission only gives the men more time to be more terrified. "Their only hope was that it would never stop raining, and they had no hope because they all knew it would

... The more it rained, the worse they suffered. The worse they suffered, the more they prayed that it would continue raining" (p. 117). Again we have a situation of entrapment, but on a crude and manifest level of experience.

But though we would describe these various levels of Catch22 as being only rough approximations to the subtle and pervasive deception of *avijjā*, as expounded by the Buddha, we must also recognise Heller's achievement in seeing the central significance of this self-replicative structure in human existence and (though he doesn't know what to do about it) in describing it in a form which has struck a deeply responsive chord in so many. Although he may lack the wisdom to resolve the dilemma he describes, yet he has sufficient wisdom to not let go of that perception; nor should we, for by being manifest, such occurrences can serve both to remind us of the subtle central dilemma which is the template upon which those coarser experiences depend and also to provide us with a model which, applied with proper attention, can indicate what action, or what sort of action, can bring that central dilemma to an end.

In the end, perhaps due to the exigencies of the novel's form, Heller does suggest a solution to Yossarian's dilemma. Whether this solution works artistically is not of concern to us here. Rather, we need to understand why this suggestion of a solution is incompatible with the Buddha's Teaching.

The Buddha's Teaching is concerned with letting go of what can be surrendered within the sphere of the unenlightened (namely, sensuality, hatred, lethargy, agitation, and doubt—the five hindrances) in order to allow for the possibility of seeing what might be let go of beyond that sphere. This further perception can be indicated by one who has already seen for himself, and must be initially accepted by the practitioner as an act of faith, until he too comes to see it. At that point it is possible for there to be a further letting go, a giving up of what can be surrendered only outside the sphere of the unenlightened, namely, all beliefs concerned with selfhood (sakkāyadiṭṭhī attavāda) and, eventually, the conceit "I am" (asmimāna). Thus the Buddha's Teaching is a course of practice concerned fundamentally with renunciation. Without giving up the world to the limits of one's ability to do so one will never be able to extend those limits: one will instead remain entrapped within the world.

Heller considers this approach, but rejects it. Yossarian certainly sees the problem: he is "unable to adjust to the idea of war" (p. 297) and repeatedly flees the oppressiveness of the world by running to "the cloistered shelter of a hospital" (p. 177) with a supposititious liver ailment. That this flight is meant to be seen as (at least in a sense) religious is borne out by a doctor who tells Yossarian that the family of a just-deceased soldier have "travelled all the way from New York to see a dying soldier, and you're the handiest one we've got."

"What are you talking about?" Yossarian asked suspiciously. "I'm not dying."

"Of course you're dying. We're all dying. Where the devil else do you think you're heading?"

"They didn't come to see me," Yossarian objected. "They came to see their son."

"They'll have to take what they can get. As far as we're concerned, one dying boy is just as good as any other, or just as bad. To a scientist, all dying boys are equal ..." (p. 181)

Thus the doctors, the staff of that cloistered shelter, perform the essentially religious function of reminding Yossarian ("how could he have forgotten") of his mortality; and they also insist that he observe the celibacy normally associated with monastic institutions: "How do you expect anyone to believe you have a liver condition if you keep squeezing the nurses' tits every time you get a chance? You're going to have to give up sex if you want to convince people you've got an ailing liver."

"That's a hell of a price to pay just to keep alive …" (p. 181) Precisely: giving up sensuality (to say nothing of hatred, lethargy, agitation, and doubt) is a price Yossarian is not prepared to pay. He wants the sybaritic salvation sought also by Hungry Joe, to whom women were "lovely, satisfying, maddening manifestations of the miraculous, instruments of pleasure" (p. 52), and he dreams of being interred for the duration of the war (i.e., for all eternity) in Sweden, an earthly (and earthy) paradise where he could keep himself busy siring dozens of illegitimate little Yossarians. Yossarian wants the world's pleasures without having to endure the world's drawbacks, and he fails to see the essence of the world's dangers. (Hungry Joe is more consistent than Yossarian on this point, for he goes to pieces each time he finishes flying the number of missions Headquarters requires, and recovers only when Headquarters raises the number of missions required, as it inevitably does, throwing him back on combat status.)

If any character in Catch-22 comes close to accepting the Buddha's advice it would be Dunbar, who tries to increase his lifespan by cultivating boredom, on the grounds that when you're bored time passes slower. His idea seems to be that if only he could achieve a state of total and absolute boredom he would be, for all intents, eternal. This sounds like a rough literary approximation to meditation (although we must remember that the Buddha, unlike many Eastern teachers, quite explicitly stated that meditation by itself is an insufficient condition for enlightenment).

Dunbar, given to cultivating boredom, to seeking eternity, lies motionless in bed: he goes so far in his efforts that at one point Yossarian, looking at him, wonders whether he is still alive. This will remind us of the story of the Venerable Sañjīva who, we are told (MN 50/M I 333), was seated immersed in the highest meditative attainment when some cowherds, shepherds, and ploughmen, passing by, saw him and thought, as did Yossarian of Dunbar, that he was dead. They collected grass, wood, and cow dung, heaped it up about the Ven. Sañjīva, set his pyre alight, and went on their way. The next morning Ven. Sañjīva emerged from his meditative attainment and went wandering for alms-food. His would-be cremators were astonished at seeing him alive and gave him the name by which he became known, Sañjīva, which means "with life." Dunbar seems to have lacked the Ven. Sañjīva's meditative abilities, but each sought to escape death (Ven. Sañjīva, the Sutta tells us, successfully), and each came thereby to be taken as dead.

It is common, of course, for beginning meditators to be assailed by boredom (as well as the other four hindrances); however, this does not justify equating boredom and meditation: on the contrary, boredom is an enemy of meditation. Despite the story of Ven. Sañjīva, then, we must regard any effort to equate meditation with the cultivation of boredom as tenuous, and as being further weakened by the episode in which Dunbar becomes a fortiori. However, we must also note that it is immediately after Dunbar becomes convinced, upon re-encountering the soldier in white, that (p. 358) "There's no one inside! ... He's hollow inside, like a chocolate soldier"—thereby perhaps suggesting something of the Buddha's teaching of *anattā*, of not-self—that Dunbar "is disappeared". We never learn the meaning of this cryptic event ("It doesn't make sense. It isn't even good grammar" (p. 359), but if the parallel with meditation is accepted then the further parallel that would be suggested here is with Nibbāna, extinction. After being disappeared, Dunbar is described (p. 360) as being "nowhere to be found", which is exactly how the *sutta*s describe beings who have attained full enlightenment (arahants).[40]

Perhaps a literary parallel of an achievement that transcends literature (let alone literature, Nibbāna transcends bhava, being) could not be more closely described; but in any case we cannot allow that the parallel is more than a suggestion, and (no doubt inevitably) an inaccurate one at that. And in any case "to be disappeared" sounds, from Heller's description of it, far less desirable than extinction, from the Buddha's description of that. (Still, it would be interesting to know how much acquaintance Heller actually had, if any, with any school of Buddhism during the seven years in which he was writing Catch-22.[41])

---

40 The phrase occurs frequently in the *sutta*s. See for example the concluding lines of Vakkali Sutta (SN 22:87). Also at Dhp v 180 we find: That tangle of snares by which he'd be penned isn't found anywhere. His range has no end, that Buddha awake What track can there be to trace one who's trackless, craving-free?

41 This question was put to Mr Heller. The reply was that he knew "not an inkling." The range of the *puthujjana*, it seems, is more extensive than commonly supposed.

And if any character tries, however ineffectually, to understand the real nature of his situation, it is not Yossarian but the chaplain. The chaplain (he was named Shipman in the hardcover edition, but for some reason the name was changed in the paperback edition to Tappman—not his only identity crisis), who has an open mind, is continually wondering what everything was all about … There was no way of really knowing anything, he knew, not even that there was no way of really knowing anything. Was there a single true faith, or a life after death? … These were the great, complex questions of ontology that tormented him. Yet they never seemed nearly as crucial to him as the question of kindness and good manners. He was pinched perspiringly in the epistemological dilemma of the sceptic, unable to accept solutions to problems he was unwilling to dismiss as unsolvable. He was never without misery and never without hope (pp. 262–3).

In the chaplain's tale, the human dilemma is presented from a different point of view: it is not a question of sanity or insanity but, in Kafkaesque terms, one of guilt or innocence. Because it is the nature of beings that they are continually trying to establish an existence that continually eludes them,[42] their existence is perpetually in doubt, and they exist, if at all, in a state of guilt. This, it would seem, is the basic perception of Kafka's Trial: Joseph K. arrests himself by recognising that his existence, being unjustifiable, is essentially guilty. And the chaplain (for whom the question "Who am I?" becomes acute when he is formally charged with "being Washington Irving" (p. 378)) is also in this situation:

"You've got nothing to be afraid of if you're not guilty. What are you so afraid of? You're not guilty, are you?"

"Sure he's guilty," said the colonel. "Guilty as hell."

"Guilty of what?" implored the chaplain, feeling more and more bewildered … "What did I do?" (p. 373)

42 Thus the question "Who am I?", whether or not it is answerable, is recognised at once to be vital and fundamental to the epistemological dilemma we each face; indeed, it is thus that there is the concept of such a dilemma at all.

And later the chaplain's identity crisis and dilemma of existential guilt is expressed in the same terms that were used earlier to describe Catch-22:

"I offered it to Sergeant Whitcomb because I didn't want it." "Why'd you steal it from Colonel Cathcart if you didn't want it?"

"I didn't steal it from Colonel Cathcart!"

"Then why are you so guilty, if you didn't steal it?" "I'm not guilty!"

"Then why would we be questioning you if you weren't guilty?" (p. 377)

Thus each of us faces the question of our basic unjustifiability in a purposeless world. Some, of course, flee from these questions and deny them (by indulging in sensuality, hatred, lethargy, agitation, and doubt); but the questions return for so long as their root, the conceit "I am", exists, and the verdict is inevitable: "Guilty."

"Chaplain," he continued, looking up, "we accuse you also of the commission of crimes and infractions we don't even know about yet. Guilty or innocent?"

"I don't know, sir. How can I say if you don't tell me what they are?"

"How can we tell you if we don't know?" "Guilty," decided the colonel.

"Sure he's guilty," agreed the major. "If they're his crimes and infractions, he must have committed them."

"Guilty it is, then," chanted the officer without insignia ... (p. 379)

And "guilty" it is for all of us, if the charge is the fundamental one of being possessors, or even of simply "being": being what?

And thus Heller repeatedly and ingeniously offers us brilliant literary expressions of the dilemma of existence. The formulations are lucid and compelling, and they fully take account of the circular and self-sustaining nature of the dilemma. For this we can praise Catch-22, and perhaps find it of use as a tool in keeping to the forefront of our awareness the nature of our problem. But it would be asking too much to expect the novel to offer the means of resolving that dilemma. For that we must turn to the Buddha's Teaching.

Our Real Home

A Talk to an Ageing Lay Disciple Approaching Death

Ajahn Chah

Bodhi Leaves No. 111

First published: 1987

Our Real Home

A Talk to an Ageing Lay Disciple Approaching Death

Now determine in your mind to listen with respect to the Dhamma. During the time that I am speaking, be as attentive to my words as if it was the Lord Buddha himself sitting in front of you. Close your eyes and make yourself comfortable, compose your mind and make it one-pointed. Humbly allow the Triple Gem of wisdom, truth and purity to abide in your heart as a way of showing respect to the Fully Enlightened One.

Today I have brought nothing material of any substance to offer you, only Dhamma, the teachings of the Lord Buddha. Listen well. You should understand that even the Buddha himself, with his great store of accumulated virtue, could not avoid physical death. When he reached old age he relinquished his body and let go of its heavy burden. Now you too must learn to be satisfied with the many years you've already depended on your body. You should feel that it is enough.

You can compare it to household utensils you've had for a long time—your cups, saucers, plates and so on. When you first had them they were clean and shining, but now after using them for so long, they're starting to wear out. Some are already broken, some have disappeared and those that are left are deteriorating; they have no stable form, and it's their nature to be like that. Your body is the same way—it's been continually changing right from the day you were born, through childhood and youth, until now it's reached old age. You must accept that. The Buddha said that conditions (*saṅkhāras*), whether they are internal conditions, bodily conditions or external conditions, are not-self; their nature is to change. Contemplate this truth until you see it clearly.

This very lump of flesh that lies here in decline is saccadhamma, the truth. The truth of this body is saccadhamma, and it is the unchanging teaching of the Buddha. The Buddha taught us to look at the body, to contemplate it and come to terms with its nature. We must be able to be at peace with the body, whatever state it is in. The

Buddha taught that we should ensure that it's only the body that is locked up in jail and not let the mind be imprisoned along with it. Now as your body begins to run down and deteriorate with age, don't resist that, but don't let your mind deteriorate with it. Keep the mind separate. Give energy to the mind by realising the truth of the way things are. The Lord Buddha taught that this is the nature of the body, it can't be any other way; having been born it gets old and sick and then it dies. This is a great truth you are presently encountering. Look at the body with wisdom and realise it.

Even if your house is flooded or burnt to the ground, whatever the danger that threatens it, let it concern only the house. If there's a flood, don't let it flood your mind. If there's a fire, don't let it burn your heart. Let it be merely the house, that which is external to you, that is flooded and burnt. Allow the mind to let go of its attachments. The time is ripe.

You've been alive a long time. Your eyes have seen any number of forms and colours, your ears have heard so many sounds, you've had any number of experiences. And that's all they were—just experiences. You've eaten delicious foods, and all the good tastes were just good tastes, nothing more. The unpleasant tastes were just unpleasant tastes; that's all. If the eye sees a beautiful form, that's all it is, just a beautiful form. An ugly form is just an ugly form. The ear hears an entrancing, melodious sound and it's nothing more than that. A grating, disharmonious sound is simply so.

The Buddha said that rich or poor, young or old, human or animal, no being in this world can maintain itself in any one state for long, everything experiences change and estrangement. This is a fact of life that we can do nothing to remedy. But the Buddha said that what we can do is to contemplate the body and mind so as to see their impersonality, see that neither of them is 'me' or 'mine'. They have a merely provisional reality. It's like this house: it's only nominally yours; you couldn't take it with you anywhere. It's the same with your wealth, your possessions and your family—they're all yours only in name, they don't really belong to you, they belong to nature. Now this truth doesn't apply to you alone; everyone is in the same position, even the Lord Buddha and his enlightened disciples. They differed from us in only one respect and that was in their acceptance of the way things are; they saw that it could be no other way.

So the Buddha taught us to scan and examine this body, from the soles of the feet up to the crown of the head and then back down to the feet again. Just take a look at the body. What sort of things do you see? Is there anything intrinsically clean there? Can you find any abiding essence? This whole body is steadily degenerating, and the Buddha taught us to see that it doesn't belong to us. It's natural for the body to be this way, because all conditioned phenomena are subject to change. How else would you have it be? Actually, there's nothing wrong with the way the body is. It's not the body that causes you suffering, it's your wrong thinking. When you see the right wrongly, there's bound to be confusion.

It's like the water of a river. It naturally flows down the gradient, it never flows against it; that's its nature. If a person were to go and stand on a river bank and, seeing the water flowing swiftly down its course, foolishly want it to flow back up the gradient, he would suffer. Whatever he was doing, his wrong thinking would allow him no peace of mind. He would be unhappy because of his wrong view, thinking against the stream. If he had right view he would see that the water must inevitably flow down the gradient, and until he realised and accepted that fact, the person would be agitated and upset.

The river that must flow down the gradient is like your body. Having been young, your body has become old and now it's meandering towards its death. Don't go wishing it was otherwise; it's not something you have the power to remedy. The Buddha told us to see the way things are and then let go of our clinging to them. Take this feeling of letting go as your refuge.

Keep meditating, even if you feel tired and exhausted. Let your mind dwell with the breath. Take a few deep breaths, and then establish the mind on the breath using the mantra 'Buddho'. Make this practice habitual. The more exhausted you feel, the more subtle and focused your concentration must be, so that you can cope with the painful sensations that arise. When you start to feel fatigued then bring all your thinking to a halt, let the mind gather itself together and then turn to knowing the breath. Just keep up the inner recitation: "Bud-dho, Bud-dho."

Let go of all externals. Don't go grasping at thoughts of your children and relatives, don't grasp at anything whatsoever. Let go. Let the mind unite in a single point and let that composed mind dwell with the breath. Let the breath be its sole object of knowledge. Concentrate until the mind becomes increasingly subtle, until feelings are insignificant and there is great inner clarity and wakefulness. Then when painful sensations arise they will gradually cease of their own accord. Finally, you'll look on the breath as if it was a relative come to visit you.

When a relative leaves, we follow him out and see him off. We watch until he's walked or driven out of sight and then we go back indoors. We watch the breath in the same way. If the breath is coarse, we know that it's coarse; if it's subtle we know that it's subtle. As it becomes increasingly fine we keep following it, while simultaneously awakening the mind. Eventually the breath disappears altogether and all that remains is the feeling of wakefulness. This is called meeting the Buddha. We have that clear wakefulness that is called 'Buddho', the one who knows, the one who is awake, the radiant one. It is meeting and dwelling with the Buddha, with knowledge and clarity. For it was only the historical flesh-and-blood Buddha that entered *Parinibbāna*, the true Buddha, the Buddha that is clear radiant knowing, we can still experience and attain today, and when we do so the heart is one.

So let go, put everything down, everything except the knowing. Don't be fooled if visions or sounds arise in your mind during meditation. Put them all down. Don't take hold of anything at all. Just stay with this non-dual awareness. Don't worry about the past or the future, just be still and you will reach the place where there's no advancing, no retreating and no stopping, where there's nothing to grasp at or cling to. Why? Because there's no self, no 'me' or 'mine'. It's all gone. The Buddha taught us to be emptied of everything in this way, not to carry anything with us. To know, and having known, let go.

Realising the Dhamma, the path to freedom from the round of birth and death, is a job that we all have to do alone. So keep trying to let go, and to understand the teachings. Really put effort into your contemplation. Don't worry about your family. At the moment they are as they are, in the future they will be like you. There's no one in the world who can escape this fate. The Buddha told us to put down everything that lacks a real abiding substance. If you put everything down you will see the truth, if you don't you won't. That's the way it is and it's the same for all, so don't worry and don't grasp at anything.

Even if you find yourself thinking, well that's all right too, as long as you think wisely. Don't think foolishly. If you think of your children, think of them with wisdom, not with foolishness. Whatever the mind turns to, then think and know that thing with wisdom, aware of its nature. If you know something with wisdom, then you let it go and there's no suffering. The mind is bright, joyful and at peace, and turning away from distractions it is undivided. Right now what you can look to for help and support is your breath.

This is your own work, nobody else's. Leave others to do their own work. You have your own duty and responsibility and you don't have to take on those of your family. Don't take anything else on, let it all go. That letting go will make your mind calm. Your sole responsibility right now is to focus your mind and bring it to peace. Leave everything else to others. Forms, sounds, odours, tastes— leave them to others to attend to. Put everything behind you and do your own work, fulfil your own responsibility. Whatever arises in your mind, be it fear of pain, fear of death, anxiety about others or whatever, say to it: "Don't disturb me. You're not my business any more." Just keep saying this to yourself when you see those dhammas arise.

What does the word 'dhamma' refer to? Everything is a dhamma. There is nothing that is not a dhamma. And what about 'world'?

The world is the very mental state that is agitating you at this moment. "What will this person do? What will that person do? When I'm dead, who will look after them? How will they manage?" This is all just 'the world'. Even the mere arising of a thought of fearing death or pain is the world.

Throw the world away! The world is the way it is. If you allow it to arise in the mind and dominate consciousness then the mind becomes obscured and can't see itself. So, whatever appears in the mind, just say: "This isn't my business. It's impermanent, unsatisfactory and not-self."

Thinking you'd like to go on living for a long time will make you suffer. But thinking you'd like to die right away or die very quickly isn't right either; it's suffering, isn't it? Conditions don't belong to us, they follow their own natural laws. You can't do anything about the way the body is. You can prettify it a little, make it look attractive and clean for a while, like the young girls who paint their lips and let their nails grow long, but when old age arrives, everyone's in the same boat. That's the way the body is, you can't make it any other way. But what you can improve and beautify is the mind.

Anyone can build a house of wood and bricks, but the Buddha taught that that sort of home is not our real home, it's only nominally ours. It's a home in the world and it follows the ways of the world. Our real home is inner peace. An external material home may well be pretty, but it is not very peaceful. There's this worry and then that, this anxiety and then that. So we say it's not our real home, it's external to us; sooner or later we'll have to give it up. It's not a place we can live in permanently because it doesn't truly belong to us, it's part of the world. Our body is the same; we take it to be self, to be 'me' and 'mine', but in fact it's not really so at all, it's another worldly home. Your body has followed its natural course from birth until now it's old and sick and you can't forbid it from doing that, that's the way it is. Wanting it to be different would be as foolish as wanting a duck to be like a chicken. When you see that that's impossible, that a duck has to be a duck, that a chicken has to be a chicken and that bodies have to get old and die, you will find strength and energy. However much you want the body to go on and last for a long time, it won't do that.

The Buddha said:

Anicca vata saṅkhārā
Uppāda vayadhammino
Uppajjitvā nirujjhānti
Tesaṃ vūpasamo sukho.

Conditions are impermanent,
subject to rise and fall.
Having arisen they cease—
their stilling is bliss.

The word *saṅkhāra* refers to this body and mind. Saṅkhāras are impermanent and unstable, having come into being they disappear, having arisen they pass away, and yet everyone wants them to be permanent. This is foolishness. Look at the breath. Having come in, it goes out; that's its nature, that's how it has to be. The inhalation and exhalation have to alternate, there must be change. Saṅkhāras exist through change, you can't prevent it. Just think: could you exhale without inhaling? Would it feel good? Or could you just inhale? We want things to be permanent, but they can't be; it's impossible. Once the breath has come in, it must go out; when it's gone out, it comes in again, and that's natural, isn't it? Having been born, we get old and sick and then we die, and that's totally natural and normal. It's because *saṅkhāra*s have done their job, because the in-breaths and out-breaths have alternated in this way, that the human race is still here today.

As soon as we're born, we're dead. Our birth and death are just one thing. It's like a tree: when there's a root there must be twigs. When there are twigs there must be a root. You can't have one without the other. It's a little funny to see how at a death people are so grief-stricken and distracted, tearful and sad, and at a birth how happy and delighted. It's delusion; nobody has ever looked at this clearly. I think if you really want to cry, then it would be better to do so when someone's born. For actually birth is death, death is birth, the root is the twig, the twig is the root. If you've got to cry, cry at the root, cry at the birth. Look closely: if there was no birth there would be no death. Can you understand this?

Don't think a lot. Just think: "This is the way things are." It's your work, your duty. Right now nobody can help you, there's nothing that your family and your possessions can do for you. All that can help you now is the correct awareness.

So don't waver. Let go. Throw it all away.

Even if you don't let go, everything is starting to leave anyway. Can you see that, how all the different parts of your body are trying to slip away? Take your hair: when you were young it was thick and black, now it's falling out. It's leaving. Your eyes used to be good and strong, and now they're weak and your sight is unclear. When the organs have had enough they leave, this isn't their home. When you were a child your teeth were healthy and firm; now they're wobbly, perhaps you've got false ones. Your eyes, ears, nose, tongue—everything is trying to leave because this isn't their home. You can't make a permanent home in a *saṅkhāra;* you can stay for a short while and then you have to go. It's like a tenant watching over his tiny little house with failing eyes. His teeth aren't so good, his ears aren't so good, his body's not so healthy, everything is leaving.

So you needn't worry about anything, because this isn't your real home, it's just a temporary shelter. Having come into this world, you should contemplate its nature. Everything there is, is preparing to disappear. Look at your body. Is there anything there that's still in its original form? Is your skin as it used to be? Is your hair? It's not the same, is it? Where has everything gone? This is nature, the way things are. When their time is up, conditions go their way. This world is nothing to rely on—it's an endless round of disturbance and trouble, pleasures and pains. There's no peace.

When we have no real home we're like an aimless traveller out on the road, going this way for a while and then that way, stopping for a while and then setting off again. Until we return to our real home we feel ill-at-ease whatever we're doing, just like the one who's left his village to go on a journey. Only when he gets home again can he really relax and be at ease.

Nowhere in the world is any real peace to be found. The poor have no peace and neither do the rich. Adults have no peace, children have no peace, the poorly-educated have no peace and neither do the highly-educated. There's no peace anywhere. That's the nature of the world.

Those who have few possessions suffer and so do those who have many. Children, adults, the aged, everyone suffers. The suffering of being old, the suffering of being young, the suffering of being wealthy, and the suffering of being poor—it's all nothing but suffering.

When you have contemplated things in this way you'll see *anicca*, impermanence, and *dukkha*, unsatisfactoriness. Why are things impermanent and unsatisfactory? It's because they're *anattā*, not-self.

Both your body that is lying here sick and painful, and the mind that is aware of its sickness and pain, are called *dhamma*s. That which is formless, the thoughts, feelings and perceptions, is called *nāmadhamma*. That which is racked with aches and pains is called *rūpadhamma*. The material is dhamma and the immaterial is dhamma. So we live with dhammas, in dhamma, we are dhamma. In truth there's no self anywhere to be found, there are only dhammas continually arising and passing away, as is their nature. Every single moment we're undergoing birth and death. This is the way things are.

When we think of the Lord Buddha, how truly he spoke, we feel how worthy he is of salutation, reverence and respect. Whenever we see the truth of something, we see his teachings, even if we've never actually practised Dhamma. But even if we have a knowledge of the teachings, have studied and practised them, but still haven't seen their truth, then we're still homeless.

So understand this point that all people, all creatures, are about to leave. When beings have lived an appropriate time they go their way. The rich, the poor, the young, the old, all beings must experience this change.

When you realise that that's the way the world is, you'll feel that it's a wearisome place. When you see that there's nothing stable or substantial you can rely on, you'll feel wearied and disenchanted. Being disenchanted doesn't mean you're averse. The mind is clear. It sees that there's nothing to be done to remedy this state of affairs, it's just the way the world is. Knowing in this way, you can let go of attachment, let go with a mind that is neither happy nor sad, but at peace with *saṅkhāra*s through seeing with wisdom their changing nature.

Anicca vata saṅkhārā—all *saṅkhāra*s are impermanent. To put it simply: impermanence is the Buddha. If we see an impermanent phenomenon really clearly, we'll see that it's permanent, permanent in the sense that its subjection to change is unchanging. This is the permanence that living beings possess. There is continual transformation, from childhood through youth to old age, and that very impermanence, that nature to change, is permanent and fixed. If you look at it like that your heart will be at ease. It's not just you that has to go through this, it's everyone.

When you consider things thus, you'll see them as wearisome, and disenchantment will arise. Your delight in the world of sense pleasures will disappear. You'll see that if you have a lot of things, you have to leave a lot behind; if you have few you will leave behind few. Wealth is just wealth, long life is just long life, they're nothing special.

What's important is that we should do as the Lord Buddha taught and build our own home, building it by the method that I've been explaining to you. Build your home. Let go. Let go until the mind reaches the peace that is free from advancing, free from retreating and free from stopping still. Pleasure is not our home, pain is not our home. Pleasure and pain both decline and pass away.

The Great Teacher saw that all *saṅkhāra*s are impermanent, and so he taught us to let go of our attachment to them. When we reach the end of our life, we'll have no choice anyway, we won't be able to take anything with us. So wouldn't it be better to put things down before that? They're just a heavy burden to carry around; why not throw off that load now? Why bother to drag them around? Let go, relax, and let your family look after you.

Those who nurse the sick grow in goodness and virtue. One who is sick and giving others that opportunity shouldn't make things difficult for them. If there's a pain or some problem or other, let them know, and keep the mind in a wholesome state. One who is nursing parents should fill his or her mind with warmth and kindness, not get caught in aversion. This is the one time when you can repay the debt you owe them. From your birth through your childhood, as you've grown up, you've been dependent on your parents. That we are here today is because our mothers and fathers have helped us in so many ways. We owe them an incredible debt of gratitude.

So today, all of you children and relatives gathered here together, see how your parents become your children. Before, you were their children; now they become yours. They become older and older until they become children again. Their memories go, their eyes don't see so well and their ears don't hear, sometimes they garble their words. Don't let it upset you. All of you nursing the sick must know how to let go. Don't hold on to things, just let go and let them have their own way. When a young child is disobedient, sometimes the parents let it have its own way just to keep the peace, to make it happy. Now your parents are like that child. Their memories and perceptions are confused. Sometimes they muddle up your names, or you ask them to give you a cup and they bring a plate. It's normal, don't be upset by it.

Let the patient remember the kindness of those who nurse and patiently endure the painful feelings. Exert yourself mentally, don't let the mind become scattered and agitated, and don't make things difficult for those looking after you. Let those who nurse the sick fill their minds with virtue and kindness. Don't be averse to the unattractive side of the job, to cleaning up mucus and phlegm, or urine and excrement. Try your best. Everyone in the family give a hand.

These are the only parents you've got. They gave you life, they have been your teachers, your nurses and your doctors—they've been everything to you. That they have brought you up, taught you, shared their wealth with you and made you their heirs is the great beneficence of parents. Consequently the Buddha taught the virtues of *kataṭṭu* and *katavedī* of knowing our debt of gratitude and trying to repay it. These two virtues are complementary. If our parents are in need, if they're unwell or in difficulty, then we do our best to help them. This is *kataṭṭu-katavedī*; it is a virtue that sustains the world. It prevents families from breaking up, it makes them stable and harmonious.

Today I have brought you the Dhamma as a gift in this time of illness. I have no material things to give you; there seem to be plenty of those in the house already, and so I give you Dhamma, something which has a lasting worth, something which you'll never be able to exhaust. Having received it from me you can pass it on to as many others as you like and it will never be depleted. That is the nature of Truth. I am happy to have been able to give you this gift of Dhamma, and I hope it will give you strength to deal with your pain.

The Problem of Fear *and* In Time of Grief

Two Letters on Dhamma

Nina Van Gorkom

Bodhi Leaves No. 112

First published: 1987

The Problem of Fear

Dear Khun Charūpan,
15 July 1983,

You asked my comment on a few Dhamma questions. These are questions we all have and I find it helpful to think about the answers since this gives me an opportunity to consider Dhamma. I will repeat your questions and comment on them.

Question: What is the characteristic of fear and how can it be overcome? I have fear of old age, sickness and death. I fear sickness and death of those who are dear to me. I have many kinds of fears. I also fear an unhappy rebirth. So long as one is not a "stream enterer" (*sotāpanna*), the noble person who has attained the first stage of enlightenment, one may be reborn in an unhappy plane where there is no opportunity to develop right understanding of the phenomena of our life. The good deeds one performs in this life are no guarantee of a happy rebirth. A bad deed performed even in a past life may condition an unhappy rebirth.

Answer: Fear can be a form of aversion and then it is unwholesome. When there is aversion we do not like the object experienced at that moment. We tend to cling to pleasant objects and to have aversion towards unpleasant objects. Aversion may be slight or it can be stronger, it may amount to hate. It can also take the form of fear and dread. When there is fear we shrink back from the object experienced and would like to flee from it. Or we may think with worry and dread about an unpleasant event which may happen in the future, such as old age, sickness and death, or an unhappy rebirth.

Fear arises so long as there are still conditions for its arising. It cannot be eradicated at once. Only the "non-returner" (*anāgāmi*), the noble person who has attained the third stage of enlightenment, has fully uprooted it. The development of right understanding of the phenomena that appear in our life is the only way leading to the eradication of fear. When fear appears we can learn to see it as it is: only a reality which arises because of its own conditions and which does not belong to a self.

Fear is conditioned by ignorance and by clinging. We cling to all the pleasant objects and we fear to lose them. We read in the

Gradual Sayings (Book of the Sixes, Ch. III, par. 3, Fear) about different names given to sense-desires, in order to show their dangers. One of these names is fear:

> And wherefore, monks, is fear a name for sense-desires? Monks, impassioned by sensuous passions, bound by passionate desire, neither in this world is one free from fear, nor in the next world is one free from fear. Therefore "fear" is a name for sense-desires.

In order to develop right understanding we should be aware of any reality that appears and we should not reject anything as an object of awareness. When fear appears it can be an object of awareness.

We may have theoretical understanding of the fact that we cannot control any reality that arises and that we thus cannot control the rebirth-consciousness of the next life. However, we still may be troubled by fear of rebirth. It is love of "self" which conditions this fear. We are worried about what will happen to the "self" after we die and we are afraid that this "self" will not be successful in developing understanding of realities in the next life. The stream-enterer does not worry about what will happen to a self, because he has eradicated belief in a self. Moreover, he has no more conditions for an unhappy rebirth. So long as one is not a stream-enterer one clings to a self and there are conditions for an unhappy rebirth.

It is understandable that we worry about the possibility of developing right understanding in the next life. However, we should remember that no moment of awareness is ever lost; each conditions the arising of awareness again later on. Also, awareness which arises now is conditioned: it is conditioned by moments of listening to the Dhamma and considering it, moments which arose in the past, even in past lives. Even so, awareness which arises now, although it does not stay, conditions awareness in the future because it can be accumulated from moment to moment.

Even if the next birth should be in an unhappy plane where there is no opportunity to develop right understanding, there will be following lives again in other planes where the development of understanding can continue. Even the *Bodhisatta* was reborn in the hell plane, but after that life he was reborn in the human plane where he continued to develop right understanding of realities.

Unwholesome fear, which is a form of aversion, is harmful for mind and body. However, there is also wholesome fear, that is, fear of unwholesomeness and its consequences. This fear is different from aversion. Unwholesome consciousness (*akusala citta*) is accompanied by unwholesome mental factors (*akusala cetasika*) and wholesome consciousness (*kusala citta*) is accompanied by beautiful mental factors (*sobhana cetasika*). Mental factors each perform their own function while they assist the consciousness they accompany.

Among the beautiful mental factors which accompany each act of wholesome consciousness are "moral shame" (*hiri*), shame of unwholesomeness (*akusala*), and "fear of blame" (*ottappa*), fear of the consequences of unwholesomeness. When these two mental factors perform their functions there cannot be unwholesome consciousness at that moment. There can be wholesome fear of the danger of the cycle of birth and death. With right understanding we can see the disadvantages of the imperfections and defilements that lead to rebirth. So long as there is ignorance and clinging, there has to be rebirth again and again. Wholesome fear of the danger of rebirth can urge us to persevere with the development of right understanding until all defilements are eradicated. Then there will be no more rebirth.

When the Buddha was still a *Bodhisatta* he developed right understanding with patience and perseverance in order to attain Buddha-hood so that he could teach other beings the way leading to the end of birth. The Mugapakkha Jātaka (VI, No. 538) gives an impressive account of the *Bodhisatta*'s heroism.

He never was neglectful of his task of developing wisdom, since he had a wholesome fear of rebirth in hell. He had to suffer severe tribulations, but he was always perfectly composed and never showed any weak point. When we are in difficult situations do we have perseverance to develop right understanding of realities?

We may find it difficult to be aware of whatever reality appears through one of the six doors, in particular when we are very busy or when we are in the company of other people. We could consider such circumstances as a test or an examination we have to pass. If we fail we have to begin again and again.

We read in the Mughapakkha Jātaka that the *Bodhisatta* was born as the son of the King of Kasi and received the name Temiya. He remembered that in a former life when he was a king he condemned people to death. As a result of his unwholesome *kamma* he was reborn in hell. After that he was reborn as Prince Temiya. When he remembered his former lives he decided that he did not want to succeed his father as king and therefore he pretended to be a cripple, deaf and dumb. Five hundred infants born to the concubines of the king were his companions. When they cried for milk he did not cry, reflecting that to die of thirst would be better than to reign as king and risk rebirth in hell. Milk was given to him after the proper time or not at all, but he did not cry. The nurses spent one year in trying him but did not discover any weak point. In order to test him the other children were given cakes and dainties and they quarrelled and struck one another. The *Bodhisatta* would not look at the cakes and dainties. He told himself, "O Temiya, eat the cakes and dainties if you wish for hell!" People kept on trying him in many ways but he was always patient and composed, realising the danger of an unhappy rebirth. People tried to frighten him with a wild elephant and with serpents but they did not succeed. They tempted him with pleasant objects. Performances of mimes were given and the other children shouted "bravo" and laughed, but Temiya did not want to look and remained motionless, reflecting that in hell there never would be a moment of laughter and joy. In order to know whether he was really deaf they tested him by a burst of sound made by conchblowers, but they "could not through a whole day detect in him any confusion of thought or any disturbance of hand or foot, or even a single start." They smeared his body with molasses and put him in a place infested with flies which bit him, but he remained motionless and perfectly apathic. When he was sixteen years old they tried to tempt him with beautiful women who were dancing and singing, "but he looked at them in his perfect wisdom and stopped his inhalations and exhalations in fear lest they should touch his body, so that his body became quite rigid."

The *Bodhisatta* looked with perfect composure and with wisdom at the beautiful women. While he was motionless during his trials and tests he was not idle, he was mindful. In order to attain Buddhahood he had to develop right understanding with perseverance. He was mindful of whatever reality appeared, no matter in what situation. Although this is not always mentioned in the Jātaka's, it is implied.

Finally the king was advised to bury him alive. When the charioteer was digging the hole for his grave, Temiya was adorned by Sakka, king of the gods, with heavenly ornaments. He then told the charioteer that he was not a cripple, deaf and dumb. He became an ascetic and preached to his parents about impermanence:

"It is death who smites this world,
old age who watches at our gate,
And it is the nights which pass and win their purpose soon or late.
As when the lady at her loom sits weaving all the day
Her task grows ever less and less—so waste our lives away.
As speeds the hurrying river's course on, with no backward flow,
So in its course the life of men does ever forward go;
And as the river sweeps away trees from its banks uptorn,
So are we men by age and death in head-long ruin born."

He explained to his father that he did not want the kingdom, stating that wealth, youth, wife and children and all other joys do not last:

"Do what you have to do today
Who can ensure the morrow's sun?
Death is the Master-general
Who gives his guarantee to none."

These words can remind us not to put off our task of developing right understanding. The *Bodhisatta* was unshakable in his resolution to develop right understanding. Also, when he was put to severe tests he did not prefer anything else to the development of wisdom. Are we resolute as well? Or are we forgetful of what is really worthwhile in our life? Wisdom is more precious than any kind of possession, honour or praise.

When we acquire wisdom, when we learn to see realities as they are, as mere mental and physical phenomena which arise due to conditions, we will no longer think ourselves to be so very important, and we will be less anxious about our "self." The Buddha's teachings remind us to consider the danger of the cycle of birth and death. If we do so, instead of unwholesome fear, there will arise wholesome fear urging us to be aware of the present moment.

Question: In order to lead a wholesome life is it sufficient to keep the Five Precepts? I feel that so long as one does not harm others there are no defilements. Is that right?

Answer: We may keep the precepts but that does not mean that we have eradicated defilements. Only the noble persons who have attained the fourth and last stage of enlightenment, the *arahat*s, are without defilements. We should develop understanding of our different types of consciousness. Then we will discover that there are many more unwholesome moments of consciousness than wholesome ones.

There are different degrees of defilements: they can be coarse, medium or subtle. Evil deeds by body, speech and mind are coarse defilements. But even when we do not commit evil deeds there are countless moments of unwholesome consciousness: these are medium defilements. For example, attachment and aversion may not motivate unwholesome deeds, but they are still unwholesome and thus dangerous. Unwholesome consciousness which arises falls away, but the unwholesome tendency is accumulated and it can condition the arising of unwholesomeness again. The unwholesome tendencies which are accumulated are subtle defilements. Even though they are called subtle, they are dangerous. Like microbes infesting the body, they can become active at any time. So long as they have not been eradicated they can condition the arising of unwholesome consciousness and of unwholesome deeds, and thus keep us in the cycle of birth and death.

Different objects are experienced through the five sense-doors of eyes, ears, nose, tongue and body-sense, and through the mind-door. On account of the objects which are experienced defilements tend to arise. A visible object, for example, is experienced by seeing-consciousness through the eye-door. Seeing-consciousness experiences only the visible object, it does not know anything else and at that moment there is no like or dislike of the object. However, shortly after the seeing has fallen away there are moments of consciousness which are either wholesome or unwholesome. When we are not engaged with generosity, with morality or with other kinds of wholesomeness, unwholesome consciousness has the opportunity to arise. Clinging is likely to arise very often after seeing, after the other sense-cognitions and also when we think.

When we think about events or people, the thinking is done either with wholesome consciousness or with unwholesome consciousness. We often think with clinging or attachment. Attachment can be accompanied by pleasant feeling or by indifferent feeling. When it is accompanied by indifferent feeling we may not notice it. We like to perceive all the familiar things around us, and we don't want to miss out on anything. This shows our clinging. Do we like softness? When we sit on a hard floor, there may be aversion. Aversion is conditioned by clinging. When we are aware of different realities we will know that there are many more unwholesome moments of consciousness than we ever thought. It is better to know the truth than to deceive ourselves.

Even when we keep the precepts and do not transgress them for a long time, it does not mean that we will never neglect them. So long as we have not become stream-enterers there are still conditions for unwholesome deeds which may produce an unhappy rebirth. When there is, for example, danger to our life, we may neglect the precepts. Only when one has attained to the stage of the stream-enterer can right understanding of the mental and physical phenomena of our life condition purity of morality to the degree that one never again neglects the Five Precepts.

Question: Although I know that gain, honour and praise do not last and can only arise when there are conditions for their arising, I cannot help being distressed when I do not get the rank or position I believe I deserve. What can I do in order to have less ambitions?

Answer: We are ambitious because we think ourselves to be important. Our clinging makes us unhappy. While we strive to get something there is clinging. Also, when we obtain what we want we hold on tightly. Clinging is the cause of endless frustrations. We want the "self" to become more important, but then it will be all the harder to eradicate the idea of self. If we think more of others the self will become less important.

We may have reflected on the impermanence of realities which arise because of conditions, or on the impermanence of all pleasant objects, but if we do not develop direct understanding of the realities which appear, understanding will not be strong enough to overcome clinging.

We should not only develop understanding when we are disappointed and unhappy, but we should begin right now. If we do not begin now how can there ever be less clinging to the self? We cling so much to our body, but in reality there are only different elements: solidity, cohesion, temperature and motion. The element of solidity, for example, which appears as hardness or softness, can be directly experienced through the body-sense without there being the need to think about it or to give it a name. When hardness appears there can be awareness of it and then understanding can see that it is only hardness, not a body that belongs to us. Hardness is only hardness, it does not matter whether it is hardness of what we call the body or hardness outside. If there is awareness of it when it appears we will begin to see it as an element, not self.

When right understanding is being developed we will also see that realities such as honour or praise are only elements and that they do not belong to a self. Thus there will be more confidence in the Dhamma and we will consider the Dhamma more precious than honour or praise.

We can easily be infatuated by gains, favours or flattery. They are treacherous because they seem desirable, but they lead to misery. In the Kindred Sayings (II, Nidana Vagga, Ch. XVII, Kindred Sayings on Gain and Favours) there are forty-three *sutta*s which point out to us the dangers of gains, favours and flattery. They are as dangerous as a fisherman's hook to the fish, as a thunderbolt, as a poisoned dart which wounds a man, as a hurricane which hurls a bird apart. People who do not easily lie tell deliberate lies when they are overcome by desire for gains, favours and flattery. We read in par. 10 of this section:

> Dire, monks, are gains, favours and flattery a bitter, harsh obstacle in the way of arriving at uttermost safety Concerning this matter, I see one person overcome, and whose mind is possessed by favours, another who is overcome and possessed by lack of favours, yet another who is overcome and possessed by both favours and the lack of them—I see one and all, at the separation of the body after death, reborn in the Waste, the Woeful Way the Downfall, Hell. So dire, monks, are gains ... Verily thus must you train yourselves: "When gains, favours, and flattery come to us, we will put them aside, nor when they come shall they take lasting hold on our hearts."
>
> In whom, when favours fall upon him or
> When none are shown, the mind steadfast, intent,
> Sways not at all, for earnest is his life,
>
> Him of rapt thought, (of will) unfaltering,
>
> Of fine perception, of the vision seer,
> Rejoicing that to grasp is his no more:
> Him let the people call in truth Good Man.

With mettā, Nina

In Time of Grief

Dear Maud, March 1979

You asked me whether the Buddha's teachings could console our friend Ina, who lost her husband and who has to bring up her children all by herself.

The Buddha's teachings can help us to have right understanding about life and death. What is life? Why must we die? We make ourselves believe that life is pleasant, but there are many moments of pain and sickness, sorrow and grief. And inevitably there is death.

Everything which arises must fall away, it cannot stay. We are born and therefore we have to die. The body does not disintegrate only at the moment of death, there is decay each moment. We notice that we have become older when we see a photograph taken some time ago. But the change which is noticeable after some time proves that there is change at each moment.

There are many phenomena taking place in our body, and they change each moment. Temperature changes: sometimes we feel hot, sometimes cold. We feel motion or pressure in our body time and again. What we take for "our body" is a compound of many different elements which arise and then fall away, but we are so ignorant that we do not notice it. The Buddha reminds us that our body is like a corpse, because it is disintegrating, decaying each moment. Our body does not belong to us but we cling to it: we are ignorant of the truth.

We may understand intellectually that the body does not really exist as a unitary whole and that it is only a composite of physical elements which change all the time. However, intellectual understanding is thinking, and thinking, even if it is right thinking, cannot eradicate wrong understanding of reality. We should learn to experience the truth directly.

Can we experience the body as it really is? Let us for a while forget about our theoretical knowledge of the body and ask ourselves whether there is not a bodily phenomenon now, which we can experience directly, without having to think about it. While we are sitting or walking, is there no hardness? Can it be experienced now, just for a moment, without having to think about it? These are physical elements which can be directly experienced, one at a time, through the body-sense.

There are many different kinds of elements. The element which is solidity can be directly experienced as hardness or softness, when it appears through the body-sense. Body-sense is all over the body. In order to experience hardness and softness, we do not have to think of the place where they appear.

Temperature is another physical phenomenon, an element that can be directly experienced. It can be experienced as heat or cold when it appears through the body-sense. There is change of temperature time and again. Is there not sometimes heat, sometimes cold? We do not have to think about it in order to experience it.

I have given only a few examples of bodily phenomena, physical elements which constitute the body. These examples may help us to see that all the Buddha taught can be proven through direct experience. Knowledge developed through direct experience is clearer than theoretical knowledge. The knowledge acquired through direct experience is the wisdom the Buddha taught his disciples to develop, so that all ignorance and clinging can be eradicated.

When we gradually learn through direct experience that what we take for our body is only physical elements which do not stay, we will be less taken in by an idea of our body as belonging to ourselves. We will see more clearly that all that arises, be it dead matter or a living being, is subject to decay.

Not only bodily elements arise and fall away, also what we call mind arises and falls away each moment. There is no lasting mind or soul, there is only a moment of consciousness now, and this falls away to be succeeded by the next moment. There may be thinking now, but it falls away to be succeeded by the next moment. Don't we think now of this, now of that? Thinking never stays the same. Can we control our thinking? Now we may have attachment, then aversion, then a moment of generosity. Is there generosity all the time? It falls away and very soon afterwards there may be pride, or stinginess.

What we call mind consists of many different elements which arise and then fall away immediately. The birth and death of consciousness occurs time and again all through life. Thus, we may understand that what we call in conventional language "dying" is in fact not different from what takes place each moment of our life.

The Buddha and the disciples who had attained to full enlightenment felt no grief about anything, whatever happened to them. So long as we have not attained to full enlightenment, we are still capable of feeling deep grief when those who are dear to us die, and at times we think with fear of our own death. Does the Buddha have a message for us who are only beginners on his path? The Buddha has a message for all those who are afflicted by grief and are disturbed by the thought of death. He teaches us to develop clear comprehension of the present moment. The wisdom the Buddha taught us to develop is knowledge acquired from direct experience of the physical elements and mental elements of which our life consists. Mental elements are moments of consciousness, feelings and other mental qualities such as anger and attachment.

We can have clear knowledge only of what occurs at the present moment, not of what is past already. Is there hardness now? Is there heat or cold now? These are only physical elements. Is there pleasant feeling now? Is there dislike of something now? Those are only mental elements. We are not used to considering the world in us and around us as elements. We may be inclined to say, "How can this kind of understanding help me now? It will not return to me my husband or wife, my child or my friend who has died. It will not alleviate my bodily pain, it cannot make me healthy again."

When we learn to see realities as elements which do not belong to us and which are beyond control, there will be less ignorance in our lives and we will then suffer less from life's adversities.

We still may have sorrow, but we should know sorrow as it is. Sorrow or grief is a kind of aversion, it is dislike of something we experience. It is natural that we feel grief. It is bound to arise when there are conditions for it. We had aversion in the past and this conditions the arising of aversion today. Ignorance of realities conditions everything unwholesome including aversion. Aversion is also conditioned by attachment. We are attached to the pleasant feeling we have when we are in the company of someone dear to us. When that person isn't around anymore we experience grief. Thus, it is actually a selfish clinging to our own pleasant feeling that conditions grief. This may sound crude, but if we are honest with ourselves we can see that it is true.

When we know more about the conditions for grief, we can understand that grief is only a mental element. Grief does not last, it falls away as soon as it has arisen. It may arise again, but then it is a different moment of grief. When we learn to see grief as a conditioned phenomenon, we will think less in terms of "my grief," and thus we will be less often overpowered by it. Our life consists not only of grief; there are many other realities which arise. When there is, for example, seeing or hearing, there cannot be grief at the same time.

When we learn to know the present moment, we will worry less about the past. What has happened, has happened already, how can we change it now? What can be done now is the development of right understanding of the present moment.

We read in one of the Jātakas, the Birth Stories of the *Bodhisatta*, in the "Birth Story about Desire" (Kāma Jātaka, No. 467) about grief conditioned by clinging. In the commentary to this story we read that a brahmin cultivated corn with the greatest care, intending to offer it when ripe as alms to the Buddha and his disciples. However, the night before he was to reap it, a great flood carried away the whole crop. The brahmin pressed his hand to his heart; overcome with grief, he went home weeping and lay down lamenting. The Buddha came in order to console him and said: "Why, will what is lost come back when you grieve?" The brahmin answered: "No, Gotama, it will not." The Buddha then said:

> "If that is so, why grieve? The wealth of beings in this world, or their corn, when they have it, they have it, and when it is gone, it is gone. There is no composite thing that is not subject to destruction: do not brood over it."

After the Buddha's discourse the brahmin could see realities as they are and attained enlightenment.

> "For each desire that is let go
> A happiness is won:
> He that all happiness would have,
> Must with all lust have done."

With *mettā*, Nina

—§§§—

The Walking Meditation

A Story

Suvimalee Karunaratna

Bodhi Leaves No. 113

First published: 1988

The Walking Meditation

A Story

When I place my feet one after the other, first the left front foot, then the right hind foot, then the right front foot and then the left hind foot, I try to be mindful. I do this meditation when I walk in the festival procession held every year in Kandy in the month of Esala.

I heard about this walking meditation from a nun who preached a sermon at the temple where I am tethered. At first, when I started on this meditation, I was not very successful. I kept recalling various incidents in the past and fragments of conversation, but I persevered. When I place my foot forward, I make a determined effort to be mindful and I try to sense the feeling of contact with the road surface and the weight of my body pressing down on the foot. I also try to see whether I can feel anything underfoot—grains of sand, for instance, or whether it feels hot or cold, rough or smooth. This was difficult, for, as you know, my feet are by no means tender, but after some time ... yes, I was able to feel these things and that gave me a great deal of encouragement.

At the same time, I try to be mindful of my body elsewhere, as, for instance, the folds of the caparison flap against my legs and even the weight on top. Invariably, that isn't much, considering only two men usually sit there holding the flag of the temple I belong to; but I always go back to my feet.

I am also mindful of the mahout at my side with his goad. I never can fathom why my mahout thinks I understand only that silly "elephant language" he uses to talk to me, and not his own, as if it had some special mystique to it. He thinks it is this language and my training that make me obey him. He little realizes that I obey him because I want to obey and that I have used that training and that language merely as tools to discipline myself.

When I was young, I used to love to be scrubbed, washed and got ready for the perahera, the annual festival procession. There was such a sense of anticipation among all the elephants brought to the Temple of the Tooth and the four main devales in Kandy from the outlying temples. Once, I remember, my mahout became angry with the organizer of our temple procession for giving him a torn caparison to put on me. He was greatly insulted and refused to dress me in it and squatted in a corner of the temple courtyard chewing betel, muttering and grumbling to himself.

I watched the others being dressed. What an operation it was! One man had to get on top of the elephant that was being dressed and the heavy material of lined silk or batik had to be gathered into a bundle and thrown up to him. Then the man on top would drape it over the animal's wide back and adjust it and strap it in place. Then the ear covers and the trunk covers would be put on, the small box which contained batteries for the electric lights on the trunk cover and howdah would be strapped on to the neck, and so on and so forth. As I watched, indignation mounted in me too, that I had been given torn clothes to wear. Finally, when the mahout made a ball of the material and threw it away with curses and took me off, I had likewise worked myself up to a fine pitch of anger.

Now when I look back on that episode I smile to myself. I would not react like that now. The change came over me after I heard the nun giving a sermon at the temple. She said one gets hurt when one's ego-supporting delusion gets shattered. I had only a vague idea then of what those words meant. I have a better idea now.

As I was saying, in those days I loved to get all dolled up and walk in the perahera. I loved the excitement in the air, the scent of flowers and incense all over the town, the streets agog with vendors with their bleating horns and happy hub-bub of chattering holiday crowds.

In the night the procession began with the rhythmic staccato drat-tattertat, tattertat, tattertat beating of kettle drums and the melodious wailing of oboes. The happy sound of anklets on the feet of the dancers and the silver spangles dangling from the rim of their metal headdresses fractured the air with an icy exhilaration. When I saw the bearers of flaring copra torches being lined up along the main road in front of our temple, and likewise the bearers of standards, banners, pennants and spears coming up, I used to feel such elation that I almost became dizzy.

In those days I used to have anklets tied round my feet too. I must have looked quite a giddy sight as I swayed my rump about, shook my head, flapped my ears and waved my tail and trunk as I walked. I was pleased no end to see the effect on the young bucks around me, whose eyes were always roaming around for such entertainment. At first the big one in front of me in the procession pretended not to notice me at all. He was standing next to Raja, the Maligawa Tusker, who carried the golden howdah in which is kept the casket containing the Buddha's tooth relic. He — that is, the big one next to Raja — was very tall and lordly and handsome, with fearsome looking tusks, but he took great pains to ignore me, sometimes giving me even disdainful looks when I got up too close to him.

Once, out of sheer devilry, I gave his tail a playful tug with my trunk and received from him an instant response. He halted in his tracks, turned the fore part of his body in a slow, dignified awesome manner, and gave me such a glare that I immediately froze with fright. My mahout too gave me a sharp reprimand for my saucy behaviour and I felt thoroughly chastised, so much so that my ears began to burn with shame. So many years later, I see other saucy creatures swaying their backs about, their anklets tinkling away, all dressed up like tarts and I think how silly they look. I even want to go up to some and give them a good shaking. I wish they could see themselves the way I see them. But did I see myself then, the way I see them now? I am quietened by that thought and a feeling of amused tolerance comes over me.

To tell the story of the lordly big one who glared at me: some time later, he was brought to our temple. There were ample meadows around and he was allowed to graze there, tethered to a long chain and I was tethered close by. His demeanour towards me had changed. He was even kindly. When he looked in my direction, which he did very often, an extraordinary heat coursed through my body, making my heart pound and my pulse beat fast. Once he came up quite close to me and this caused in me such turmoil that I actually thought I would swoon. Then he looked at me with such deep understanding, as if he knew exactly how I felt and rubbed me gently with his trunk. I cannot explain what I felt when his trunk touched me; it was as though electric flashes sparked all over me and shafts of lightning drove down deep into my groin.

I was very happy to be in his company and the days went by fast, but one day his mahout came and took him away. I protested, I wailed, I nearly charged the mahout but no one took any notice of my tantrum, least of all he. I had to watch with tears of rage as he was led away. What infuriated me most was that he did not even turn his head once to look back at me. He left me, rather, as if he were in a great hurry to leave, seeming even somewhat abashed at my outburst. I thought I heard him exclaim something like "Aah, these silly women! How they do carry on!"

I moped for days after that. I was so depressed and such a feeling of rejection came over me that I felt desperately frustrated. My mahout was very good to me in those days of my dejection, as though he understood me perfectly well.

"That's the way it is, old girl," he would say to me in his own language, which I had no difficulty following. "That's the way it is

—attachment, separation and the result is *dukkha*—pain, grief, lamentation and despair."

Sometime later as I worked out my grief in the day's labour at a dam site, I became aware of something new inside of me. I felt very hungry and was always demanding more fodder — coconut palms or kitul palms — from my mahout. He brought me what I wanted readily enough. There was such an intense driving force in my hunger that my mahout, after watching me for a few minutes, squatted on his haunches, began to feel my belly, and soon located a bulge.

"Aha! So you are to be a mother, eh?" he cried, his tone carrying with it a note of jubilation.

I did not know quite what to say or do.

I think I must have blushed and looked pleased, but after the mahout went away, I slowly felt my belly with my trunk. It was definitely swollen and harder. Oh yes. How wonderful! Me a mother? The whole day I thought of my being a mother and what the baby would be like, whether it would be like him or me. A hundred times a day I asked myself "Me, a mother?" and each time the question gave me a pleasant start. Thinking these thoughts, I grazed and grazed in the meadow and I hardly felt the time go by, because I was so consumed by thoughts and feelings of motherly love for my unborn babe and grandiose ideas of what he would be.

Then I began to crave for certain kinds of trees and leaves and fruit. As I foraged around, stuffing myself unceasingly, knowing I now had to eat for another as well, I indulged myself completely in the act of eating. The mahout was very considerate and brought me all kinds of different branches and leaves and even the monk in the temple came and fed me sugar cane, jaggery, wood apples and plantains. Even the villagers round and about heard of the news and came to see me, bringing with them all kinds of different delicacies. I was quite spoilt by their attentions and concern and the good will they lavished on me. How kind and generous they were!

I had no idea that the birth would cause me so much pain and discomfort. However, there was no dearth of well-meaning people around to give me moral support. I would have preferred if only my mahout was there. He was such a good midwife. After the birth, he brought some roots and leaves which he boiled and with which he fomented me all over. This took away all the tiredness from my body so that I felt very relaxed and content.

When I saw the helpless newborn baby, I felt a fierce love of protection for the funny puny thing with its fuzzy down all over him. I felt now as if I were the sole entity responsible for its birth, brought forth from my own womb where for so long it had gestated and been nourished by my body. As it tentatively felt me all over with its tiny trunk, searching and seeking out my teats to suckle, I felt such love for it, such sublime love, that my whole being was suffused with a gentle tingling warmth and the milk gushed out at his merest touch.

It was such a joy to watch him grow and become aware of the world around him. He would pay close attention to the smallest of creatures and I would be quite amused watching him. Even an ant crawling, a butterfly fluttering by or a bird calling on a branch above his head would enthrall him. Then, there was such gallantry and chivalry in him too when he thought there was danger about that threatened our safety. Once when a faint glimmer of lightning crackled over the horizon, he dashed out a few yards from me and made such a snorting, trumpeting racket, such a stamping of feet and a pawing of the earth, such a show of bravado, that he looked really comic. I had to turn away so he could not see that I was laughing. But all I said was, "Come here. It's only thunder and lightning and soon it will pass. Come under the shelter of this big tree and we will be safe from the rain."

One year when the festival came around, he was old enough to take part in the perahera. I think he must have been the youngest elephant in it that year. The mahout kept him very close to me and I had to be very stern-faced and firm because he was so playful and frisky. Behind my facade, however, I was brimming over with pride and it was with the greatest of difficulty that I held it all in.

All the time as I walked, I kept looking to see if his father would be there. I wanted to show off to him this marvel, this wonderful creation of ours. Would he show surprise and interest ... even joy? Then I saw him only a few paces ahead. As usual he stood next to Raja, the Maligawa Tusker, who carried the golden howdah with the holy Tooth Relic inside.

A young filly was trying to flirt with him, giving his tail sly tugs with her trunk. I froze all over and stonily watched what she was doing. I thought any minute he'll turn his lordly head and give her a stare, but to my astonishment I began to see that he was enjoying it. Once when we had paused for the dancers to complete their climactic sequence, he even turned around and swinging his trunk out, caught hers in his and swung it back and forth as though he were a teenager in love for the first time. He looked so foolish that my temper began to rise. It was really too much for me to bear.

Before I knew what I was doing, I charged and gave her a hefty whack with my trunk. Instantly he turned and shouldered me aside with such a sudden powerful swinging movement that I was sent staggering back and was spun half-way round. It all happened very quickly and I had barely recovered my balance when I became aware of the mahout shouting, tugging at my ear and I found the goad a full three inches inside my shank. I screamed and trumpeted, more from the pain of mind than anything else, and this caused still more pandemonium. Mahouts shouted to their animals to get them under control and a wave of panic went through the standing crowds alongside the road like a snake suddenly uncoiling itself.

"Kapuri! Behave yourself!" the mahout shouted at me. Then he led me out of the procession, the little one trotting behind me, cowering against my hind legs.

"You are not in a fit condition to take part in the perahera any more. I shan't bring you again!" he threatened. I felt so humiliated! Back in the temple grounds, I brooded for days. Inside me, I felt all bruised and shattered and there was a constant constriction in my throat so I could scarcely eat. For a few days the mahout left me severely alone and the little one hovered about me, anxious, frightened and baffled, but I was hardly aware of his existence. I was so absorbed in my hurt.

After a few days, the mahout softened towards me. The anger left his tone and he was even kind. "You are like my old woman," he told me, sitting down on the ground under the shade of the broad leaved breadfruit tree where I was tethered. He squatted there chewing his betel leaf, now and then spitting out the red juice. He was a man of few words but I felt his sympathy. "She used to behave just like you," he confided. I waited to see if he would say anything more but that was all. I continued to pick at the leaves he had brought me and pretended I hadn't heard him, though his words consoled me. In due course, I recovered from my bruised ego.

The following year I was led away again to take part in the perahera. Throughout that night I kept my eyes peeled on the lookout for him. Usually he walked by the side of the majestic Maligawa Tusker, but I saw another in his place. I wondered where he could be and why he hadn't come.

The year after that, however, I saw my little one's father again. He was there by Raja, the Maligawa Tusker, but what a change had come over him! I had to blink hard and look again to be doubly sure it was him I saw. He had become gaunt and grey and he held himself in a peculiar slouching fashion, his head sunk low. I then noticed the angry pink marks round his feet where his chains had cut into his flesh. In those places, the flesh looked raw and innumerable flies kept settling on the wounds. I felt sad to see him looking old and ill and in such obvious pain. Slowly, I moved up to him. I looked into his drawn face and sunken eyes and felt a pang of grief. "Is this him, this shadow, this ghost of that former giant?" I touched him, very tenderly with great sorrow in my heart and I rubbed my trunk all over his body as I had done in earlier years.

"I still love you, my lord master," I said. "I still love you. Do you love me?"

He responded by taking my trunk and curling his trunk round mine in a firm grip but the grip trembled and soon I felt the strength going out of it. Then I felt my mahout pulling me away.

Some days later, when I was in the temple compound, I overheard the monk calling out to the mahout from the verandah of the monastery that Skanda had died. I knew Skanda was his name. It gave me a start. I felt the mahout's gaze on me. I must have looked quite stricken because he patted my trunk.

"There, there, now, old girl. Don't take it so hard," he said gruffly. He had seen that I had not been eating ever since I saw my little one's father looking so sickly in the perahera and I think the mahout had realized why I was depressed. I cannot explain how I grieved for him — for what had become of him. When I thought of that last good-bye clasp he had given me, my grief knew no bounds.

"Come, eat this sugarcane I brought for you," the mahout said in a matter of fact voice that somehow comforted me. "We've got plenty of work to do tomorrow morning."

So I ate absentmindedly, without pleasure, just to please him, to show him that I appreciated his sympathy.

They took my little one away the following year. The monk had sold him to a rich landlord who lived in another area. They had taken him away when I was out at work in a patch of jungle where logging was in progress. I was so upset I thought I'd lose my reason. My loss kept whirling round and round in my head and then, when I thought nothing worse could happen to me, the mahout fell ill. He didn't come for days and meanwhile another mahout was brought in his place. I thought this was going to be a temporary arrangement, but as the days went by I realized the old mahout was never going to return. The awful thought came into my head that he might have died. As a matter of fact, he had, as I came to know later.

The new mahout was a raw recruit and very young. It was more as if I had to take him in hand and train him in his work. For instance, I would wait very patiently for his instructions, even if I knew well beforehand what they would be. When I was taken into the jungle where trees were being felled and I was required to drag away the trees or pile up the sawn logs neatly, I knew exactly what to do. It involved piling the pieces of timber one on top of the other and adjusting them, sometimes with the help of my leg, so they would be in a perfectly straight line. It required not only effort but concentration. Still, I had to wait for the mahout's fumbling instructions without jumping the gun, and that required much patience and self-control.

In time, we developed a rapport. He came to know what leaves and trees and fruits I liked best. Sometimes I'd tease him by not eating at all until he went and got me what I liked. Not that I really cared what I ate but I had to train him to look after me.

Training the young mahout took my mind off my own misery and I made him feel he was getting good results out of me entirely from his own efforts. When he tethered me at the end of the day and went away. I was left to myself to brood and ruminate, reflect, contemplate and meditate. This was the twilight hour I like best. At this time various rituals were conducted at the temple. Refreshing drinks, flowers, incense and lighted oil lamps would be offered in honour of the Buddha or the Bodhi tree and many devotees would come and participate in them. After these poojas, I would listen very carefully to the monk's sermons. No one knew I was listening or that I could understand, yet I understood perfectly. While I munched on my kitul palm branches, breaking them on my knee, sometimes waving them this way and that to get the sand off. I was aware as well of the gentle swishing and munching sounds I was making in the silence while the devotees listened to the monk giving a sermon or sat in meditation.

Actually, it was the nun who taught us to meditate. The nun had been invited to the temple by the monk to teach meditation on full moon days, for meditation was not his forte, though he could expound other aspects of the Teaching. It was the nun who explained about the ego-supporting delusion which we call "I" and "me."

It is difficult for one such as I, with all my bulk, to believe I am nothing. The *anattā* doctrine—that one does not have an ego as such—is beyond me. It is easy enough to understand *dukkha*, the unsatisfactoriness of existence, and *anicca*, change. My whole life has been a lesson in that. But she said one's understanding of these truths should go much deeper and that the "I" delusion is nothing but a host of wants resulting in clinging. When we rid ourselves of wants one by one, she said, like peeling off a plantain tree which has no core, we come to a nothingness at the centre.

I contemplate on this when I am given a plantain tree to munch. While I peel off and chew it skin by skin, I reflect and try to arrive at the "nothing" core with a start of realization. Once the young mahout, watching me and seeing what I did, expressed surprise that I was taking so much pains to peel the bark off layer by layer, daintily with my trunk, instead of putting it all in my mouth. No doubt he thought I was cranky.

When I first heard the nun talk of non-self, it made no sense to me at all. In fact, it made me laugh. Once the mahout gave me an order. "Kapuri! Come, let's go!" he shouted.

I pretended not to hear him and went on chewing my kitul palm tree. "There is no such person as Kapuri here," I said to myself, enjoying the joke as much as I did the kitul, turning over and over the juicy pulp in my mouth.

"Huh, so you are enjoying a joke by yourself, arh?" the mahout called out to me angrily. "Go on then. Pretend you don't hear me, but remember, if you let that training slip away from you, you lose the only thing worth having in this life."

Huh, look at him, that young whipper-snapper, coming to tell me about training! Anyway, it made my ears twitch and I soon turned towards him and began to follow him like a puppy.

The meditation on the breath as it touches the upper lip while one breathes in and out, which the nun taught, presented a problem to me; my anatomy is such that it didn't work at all, for you see, I have no upper lip. But I had no difficulty in doing the body meditation, first contemplating on top of my head and then slowly going further up to the crown, pressing down with my mental eye on the surface of my head till I got a sensation—any sensation—and then slowly working down to my forehead, the sides of the head, the shoulders, and so on all the way down.

I can do the meditation on the body better now because now I have many rheumatic aches and pains. Some time ago, I used to like to groan to excite and alarm the mahout. He'd show great concern, touching my body here and there and examining me all over. Then I would indicate where it hurt me by lifting my leg slightly and making it limp and dangle in front of him. Then he'd touch the knee and press it and even if I felt no pain, I'd groan and make out as if I were in great agony. He would then run off to get me some suitable medicinal herbs, which he would boil and rub over me and then tie around my leg. I shouldn't tease him so much. He's really a good boy.

When I do the walking meditation also, I become aware of my rheumatic pains

They may be ever so excruciatingly painful but when my concentration deepens the pain vanishes and then sometimes starts elsewhere. By doing this meditation constantly I have grown so adept at it that I can watch as the pain begins, becomes redder and redder on my mental screen, and then starts to wane. The nun said we must reflect on impermanence as we meditate, taking those feelings as our subjects. After all, what are we but a conglomeration of the physical elements that make up the body along with the mind, which consists of feeling, perception, mental formations and consciousness? And they are never static, but only a continual arising and passing away from moment to moment.

And so, when I walk in the perahera and I place my feet, one after the other, I concentrate on the sensations I feel as my foot comes in contact with the road surface, whether hot or cold, whether rough or smooth; and when a pain arises in my knee, I shift my concentration there, till it passes off, then I go back to the act of placing my feet one after the other as I move forward. As I do so, I reflect on the transience of feelings—ever-changing like this whole conglomeration of changing phenomena that we are. Then I think that my thoughts, like my feet, also follow one after the other in a chain, a perpetual progression of karma-forming mental acts that keep us instinctively clinging to existence.

Then I see before me the golden how-dah with the shining casket inside it, strapped on to Raja's back. It glows with a thousand lights in the night and I feel as if the Buddha's all-compassionate eyes were radiating from it, penetrating me with infinite compassion, seeking out every corner of my being, filling me with light and warmth and loving-kindness for all beings, who, like myself, are fleeting, changing phenomena whirling round and round, chained to the wheel of birth and rebirth. And as I walk on, the feeling of loving-kindness in me deepens and suffuses my whole being. It radiates outward, encompassing all the other elephants in the perahera and the people on the pavement, the whole town, and rising above the hill, it radiates in every direction, north, south, east, west and beyond the seas to all the world.

Going Into Homelessness

George Grimm

Translated by Bhikkhu Sīlācāra

Bodhi Leaves No. 114

First published: 1988

Going Into Homelessness

Preface

This Bodhi Leaf is an extract from Georg Grimm's magnum opus, The Doctrine of the Buddha: the Religion of Reason and Meditation (2nd revised ed., Berlin: Akademie-Verlag, 1958), translated by Bhikkhu Sīlācāra.

Grimm (1868–1945), known in his day as 'Bavaria's most benevolent judge', was an early German Buddhist who wrote on the Dhamma from deep personal conviction. Despite a controversial interpretation of the *anattā* or 'not-self' doctrine, his book remains a brilliant pioneering attempt to comprehend from within the Master's teaching as a unified whole.

This extract was chosen because it deals with a crucial topic which today is in danger of being brushed aside with too much haste, namely, the 'going forth into homelessness', the adoption of the monastic way of life. In our own secular age, this momentous step—always placed by the Buddha at the very start of the gradual training—is being trivialised by being reduced to a choice of 'lifestyle' or a cultural convention possessing no intrinsic value. Grimm's essay, building upon the Pali *sutta*s, offers a powerful and cogent reply to the contrary: that monasticism is not a mere dispensable appendage of the Dhamma but a natural and necessary outgrowth rooted in its transcendental core.

Grimm does not overlook the Buddha's declaration that the Dhamma can be practised with deep commitment by the laity or that a dedicated lay person may far surpass a slack and negligent monk. But he eloquently reminds us, by appeal to the Buddha's own word, that those who earnestly seek for full deliverance itself within this very life must be prepared to sever their ties to the world, including those that keep them in the home life. The Buddha in his great compassion founded the Sangha to encourage this step and to give it full support.

Bhikkhu Bodhi

Going Into Homelessness

The more exalted anything is, all the less is it generally understood, because it exceeds the mental capacity of the average man; and all the more is it exposed to misinterpretations. Indeed, because the cause cannot be removed, it is also quite impossible to meet these misinterpretations successfully. Hence it has always been the fate of the highest truths not only to be misunderstood, but also to be ridiculed.

It is therefore not astonishing that the doctrine of the Buddha too, the highest truth ever communicated to mankind, has frequently met this fate, especially in the countries of the West. This has been the case to a high degree from the fact that in its full, practical realisation, it issues in monasticism, an institution against which the ordinary man of the world instinctively revolts, because if it were in accord with the truth, it would mean the severest condemnation imaginable of his own way of living, which is entirely given up to the pleasures of the senses.

There are even in the West 'Buddhists', in all seriousness believing themselves to be such, who consider this institution of the Buddha superfluous! Of course they thereby only prove the truth of the old Indian proverb: "Even in the ocean, a jug cannot hold more than its own measure."

But to those who understand the way of freedom taught by the Buddha, it will be clear that this path cannot possibly be trodden in its entirety in the world. It demands nothing more and nothing less than the cultivation of the deepest contemplation and ceaseless watchfulness with regard to every single act, even the most insignificant, in the activity of the senses, so as to recognise as such every motion of thirst for the world in all its perniciousness, and thus allow no kind of grasping to arise any more.

But how should such unceasing control of all the impressions of the senses be possible within the world? It is impossible, because in the world these impressions are far too numerous for us to be able to maintain complete watchfulness over every single one of them. In the world, it is only on the rarest occasions, and then only for a brief period that we attain thoughtfulness, to say nothing of unbroken watchfulness.

As Raṭṭhapāla says to the Master: "If I really understand the doctrine expounded by the Exalted One, it is not possible, living the household life, to carry out point by point the perfectly purified, perfectly stainless holy life" (MN 82). Not even the fundamental precepts can be constantly kept: "Who lives at home is much busied, much occupied, much concerned, much harassed, not always wholly and entirely given to truthfulness, not always wholly and entirely restrained, chaste, devout, detached" (MN 99).

Certainly, also in the world, we may restrict our relations to it as much as possible; for instance, we may enter no profession, found no family, but these relations will never allow of being cut off entirely. For to live in the world just means to maintain relations with the world. So far, however, as these relations extend, to that extent we are occupied with worldly things; to this extent, therefore, we are cultivating and strengthening the fetters that chain us to the world. In so far, therefore, the ties cannot be definitively severed; and hence, to this extent, complete deliverance is impossible. For, wholly delivered he only is who "has cut through every tie."

On this point there can be no reasonable doubt. And thus it is really only a self-evident thing when the Buddha expressly asserts the impossibility of reaching Nibbāna while living the ordinary life of the world. "Is there, O Gotama, any householder, who, not having left off household ties, upon the dissolution of the body, makes an end of suffering?" "There is no householder whatever, Vaccha, who, not having left off household ties, upon the dissolution of the body, makes an end of suffering" (MN 71).

Precisely in consequence of this point of view the Buddha founded the Sangha as the Order of all those who have left home for the life of homelessness, in order, under his guidance, to strive as noble disciples towards the great goal of complete departure out of this world. In this Sangha of the selected ones, therefore, not less than in the Buddha and in his Doctrine itself, as the Three Jewels, *Tiratana*, must those take their refuge who wish to tread the most direct road to deliverance, as it is expressed in the formula of confession which up to the present day constitutes the actual confession of faith of all Buddhists:

To the Buddha I go for refuge.
To the Dhamma I go for refuge.
To the Sangha I go for refuge.

After this, the utter folly will probably be apparent of all those who think they must advocate a Dhamma without a Sangha. For they take away the blade from the knife; or, what is the same thing, they would have us believe that a bather might become dry before he has got out of the water. Such a standpoint, of course, they can only adopt because they are unable to grasp the kernel of the Buddha's doctrine, and with it, their own eternal destiny. That is to say, they are unable to comprehend that "the whole world is really a burning house, from which we cannot save ourselves quickly enough" (MN 52). For if they did understand this, then it would be simply impossible that instead of speaking contemptuously of "flight from the world," they should not draw a breath of relief every time they saw yet another person flee out of this burning house, and only regret that they themselves cannot find the courage to do the same.

What about the complaints that, according to this, all men ought to become monks and nuns, and that the world would thus be in danger of dying out? Such complaints amount to just this, that one would regard it as a calamity if all men were to be cure of their bodily ailments because then there would be no more hospitals. Certainly, the world would cease to exist if all beings could be brought to realise their eternal destiny; but thereby it would only be suffering that would reach its definitive end. However, those who are so intensely concerned about the continuation of the world may console themselves, since this will not happen. For there will always be those who, far from leaving the world themselves, will even throw stones at those who set them the example.

Assuredly, certain scruples are difficult to set aside, even for earnest strivers, as regards the so-called collision of duties brought about by the way into homelessness as it affects one's own relatives, especially wife and children. Though the Buddha does not permit ordination to anyone who does not have the permission of his parents, he is not opposed to a man's leaving wife and children in order to seek his eternal deliverance. This standpoint comes out most clearly in the following narrative.

One time the Exalted One was staying at Sāvatthī, in the Jeta forest grove of Anāthapiṇḍika. At that time Venerable Saṅgāmaji had come to Sāvatthī in order to see the Exalted One. Now the former wife of the Venerable Saṅgāmaji had heard that the Venerable Saṅgāmaji had arrived in Sāvatthī. Thereupon she took up her child and went to the Jeta forest. Now at this time the Venerable Saṅgāmaji was seated at the foot of a tree in order to spend the afternoon there in meditation.

The former wife of the Venerable Saṅgāmaji went to him and said: "Look here, ascetic, at your little son and support me!" At these words the Venerable Saṅgāmaji remained silent. A second and a third time she said to him: "Look here, ascetic, at our little son and support me!" And for the second and the third time the Venerable Saṅgāmaji remained silent.

Then the former wife of the Venerable Saṅgāmaji laid down the child before the Venerable Saṅgāmaji and went off, saying: "This is your son, ascetic. Support him!" But the Venerable Saṅgāmaji neither looked at the child nor spoke a word.

As the former wife of the Venerable Saṅgāmaji watched from a distance, she saw that the Venerable Saṅgāmaji neither looked at the child nor said a word. Thereupon she thought: "Not even for this child does this ascetic care." And so she returned, took the child and went away. But the Exalted One, with the divine eye, purified and superhuman, saw this meeting between the Venerable Saṅgāmaji and his wife. And the Exalted One perceived the meaning (of this meeting) and on this occasion uttered the following verse:

> The coming does not make him glad,
> The going does not make him sad;
> The monk, from longings all released,
> Him do I call a brahmin.

Ud I.8

There are many who are honest friends of the doctrine of the Master, but nevertheless are unable to understand this standpoint. And yet it is perfectly clear if only understood from the heights of pure cognition.

If the Buddha is right in this, that the eternal destiny of every being lies in his outgrowing the world, and at last leaving it entirely, then from the nature of this destiny also must be taken the criterion for the evaluation of every action from a moral point of view. Good or moral, in the highest sense, can only be what serves for the reaching of this ultimate goal; bad or immoral is everything that hinders this or directly makes it impossible. If this indubitably correct principle is taken as basis, then he certainly is not acting immorally who for the sake of his eternal welfare leaves the world and with it also wife and child. What he does is good for him, for it lies in the line of his eternal destiny; it is even extraordinarily good, for it lies upon the nearest way to it.

But if, on his side, it is something extraordinarily good that he wishes to do, then just because of this, every obstruction of this step, from whatever side it may come, appears as something immoral—this word used, of course, from the highest standpoint now adopted by us. In short: it is not he who wishes to become a saint who acts immorally; but those who act immorally are his wife and children who out of selfishness wish to hinder him from achieving his eternal liberation.

In order to recognise clearly this distribution of the guilt, the following points ought to be considered. He also is moved by love of wife and child, perhaps more than those who condemn him, for he is unquestionably a noble man. But with the severest mental struggles he opposes this love as well as any other inclination leading back to the world, and presses forward to do the most difficult thing a man can ever do, to take up the struggle against himself to its full extent. Compared to this struggle, every other is mere child's play, for he aims to learn to renounce the satisfaction of every motion of craving, and in time, to become entirely free from craving.

But all that the others want is not to lose their supporter. They are unable to master their inclination towards him who is leaving them, which presents itself in the guise of love; in a word, they are the slaves of their own craving.

Who now is great, and how small? But is the great to abandon his goal for the sake of the small? May a warrior going to battle allow himself to be kept back by the complaints of wife and children? Wouldn't the whole world cry out at him: "Weakling!"?

From this, it obviously follows that is not advisable to neglect to do something morally good out of regard for the lack of understanding of others. For it is nothing else but lack of understanding that here stands obstructively in the way.

During their endless pilgrimage through the world, some few persons have found themselves together for a brief time in one family, to be separated again very soon in death, and then each must continue the pilgrimage alone, perhaps on through a terrible future. Looked at from this point of view, is it not unreasonable if one of them wishes to hinder another from putting an end to this unhappy wandering through the worlds only in order that he may enjoy this present fleeting existence as free from care and pain as possible, unconcerned about his own fate or about the future fate of the other?

Is not this at bottom really irresponsible? Who is here the egoist—he who wishes radically to annihilate everything that makes him an ego existing in the world; or the other who, not satisfied merely with the affirmation of his own ego, desires also to force the other into his service?

Since, therefore, the going into homelessness is moral, every impediment to it is an immorality; hence none can claim treaty rights as impediments against it. For every claim to such a restriction by treaty-right of the other party would itself mean an immorality, inasmuch as the character of the action that is immoral in itself cannot be altered by a claim to its being reserved to the person against whom it is to be committed, moreover, under conditions quite different from those at present prevailing. In the same way that public law takes precedence over private law, and thus a private claim must give way to a public one, in the same way, every claim derived from a contract or from some other legal ordinance must give way to the demands of ethics, if law is not to become an instrument for the triumph of immorality.

By this, however, we do not mean that the claim to go into homelessness is one that is free of all conditions. Rather does it find its limits in the very moral demands out of which it arises.

Whoever seeks his own eternal welfare may not endanger the true welfare of others.

Of course, the sorrow he causes to those belonging to him without further ado may be excluded as regards him who leaves home; for it is not he who is the cause of this, but simply their own ignorance. Accordingly, he has not to bear the consequences of this. For the rest, however, it is, of course, only a question of the true welfare of those belonging to him, not what these themselves hold to be their welfare.

Hence it is no great matter if now they should lose that carefree, perhaps comfortable life they have hitherto been leading. For such a life, regarded from the highest standpoint, is to be regarded as more of a misfortune than a blessing, since, as a rule, it only strengthens attachment to this world, and thereby future suffering.

"If, householder, you will do what I advise, then you will put this heap of gold and jewels on carts and have them taken out of town and thrown into the middle of the Ganges. And why so? Surely, householder, you will experience through them woe and sorrow, grief and pain and despair," Raṭṭhapāla tells his father who tries to persuade him to renounce monkhood by calling attention to his great wealth (MN 82).

It does not matter even if those left behind lose their supporter, if only they are just able to support themselves, be it only with the help of others. For this, regarded from the highest standpoint, may be more a blessing than a misfortune, since it is particularly effective in making men think about their true relation to the world. Hence there remain only as cases demanding consideration of him who wishes to become a monk, those where without him even the minimum amount of support necessary to his relatives, or even their eternal liberation, would be jeopardised. An example of the latter would be the case where his children were in danger of being morally neglected.

The former standpoint is adopted by Ghaṭīkāra the potter in the 81st Discourse of the Majjhima Nikāya. In reply to the exhortation of his friend Jotipāla to enter the Order of the Master, he says: "Don't you know, dearest Jotipāla, that I have to support my old and blind parents?" But that in no case may a man put in jeopardy the eternal welfare of those he leaves behind by going into homelessness becomes clear precisely through the story from the Udāna quoted above, where Saṅgāmaji maintains a passive attitude only towards the demand of his former wife that he shall support her and her child. If her eternal welfare had been in question, that pity for all beings, dwelling in him as in every saint, would have determined him to save her. To be sure, this pity, in the case before him, would probably have been confined to the 'miracle of instruction' as the only means promising real success.

To bring under one principle, in harmony with the intentions of the Buddha, the cases in which the going into homelessness had better not be undertaken out of regard for others, we might say: whoever wants to enter the Order of the Master, his relations towards those belonging to him must be of such a kind that his step would be approved by them if they stood upon the same high moral level as he himself. If, after having carefully examined himself, he finds these relations to be of this sort—in other words, if, their roles being exchanged, he could say that he, in their place, would consider himself obliged to give his consent—then, if now he actually goes away, he acts in entire harmony with the moral law decisive for him, and therefore cannot be doing anything in any way blameworthy.

For the real cause of all the suffering entailed upon those belonging to him through the step he takes, lies not in him but in their own lack of understanding or defective cognition. Thus, rightly regarded, the blame is not his but their own, and by them must be borne. If they were on the same level as he, instead of their making the event a source of suffering, it would be followed by the most wholesome consequences for them also.

"If, Dīgha, the family whence have come these three well-born ones who have left home behind and vowed themselves to the homeless life shall think upon them with hearts filled with faith, long will it make for the welfare and happiness of that family," is said in the 31st Discourse of the Majjhima Nikāya, with reference to three youths who had followed the Buddha.

If thus there may be external circumstances detaining one from going into homelessness, the chief hindrance generally lies in the man himself. The man must be ripe for this, that is to say, his entire willing must already be so ennobled that nothing within this world is able any longer entirely to satisfy him, so that the eternal, as soon as in any comprehensible fashion it enters his range of vision, powerfully attracts him and causes all his earthly possessions to appear to him as empty and insipid, no further able seriously to fetter him.

"Just as if, Udāyi there was a householder or the son of a householder, rich, greatly endowed with money and valuables, many heaps of gold, many masses of corn, many fields and meadows, many multitudes of women, many servants, many handmaids. And he would see in a grove a monk, with clean-washed hands and feet, cheerful of countenance, after having taken his meal, sitting there in the cool shadow, giving himself to exalted heedfulness.

"And he would feel thus: 'Blissful, truly, is the holy life! Free from suffering, truly, is the holy life! Oh, that I were such a man who, with hair and beard shaved off, clad in yellow robes, might go forth from home into homelessness!' And he would be able to leave the many heaps of gold, the many masses of corn, the many fields and meadows, the many houses and farms, the many multitudes of women, the many servants, the many handmaids, and go with hair and beard shaved off, clad in yellow robes, from home to homelessness ... These for him are no strong fetters, but weak fetters, rotten fetters, fetters unable to hold" (MN 66).

But on this height stand only the very tiniest minority of men. The immense majority still cleave so tightly to the world that the message of a supramundane happiness and peace is at best only able to arouse in them, even if they live in the most miserable circumstances, a feeble and indefinite feeling of the unworthiness of their present situation, which of course can furnish no motive to corresponding action.

"As if, Udāyi there was a man, poor and neither free nor independent, and owning but a single hut, decayed and dilapidated, open to the crows, not at all beautiful, a single resting place, decayed and dilapidated, not at all beautiful, a single bushel of corn-seed, not at all beautiful, a single woman, not at all beautiful; and in a grove he would see a monk, with clean-washed hands and feet, cheerful of countenance, after having taken his meal, sitting in the cool shade, giving himself to exalted heedfulness.

"And he would feel thus: 'Blissful, truly, is the holy life! Free from suffering truly is the holy life! Oh, that I were such a man who, with hair and beard shaved off, clad in yellow robes, might go forth from home to homelessness!' And he would not be able to leave his one single hut, decayed and dilapidated, open to the crows, not at all beautiful, his one single resting-place, decayed and dilapidated, not at all beautiful, his one bushel of corn-seed, not at all beautiful, his one woman, not at all beautiful, and go forth, with hair and beard shaved off, clad in yellow robes, from home to homelessness ... These are strong fetters for him, tight fetters, tough fetters, not rotten fetters, but a heavy clog" (MN 66).

According to this, the Order of the Master comes into question only for very few men, for so very few that the Buddha, after having come to full awakening, doubted if he ought to communicate to the world the Dhamma that had unveiled itself before him, since it was a truth "going against the stream, deep, intimate, delicate, hidden, not to be reached by mere reasoning, imperceptible to those delighting in the senses" (MN 26).

But at last, consideration for those few "noble beings who would be lost if they heard not the Doctrine," determined him to found the Sangha. So very few minds of the highest order did the Buddha find even in his own favoured age when care for their eternal welfare exerted an influence over the actions of men as at no other time. How many, then, in our 'evil age', and moreover, in the West, may be ripe to walk the highest path on to its end?

The question therefore arises as to what all those are to do who in consequence of their previous *kamma*, for external or internal reasons are not ripe for the Sangha, and yet in whom, more or less, a "Divination of the truth" has arisen, and thereby "trust in the perfected One and in his Doctrine has become rooted and sent forth shoots" (MN 109).

To them also, as we know, the Buddha shows the way, and precisely in the Noble Eightfold Path, points out to them also the only possibility of moral progress. Even in the world they may live in accordance with it in the measure of their capacity for doing so, and so far as the conditions under which they have to live permit. Some may have to confine themselves merely to creating the conditions for a favourable rebirth, some may also strive towards the great final goal of the complete overcoming of the circle of rebirths.

Though they do not reach the highest goal of holiness in this life—in this embodiment, according to what we have said above, Nibbāna can only be attained within the Sangha—nevertheless they may thus far curb and refine their passions and thereby their thirst for the world, that even in them the inner certainty may arise that at the moment of their approaching death they will never again attach themselves to a germ below the human kingdom; so that with every existence still in store for them, they come nearer to their eternal liberation.

Having "entered the stream, they are safe from torment in the lower worlds and sure of the Full Awakening." They may even completely cast off "the five fetters of the low earthly life" that ever and again lead back to this our world of the five senses, namely, sensual desire, ill will, belief in personality, faith in the efficaciousness of ritual ceremonies and customs, and doubt, so that after death they will no more return to this world, but in one of the highest worlds of light will attain Nibbāna.

The Sangha is nothing but an institution for clearing away, in advance, all those external hindrances that in the world generally make it impossible to keep closely and steadily to the Noble Eightfold Path. In so far as we know how to avoid these hindrances as much as possible in the world, and thus to restrain them, successful progress may also take place here. And it may even happen that one who remains in the household life may progress further than another who has left it.

But of course one who withdraws from household life, other circumstances being the same, will make much easier and quicker progress than one who remains in the household life. Often, in fact, one's household and business duties will be of such a kind that only a complete break with them will provide even the possibility of working earnestly for deliverance. But even where they are exceptionally favourable, they can never be of such a kind as to make possible complete deliverance during this present lifetime, and the unshakable certainty of the same. Therefore to those who make this highest goal their aim, it only remains to enter the Sangha.

To these elect ones the Buddha appeals first. Hence, it will be clear without further argument that he makes the going into homelessness the starting-point for the realisation of the Noble Eightfold Path, and bases this Path in all its parts upon this going forth, by leaving it to all who are not able or willing to fulfil this fundamental antecedent condition to hold to the several stages of the Path, as far as it is possible to them in their individual circumstances. And so he begins his description of the Path to deliverance, as it takes practical shape, with the going forth into homelessness.

Ānāpānasati: Meditation on Breathing

Ven. Nauyane Ariyadhamma Mahāthera

Bodhi Leaves No. 115

First published: 1988

Ānāpānasati: Meditation on Breathing

Homage to the Blessed One, Accomplished and Fully Enlightened

Ānāpānasati, the meditation on in-and-out breathing, is the first subject of meditation expounded by the Buddha in the Mahāsatipaṭṭhāna Sutta, the Great Discourse on the Foundations of Mindfulness. The Buddha laid special stress on this meditation, for it is the gateway to enlightenment and Nibbāna adopted by all the Buddhas of the past as the very basis for their attainment of Buddhahood. When the Blessed One sat at the foot of the Bodhi Tree and resolved not to rise until he had reached enlightenment, he took up *ānāpānasati* as his subject of meditation. On the basis of this, he attained the four *jhānas,* recollected his previous lives, fathomed the nature of *saṃsāra,* aroused the succession of great insight knowledges, and at dawn, while 100,000 world systems trembled, he attained the limitless wisdom of a Fully Enlightened Buddha.

Let us then offer our veneration to the Blessed One, who became a peerless world-transcending Buddha through this meditation of *ānāpānasati.* May we comprehend this subject of meditation fully, with wisdom resplendent like the sun and moon. Through its power may we attain the blissful peace of Nibbāna.

The Basic Text

Let us first examine the meaning of the text expounded by the Buddha on *ānāpānasati.* The text begins:

"Herein, monks, a monk who has gone to the forest, or to the foot of a tree, or to an empty place, sits down cross-legged, holding his back erect, arousing mindfulness in front of him."

This means that any person belonging to the four types of individuals mentioned in this teaching—namely, *bhikkhu* (monk), *bhikkhunī* (nun), *upāsaka* (layman) or *upāsikā* (laywoman)—desirous of practising this meditation, should go either to a forest, to the foot of a secluded tree, or to a solitary dwelling. There he should sit down cross-legged, and keeping his body in an erect position, fix his mindfulness at the tip of his nose, the locus for his object of meditation.

If he breathes in a long breath, he should comprehend this with full awareness. If he breathes out a long breath, he should comprehend this with full awareness. If he breathes in a short breath, he should comprehend this with full awareness. If he breathes out a short breath, he should comprehend this with full awareness.

"He breathes in experiencing the whole body, he breathes out experiencing the whole body"—that is, with well-placed mindfulness, he sees the beginning, the middle and the end of the two phases, the in-breath and the out-breath. As he practises watching the in-breath and the out-breath with mindfulness, he calms down and tranquillises the two functions of in-breathing and out-breathing.

The Buddha illustrates this with a simile. When a clever turner or his apprentice works an object on his lathe, he attends to his task with fixed attention: in making a long turn or a short turn, he knows that he is making a long turn or a short turn. In the same manner if the practitioner of meditation breathes in a long breath he comprehends it as such; and if he breathes out a long breath, he comprehends it as such; if he breathes in a short breath, he comprehends it as such; and if he breathes out a short breath, he comprehends it as such. He exercises his awareness so as to see the beginning, the middle and the end of these two functions of breathing in and breathing out. He comprehends with wisdom the calming down of these two aspects of in-breathing and out-breathing.

In this way he comprehends the two functions of in-breathing and out-breathing in himself, and the two functions of in-breathing and out-breathing in other persons. He also comprehends the two functions of in-breathing and out-breathing in himself and in others in rapid alternation. He comprehends as well the cause for the arising of in-breathing and out-breathing, and the cause for the cessation of in-breathing and out-breathing, and the moment-by-moment arising and cessation of in-breathing and out-breathing.

He then realises that this body which exercises the two functions of in-breathing and out-breathing is only a body, not an ego or 'I'. This mindfulness and wisdom become helpful in developing greater and more profound mindfulness and wisdom, enabling him to discard the erroneous conceptions of things in terms of 'I' and 'mine'. He then becomes skilled in living with wisdom in respect of this body and he does not grasp anything in the world with craving, conceit or false views. Living unattached, the meditator treads the path to Nibbāna by contemplating the nature of the body.

This is an amplified paraphrase of the passage from the Mahāsatipaṭṭhāna Sutta on *ānāpānasati*. This meditation has been explained in sixteen different ways in various *suttas*. Of these sixteen, the first tetrad has been explained here. But these four are the foundation for all the sixteen ways in which *ānāpānasati* can be practised.

The Preliminaries of Practice

Now we should investigate the preliminary stages to practising this meditation. In the first place the Buddha indicated a suitable dwelling for practising *ānāpānasati*. In the *sutta* he has mentioned three places: the forest, the foot of a tree, or an isolated empty place. This last can be a quiet restful hut, or a dwelling place free from the presence of people. We may even consider a meditation hall an empty place. Although there may be a large collection of people in such a hall, if every one remains calm and silent it can be considered an empty place.

The Buddha recommended such places because in order to practise *ānāpānasati* silence is an essential factor. A beginning meditator will find it easier to develop mental concentration with *ānāpānasati* only if there is silence. Even if one cannot find complete silence, one should choose a quiet place where one will enjoy privacy.

Next the Buddha explained the sitting posture. There are four postures which can be adopted for meditation: standing, sitting, reclining and walking. Of these the most suitable posture to practise *ānāpānasati* at the beginning is the seated posture.

The person wishing to practise *ānāpānasati* should sit down cross-legged. For *bhikkhus* and laymen, the Buddha has recommended the cross-legged position. This is not an easy posture for everyone, but it can be gradually mastered. The half cross-legged position has been recommended for *bhikkhunīs* and laywomen. This is the posture of sitting with one leg bent. It would be greatly beneficial if the cross-legged posture recommended for *bhikkhus* and laymen could be adopted in the 'lotus' pattern, with the feet turned up and resting on the opposite thighs. If that is inconvenient, one should sit with the two feet tucked underneath the body.

In the practice of *ānāpānasati* it is imperative to hold the body upright. The torso should be kept erect, though not strained and rigid. One can cultivate this meditation properly only if all the bones of the spine are linked together in an erect position. Therefore, this advice of the Buddha to keep the upper part of the body erect should be clearly comprehended and followed.

The hands should be placed gently on the lap, the back of the right hand over the palm of the left. The eyes can be closed softly, or left half-closed, whichever is more comfortable. The head should be held straight, tilted a slight angle downwards, the nose perpendicular to the navel

The next factor is the place for fixing the attention. To cultivate *ānāpānasati* one should be clearly mindful of the place where the incoming and outgoing breaths enter and leave the nostrils. This will be felt as a spot beneath the nostrils or on the upper lip, wherever the impact of the air coming in and out the nostrils can be felt most distinctly. On that spot the attention should be fixed, like a sentry watching a gate.

Then the Buddha has explained the manner in which *ānāpānasati* has to be cultivated. One breathes in mindfully, breathes out mindfully. From birth to death this function of inbreathing and out-breathing continues without a break, without a stop, but since we do not consciously reflect on it, we do not even realise the presence of this breath. If we do so, we can derive much benefit by way of calm and insight. Thus the Buddha has advised us to be aware of the function of breathing.

The practitioner of meditation who consciously watches the breath in this manner should never try to control his breathing or hold back his breath with effort. For if he controls his breath or holds back his breath with conscious effort, he will become fatigued and his mental concentration will be disturbed and broken. The key to the practice is to set up mindfulness naturally at the spot where the in-breaths and the out-breaths are felt entering and leaving the nostrils. Then the meditator has to maintain his awareness of the touch sensation of the breath, keeping the awareness as steady and consistent as possible.

The Eight Steps

To help practitioners in developing this meditation, the commentators and meditation masters have indicated eight graduated steps in the practice. These eight steps will first be enumerated, and then they will be explained in relation to the actual meditative process.

The eight steps are named: counting (*gaṇaṇa*); following (*anubandhana*); contact (*phusana*); fixing (*ṭhapana*); observing (*sallakkhaṇa*); turning away (*vivaṭṭana*); purification (*pārisuddhi*); and retrospection (*paṭipassana*). These eight cover the whole course of meditative development up to the attainment of arahantship.

Counting

Counting is intended for those who have never before practised *ānāpānasati*. It is not necessary for those who have practised meditation for a considerable period of time. However, as it is expedient to have a knowledge of this, counting should be understood in the following manner.

When the meditator sits down for meditation, he fixes his attention at the tip of his nose and consciously attends to the sequence of in-and-out breathing. He notes the breath as it enters, and notes the breath as it leaves, touching against the tip of the nose or the upper lip. At this time he begins to count these movements.

There are a few methods of counting. The easiest is explained thus: The first breath felt is counted as "one, one"; the second as "two, two"; the third as "three, three"; the fourth as "four, four"; the fifth as "five, five" and so on up to the tenth breath which is counted as "ten, ten." Then he returns to "one, one" and continues again up to "ten, ten." This is repeated over and over from one to ten.

The mere counting is not itself meditation, but the counting has become an essential aid to meditation. A person who has not practised meditation before, finding it difficult to understand the nature of his mind, may think he is meditating while his mind runs helter skelter. Counting is an easy method to control the wandering mind.

If a person fixes his mind well on his meditation, he can maintain this counting correctly. If the mind flees in all directions, and he misses the count, he becomes confused and thus can realise that his mind has wandered about. If the mind has lost track of the count, the meditator should begin the counting over again. In this way he should start the counting again from the beginning, even if he has gone wrong a thousand times.

As the practice develops, there may come a time when the in-breathing and out-breathing take a shorter course and it is not possible to count the same number many times. Then the meditator has to count quickly "one," "two," "three," etc. When he counts in this manner he can comprehend the difference between a long in-breath and out-breath and a short in-breath and out-breath.

Following

'Following' means following the breath with the mind. When the mind has been subdued by counting and is fixed on the in-breathing and out-breathing, the counting is stopped and replaced by mentally keeping track of the course of the breath. This is explained by the Buddha in this manner:

"When the meditator breathes in a long breath, he comprehends that he is breathing in a long breath; and when he is breathing out a long breath, he comprehends that he is breathing out a long breath."

Herein, one does not deliberately take a long in-breath or a long out-breath. One simply comprehends what actually takes place.

The Buddha has declared in the next passage that a meditator trains himself thinking: "I shall breathe in experiencing the whole body, and I shall breathe out experiencing the whole body." Here, what is meant as "the whole body" is the entire cycle of breathing in and breathing out. The meditator should fix his attention so as to see the beginning, the middle and the end of each cycle of in-breathing and out-breathing. It is this practice that is called "experiencing the whole body."

The beginning, middle and end of the breath must be correctly understood. It is incorrect to consider the tip of the nose to be the beginning of the breath, the chest to be the middle, and the navel to be the end. If one attempts to trace the breath from the nose through the chest to the belly, or to follow it out from the belly through the chest to the nose, one's concentration will be disrupted and one's mind will become agitated. The beginning of the in-breath, properly understood, is the start of the inhalation, the middle is continued inhalation, and the end is the completion of the inhalation. Likewise, in regard to the out-breath, the beginning is the start of the exhalation, the middle is the continued exhalation, and the end is the completion of the exhalation. To "experience the whole body" means to be aware of the entire cycle of each inhalation and exhalation, keeping the mind fixed at the spot around the nostrils or on the upper lip where the breath is felt entering and leaving the nose.

This work of contemplating the breath at the area around the nostrils, without following it inside and outside the body, is illustrated by the commentaries with the similes of the gatekeeper and the saw.

Just as a gatekeeper examines each person entering and leaving the city only as he passes through the gate, without following him inside or outside the city, so the meditator should be aware of each breath only as it passes through the nostrils, without following it inside or outside the body.

Just as a man sawing a log will keep his attention fixed on the spot where the teeth of the saw cut through the wood, without following the movement of the teeth back and forth, so the meditator should contemplate the breath as it swings back and forth around the nostrils, without letting his mindfulness be distracted by the breath's inward and outward passage through the body.

When a person meditates earnestly in this manner, seeing the entire process, a joyous thrill pervades his mind. And since the mind does not wander about, the whole body becomes calm and composed, cool and comfortable.

Contact and (iv) Fixing

These two aspects of the practice indicate the development of stronger concentration. When the mindfulness of breathing is maintained, the breathing becomes more and more subtle and tranquil. As a result the body becomes calm and ceases to feel fatigued. Bodily pain and numbness disappear, and the body begins to feel an exhilarating comfort, as if it were being fanned with a cool gentle breeze.

At that time, because of the tranquillity of the mind, the breathing becomes finer and finer until it seems that it has ceased. At times this condition lasts for many minutes. This is when breathing ceases to be felt. At this time some become alarmed thinking the breathing has ceased, but it is not so. The breathing exists but in a very delicate and subtle form. No matter how subtle the breathing becomes, one must still keep mindful of the contact (*phusana*) of the breath in the area of the nostrils, without losing track of it. The mind then becomes free from the five hindrances— sensual desire, anger, drowsiness, restlessness and doubt. As a result one becomes calm and joyful.

It is at this stage that the 'signs' or mental images appear heralding the success of concentration. First comes the learning sign (*uggahanimitta*), then the counterpart sign (*paṭibhāganimitta*). To some the sign appears like a wad of cotton, like an electric light, a silver chain, a mist or a wheel. It appeared to the Buddha like the clear and bright midday sun.

The learning sign is unsteady, it moves here and there, up and down. But the counterpart sign appearing at the end of the nostrils is steady, fixed and motionless. At this time there are no hindrances, the mind is most active and extremely tranquil. This stage is expounded by the Buddha when he states that one breathes in tranquillising the activity of the body, one breathes out tranquillising the activity of the body.

The arising of the counterpart sign and the suppression of the five hindrances marks the attainment of access concentration (*upacārasamādhi*). As concentration is further developed, the meditator attains full absorption (*appanāsamādhi*) beginning with the first *jhāna*. Four stages of absorption can be attained by the practice of *ānāpānasati* namely, the first, second, third and fourth *jhānas*. These stages of deep concentration are called 'fixing' (*ṭhapana*).

(v) Observing—(viii) Retrospection

A person who has reached *jhāna* should not stop there but should go on to develop insight meditation (*vipassanā*). The stages of insight are called 'observing' (*sallakkhaṇa*). When insight reaches its climax, the meditator attains the supramundane paths, starting with the stage of stream-entry. Because these paths turn away the fetters that bind one to the cycle of birth and death, they are called 'turning away' (*vivaṭṭana*).

The paths are followed by their respective fruitions; this stage is called 'purification' (*pārisuddhi*) because one has been cleansed of defilements. Thereafter one realises the final stage, reviewing knowledge, called retrospection (*paṭipassana*) because one looks back upon one's entire path of progress and one's attainments.

This is a brief overview of the main stages along the path to Nibbāna, based on the meditation of *ānāpānasati*. Now let us examine the course of practice in terms of the seven stages of purification.

The Seven Stages of Purification

The person who has taken up the practice begins by establishing himself in a fitting moral code. If he is a layman, he first establishes himself in the five precepts or the ten precepts. If he is a *bhikkhu*, he begins his meditation while scrupulously maintaining the moral code prescribed for him. The unbroken observance of his respective moral code constitutes purification of morality (silāvisuddhi).

Next, he applies himself to his topic of meditation, and as a result, the hindrances become subjugated and the mind becomes fixed in concentration. This is purification of mind (cittavisuddhi)— the mind in which the hindrances have been fully suppressed—and this includes both access concentration and the four *jhānas*.

When the meditator becomes well established in concentration, he next turns his attention to insight meditation. To develop insight on the basis of *ānāpānasati* the meditator first considers that this process of in-and-out breathing is only form, a series of bodily events—not a self or ego. The mental factors that contemplate the breathing are in turn only mind, a series of mental events—not a self or ego. This discrimination of mind and matter (nāmarūpa) is called purification of view (diṭṭhi-visuddhi).

One who has reached this stage comprehends the process of in-and-out breathing by way of the conditions for the arising and cessation of the bodily and mental phenomena involved in the process of breathing. This knowledge, which becomes extended to all bodily and mental phenomena in terms of their dependent arising, is called the comprehension of conditions. As his understanding matures, all doubts conceived by him in respect of past, future and present times are dispelled. Thus this stage is called 'purification by the transcending of doubt'.

After having understood the causal relations of mind and matter, the meditator proceeds further with insight meditation, and in time there arises the wisdom 'seeing the rise and fall of things'. When he breathes in and out, he sees the bodily and mental states pass in and out of existence moment after moment. As this wisdom becomes clearer, the mind becomes illumined and happiness and tranquillity arise, along with faith, vigour, mindfulness, wisdom and equanimity.

When these factors appear, he reflects on them, observing their three characteristics of impermanence, suffering and egolessness. The wisdom that distinguishes between the exhilarating results of the practice and the task of detached contemplation is called 'purification by knowledge and vision of the true path and the false path'. His mind, so purified, sees very clearly the rise and cessation of mind and matter.

He sees next, with each in-breath and out-breath, the breaking up of the concomitant mental and bodily phenomena, which appears just like the bursting of the bubbles seen in a pot of boiling rice, or like the breaking up of bubbles when rain falls on a pool of water, or like the cracking of sesame or mustard seeds as they are put into a red-hot pan. This wisdom which sees the constant and instantaneous breaking up of mental and bodily phenomena is called 'the knowledge of dissolution'. Through this wisdom he acquires the ability to see how all factors of mind and body throughout the world arise and disappear.

Then there arises in him the wisdom that sees all of these phenomena as a fearsome spectacle. He sees that in none of the spheres of existence, not even in the heavenly planes, is there any genuine pleasure or happiness, and he comprehends misfortune and danger. Then he conceives a revulsion towards all conditioned existence. He arouses an urge to free himself from the world, an all consuming desire for deliverance. Then, by considering the means of releasing himself, there arises in him a state of wisdom which quickly reflects on impermanence, suffering and egolessness, and leads to subtle and deep levels of insight.

Now there appears in him the comprehension that the aggregates of mind and body appearing in all the world systems are afflicted by suffering, and he realises that the state of Nibbāna, which transcends the world, is exceedingly peaceful and comforting. When he comprehends this situation, his mind attains the knowledge of equanimity about formations. This is the climax of insight meditation, called 'purification by knowledge and vision of progress'.

As he becomes steadfast, his dexterity in meditation increases, and when his faculties are fully mature he enters upon the cognitive process of the path of stream-entry (*sotāpatti*). With the path of stream-entry he realises Nibbāna and comprehends directly the Four Noble Truths. The path is followed by two or three moments of the fruit of stream-entry, by which he enjoys the fruits of his attainment. Thereafter there arises reviewing knowledge by which he reflects on his progress and attainment.

If one continues with the meditation with earnest aspiration, one will develop anew the stages of insight knowledge and realise the three higher paths and fruits: those of the once-returner, non-returner, and arahant. These attainments, together with stream-entry, form the seventh stage of purity, 'purification by knowledge and vision'. With each of these attainments one realises in full the Four Noble Truths, which had eluded one throughout one's long sojourn in the cycle of rebirths. As a result, all the defilements contained within the mind are uprooted and destroyed, and one's mind becomes fully pure and cleansed. One then realises the state of Nibbāna, wherein one is liberated from all the suffering of birth, ageing and death, sorrow, lamentation, pain, grief and despair.

Conclusion

Births like ours are rare in *saṃsāra*. We have been fortunate to encounter the Buddha's message, to enjoy the association of good friends, to have the opportunity to listen to the Dhamma. As we have been endowed with all these blessings, if our aspirations are ripe, we can in this very life reach the final goal of Nibbāna through its graduated stages of stream-entry, once-returner, non-returner and arahantship. Therefore, let us make our life fruitful by developing regularly the meditation of *ānāpānasati*. Having received proper instructions on how to practise this method of meditation, one should purify one's moral virtue by observing the precepts and should surrender one's life to the Triple Gem.

One should choose a convenient time for meditation and practise with utmost regularity, reserving the same period each day for one's practice. One may begin by briefly reflecting on the abundant virtues of the Buddha, extending loving kindness towards all beings, pondering the repulsiveness of the body, and considering the inevitability of death. Then, arousing the confidence that one is walking the very road to Nibbāna walked by all the enlightened ones of the past, one should proceed forth on the path of meditation and strive with diligent effort.

—§§§—

Essential Advice of the Kadampa Masters

from The Door of Liberation by

Geshe Wangyal

Translated from the Tibetan

Bodhi Leaves No. 116

First published: 1988

Essential Advice of the Kadampa Masters

Introduction

The Kadampa tradition of Tibetan Buddhism arose during the highly active and creative eleventh century. The school was founded by the Indian master Atisha (982–1054) who came to Tibet in 1042. Although this school did not survive for very long as an independent tradition, it was absorbed into the other schools and thereby left a lasting influence.

The short text presented here is a compilation of dialogues, words of advice, and reflections of several of the major figures in the Kadampa tradition, including Atisha and his foremost Tibetan disciple, Geshe Drom. These sayings are typical of the Kadampa school in emphasising the basic insights of Buddhism as a foundation for the entire Buddhist path to enlightenment.

The teachings of the Kadampa masters are noted for their straight-forwardness, their almost uncompromising simplicity. These masters continually confront us with the basic facts of our existence and challenge us to adopt a meaningful and practical response to them. They repeatedly point out that the spiritual path is fraught with as many possibilities of self-deception as is our life in the world. To avoid such pitfalls we must be constantly mindful of our innermost motives, our aims, our commitments, and most significantly, our death.

This text was first translated into English under the guidance of the Mongolian lama, Geshe Wangyal, by some of his American students. It was published as part of a collection of Tibetan Buddhist writings entitled The Door of Liberation in 1975. The text presented here contains about half of the original.

Stephen Batchelor

Advice from Atisha

One time Atisha was asked by his disciples, "What is the highest teaching of the path?" Atisha replied:

"The highest skill is in the realisation of egolessness.
The highest nobility is in subduing your own mind.
The highest excellence is in having a mind which seeks to help others.
The highest precept is continual mindfulness.
The highest remedy is in understanding the naturelessness of everything.
The highest activity is not to conform with worldly concerns.
The highest accomplishment is the lessening and transmutation of the passions.
The highest giving is found in non-attachment.
The highest moral practice is a peaceful mind.
The highest patience is humility
The highest effort is to abandon attachment to activities.
The highest meditation is the mind without pretension.
The highest wisdom is not to grasp anything as it appears."

Upon leaving the Western province of Narī, Atisha gave the following parting advice to his assembled disciples:

"Friends, until you have obtained enlightenment, the spiritual teacher is needed; therefore depend upon the holy spiritual teacher. Until you fully realise the nature of voidness, you must listen to the Teaching; therefore listen closely to the precept of the teacher. Merely understanding the Dharma is not enough to become enlightened, you must practise constantly.

"Go far away from any place that is harmful to your practice; always stay in a place that is conducive to virtue. Clamour is harmful until you obtain a firm mind; therefore, stay in an isolated place. Abandon friends who increase your fettering passions; depend on friends who cause you to increase virtue. Bear this in mind. There is never an end of things to do, so limit your activities. Dedicate your virtue day and night, and always be mindful.

"Once you have obtained the precept of the teacher, you should always meditate on it and act in harmony with his speech. When you do this with great humility, the effects will manifest without delay. If you act according to the Dharma from the depths of your heart, both food and necessities will come naturally.

"Friends, there is no satisfaction in the things you desire. It is like drinking seawater to satisfy thirst. Therefore be content. Annihilate all forms of pretentiousness, pride and conceit; be subdued and peaceful. Abandon all that which some call virtue, but which is really an obstacle to the practice of Dharma. As if they were stones on a narrow slippery path, you should clear away all ideas of gain and respect, for they are the rope of the devil. Like snot in your nose, blow out all thoughts of fame and praise, for they serve only to beguile and delude.

"As the happiness, pleasure and friends you have accumulated are of but a moments duration, turn your back on them. Future life is longer than this life, so carefully secure your treasure of virtue to provide for the future. You leave everything behind when you die; do not be attached to anything.

"Leave off despising and deprecating others and generate a compassionate mind to those who are your inferiors. Do not have deep attachment to your friends and do not discriminate against your enemies. Without being jealous or envious of others' good qualities, with humility take up those good qualities yourself. Do not bother examining the faults of others, but examine your own faults. Purge yourself of them like bad blood. Nor should you concentrate on your own virtues; rather, respect those as a servant would. Extend loving kindness to all beings as though they were your own children.

"Always have a smiling face and a loving mind. Speak honestly and without anger. If you go about saying many senseless things, you will make mistakes; thus speak in moderation. If you do many senseless things, your virtuous work will cease; give up actions that are not religious. It is useless to make effort in unessential work. Because whatever happens to you comes as a result of your karma from long ago, results never match your present desires. Therefore, be calm.

"Alas, it is far better to die than to cause a holy person shame; you should therefore always be straightforward and without deceit.

All the misery and happiness of this life arise from the karma of this and previous lives; do not blame others for your circumstances.

"Until you subdue yourself, you cannot subdue others; therefore, first subdue yourself. As you are unable to ripen others without clairvoyance, make a great effort to achieve clairvoyance.

"You will surely die, leaving behind whatever wealth you have accumulated, so be careful not to gather defilement due to wealth. As distracting enjoyments are without substance, adorn yourself with the virtue of giving. Always keep pure moral practice, for it is beautiful in this life and ensures happiness in future lives. In this world age of the Kaliyuga, where hatred is rampant, don the armour of patience, which nullifies anger. We remain in the world by the power of sloth; thus we must ignite like a great fire the effort of achievement. Moment after moment your life is wasted by the lure of worldly activities; it is time to meditate. Because you are under the influence of wrong views, you do not realise the nature of voidness. Zealously seek the meaning of reality.

"Friends, *saṃsāra* is a vast swamp in which there is no real happiness; hurry to the place of liberation. Meditate according to the precept of the teacher and dry up the river of saṃsāric misery.

"Always keep this in mind. Listen well to this advice, which is not mere words but comes straight from my heart. If you follow these precepts you will make not only me happy, but yourselves and all others as well. Though I am ignorant, I urge you to remember these words."

When the venerable Atisha was staying in Yerpadrak near Lhasa, he gave the following precept:

"Noble sons, reflect deeply on these words. In the Kaliyuga, lives are short and there is much to be understood. The duration of life is uncertain; you do not know how long you will live. Thus you must make great effort now to fulfil your right desires.

"Do not proclaim yourself a monk if you obtain the necessities of life in the manner of a layman. Though you live in a monastery and have given up worldly activities, if you fret about what you have given up, you have no right to proclaim, 'I am a monk living in a monastery.' If your mind still persists in desire for pretty things and still produces harmful thoughts do not proclaim, 'I am a monk living in a monastery.' If you still go about with worldly people and waste time in worldly, senseless talk with those with whom you live, even though you are living in a monastery, do not proclaim 'I am a monk living in a monastery.' If you are impatient and go about feeling slighted, if you cannot be even the least bit helpful to others, do not proclaim 'I am a Bodhisattva-monk.' If you speak thus to worldly people, you are a great liar. You may get away with saying such things. However you cannot deceive those who have the boundless sight of clairvoyance, nor can you deceive those who have the Dharma eye of great omniscience. Neither can you deceive yourself, for the effects of karma follow after you.

"To stay in a monastery it is necessary to give up worldly ways and attachment to friends and relatives. By renouncing these, you are getting rid of all the cooperating causes of attachment and longing. From then on, you must seek the precious mind of enlightenment. Not even for an instant should you allow your past obsession with worldly concerns to arise. Formerly you did not properly practise the Dharma, and under the influence of past habits that sapped your strength, you continually produced the concepts of a worldly person. Because such concepts are predominant, unless you make use of strong antidotes to them, it is useless to remain in a monastery. You would be like the birds and the wild animals that live there.

"In short, staying in a monastery will not be helpful if you do not reverse your obsession for fine things and do not renounce the activities of this life; for if you do not cut off these inclinations, thinking that you can work for the aims of both this and future lives, you will perform nothing but incidental religious practice. This type of practice is nothing but hypocritical and pretentious practice done for selfish gain.

"Therefore you should always seek spiritual friends and shun bad company. Do not become settled in one place or accumulate many things. Whatever you do, do in harmony with the Dharma. Let whatever you do be a remedy for the fettering passions. This is actual religious practice; make great effort to do this. As your knowledge increases, do not be possessed by the demon of pride.

"Staying in an isolated place, subdue yourself. Have few desires and be contented. Neither delight in your own knowledge nor seek out the faults in others. Do not be fearful or anxious. Be of good will and without prejudice. Concentrate on the Dharma when distracted by wrong things.

"Be humble, and if you are defeated, accept it gracefully. Give up boastfulness; renounce desire. Always generate the compassionate mind. Whatever you do, do in moderation. Be easily pleased and easily sustained. Run like a wild animal from whatever would entrap you.

"If you do not renounce worldly existence, do not say you are holy. If you have not renounced land and agriculture, do not say you have entered the Sangha. If you do not renounce desire, do not say you are a monk. If you are without love and compassion, do not say you are a bodhisattva. If you do not renounce activity, do not say you are a great meditator. Do not cherish your desires.

"In short, when you stay at a monastery, engage in few activities and just meditate on the Dharma. Do not have cause for repentance at the time of death."

At another time, Atisha stated:

"This Kaliyuga is not the time to display your ability; it is the time to persevere through hardship. It is not the time to take a high position, but the time to be humble. It is not the time to rely on many attendants, but the time to rely on isolation. Nor is it the time to subdue disciples; it is the time to subdue yourself. It is not the time to merely listen to words, but the time to contemplate their meaning. Nor is it the time to go visiting here and there; it is the time to stay alone."

Advice from Other Masters

On one occasion Geshe Drom was asked: "Which is more important, to help living beings by means of the teaching, or to practise in an isolated place?"

The teacher answered:

"Beginners who have no internal realisation cannot help living beings with the teaching. Their blessing is like pouring from an empty jar—nothing will come out. Their advice is like unfermented beer—it has no essence.

"Those of admirable deeds who have not yet obtained the firmness of wisdom do not have the ability to act for the benefit of living beings. Their blessing is like pouring from a full vessel— when it has filled another, it itself is empty. Their advice is like a butter lamp held in the hand: it may illuminate others, but the holder remains in the shadows.

"However, when they have entered the stages of the noble ones, whatever they do brings benefit to living beings. Their blessing is like a magic vessel—though it fills countless vessels, it does not empty itself. Their advice is like a butter lamp held by the base—it illuminates others and the one who holds it as well.

"Therefore this Kaliyuga is not the time for individuals to be of help to living beings unless they have cultivated love, compassion and the aspiration for enlightenment in isolation. It is the time to guard against fettering passions. It is not time to cut down the seedling of the magical medicine tree, but the time to cultivate it."

One day an old gentleman was walking round the monastery. Geshe Drom said to him, "Sir, I am happy to see you walking round, but wouldn't you rather be practising the Dharma?"

Thinking this over, the old gentleman felt it might be better to recite the holy sutras. While he was reading in the temple courtyard, Geshe Drom said, "I am happy to see you reciting sutras, but wouldn't you rather be practising the Dharma?"

At this, the old gentleman thought that perhaps he should meditate. He sat cross-legged on a cushion, with his eyes halfclosed. Drom said again, "I am so happy to see you meditating, but wouldn't it be better to practise the Dharma?"

Now totally confused, the old gentleman asked, "Geshela, please tell me what I should do to practise the Dharma."

Drom replied, "Renounce attraction to this life. Renounce it now. For if you do not renounce attraction to this life, whatever you do will not be the practise of the Dharma, as you have not passed beyond worldly concerns. Once you have renounced this life's habitual thoughts and are no longer distracted by worldly concerns, whatever you do will advance you on the path of liberation."

The teacher Drom was asked by Potowa, "What is the difference between Dharma and non-Dharma?"

"If something is in opposition to fettering passions, it is Dharma. If it is not, it is not Dharma. If it does not accord with worldly people, it is Dharma. If it does accord, it is not Dharma. If it accords with the teachings of Buddha, it is Dharma. If it does not accord, it is not Dharma. If good follows, it is Dharma. If bad follows, it is not Dharma."

Yerbay Shangtsun said: "When we desire liberation from the depths of our hearts, we should, through continuous contemplation of the imminence of death, always abide in thoughts and deeds in the four qualities of the noble ones.

"These four qualities of the noble ones are: to be satisfied with simple religious dress, to be satisfied with meagre food, to be satisfied with a poor cushion, and to be satisfied with the minimum of medicine.

"Put another way, these four are: to be desireless, to be content, to be easily sustained, and to be easily satisfied. To be desireless is to be unattached to all possessions and not to desire many or good things to maintain oneself. Contentment is to be happy with simple things. To be easily sustained means to subsist with meagre and poor food, a poor cushion, and simple dress. To be easily satisfied means to be content with scant alms and recognition.

"A person who lives in this way is said to be abiding in the four qualities of the noble ones, as all his practice of Dharma is directed towards enlightenment. A person who is completely taken up with worldly desires is not abiding in the four qualities of the noble ones. Instead, he is said to be abiding in the qualities of the devil, for abiding in non-virtuous activities is the cause of rebirth in *saṃsāra*'s lower states.

"If we do not give up the desires of this life now, we will come under the influence of attachment again in future lifetimes. To give up the desires of this life, the most potent countermeasure is continual meditation on impermanence. If you do not meditate on impermanence in the early morning, by midday you will have many desires."

Geshe Potowa was asked by a lay disciple: "To actually practise the Dharma, what is most important?"

"The most important thing is the meditation on impermanence. Meditate on impermanence, the imminence of death; it will cause you to begin practising the Dharma. This will create conditions impelling you to do virtuous work, which will then assist you in realising the equality of all things in their nature of existence.

"Meditation on impermanence will also cause you to decide to renounce the enjoyments of this life, which will create the conditions for ridding yourself of all worldly desires, and thus assist you to enter the path of Nirvana.

"When you have meditated on impermanence and have gained some understanding, you will seek the Dharma. This will create the conditions for the achievement of Dharma and thus assist in its final accomplishment.

"Meditating on impermanence and finding some understanding of it will also cause you to begin to arm yourself, which will create the conditions for beginning religious practice. This will assist you in initiating the stage of non-returning."

Geshe Chennawa, while speaking to a gathering of his disciples said: "In brief, the Dharma can be divided into abandoning harmful activities and taking up helpful ones. All the teachings are included within this precept.

"To apply this precept, patience is most important. If you are without patience and someone harms you, you will feel vengeful. Should you act on that feeling, you will not cease from harmful activities, much less be helpful to others. Therefore, patience is necessary to begin religious practise.

"To meditate on patience, there are four methods: setting up the target for the arrow; love and compassion; teacher and disciple; and on the nature of existence.

"First comes meditation on the setting up of the target for the arrow: if you have not set up a target, it cannot be hit by an arrow. The arrow of harm strikes in this life because we have set up a target by the bad karma we accumulated in previous lives. If you set up a target of bad activities and hateful speech, it will be struck by arrows of retribution. We set up targets ourselves: understand that the arrows come from our own harmful acts and do not be angry with others.

"Next comes the meditation on love and compassion. When a lunatic harms a sane person, the sane person should not return the harm by fighting him, but should say, 'How sad!' The person who harms you is also insane, possessed by the madness of the powerful fettering passions. Think, 'How sad!' and meditate on compassion for him.

"The third meditation on patience is on teacher and disciple. If there is no teacher to impart instruction, there can be no realisation. Similarly, if there is no enemy who harms you, there can be no practice of patience: therefore you should feel that those who abuse you are the teachers of patience. Be happy at this opportunity and concentrate on repaying their kindness. Meditating that you are a disciple being taught patience, do not be angry.

"To meditate on the nature of existence as voidness, contemplate that all three aspects of harmfulness—the agent of harm, the recipient of harm, and the act of harming—are all void of self-nature. As your actual enemy is without self-nature, do not be angry with him, and meditate on patience."

Geshe Puchungwa said:

"Though we have obtained the indispensable human body with its leisure and opportunity, we do not have the power to stay in it—we have to die. At the time of death, we cannot take with us any of the enjoyments or the concepts of this life, just as a tree sheds all its leaves. At that time the measure of our knowledge, our strength, and the wisdom of our goals will be clear. When we face death happily and with joyful anticipation, we are wise and strong: our goals are noble, and we will enter death clear-headed. But if at that time the form of Yama and the distinct sign of lower states of birth appear, our goals were foolish and we are without selfmastery.

"We, for the most part, follow the wrong path, seeking to fulfil the desires of this life. The perfect Buddha never spoke falsely. The authors of the commentaries never spoke falsely. The holy spiritual friends do not speak falsely. Then how do we enter the wrong path? By the desires of this life. Thus we should always contemplate death, for remembering the imminence of death we understand the need for non-attachment to this life. We should contemplate the perniciousness of all *saṃsāra*, for then we understand the need to be unattached to the whole of it. By remembering living beings in the meditation on love, compassion and the aspiration for enlightenment, we understand the need to be unattached to our selfish goals. By remembering egolessness in the meditation on the voidness of all things, we understand the need to be unattached to objects and attributes."

Geshe Nyugrumpa said:

"You who wish to obtain rebirth as a human being or god, and also wish to obtain perfect enlightenment, must think of *saṃsāra* as a prison. You should see this life and body as a bubble of water, bad company as an enemy, the spiritual teacher as a wish-fulfilling jewel, the fettering passions as a poisonous snake, sinful activities as strong poison, the aspects of desire as the embers of a fire, sweet words and fame as an echo, respect and gain as an entangling snare, bad friends as a contagious disease, good friends as beautiful and fortified palace, all sentient beings as your mother and father. You should feel that giving is the wish-fulfilling cow, that moral practice is a precious jewelled ornament, that patience is strong armour, that effort is the wish-fulfilling wisdom-horse, that meditation is a great treasure, and that the wisdom of hearing, thinking and meditation is a bright lamp."

Geshe Tolungpa said:

"If you desire liberation from the depths of your heart, you must follow the holy, rather than the clever teacher. You must follow those who devote themselves to the teaching rather than those who explain it, those who are humble rather than those who have great position, those of faith rather than those famous for their intelligence. There is no harm if you do not know the teaching, but misfortune will come if you follow those whose actions are contrary to the Dharma."

Geshe Shabogaypa said:

"As the desires of this life cause all the misery of this and future lives, we must not seek the fulfilment of our desires. When we try to fulfil our desires, we are not happy. We become unsure of the direction of our life, and wrong speech, wrong mind and wrong actions all surface at once.

"Therefore we must turn away from our many desires. When we are able to do this, we establish the beginnings of happiness and pleasure. The best sign of happiness in this and all future lives is not desiring or accumulating anything at all. When we do not desire gain, we have the greatest gain. When we do not desire reputation, we have the best reputation. When we do not desire fame, we have the greatest fame. When we do not desire companions, we have the best companions.

"If we are to sincerely practise the Dharma, we must entrust ourselves wholeheartedly to the life of a mendicant, for mendicants are those who entrust themselves to death. When we can produce this feeling, neither gods nor devils can conquer us. But when we indulge in the desires of this life, we lower ourselves and make ourselves completely miserable. We bring censure on ourselves in this life and rebirth in lower states in future lives.

"Therefore, when not wishing our own happiness, we limit our criticism of others, humble ourselves, limit our desires, and avoid all activities that are not religious, we will then obtain enlightenment in the future.

"In short, we are always beginning what is not necessary to begin, realising what is not necessary to realise, doing what is not necessary to do. Though we say all this, if we do not actually turn away from the desires of this life, there is no way of seeking happiness now or in future lives. If we turn away from all desires, we do not need to seek happiness at all."

Finally, Geshe Shabogaypa chastised himself:

> "You old fool—you wish for high teachings, though your nature is low
> You charlatan—you desire to improve others, but do not improve yourself.

You sham—you act as if Dharma were meant only for others to follow and not for yourself.
You blunderer—you have charged others to act correctly but act incorrectly yourself.
You shiftless bum—each rise precedes a greater fall.
You politician—you make extensive promises but abbreviated application.
You rascal—you seek fettering passions and at the same time pretend to apply their counter-measures.
You coward—you are fearful of others seeing your faults and hope that they will see only your good qualities.
You involve yourself with your relatives instead of cultivating spiritual friends.
You involve yourself with fettering passions instead of cultivating their antidotes.
You leave practice for future lives instead of cultivating it in this life.
You involve yourself with those who help you rather than cultivating those who harm you.
You idiot—you harm others, not knowing you harm yourself.
You do not know that to help others is to help yourself.
You do not see that misery and harm which come to you are conducive to practising Dharma.
You do not see that desire and happiness are not conducive to the practice of Dharma.
You say to others that practising Dharma is very important, yet do not follow the teaching yourself.
You despise others who are sinful, yet do not stop your own wrongdoing.
You see the slightest faults in others, yet do not perceive great faults in yourself.
You soon stop helping others when you get nothing in return.
You cannot bear to see other teachers receive respect.
You are subservient to those in high positions while contemptuous of those beneath you.
Talk of future lives is not pleasing to your ears.
You act holy and disdainful when corrected by others.
You want others to see your virtues and are content when they do not see your faults.

You are satisfied with a good facade while what is inside is not so good.
You like to be given things. Not seeking happiness within yourself, you seek it externally
Having vowed to learn Buddha's teaching, you learn worldly affairs instead.
Though you agree with the advice of the bodhisattvas, your actions are preparing you for hell.
Though you have dedicated your body, enjoyment, and virtuous activities of the past present and future for the benefit of all living beings, you refuse to give up your ego.
You like sinful friends, forgetting that they lead to ruin.
You do not know that a scolding from a spiritual friend is helpful.
Do not waste time in pointless debate.
Do not build castles in the air, increasing your cravings. Do not delight in dangerous activities.
Do not do those many things which senselessly hinder virtuous work."

Feeling self-reproach, he scolded himself in this way.

—§§§—

A Buddhist View of Abortion

Bhikkhu Nyanasobhano

Bodhi Leaves No. 117

First published: 1989

A Buddhist View of Abortion

Modern life, with its fierce shifts and starts in social custom and technological capability, increasingly presents us with painful problems of conscience. If religion is to be of practical use it should, if not provide us with complete answers, at least make clear to us those principles of conduct that can safely guide us through this new wilderness. Buddhism responds especially well to the sceptical temper of the times, as it does not attempt to command but gently and reasonably appeals to the individual's own powers of understanding. There are right ways and wrong ways of acting, the Buddha taught, but the moral precepts he set up are perfectly available to inquiry and analysis, and will in time, to the sincere mind, reveal their rightness.

A thorny question that has roused passion in recent years is that of abortion. Withdrawing for a while from the public din, we might gain fresh insight by examining abortion from a Buddhist perspective, on moral grounds, leaving aside the social, political, and legal aspects of the matter. What does Buddhism teach that may be useful to an individual's private reflections on the rightness or wrongness of abortion? Regardless of what the State says, should we ever consider seeking an abortion for ourselves or someone else?

Students of religion are sometimes surprised to learn that the Dhamma, the teaching of the Buddha, far from being an esoteric, morally indifferent exercise in contemplation, is a practical and highly moral religion. The three levels of training detailed in the ancient Pali Canon are *sīla*, *samādhi*, and *paññā*—moral discipline, concentration, and wisdom. The second and third levels, culminating in liberating understanding, cannot be attained without the support of the first. In this world of dependency and interrelationship there must always be a sound foundation to one's efforts, so Buddhists believe that keeping moral precepts is a practical necessity for one's own well-being and progress, quite apart from altruistic motives.

How such precepts and the higher mental training that follows them relate to the question of abortion is a matter that requires serious reflection. Although abortion has been practised throughout human history, inefficacious methods and strong prohibitions against it made it relatively uncommon, so that the average person was unlikely to be confronted with it as a possibility or a problem. But recently with new technology and diminished opposition, abortion has become a much more frequent practise, with fervent defenders and detractors. Since it has the potential to touch any of our lives, and since it raises profound moral dilemmas, many of us find it a subject not easy to dismiss, one that causes us unease and doubt. Indeed, we should not pass over it lightly.

A number of Buddhist teachings bear directly on the problem of abortion. Over and above everything is the principle of causation. According to the Buddha, the universe is not a field of spontaneous happenings, but an infinitely complex web of causes and effects stretching from limitless past to limitless future. Within this matrix, human beings are not hapless victims of fate but primary players in the drama of existence, possessing the power to shape their own fate by acts of body, speech, and mind. This power entails responsibility. Volitional action or *kamma* (*karma* in Sanskrit) rebounds upon the doer according to its nature: good actions produce good results and evil actions produce evil results. Actions we conventionally call "evil" spring from three unwholesome roots: greed, hatred, and delusion. Whenever we allow thoughts, words, or deeds to arise from these roots we set in motion the natural processes that will in time bring us equivalent results. It follows that to avoid experiencing pain we should avoid inflicting pain; to avoid misfortune for ourselves we should avoid causing misfortune to others. The basic moral precepts described by the Buddha are logically founded on this relationship between actions and the results of actions (*kamma* and *kammavipāka*).

The first Buddhist precept is to refrain from taking life. This precept refers to all sentient creatures, from the lowest animals on up to human beings. All intentional killing is unwholesome *kamma* which generates unwholesome results, but the killing of a human being is considered especially serious, one of the gravest actions that one can commit. It is immoral, foolish, and wrong not only because of the immediate suffering of the victim but also because of the tremendous kammic debt that is engendered and must sooner or later be paid by the doer. Any person with the slightest interest in the Buddhist path must recognise the danger of violating the first precept by killing a human being.

Civilised people will agree that the killing of innocent human beings is immoral; thus the debate on abortion often hinges on the question of whether or not a foetus in the womb should be considered a human being—a person—and given any concern or protection. In the light of Buddhist teaching, the question "When does life begin?" is misleading because, strictly speaking, it does not begin—it only continues. At death, the aggregates that make up the person break down and the accumulated kammic energy springs up again with a new body as its physical base. The last moment of consciousness in one life is followed by the first moment of consciousness in the next life in the mother's womb, in the case of human rebirth. This is the moment of conception, the simultaneous conjunction of sperm, egg, and gandhabba, or stream of consciousness from the previous existence. At this moment there are again present, embryonically, the same five aggregates: material form, feelings, perceptions, mental formations, and consciousness. Therefore we say that what is conceived of human parents is a human being and to kill such a being will bring on the appropriate result of *kamma*.

Those who support the option of abortion might say that this explanation is simply a religious belief that they do not share, that they choose to believe that an embryo or foetus is not a human being, and that it is all a matter of personal conviction, anyway. Let us examine this view briefly. If we are presented with the proposition that a foetus is not a human being, we are justified in asking, at what point does it become one? On this there are innumerable arbitrary opinions. Some people would say, after two weeks, or twelve weeks, or six months, or not till birth itself. If the latter is proposed, we may inquire, what is it about passage through the birth canal that confers humanity on the foetus? If it becomes a "person" only at birth, then would we not be blameless of taking a human life if we killed it five minutes before that event? So logic would dictate, though the thought is hideous.

Take any time after conception and apply the same test. Whatever time we fix on has the same liability. If the end of six months (or three or one or whatever) is the magic, humanising moment, then can we not assume an abortion would be permissible even two minutes, or two seconds, before? But who among us would not be driven frantic by this insane mincing of time, as if the licking of a second hand should turn tissue-removal into murder?

To come down to a critical problem, if a foetus becomes a fully human person at a certain point in its development, who is to say precisely when such a transforming instant occurs?—for we must be precise in dealing with something as serious as abortion. Truly, there is no authority to say; there is only a storm of opinions. No one can unequivocally determine that such-and-such a condition is the dividing line on one side of which is a lump of protoplasm and on the other a human baby deserving love and protection. "Well, in that case," many would conclude, "the matter must be left to individual discretion." Now we come to a very, very important point. Certainly we may all entertain personal beliefs as to when a foetus might become a human being, but there is—somewhere—only one truth. If a foetus at some point in its development becomes a human being, a morally significant person, our beliefs do not make it so. Its essential nature—as sentient or non-sentient or whatever— is quite independent of our views. This is a philosophical realisation that must be kept in mind for any rational inquiry. We are quite free to believe what we choose, but we must understand that possibly we are wrong and the truth is something else altogether.

If, as the Buddha teaches, there are grievous consequences to taking a human life, we had best be careful in defining the period in which we would sanction abortion. But, as we have seen, it is impossible to fix an exact time before which a foetus is unquestionably not human, not of the same essence as we. Furthermore, who can agree on what constitutes a "human being," anyway? We are left in a profound uncertainty that should warn us against rash action.

The Buddhist view of sentient existence as a shifting but unbroken continuum flowing from life to life is rational and intellectually sound, and gives us a standard with which to judge the matter of abortion. But if one still finds it hard to admit the idea that a tiny foetus might possibly be as human and as significant as oneself, there is still a quite practical reason for refraining from having an abortion: we might in our uncertainty take a human life and thereby bring down on our heads a train of misfortune worse than what we suffer at present. Ignorance of the law is, unhappily, no protection.

The law in this case is the law of *kamma*, a quite impersonal function of nature which, rightly speaking, neither rewards nor punishes. It simply reflects our own actions back upon us with complete indifference. When we intentionally take a life our beliefs, opinions, and rationalisations are irrelevant. It does no good to pretend, as people often do, that one can perform the act, or have it performed, without hostility to the unborn child. Buddhist psychology points out, with acute insight, that for any intentional act of killing to be carried out there must always be a degree of hatred or aversion in the mind. When the deed is done a seed is planted which will sooner or later yield a fruit. Because volitional acts have consequences for the doer, and because killing is a cruel and violent act, painful results are to be expected. We cannot predict exactly what they will be, because acts of killing and harming have different weights and outcomes depending on many factors especially the volition or will behind the acts. Where there is no volition, there is no responsibility: a woman who is compelled, entirely against her will, to submit to an abortion, would not commit the *kamma* of killing. But in all cases, those who act consciously and intentionally to take life generate unwholesome *kamma* to one degree or another, and we can be sure that no good will come of it. All the universe proceeds according to causes and conditions. A deluded man may believe that he can fly, but if he steps off the roof of a building he will be dashed to the ground. The law of gravity means him no harm; it merely operates according to its nature, and if he is so foolish as to ignore it he will suffer. Likewise the law of *kamma* is a natural law which, for our own welfare, we will do best to heed.

We have spoken thus far only of the principle of causation and its ramifications. Let us now turn to another great pillar of Buddhism. This is compassion, that queen of virtues. The Buddha is said to represent in his person the perfect fusion of wisdom and compassion, wisdom meaning a limpid understanding of the working of all phenomena and compassion, an open-hearted benevolence toward all beings caught in *saṃsāra,* the round of birth and death. The enlightened person not only knows and sees the world without delusion, but naturally feels sympathy for those who struggle in the dark without understanding. Such a person, having lost the sense of "I" or ego, practises *ahiṃsa*—harmlessness—and leans with boundless good will toward all beings, ever desirous of their happiness and security. All Buddhists, if they are worthy of the name, take the Buddha and his enlightened disciples as their guides and models and strive to emulate their wisdom and compassion. All beings, the Buddha said, love life and fear death. Therefore one should not kill or cause to kill, but rather stoop to defend the helpless and point out the way to the lost.

Compassion is a virtue to cultivate so that it will grow in us and through us at all times like a blossoming tree that yields its fragrance to all, without distinction. It is unworthy to suppress compassion with the cold calculation that our own self-interest outweighs the negligible life of a foetus. But this is what we indulge in when we consider and carry out "pregnancy termination." The procedure might be quick, the room cheery, the attendants reassuring, but it is always a sorry deed, and in those minutes there must be a deadening of charity, a loss of honour, a pall on the heart, for compassion can never co-exist with killing.

"Wait a minute!" the defenders of abortion cry with one voice of indignation. "All this talk of compassion! How about some compassion for the woman who suffers an unwanted pregnancy?" There is no question that an unwanted pregnancy can cause grief and suffering to a woman and her family. But Buddhist compassion does not overlook anybody. As for any misfortune, the proper response is to give comfort, sympathy, encouragement, and love. An unexpected, unwelcome pregnancy can indeed be very trying, causing depression and intense worry. It is very difficult for someone who has not experienced the problem to appreciate the emotional upset and unhappiness involved, and women justifiably object to a cavalier dismissal of their predicaments. An unhappily pregnant woman wants to know what options are open to her, how she might lift her anxiety and gloom, and why she should not seek an abortion as the obvious solution. We have already attempted to show that abortion is an unwholesome act, certain to bring unwholesome consequences, but when people are in the grip of strong aversion or desire or confusion they may think only of present misery and reach for the nearest seeming remedy. Thus it happens that some of us may grant that abortion is a nasty business but maintain that under the circumstances it is the lesser of two evils, and that, anyway, for good or ill, what a woman does with her body is her own personal business.

Here again we should carefully analyse and not be swept along emotionally and unthinkingly. First of all, it is only in a conventional and relative sense that our bodies are "ours" at all. Buddhist doctrine recognises three basic characteristics of existence: impermanence, suffering, and selflessness. This last means that ultimately there is no real self or ego that possesses a body or anything. Thus our claim to dominion over "our" bodies is not altogether accurate. Second, and more important, a developing baby, while enclosed in and nourished by the mother's body, is nevertheless a separate entity, another stream of life with its own history and future. It is in fact somebody else whose existence is of consequence.

But surely, it might be argued, the happiness of a woman is infinitely more important than the life of a foetus; it is absurd to grant a foetus rights equal to those of a grown woman. But Buddhism does not suggest any such equality for an undesired foetus. It simply teaches that mercy benefits everyone in the long run, while violence causes sorrow. Both sides in the public abortion debate have unfortunately cast the argument in terms of right-to-life versus right-to-free-choice. Unlike those whose interest is entirely or chiefly in protecting the unborn, Buddhists are as much concerned with the welfare of the parents. In the case of unwanted pregnancy the interests of the affected parties are not so incompatible as they are made out to be. Any being, human or other, desires life and happiness—that is to say, lasting well-being. What will really accomplish that? Buddhism teaches that happiness is in the long run increased, not diminished, by compassionate restraint.

Confirmation of this truth can be found by observing our own minds, here and now, by noting changing mental conditions when we are intending harm and when we are inclined toward benevolence and mercy. In the former case the mind is rigid, hostile, full of grievance. In the other case the mind is supple, peaceable, and compassionate. Now, in which sort of mind can wisdom be expected to grow? In which might joy take root? Thoughts of mercy and tenderness make us feel good because they are good; they rise out of good will and, as they develop into speech and action, yield benefits such as confidence, relief of anxiety, and peace of mind. No matter what euphemisms we employ, we know that abortion is a planned killing, and the intention to carry it out or order another to do it stimulates the states of mind associated with killing—hatred, agitation, fear, guilt, self-loathing.

We should refer to our own experience: have we ever regretted an act of kindness and mercy? Then think: have we ever regretted killing or harming? Common sense, let alone the weight of Buddhist teaching, will tell us that if only for our own peace of mind we should restrain violent impulses and instead trust the pull of our hearts toward compassion.

Nevertheless, in the dark of misfortune many women and men may wish strongly to put an end to a pregnancy, to make it as if it never were, and hence may be drawn to abortion. Even though they might be moved by such arguments as presented here, they still might feel that their own circumstances justify the deed. Here we approach a very old moral problem which we should scrutinise carefully: to what extent does one's suffering entitle one to commit an unwholesome act? In this case, does the distress of a pregnant woman make it all right for her to resort to abortion? May we allow, excuse, or condone such an action? Perhaps we may; perhaps society may; but that is really beside the point in seeking for moral understanding.

According to Buddhism, the end can never be used as justification of the means. *Kamma* is not a god with discretion and understanding who might impose or withhold a punishment; it is an impersonal law, a function of nature, and it does not make exceptions for anybody. Mahā Moggallāna, one of the Buddha's foremost disciples, was an enlightened one, an *arahat*, yet even he, on account of evil deeds long past, could not escape the kammic result of a painful death. The fact that we are suffering now does not make us immune from future harm if we do harm to someone else. We cannot, in the long run, get out of suffering by causing more suffering.

To gain a wider view of the situation we should take a look at how an unwanted pregnancy comes about. Originally, it rises from the unfathomable depths of *kamma*, perhaps from many lives ago. The results of *kamma*, it should be noted, are not absolutely fixed to any target in time, but remain as pure potential until conditions are right for them to come to fruition. The immediate or enabling cause of pregnancy is volitional actions by mother and father. We have to do something to get pregnant. In this day of effective contraceptives (and Buddhism has no objection to procedures that prevent conception) it is becoming less credible to treat the event as something entirely out of our hands. We must frankly admit our responsibility in the matter. According to Buddhism, men and women have the freedom to make their own destinies, to rise toward final liberation, and the equal freedom to fall into misery. Freedom and responsibility cannot be separated.

But what about the cases of poor women with many children already, or ignorant teenagers, or frightened women whose careers or family lives may suffer? We must agree that such pregnancies present woeful difficulties and genuine suffering. This world, the Buddha taught, is bound up with suffering and steeped in suffering. It is for this very reason that we tread the path toward deliverance.

How do we tread this path? With wisdom and compassion, with forbearance, courage, and humility, which are all of great benefit even when dealing with the hardest problems. In all cases of unwanted pregnancy it should be borne in mind that things change. Circumstances change, desires and aversions arise and fall away, and what is unwelcome today may be welcome tomorrow. Doubtless there are many parents who considered abortion, decided against it, and subsequently rejoiced in their children. We cannot predict the future. Courage and resolve may awake in us. Our pains may be shorter than we expect, so we should not rush into error but rather be patient and watch our own minds. If after giving birth a woman still does not want or is unable to keep a baby she may certainly give it up for adoption. With so many childless couples desperately seeking children, this course is an honourable one, yielding life and loving home to the baby and saving the mother from the pain, humiliation, and grief likely to follow an abortion.

It is only natural to wish to escape a distressing dilemma at once, completely, but how often is this really possible? The owner of a business, whose partner absconds, leaving him in debt, cannot at once tear up his bills and proclaim himself free. A couple having trouble making mortgage payments on a house cannot restore prosperity by a single stroke. An athlete who has suffered a heart attack cannot immediately resume playing tennis. A time for recovery is required. Bad situations—even apparently undeserved ones—have to be faced with patience and intelligence, first, so that they will not get worse, and second, so that they will get better.

Abortion does not solve the problem of unwanted pregnancy. It eliminates the foetus, but leaves in its place untold regret, remorse, and unwholesome potential. The driving stream of *kamma* which has led to the situation in the first place is given new impetus. But if a woman chooses to go ahead with the pregnancy with whatever courage, fortitude, and grace she can muster, then that particular stream must spend its force and subside. To refrain from striking out—even when greatly provoked—not only avoids future suffering but positively advances one's virtue and strength of character. Furthermore, as the well-known tales of the Buddha's former lives testify, to willingly endure suffering out of sympathy for another is magnificent and potent merit sure to result in benefit.

It is often argued that some cases of suffering seem so severe as to demand immediate relief in the form of abortion, as drastic and unpleasant as it may be. While it is impossible here to deal with every real or hypothetical special case, we ought to mention the most common types that come to mind. What about pregnancies that come about as a result of rape or incest? Are these not horrible situations? Indeed they are. No sensitive person could dispute the severity of the mother's suffering here. But the searching question we might ask is, "Will an abortion do more harm than good in the long run?"

Of course, we do not know the future; we only know the painful present. But we also know from our participation in the Buddhist life that honouring the teachings has not failed us yet and has given us a start toward serenity. In our relative blindness, the best thing we can do is to rely on those principles we love and trust—the principles of basic Dhamma—which teach that self-restraint, mercy, and kindness produce benefit, whereas the taking of life does not. It certainly would require great bravery to carry on a pregnancy in such a case. All we could hope is that the afflicted woman would meet the affliction with clear sight. The unwelcome new person here is unconscious of, and not responsible for, the terrible deeds of the father. This should be remembered in making momentous decisions. We are not called on to be superhuman heroes, but just to live up to the Dhamma as well as we can, to make choices in full consciousness of all that is involved.

There are many other special cases, as of very young mothers, or the seriously ill, or women who are likely to give birth to deformed or mentally retarded babies. Again, there is no question of the intensity of the misery involved here and the deplorable nature of the problem. These are beyond dispute. What we have to be alert for, however, is the natural—the almost irresistible—tendency to assume that our very real pain authorises us to do what we would otherwise not do. Can we ever honestly separate positive need from desire for convenience? Babies who come into this world deformed or sick or unwanted are experiencing the fruits of their past *kamma*, and they have their own destinies, happy or unhappy, to live out. It is always disingenuous for us to say, when inclined toward abortion, that such babies are better off not being born. It is better to recognise forthrightly that we are concerned principally about our own well-being. And, in a higher sense, there is nothing at all wrong with this, if we carry our concerns to the fullest extent. Why? Because we should see by the light of the Dhamma that our own well-being is ultimately indivisible from the well-being of others. We lose nothing—we only gain—by giving the gift of compassion.

The most extreme special case is that in which the mother's life is imminently threatened by the continuation of a pregnancy. What is to be done? We know that saints do not take life under any circumstances, but if we are not saints yet then we must decide what to do according to the urgency of the situation and according to our strength, compassion, and understanding of conflicting needs. The same principles apply, *saṃsāra* rolls on according to its laws (and if nothing else, one may see here that conflict is the very essence of this grim round of becoming). In medical crises, a physician's duty is always to protect the life of the mother. This goes without saying. He or she should also try to save the baby. If both cannot be done then it would seem only reasonable to take necessary measures to guard the mother. If the baby or foetus does not survive, then perhaps so it must be.

But probably it is rare for matters to come to an absolute either-or situation. More likely a pregnancy may pose some degree of medical risk to a woman, which she must judge as best she can, paying particular attention to the state of her own mind. What sort of volitions are stirring there? How much risk can she accept? All intentional taking of life is unwholesome *kamma* though many factors enter into (and sometimes mitigate) the process, chiefly the fundamental volition underlying the action. Killing in self-defence is doubtless of lesser weight than killing for baser motives, though it is still significant. In all cases Buddhism asks that we look clearly at the situation, remember our duties, balance wisdom and compassion, suppress selfishness, and act as nobly as we can.

But what advice or consolation can Buddhism offer to woman or couples who have already carried out an abortion? Certainly such a deed generates unwholesome *kamma,* but it must not be thought that this is the end of the story and that there is nothing more to be done about it. As we said, *kamma* remains as potential until conditions are right for its ripening. But how it ripens, and when, and to what degree, are entirely unpredictable, as the process depends on innumerable other conditions. And chief among these conditions are our own present and future deeds. We can, to some extent, offset our bad actions by good. Thus it is that the Buddha counsels us not to torment ourselves with guilt and vain regret but simply to recognise our errors, let them go, and resolve to restrain ourselves in the future. Even the most virtuous saints and sages have, throughout the infinity of *saṃsāra*, committed countless misdeeds.

The road to perfection is a long and crooked one, so we should persevere with equanimity, learning from our mistakes and pressing onward toward final deliverance. Those of us who have procured or participated in an abortion should face up to the misdeed, acknowledge it, and resolve to live henceforth full of kindliness for all beings. This in itself will begin to lighten the mind and restore calm and self-respect. Those of us who have not had that unhappy experience should realise that we too bear an ancient load of error and that, as we hope others will be gentle with us, so we should unstintingly sympathise with them.

These reflections and arguments have only outlined the bulk of a great problem for men and women living today. We have hardly touched on the well-known social and political dimensions of the issue, focusing instead on the moral and religious implications as seen through Buddhist eyes. The conflict goes on in this world of passion, and we need to reflect deeply to avoid being caught up in it. The teaching of the Buddha, the Dhamma, should be examined with a fair mind and brought close to the heart as we gain confidence in it. In shaping our destiny we have free choice, which is both our freedom and our responsibility. We should choose with open eyes, and choose rightly.

On Pilgrimage

Susan Elbaum Jootla

Bodhi Leaves No. 118

First published: 1989

On Pilgrimage

Let me take you on a Buddhist pilgrimage. Let us visit the main places where Gotama Buddha lived and taught the Dhamma. Let us see what they look like now, recall what happened there in the days of the Buddha, and practise his Dhamma at these sites.

Before he attained *Parinibbāna*, the Buddha told his attendant monk, the Venerable Ānanda, "There are four places which should be (visited and) seen by a person of devotion." He then named his birthplace, the place where he attained Enlightenment, the place where he first taught the way to Enlightenment, and the place where he attained *Parinibbāna*.

Because of this injunction, faithful Buddhists from all over the world travel to India and Nepal to pay their respects to the Buddha at these spots which he stated "would cause awareness and apprehension of the nature of impermanence" (Ten Suttas from the Dīgha Nikāya, p. 272). Let us use the mindful approach implicit in this statement for our present purely imaginary pilgrimage. Perhaps this literary tour will one day arouse in us an urge to make such a pilgrimage a reality. For now it may provide us with a way to delve deeper into the process of mental purification taught by the Buddha to end all suffering. So, keeping in mind the transient, unsatisfactory and essenceless nature of all phenomena, let us now travel to the Indian subcontinent on a voyage of both past and present.

Lumbini

The first place the Buddha urged his followers to visit was Lumbini, where he was born, the son of King Suddhodana of the Sakyan clan. At present Lumbini is in southern Nepal, less than half an hour's drive from the Indian border. Very little remains here today to remind us of the Buddha. But Emperor Ashoka, who ruled much of India several centuries later, marked a hillock with a pillar proclaiming that he had come here on a pilgrimage because of the place's importance as the location of Gotama's birth.

There is a Japanese plan to build an elaborate garden complex in the vicinity to commemorate the great event.

His mother, Queen Mayā, had left her husband's home in Kapilavatthu to travel to her parents' residence when she knew her child was soon to be born. But on the way, quite unexpectedly, she gave birth while standing in a forest of sal trees, near Lumbini village. Soon after the baby was born, he stood on the ground, took seven steps to the north, looked around and said: "I am the foremost in the world; this is the last birth; now there is no more renewal of being in future lives" (Majjhima Nikāya 123; in Middle Length Sayings, 3:166–67).

At this time, several awe-inspiring phenomena took place in the world of nature as well, as they do whenever any *Bodhisatta* takes his final birth. A vast brilliant light appeared and it was visible on all the levels of existence of this world system, from the darkest hells up through the celestial planes. The entire area extending to 10,000 other world systems surrounding our own all trembled and shook.

We find the story of the *Bodhisatta*'s natural conception, the condition of Queen Maya while she was pregnant with the great being, and the events surrounding his birth, retold by the Venerable Ānanda as part of the discourse quoted above. The Buddha had asked Ānanda to recount all of this to a group of monks gathered at Anāthapiṇḍika's park in Sāvatthī. After Ānanda mentioned all these amazing events, the Buddha added that there was yet another wonderful quality of his which the monks should remember:

> A Perfect One's feelings of pleasure, pain or neutral are known to him as they arise … as they are present … as they subside. His perceptions and thoughts are also known to him as they arise, remain and subside.

While we are in Lumbini, let us reflect on the clarity of the Perfect One's understanding of mental processes. When we meditate here at the Buddha's birth place, we would be doing proper homage to him if we too strive to know with accurate mindfulness the rising and vanishing of feelings, perceptions and thoughts. Only Buddhas and Arahats can have perfect awareness of every mental activity, but any student of Buddhism should begin to train to see the fickle, transient, changing nature of mind and body. Slowly, if this is practised with a concentrated mind and from a sound moral base, it will develop into full insight into impermanence.

Bodh Gaya

Now let us go to Bodh Gaya in the modern Indian state of Bihar. Here Gotama became a Buddha by attaining, without the guidance of a teacher, the thorough intuitive understanding of everything in the universe.

The small town of Bodh Gaya is probably the most often visited of the four pilgrimage sites. It has become something of an international centre as many people come here to see where the *Bodhisatta* became a Buddha.

In ancient times this area was called Uruvela. It was here that Gotama sat under the Bodhi Tree beside the bank of the Nerañjara River. The broad, shallow river no longer flows close to the Bodhi Tree; its course now runs perhaps half a kilometre away. The wide branching pipal tree we see today in Bodh Gaya is, as it were, the grandchild of the original tree under which the *Bodhisatta* prepared, from a pile of grass, his seat of Enlightenment.

Right beside the tree stands the Mahā Bodhi Temple, a great monument to the greatest of achievements. But we actually approach them both by going barefoot down a long stone-flight of steps. We proceed facing the Temple's square tower which is encircled with rows and rows of small niches. Some of the alcoves contain Buddha statues, damaged, restored, or covered in gold leaf. Let us walk around the Temple on paving stones smoothed by millions of footsteps over hundreds of years. Let us sit at the base of the Bodhi Tree inside its stone-railing enclosure.

We can now, with grateful minds, pay our respects to the Buddha, whose enormous efforts over countless aeons culminated here. Let us bow to the One who in this very place agreed to share with other beings the ancient path he had discovered, the way leading to the utter cessation of suffering. Let us bow again to his Teachings, the Truth, the Dhamma. And let us bow still again to those who maintain and practise the pure Dhamma, the Sangha.

While we are at this most important place for Buddhists to visit, let us cultivate wisdom along with this faith. Starting from the confidence that the Buddha did find the Truth and that it is still being correctly taught, let us try to work our way to our own insight into the Dhamma.

Here in Bodh Gaya the *Bodhisatta* Gotama discerned, among other things: the impersonal nature of all "beings" and "things;" how they are all unsatisfactory because they are caused and conditioned by other factors; and how by eliminating the causes, the resultant suffering can be uprooted once and forever. So let us now meditate on the law of dependent origination, the chain of causes and effects through which all the suffering of existence comes about.

At the time of his Enlightenment, the *Bodhisatta* was searching for the escape from the suffering (*dukkha*) of the world, so his analysis of dependent origination on this occasion begins at old age and death, the most apparent kinds of suffering. From there he works his way back to the causes behind each step. He finds that birth is the condition for ageing and dying, that becoming is the condition for birth, and that mind's clinging lies behind becoming. He finds that clinging arises when there is craving. Craving develops out of feelings, which arise because of the contact of the six sense organs with their objects. Because of mind and body there are the sense organs. And consciousness continually brings the whole complex of mind and body into being, a role most evident in the rebirth process.

The Buddha then shows how consciousness and mind-body mutually condition each other so that if either ceases, the other must also end. Next he analyses the chain of causation in terms of the cessation of its factors. This ultimately shows how all the suffering that follows any birth can be brought to an end by breaking this cycle of dependent origination.

When the Buddha states his own profound discovery of this ancient law, he does not mention where or how the chain is to be broken. But in many other *sutta*s he advises us not to allow craving to arise in response to pleasant and unpleasant feelings. Our meditation here near the Bodhi Tree will begin to cut this link between feeling and craving if we can equanimously and closely observe the feelings, both mental and physical, as they arise and vanish. This means training the mind to know all the feelings as they come and go without getting caught up in wanting the pleasant ones to last or wishing the unpleasant ones to cease, and without ignoring the neutral feelings.

Sarnath

When the Buddha had spent seven weeks in seven spots near the Bodhi Tree in what has ever since been called Bodh Gaya, he decided to acquiesce to the entreaties of the deity Brahma and teach the Dhamma to other beings. He decided to go to Isipatana where he realised he would find competent disciples. Although the Buddha met a few individuals along the way who recognised from his demeanour that he was a special person, none of them was curious enough to ask him to show them the way to liberation.

At Isipatana, now Sarnath, in a deer park near Varaṇasi, he came to the five ascetics who had associated with him during his period of arduous asceticism before his Enlightenment. Here, to this small group, the Buddha gave his first discourse.

Modern Sarnath is almost a suburb of Varaṇasi, the holy city for India's millions of Hindus. It is a tiny village whose reason for existence is its association with the teaching of the Buddha. Amidst a large park there is a great brick stupa built by Emperor Ashoka and inscribed with the Buddha's first discourse. It has recently been renovated on its ancient foundations. Some say the monument marks the site of the Buddha's first sermon, others the site of the second sermon. The nearby ruins of the Dhamma-seat marking the spot where the other *sutta* was given are well excavated and slightly below the present ground level.

The Buddha's first discourse is called the Dhammacakkappavattana Sutta, the Discourse Setting in Motion the Wheel of the Dhamma. It was delivered on the evening of the full moon of July, just before the monsoon rains began. This discourse teaches the Four Noble Truths, the basis of all his other instructions. The second *sutta*, the Anattalakkhana Sutta, the Discourse on the Characteristic of Not-self, was given a few days later to the same five disciples. Once the five former ascetics had heard both these talks, they all became fully liberated Arahats.

Having seen Sarnath's ancient sites, let us also visit the modern temple near the stupa. It houses murals of the Buddha's life, and more important for us, some splinters of bone encased in glass in a vault beneath its shrine. These are said to be relics of the Buddha. Let us pay our respects to them, realising what proof this is of impermanence. Even the greatest of beings has left almost nothing behind after his demise.

Now let us choose a shady spot somewhere in the neat park grounds around the stupa, and sit and consider what great events took place here more than 2500 years ago. The lawns about us are scattered with numerous foundations of ancient monasteries which were used by many generations of Buddhist monks, *bhikkhus*. Each *bhikkhu* strove hard to purify his mind of all defilements to attain Arahatship. Once he had succeeded, the Arahat lived perfectly at peace, creating no new *kamma,* without the slightest trace of desire, egoism or ignorance remaining in his mind.

Here the Buddha began a long career in guiding other beings in the direction of liberation. But just one talk was not enough for the five ascetics to attain full enlightenment. In fact, at its conclusion, only one of them reached the first stage of enlightenment, stream-entry (*sotāpatti*). This is because Buddhas do not enlighten others by means of magic powers. Each individual has to do his own work. Buddhas and teachers who convey the pure Dhamma can give invaluable guidance by pointing out the way, by encouragement and instruction. But it remains the task for each one of us to actually cleanse our mind of its defiling tendencies.

The First Sermon

Let us meditate on what the Buddha taught at Isipatana. His first sermon enunciated the Four Noble Truths. In explaining the first noble truth, the truth of *dukkha* or suffering, he points out the obvious suffering in repeated birth, decay, illness, death, sorrow, grief and despair. He likewise states that we are very often unhappy because we do not get what we want, or because we find ourselves in situations we do not like. But in addition to these forms of suffering, the Buddha declares that our entire being, the mind-body which we mistakenly take as "I," is *dukkha* because it is inherently unsatisfactory due to the fact that it is constantly changing and decaying.

In the second noble truth, on the arising of suffering, the Buddha states that it is craving, *taṇhā*, that leads again to rebirth, along the chain of dependent origination. What forms does craving take and where should we look for it? Craving longs for pleasurable sights, sounds, smells, tastes, tangibles and ideas. There is also a very basic desire for life itself, and in some people, a wish for annihilation of the "self." So craving can be caught, observed and let go at any of the sense doors, whenever it arises.

The third noble truth is the ceasing of suffering. Suffering is brought to an end by giving up craving. With the elimination of all traces of desire, there is the utter passionless cessation of *dukkha*, Nibbāna.

The fourth noble truth is the way to uproot the causes of suffering, the Noble Eightfold Path. Walking on the path means eradicating the cause of craving, which lies in ignorance about these very Four Noble Truths. In this first discourse which we are now considering, the Buddha stresses that his is a moderate way of going between the extremes of sensual indulgence and asceticism, which he knew that his audience had been dedicated to for a long time.

The eight steps of the path are divided into three groups: the wisdom group of (1) Right View and (2) Right Thought; the morality group of (3) Right Speech, (4) Right Action and (5) Right Livelihood; and the concentration group of (6) Right Effort, (7) Right Mindfulness and (8) Right Concentration.

Let us work to develop this path now at Sarnath. We have to strive, initially in a theoretical way and later on through direct insight, for (1) Right View and for (2) Right Thought, the wisdom sections. The Buddha specifies in many discourses that right thoughts are those connected with the renunciation of sense pleasures and thoughts free of ill will and cruelty.

The Buddha explained over the years many aspects of Right View, or understanding, as he taught the Dhamma to different individuals. Here are four of the most central which we can consider as we sit here in the gardens of Sarnath.

1. All of our actions of body speech and mind are either good or bad depending on the quality of the volition behind them. Sooner or later in the rounds of rebirth good actions bring pleasant results while evil ones bring unpleasant results. This is the law of *kamma*.
2. What I consider "myself" is nothing more than mind and body Mind, the Buddha discovered, is a combination of the four aggregates: consciousness, feeling, perception, and other mental formations, the most central of which is volition.
3. All of these physical and mental aspects of "myself" are extremely short-lived, transient *(anicca);* they cannot give any lasting satisfaction *(dukkha),* and cannot correctly be taken as any kind of controlling or durable "being" or "self" *(anattā).*
4. All the things and beings of the world are conditioned by and dependent on many other factors, as shown in the law of dependent origination.

The second section of the Noble Eightfold Path is morality, *sīla*. We need to keep our morality perfect at all times, not just when we are on a pilgrimage or attending a meditation course. This means adhering to: (3) Right Speech (not lying), (4) Right Action (not killing, stealing or indulging in sexual misconduct) and (5) Right Livelihood (one which does not harm others). These moral steps of the path concern the active side of our lives when we interact with other people. We have to be careful of our verbal and physical actions and of our means of livelihood not only to keep from hurting others, but also to develop the concentration and wisdom required for liberation.

With a strong base of *sīla*, let us make use of this chance at Sarnath to put forth (6) Right Effort to cultivate (7) Right Mindfulness and (8) Right Concentration. Without the support of these three steps of the concentration section of the path, its wisdom phase will remain only intellectual and will not gain the impact of full liberating insight. Right Effort is steadfast exertion to develop the good and to avoid evil in order to concentrate the mind. Right Mindfulness is clear and systematic awareness of the five aggregates as they actually are, free of illusions. That is, seeing how body, consciousness, feelings, perceptions and mental formations are all impermanent, unsatisfactory and without any lasting essence or self. Right Concentration is the steady onepointedness of a mind temporarily free from the hindrances of restlessness, doubt, sensual desire, ill will and sloth. The Buddha taught *anapana,* mindfulness of breathing, as well as many other techniques for focusing one's attention. A concentrated mind is our main tool for developing *paññā,* the wisdom that liberates the mind from the causes of suffering.

We have just reviewed the Four Noble Truths and analysed briefly the Noble Eightfold Path, here at the very place where the Buddha first transmitted his discoveries of the ultimate truth to others. Next we have to train our minds to really understand these truths within ourselves. Perhaps we find that taking this pilgrimage is increasing our dedication to the long task of cultivating the mundane Noble Eightfold Path, summarised in the preceding paragraphs, until its factors grow into the supramundane path at the moment of stream-entry.

The Second Sermon

By the time the Buddha taught his second sermon, the Anattalakkhana Sutta, all the five disciples had attained the first stage of enlightenment. They were now ready to let go of the remaining mental defilements upon hearing this discourse pointing out to them the selfless nature of mind and body.

As we have already seen, the Buddha terms the body one aggregate and divides mind into four aggregates—feeling, perception, mental activities and consciousness. "I" am the combination of these five aggregates, nothing more. We all have the deluded but deep-seated idea that some aspect of this body or mind is somehow "me." Central to this notion of "I" is the concept of control, and it is the inaccuracy of this idea that the Buddha shows clearly in the Anattalakkhana Sutta. He says, if "I" cannot make "my" mind or body remain as I would like them to, it does not make any sense to consider them "my own" property. The body will get sick whether or not "I" like it or want it to. Mere wishing cannot change this fact. Nor do "I" have perfect control over the workings of mind by a simple act of will.

The next section of this *sutta* is a dialogue with the monks. The Buddha encourages the *bhikkhus* to see that all the aggregates are impermanent, unstable by nature, hence incapable of giving lasting satisfaction. They agree that ultimately it is not logical or plausible to think that the aggregates are "I" or "mine."

The Buddha wants his disciples to let go of interest in every kind of future existence. So the *sutta* proceeds in very strong terms. The Buddha states that noble ones become freed only when they are fully disgusted with and repelled by every kind of body, feeling, perception, mental activity and consciousness—be it past, present or future, be it internal or external, be it gross or subtle. At the conclusion of this discourse the five monks attained Arahatship. This talk was sufficient for them to eliminate completely the illusion "I am" at every level of their minds. We should not expect to complete the task this rapidly, however, as letting go of attachment to ourselves is a complex, difficult and long term task. But let us make good use of our time at Sarnath where the Buddha first proclaimed and rationally explained the teaching of non-self. Let us meditate on the aggregates, remind ourselves of the depth of our delusion and conceit that "I exist" and "I can do things," and begin to analyse mind and body to see the invalidity of such conceptions in the light of their utterly transient nature.

Sāvatthī and Rajgir

For the next forty-five years the Buddha ceaselessly taught others how to put an end to their misery, how to escape from the round of birth and death. An order of monks and an order of nuns developed, guided by the rules he instituted as and when a need for each of them arose. He also had many lay disciples, men and women working in the cities and villages of the Ganges valley.

Our pilgrimage could also include stops at places like Sāvatthī and Rajgir which are frequently mentioned in the *suttas*. Sāvatthī was the home of both the Buddha's chief lay disciples: the male follower Anāthapiṇḍika and the female follower Mother Visakha. It was also the capital of King Pasenadi's Kosala state and many discourses on how lay people can practise the Dhamma were given to the king here. The Buddha spent twenty-five rainy season retreats in Sāvatthī, mostly at the monastery Anāthapiṇḍika built for him and the Order of monks at Jetavana Grove, and a few at

Mother Visakha's *vihara*. Today the ruins at Sāvatthī are quite extensive. The remains of the monastic buildings are in a lovely garden of large sal trees. Here is the site of the Perfumed Chamber, the Buddha's personal residence for so many monsoons. The remains of the city itself are a few kilometres away and we can still see its gate at which the Buddha performed his unique Twin Miracle.

At and around the town of Rajgir occurred all the incidents in the Buddha's life connected with King Bimbisara, the king's son and successor, Ajatasattu, and the evil Devadatta. We can still visit the Vulture's Peak where Devadatta tried to murder the Buddha by hurling a huge boulder down on him. We can visit the mango grove of the physician Jivaka, where many discourses were given. King Bimbisara's bamboo grove, amidst which he had a vast monastery built for the Buddha and his monks, has been rediscovered by archaeologists. A park has been built around the remains of the ancient structures there.

These are two interesting side trips, but let us return to the itinerary which was determined by the Buddha's own injunction to his faithful followers—to visit the four spots most essential in his career.

Kusinara

The final place which the Buddha recommended that his followers see on pilgrimage is Kusinara, where he attained Mahāparinibbāna. This is now a small town in the Indian state of Uttar Pradesh. Here we can walk among the remains, mostly foundations of ancient monastic buildings. Let us pay respects at the golden coloured Buddha statue in the Nirvana Temple. The figure of the Blessed One is lying on his right side in the *Parinibbāna* posture, and it nearly fills the modern temple. Just behind the temple we see an ages-old stupa which was renovated by some Burmese Buddhists in the 1920's. These two structures are probably located on the actual site where the Buddha passed away, utterly relinquishing all kinds of suffering forever. There is another worn down old stupa about one or two kilometres away which probably marks the place of his cremation.

Until the Buddha's great demise, Kusinara was an unimportant village. The Venerable Ānanda had urged the Blessed One to leave this "insignificant, barren" place and to pass away in a great city full of devoted followers. But the Buddha described how long before, this very town had been the prosperous capital of the vast empire of the Universal Monarch Mahā Sudassana.

The Buddha then had Ānanda invite the local Malla princes to come and pay final homage to the Blessed One. They did this bringing their families and retinues. One wandering ascetic named Subhadda questioned the Buddha and took ordination as his last *bhikkhu* disciple.

Next the Buddha gave his final instructions to the monks, saying that the Dhamma and the Discipline he had taught them all these years would suffice as their teacher once he was gone. He made sure that none of the monks had any doubts or uncertainty about the Buddha, Dhamma or Sangha. His very last words are an exhortation to them—and to us also—to work at purifying the mind by means of insight into the ultimate truth of existence until not the slightest attachment to "me" and "mine" remains.

Let us choose a quiet spot here to meditate, perhaps inside the Nirvana Temple or beside the Cremation Stupa. Calming our minds, let us strive to comprehend deeply his final teaching: "All conditioned and compounded things have the nature of decay and disintegration. With mindfulness endeavour diligently to complete the task."

We need to experience for ourselves the utter instability and unreliability of everything in this world. Let us train ourselves to do this so thoroughly that we give up our attachment to ourselves, that we relinquish all interest in the pleasures of the senses, that we let go of our desire for continued existence in any form. If we work mindfully to know mind and body as they are, we will be putting into practise the way to the cessation of suffering taught by the Buddha.

Following his last words, the Buddha entered all the four *jhāna*s and the immaterial absorptions and then attained the cessation of all mental activity. Then he came down all the *jhāna*s in reverse order to the first *jhāna*; from the first he again rose up to the fourth *jhāna*. And "immediately after rising from the fourth *jhāna* the Bhagava passed away, realising parinibbāna," dying never to be reborn (Dīgha Nikāya, p. 290). The Venerable Anuruddha, who was beside him at this time, explained to the monks the Buddha's progress through these stages.

The Malla princes were informed and they made special arrangements for the Buddha's cremation, honouring his body for six days. They wrapped the body in many layers of finest cloth and placed it on a large funeral pyre of perfumed woods. When they thought everything was ready, they tried to light the fire, but it would not light. Some time later the Venerable Mahā Kassapa arrived with a large group of *bhikkhus*. As soon as they had paid their last homage to the Buddha's body, the funeral pyre spontaneously burst into flames and everything except a few pieces of bone and some teeth was quickly burnt up.

Followers of the Buddha arrived from many parts of the Indian subcontinent, and all wanted a share of the relics to revere. Accordingly, the remains were divided into eight parts. Later in different regions stupas were built to enshrine them. One was at Kusinara itself, but none of the archaeological sites we see here can definitely be identified as that stupa.

May all who have participated in this mental pilgrimage be inspired to actually visit the places where the Buddha was born, attained Enlightenment, first taught the Dhamma, and passed into *Parinibbāna*. May all beings come to understand the Four Noble Truths and so eradicate suffering.

Note on sources: Quotations from the Dīgha Nikāya come from the Burma Piṭaka Association's English translation of Ten Suttas from Dīgha Nikāya, Long Discourses of the Buddha, (Rangoon, 1984). All other references are to the English translations published by the Pali Text Society, London.

—§§§—

Dhamma Discourse III

The Venerable Webu Sayadaw

Translated from the Burmese by Roger Bischoff

Bodhi Leaves No. 119

First published: 1989

Introduction

The Webu Sayadaw was born on the 17th of February 1896 in Ingyinbin, a small village near Shewbo in upper Burma. He was ordained as a novice at the age of nine and was given the name Shin Kumāra. At the age of twenty he was ordained as a full member of the Sangha, now being addressed as U Kumāra. ("Webu Sayadaw" is a title meaning "the holy teacher from Webu," given to him after he became an established teacher.)

U Kumāra went to Mandalay to study at the famous Masoyein Monastery, the leading monastic university of the time. In his seventh year after full ordination he abandoned the study of the Pali scriptures and left the monastery to put into practice what he had learned about meditation.

After leaving the monastery, U Kumāra spent four years in solitude. Then he went to his native village Ingyinbin for a brief visit. He taught his former teacher at the village monastery on request the technique of meditation he had adopted. He said: "This is the shortcut to Nibbāna Anyone can use it. It stands up to investigation and is in accordance with the teachings of the Buddha as observed in the scriptures. It is the straight path to Nibbāna."

Among the thirteen *dhutaṅga* or "ascetic practices" often taken up by monks living in solitude to combat laziness and indulgence is the practice of never lying down, not even to sleep. The Webu Sayadaw is said to have followed this practice all his life. He taught that effort was the key to success not only in worldly undertakings, but also in meditation, and that sleeping was a waste of time.

The Webu Sayadaw emphasized the practice of meditation as the only way to bring the teachings of the Buddha to fulfillment. The study of the scriptures, though helpful, is not essential for the realization of Nibbāna. The technique of meditation taught by the Webu Sayadaw is *ānāpāna sati*, "mindfulness of breathing," which requires one to be aware of breathing in while breathing in, of breathing out while breathing out, and of the spot or area which the stream of air touches while the breath is entering and leaving the nostrils. Though *ānāpāna sati* is basically a way of developing *samādhi*, one-pointed concentration of mind, the Webu Sayadaw said that when concentration is developed to a sufficient degree, the meditator can gain insight into the three characteristics of nature—impermanence, unsatisfactoriness and non-self. The direct understanding of these three characteristics is called *paññā*, wisdom, which is the most essential quality required of a meditator to reach Nibbāna.

The Webu Sayadaw was not a scholar and his discourses do not cater to the intellectual who prefers the study of Buddhist philosophy to the practice. His refreshing simplicity, his patience, his lovely sense of humor, and his humility, all revealed in his dialogue with his audience, illumine a side of Buddhism which cannot be perceived by reading treatises and texts. The statements of the people in the audience offer us a glimpse of how Buddhism is practised in Burma today.

The Webu Sayadaw undertook pilgrimages to the Buddhist sites of India and Sri Lanka. He passed away on the 26th of June 1977 in the meditation centre at his native village Ingyinbin. He was believed by many to have been an *Arahat*, a person who has in practice fully understood the Four Noble Truths and attained the end of suffering.

Roger Bischoff

DHAMMA DISCOURSE III

WEBU SAYĀDAW: You have undertaken to keep *sīla*. Having taken up the training in *sīla*, practise it to the utmost. Only if you really practise morality will the aspirations you treasure in your heart be fulfilled completely.

Once you are established in moral conduct, the skilful actions you undertake will result in the fulfilment of your noble aspirations. You believe in the benefits accruing to you from giving charity, and you respect the receiver of your gift. So, straighten your mind and give to the Dhamma which has no peer. Prepare your donations yourselves and prepare them well, without employing others for the purpose.

Giving your gift, you ought to aspire to awakening by saying: "I desire to attain Nibbāna" (idaṃ me puññaṃ nibbānassa paccayo hotu). The noble ones who attained Nibbāna according to their aspirations are so numerous that they cannot be counted.

The reality one realizes and knows for oneself after penetrating the Four Noble Truths is called *bodhi*. There are different types of *bodhi*: *sammā-sam*-bodhi (the supreme self-awakening of a teaching Buddha), *pacceka-bodhi* (the self-awakening of a non-teaching Buddha), and *sāvaka-bodhi* (the awakening of a disciple of a teaching Buddha). The *sāvaka-bodhi* is divided into three levels: *agga-sāvaka-bodhi* (attained by the two chief-disciples), *mahā-sāvaka-bodhi* (attained by the eighty leading disciples) and *pakati-sāvaka-bodhi* (attained by all other Arahats). All of us have to aspire to Nibbāna, the highest blessing. Why can you bring your aspirations to Nibbāna to fulfilment now? Because the time is right, your form of existence is right, and because of the fact that all virtuous people who put forth effort can fulfil their aspirations.

The right time is the time when a Buddha arises and the time during which his teachings are available. All those who are born in the human plane or in a celestial plane are said to have the right birth. Now you have to fulfil your aspirations through your own effort.

See to it that you bring your work to a conclusion in the way so many before you have done. Once they reached their goal they were truly happy not only for a short time, or for one lifetime, but for all the remaining lives.[43]

Now that you do have this aspiration for Nibbāna, do not think that you can't attain to such happiness or that you can't fulfil such a high aspiration. Establish energy and effort sufficiently strong for you to reach the goal. If you do so, you will beyond all doubt realize your aspiration at the right time.

What will you know once you have done the work that has to be done? At the time of the Buddha, people, *deva*s, and *brahmā*s went to him to pay their respects. But no human being, *deva*, or *brahmā* was satisfied just by being in the presence of the Buddha and by

---

43 *Ariyas*, people who have experienced Nibbāna, have only a limited number of lives remaining until they reach the end of all suffering.

paying homage to him. So, the Buddha out of compassion wanted to teach them what he had discovered and understood for himself. This communicating of his knowledge we call preaching. When the Buddha preached, in one split second many people, *deva*s, and *brahmā*s attained what they had been aspiring to.

Knowing that this is the right time and the right form of existence, we should establish awareness as the wise people did before us and thus we can experience the fulfilment of our aspirations.

What are the teachings of the Buddha? The monks and the wise people have passed on the teachings of the Buddha to you out of great compassion. Every time you were instructed, you understood some of it, according to your capability to understand. You know that the teachings are enshrined in the Tipiṭaka, the Three Baskets. You know: "This is from the Sutta-piṭaka. This is from the Vinaya-piṭaka. This is from the Abhidhamma-piṭaka." All of you know a lot about the teachings.

The holy scriptures are very extensive. Even though the wise read, study, and teach these scriptures without interruption, they are too extensive for one person to study and understand them completely. It is impossible for one person to master the whole of the scriptures because these contain all the teachings of the Buddha. They are complete, wanting in nothing. They represent what the Buddha has penetrated and understood for himself. The teachings contained in the Tipiṭaka are the only way of escape from suffering, and the monks, having understood this for themselves, out of compassion point this out to you again and again. But can the wise people expound all of the sacred scriptures to you, so that not a single aspect is left out?

DISCIPLE: No, sir, this is impossible.

SAYĀDAW: How long would it take to expound all the teachings of the noble ones? How many days would you have to sit and talk in order to cover all the teachings of the noble ones that are remembered?

The purpose of all these teachings is to show the path to the end of suffering. You know quite enough of the teachings of the Buddha. In all these manifold aspects of the teachings you have to take up one and study it with perseverance. If you focus your mind on one single object, as the wise of old did, does it not stay with that object?

D: It does, sir.

S: So, select one instruction for meditation out of the many different ones the Buddha gave, and work with it, being aware always. Work with as much effort and determination as the disciples of the Buddha did in the past. If you focus your mind on one object, it will give up its habit of wandering off to objects it desires. When you are thus capable of keeping your mind on one single object, can there still be greed which is the cause of unhappiness?

D: When the mind is stable, there is no greed, sir.

S: Is there aversion?

D: No, sir.

S: Can there be delusion?

D: No, sir.

S: If there is no liking, disliking, and delusion, can there be fear, worry, and agitation?

D: No, sir.

S: If there is no fear, worry, and agitation, will you be happy or unhappy?

D: There will be happiness, sir.

S: If you choose an object of meditation given by the Buddha and practise with strong effort, will the *viriya*-iddhipāda factor hesitate to arise in you?

D: It will not fail to come, sir.

S: As soon as you establish yourselves in effort, the *viriya*iddhipāda factor will arise. But we are good at talking about the teachings. Let us instead put forth effort right away. The *viriya*iddhipāda factor will arise immediately. This is called akāliko, the immediate result that arises here and now. It doesn't arise because we think or know about it, but only because of practice. So then, focus your entire attention at the spot below the nose above the upper lip.

Feel your in-breath and your out-breath, and feel how it touches at the spot below the nose and above the upper lip.

I think you had your mind's attention focused on the spot even before I finished giving the instructions?

D: I don't think all were able to do that, sir.

S: Well, all understood what I said.

D: Some don't know yet how they have to practise, sir.

S: Oh my dear … you all have learned so much in the past. The monks taught you with great compassion time and time again, and you have grasped their instructions intelligently. When I told you to concentrate on the spot with strong determination and not to let your mind wander, you said it did stay with the breath, didn't you?

D: Those who had focused their mind on the spot answered, "It does stay, sir," but there are young people in the audience who have never heard the Dhamma before.

S: Did I say anything you haven't heard before? All of you are great lay disciples and have come so many times. All of you are capable of preaching the Dhamma yourselves.

D: Not all are, sir. Some don't know anything yet.

S: Can you others accept what he just told me?

D: Sir, I'm not talking about those people over there, I'm talking about some people not known to me.

S: In what I tell you there is nothing I have found out myself. I am only repeating to you what the Buddha preached. What the Buddha taught is without exception perfect, complete. What I preach is not complete. What the Buddha preached includes everything. His teachings are wanting in nothing, but what I am able to convey may be lacking in many aspects. Would I be able to give you all the teachings in their completeness?

D: No, sir, you can't tell us everything.

S: Well, all of you understand what the Suttas are, what the Vinaya is, and what the Abhidhamma is. Because your teachers have instructed you out of great compassion, you also understand the short and the more extensive explanation of *samatha* and *vipassanā*. But whether you know all this or not, all of you breathe, big and small, men and women. One may know all about the Pāli scriptures, but nothing about his own breath. Don't all of you breathe in and out?

D: We do breathe, sir.

S: When do you start breathing in and out?

D: When we are born, sir.

S: Do you breathe when you sit?

D: Yes, sir.

S: Do you breathe in and out when you stand upright?

D: Yes, sir.

S: When you are walking?

D: We breathe in and out then too, sir.

S: Do you breathe when you are eating, drinking, and working to make a living?

D: Yes, sir.

S: Do you breathe when you go to sleep?

D: Yes, sir.

S: Are there times when you are so busy that you have to say, "Sorry, I have no time to breathe now, I'm too busy"?

D: There isn't anybody who can live without breathing, sir.

S: In that case all of you can afford to breathe in and out. If you pay close attention, can you feel where the breath touches when you breathe? Can you feel where the air touches when it comes out of the nostrils?

D: I can feel where it touches, sir.

S: And when the the air enters, can't you feel at which point this feeble stream of air touches?

D: I can, sir.

S: Now, try to find out for yourselves at which spot the air touches gently when it goes in and when it comes out. Where does it touch?

D: It touches at a small spot at the entrance of the nostrils when it enters, sir.

S: Does the air also touch there when it comes out?

D: Yes, sir, it touches at the same spot when it comes out.

S: Wise people of the past have practised this awareness of the breath as the Buddha instructed them, and because they passed on the teachings, you too have understood now.

If you were to put your finger on the small spot under the nose, could you then feel that spot?

D: Yes, sir, I can feel it.

S: You can actually feel it when you touch it. Do you still have to talk about it?

D: No, sir, we can feel it even without talking about it.

S: As you can feel the spot when you touch it with your finger, you can also feel it when the breath touches there when it enters and leaves the nostrils. If you can feel it for yourselves, do you still have to talk about it?

D: No, sir, we don't have to.

S: If you put your finger on the spot, do you feel the touch sensation with interruptions or continuously?

D: It is a continuous touch, sir.

S: Is the stream of air entering or leaving ever interrupted?

D: No, sir.

S: As the air streams in and out we know its continuous flow and the continuous touch resulting from it. Don't follow the air to that side.

D: What do you mean by that, sir?

S: Don't let go of the sensation produced by the breath touching the skin. Remain with the awareness of touch. Don't follow the stream of air inside or outside. And why? If you do that, you won't be able to feel the touch sensation. So, let's stay with the awareness of the spot without a break.

D: Do we have to be aware of the touch of air in both nostrils or just in one?

S: Feel only one. If you try to feel two places your attention will be split. Put your undivided attention on one spot. Does your mind stay at the spot?

D: Most of the time it does, sir.

S: But not all the time?

D: Most of the time it stays, but at times the sound of coughing interrupts the continuity.

S: Is it your own coughing or is it someone else's?

D: It's someone else coughing, sir.

S: Does this disturb you because you put in too little effort or too much effort? Is the person who coughs to be blamed?

D: Well, sir, to be honest, I get a little bit angry.

S: Let's have a look at this. You have come to the Buddha to escape from suffering. Having received his teachings you begin to practise. Then someone coughs and you are upset. But of course, if you meditate, as you are doing now, people will consider you to be a good person and they will praise you. But tell me, if this good person becomes angry just before he dies, where will he be reborn?

D: He will fall into the four lower planes.

S: Yes, you should not allow this to happen. You shouldn't be impatient and short tempered. You are practising in order to escape from suffering. Hearing this coughing you should be very happy. You should say "thank you." After all, the person who is coughing shows you that your effort isn't firm enough. If you want to escape from suffering, you have to do better than this. With this type of effort, you won't make it.

We should immediately put in more effort. If we work with more determination, will we still hear this coughing?

D: No, sir, not with good effort.

S: And if there are many people, all talking loudly, will we still hear them?

D: If our effort is not of the right type, we will, sir.

S: Should we become angry at them if we hear them?

D: Most times I do get angry, sir.

S: You should not allow this to happen. You should not be short tempered. You should think of the people who disturb you as being your friends: "They are concerned with my welfare, I should thank them. I don't want everyone to know that my effort is so weak. I will meditate and improve myself and if they begin to talk still louder, I have to put in even more effort." If we improve ourselves until we are equal in effort to the wise who have practised before us, we will attain the goal to which we aspired.

If you don't hear any sounds at all, you become filled with pride, thinking that your effort is perfect. That is why we should be very happy if someone disturbs us. If we go to another place, there may be disturbances again. If we change from one place to another, we just lose time. But if we establish our mindfulness firmly, do we still have to change place or complain to others?

D: No, sir.

S: Is it not proper to say "thank you" to those who disturb us? They help us to learn how to overcome our wishes and desires, and we have to thank all who are our friends. If our effort becomes as strong as that of our teachers, we will not hear anything any more. We will be aware of one thing only: this small spot and the touch sensation. Once we have gained good awareness of this, we will apply our attention fully to this awareness.

If we attain to the happiness to which we aspire through this practice, are the contents of the Tipiṭaka, the ten *pāramī*s, the threefold training, the aggregates, the sense bases, and the relative and ultimate truths not all contained in this awareness?

D: Yes, sir, the awareness of this touch sensation contains everything that the Buddha taught.

S: You have been talking about the three Piṭakas, about the Four Noble Truths, about mind and matter, and other technical terms. But do you actually know how to distinguish between mind and matter? Is the small spot under your nose mind or matter?

D: It is matter, sir.

S: And what is the awareness of the spot?

D: That is mind, sir.

S: And if you are as clearly aware of this spot under your nose as when you touch it with your finger?

D: Then we are aware of mind and matter, sir.

S: Is it good or bad to be aware of mind and matter simultaneously?

D: It is good, sir.

S: Is this called understanding or ignorance?

D: It is understanding, sir.

S: And what if we don't have this awareness?

D: Then we live in ignorance, sir.

S: Which is more powerful, knowledge or ignorance?

D: Knowledge has more power, sir.

S: Yes, it is understanding that has power. The whole of the cycle of birth and death is full of ignorance, but now that you have received the teachings of the Buddha, be aware. Skilful people gain awareness because they are able to accept the teachings of the Buddha and direct their attention here only. As they gain awareness, knowledge comes to them. When you are aware in this way, what happens to ignorance?

D: It is cut off and disappears, sir.

S: Where can we find it, if we look out for it?

D: It is gone, sir.

S: Though ignorance has had so much power over you in the past of *saṃsāra*, when you receive the teachings of the Buddha and achieve understanding, you don't even know where your ignorance has gone. So, really, understanding has much more power than ignorance, and still you complain that ignorance has such a strong hold over your minds.

D: But, sir, we have been associated with ignorance for so long that we are reluctant to let go of it.

S: Still, if you apply the teachings of the Buddha, ignorance will disappear. Which of the two is more agreeable to you?

D: For us, sir, ignorance is more agreeable.

S: Would you like to sustain a state of understanding?

D: Yes, sir, but we can't let go of ignorance.

S: Does ignorance force its way into your mind?

D: We call it into our minds by force, sir.

S: All of you have had an education, and you know many things about the teachings of the Buddha, and you can talk about them, and you practise them. You meditate and keep up your awareness all the time. But tell me, what preparations do you have to make in order to meditate?

D: We have to take a cushion and a mat to lie down, sir.

S: If you have all these things, will your meditation be good as a matter of course?

D: We have to stay away from other people too, sir.

S: What happens if you are negligent?

D: We fall asleep, sir.

S: You are disciples of the Buddha. You know that ignorance is your enemy. And though you know that, you start meditating only after preparing a bed for yourself. After meditating for some time you will become bored, and sloth and torpor will creep in. What will you do then?

D: We will endure them.

S: And if sloth and sleepiness are very strong, will you still resist?

D: No, sir, we will say to them, "Now only you come!"

S: Yes, that's just like you! "Now only do you come! I have had the bed ready for a long time." That's what you are going to think, aren't you?

D: Yes, sir.

S: When will you wake up again after going to sleep?

D: We will get up when it is day and time for breakfast, sir.

S: If you go on speaking in this way, this will have the effect that the dangers of ignorance will never be overcome. You don't praise understanding and wisdom, but ignorance. If you work like this, will you ever obtain the happiness to which you have aspired?

D: No, sir.

S: Will you just pretend to work then?

D: If we just pretend, we won't get anywhere, sir.

S: So, if you can't achieve your goal, what will you do?

D: I think we will have to continue with this practice until we reach the goal, sir.

S: Good. Yes, you know the difference between understanding and ignorance. Knowing what to do to achieve understanding, focus your attention on the spot and then keep it there. If you live with this awareness, do you still have to fear and be worried about the moment of death?

D: No, sir.

S: Tell me, what happens if you die without this awareness?

D: I will be reborn in one of the four lower planes.

S: Do you want this to happen?

D: No, sir.

S: Do you really not want to go, or are you telling me a lie?

D: You are right, sir, I have fallen into telling lies. I am walking on the path that leads straight to the lower worlds. I am speaking only empty words when I say that I don't want to go to hell and am still staying on the broad highway leading downwards.

S: Very good. You have understood. If you know for yourself whether you have got some understanding or not, then you are on the right path. If you know when you don't understand, you have understood. But if you think you have understood though you haven't understood a thing, then there is not the slightest hope for you to acquire any understanding.

You see, he knows that he is lazy when he is lazy; he knows that he is useless when he is useless. If you can see yourself in the correct light, then you will achieve understanding, because you are able to correct yourselves.

"I don't want to go to the lower worlds. Well, with all the meditation I'm doing I'll be alright. After all it doesn't take that much." Do you still think in this way, assuming that you needn't work much anymore, when really you do?

D: No, sir, I don't take what is wrong to be right and what is right to be wrong.

S: If you firmly fix your attention on the spot and are aware of mind and matter, you practise understanding. If you have no awareness, you are living in ignorance. If you die with your mind steeped in ignorance, you will go down, even if you are observing the *Uposatha* precepts. Tell me, where would you be reborn if you happened to be at a pagoda or under a Bodhi tree when you die?

D: Wherever I am, if I can't concentrate my mind when I die, I will go down, sir.

S: What about monks? Suppose I think, "Ha, my stock of merit is quite great, much greater than the merit of those lay people," and then I wander about here and there with a smile on my face. If I were to die, where would I be reborn?

D: We don't dare to say anything about monks, sir.

S: You needn't say anything about monks, just take me as an example.

D: Sir, we would dare even less say anything about you.

S: I'm assuming that my mind wouldn't stay with any object and I had to die, what would happen, my disciple?

D: Sir, I don't think there is a time when you are not aware of this spot.

S: But if I were to die without this awareness?

D: If it were me, I would fall into the lower planes.

S: Whoever it is, if there is no awareness at the moment of death, the result will be rebirth in hell. Therefore, establish your mindfulness so that you never forget this small spot. If I were to wish to be reborn in hell after having reached complete understanding due to this awareness, would there be a possibility of my going to hell?

D: Such a wish couldn't come true, sir.

S: If we don't understand what should be understood, and then start praying for Nibbāna, will we get it?

D: No, sir. However long we pray for Nibbāna, we will go down.

S: Ignorance leads to the four lower worlds. But if you take up this training of awareness of in-breath and out-breath, you will gradually develop towards the attainment of Nibbāna to which you have aspired. So, place your attention at this small spot steadfastly so that it doesn't budge.

Isn't it possible for you to fix your mind on this small spot while you are sitting in front of me?

D: It is, sir.

S: Can it be done while standing and walking?

D: Yes, sir.

S: Can you practise while eating, drinking, or working?

D: It is possible, sir.

S: Can you practise *Ānāpāna* when you are alone?

D: Yes, sir.

S: Or when you are in a crowd?

D: Even then it is possible to keep up the awareness, sir.

S: Do you get tired if you keep your attention at the spot all the time?

D: No, sir, it is not tiresome.

S: Does it cost you anything?

D: No, sir, it doesn't cost anything.

S: Is your work interrupted or disturbed?

D: No, sir, it isn't.

S: Are you more efficient in your work if you let your mind wander here and there or if you keep your attention focused on the spot?

D: It takes the same amount of time, sir.

S: Who is more efficient, the one with a wandering mind or the one who keeps his mind under control?

D: The one who keeps his attention at the spot does his job, and at the same time he is working for the attainment of Nibbāna.

S: One may earn one hundred thousand, but the one who works and practises awareness at the same time earns twice as much. From now on you will earn two hundred thousand. But, tell me, when we make our mind firm and tranquil, will our reward be only this much?

D: No, sir, when the mind is clear it becomes stable, firm, and strong.

S: The housewives here are surely all experienced in cooking.

You have to cook at times though you are very tired.

D: Yes, sir, at times we just stare into the fire and nod from fatigue. Then the rice is burned sometimes, sir.

S: Why does this happen?

D: Because our mind is not on the job, sir. Just yesterday I was thinking of some scene I had seen in a show and I burned the rice, sir. If my mind didn't wander, I would be able to do my work more quickly, and I wouldn't burn the food.

S: What happens if you eat rice that isn't properly cooked?

D: Some people get an upset stomach, sir.

S: If you cook in a haphazard manner, you are slow, you get tired easily, and the food isn't good. The fire burns down, and you have to kindle it anew. The water for the rice cools down, and you have to bring it to a boil again. Nothing is improved by not being attentive. When we improve our awareness, so many other things improve. I am only telling you what the Buddha taught, but of course I can't tell you all he taught. There are many more advantages resulting from this practice. The Buddha's teachings are complete and without a flaw. It is impossible to teach every aspect of the Dhamma. But if you keep your attention focused on the spot and are aware from moment to moment, then you will reach your goal. The Buddha did teach this, and the wise people of old did reach their goal by this practice, and yet there are many things the Buddha realized that are not contained in this. But you can reach your goal if you keep knowing in-breath and out-breath at the spot. You will become really happy.

I am talking only about this little spot. You know all the theories about meditation for tranquillity (*samatha*) and insight meditation (*vipassanā*) and how they come about. Yes, there is *samatha* and there is *vipassanā*, but the Buddha did say that you have to establish yourselves well in one practice: If you practise one, you accomplish one.

If you practise one, you accomplish two. If you practise one, you accomplish three.

But these are mere words. We have to practise with effort equal to the effort of the wise people of old.

When we teach the Dhamma we have to distinguish between Sutta, Abhidhamma, and Vinaya according to the established order, but only after having practised meditation to the same extent and with the same effort as the noble disciples of the Buddha will you really be able to explain the teachings.

Though I have explained the technique to you in the proper way, some of you may remain closed to it and without understanding. If I ask you about the house in which you are living, you will describe it to me accurately. If I were to think and ponder about your house, would I be able to visualize how it really is?

D: No, sir.

S: If I were to think and ponder all day and all night without even sleeping, would I find out about your house?

D: No, sir.

S: Tell me then, how can I find out for myself what your house looks like?

D: If you come to my house yourself, you will immediately know all about it even if no one says a word to you.

S: So, you too should proceed in such a way that you reach your goal. When you get there you will know, "Ah, this is it." Will you continue to put off practising? No, of course not. You can attain the Dhamma here and now.

Understanding all this, practise, make effort. You told me just now that meditation doesn't tire you. You said that it didn't cost anything, it didn't disrupt your work, and that you were able to practise it while alone and while you are with your family. Can you still find excuses for not practising, or are you going to continue living in the same way as you have been, without even trying to find excuses?

D: Most of the time we just carry on as usual, sir.

S: Those who take up this practice will receive the answers to their questions. So, keep your mind focused and your cooking will be done quickly; the rice is not going to be burned, and no wood is wasted. Your whole life will improve, and the time will simply fly.

There is right conduct, and there is understanding. Both are important. Right conduct is the fulfilment of your manifold duties and your giving of the four requisites for the support and furthering of the Buddha's teaching. The control over your mind gives you understanding.

There are these two elements of training, and you have to train yourselves in both simultaneously. Is it not possible to be aware of the breath while you are preparing and giving the four requisites to the community of monks?

D: It is possible, sir.

S: Under which of the two disciplines does sweeping fall?

D: Sweeping is part of right conduct.

S: Can't you keep your attention at the spot while you are sweeping?

D: We can, sir.

S: Under which of the two trainings does serving your parents fall, to whom you are deeply indebted for the love, compassion, and support they have given you?

D: That is right conduct, sir.

S: What do you accomplish if you keep your attention focused at the spot while you are serving and helping your parents?

D: We develop our understanding, sir.

S: So you can train yourselves both in right conduct and understanding at the same time. Sometimes you may say that you can't meditate, though you would like to, because you can't ignore your old father and mother. Does this happen to you?

D: Young people often think in this way and put off meditation, sir.

S: What about older people?

D: They often say they can't meditate because they have to look after their children, sir.

S: To fulfil our duties is part of moral conduct. If you don't fulfil your duties, your conduct is not perfect. At the same time that you fulfil your duties, admonishing your children, for example, you can train yourself in the awareness of the spot. Isn't this wonderful? Now you have the time to train yourselves in both moral conduct and understanding.

Venerate and respect your benefactors—your parents, your teachers, and the community of monks—without ever resting. From now on work without ever resting, with firm effort, as the wise of old did before you. Your aspirations will be realized as were the aspirations of the wise disciples of the Buddha.

—§§§—

The Self Made Private Prison

Lily de Silva

Bodhi Leaves No. 120

First published: 1990

The Self Made Private Prison

According to the teachings of the Buddha the human personality comprises five 'aggregates of grasping', called in Pali *pañc'upādānakkhandha*. They are enumerated as:

1. the aggregate of body;
2. the aggregate of feelings;
3. the aggregate of perception;
4. the aggregate of volitional activities; and
5. the aggregate of consciousness.

We may wonder why the Buddha mentions only five aggregates, no more and no less. We can attempt to answer this question by analysing any unit of experience in our day-to-day life. Suppose, for instance, we hear a big noise on the road, and we rush to the spot and recognise that a motorcycle accident has taken place; we feel sorry for the victim and want to rush him to the hospital. If we look at this experience and analyse the physical and mental phenomena involved, we will notice that they can be accommodated within the five aggregates of grasping. Of course, we all know the body or the material aspect of our personality. It is this body which approached the site of the accident. We heard the noise and saw the scene of the accident; that means we have had auditory and visual consciousness. We recognised that it is a motorcycle accident; that is the aggregate of perception and ideation. We felt sorry for the victim, and our sorrow is the feeling aspect of our personality. We wanted to take the victim to hospital, and that is the volitional aspect. Thus we have found all five aggregates of grasping in this unit of experience.

Likewise, the physical and mental phenomena involved in all our varied experiences can be included within these five aggregates. It is very likely that the Buddha too discovered these five aggregates of grasping by analysing experience through objective awareness (*sati*) and intuitive wisdom (*paññā*).

Why are they called aggregates, *khandha*? Khandha means 'heap' or 'accumulation'. It is easy to understand that the body is a heap of material elements. We maintain its process of growth by heaping it up with gross material food. In the mental sphere, too, through our experiences we accumulate feelings, perceptions and ideas, volitions, and consciousness. Therefore all five aspects of the personality are called heaps, accumulations, or aggregates.

Since they are intimately interconnected and act on one another, the processes are extremely complex and complicated. According to one commentarial simile they are like the waters at a confluence where five rivers meet. One cannot take a handful of water and say that it came from such and such a river. The aggregates are ever-changing and are constantly in a state of flux. They are so volatile and dynamic that they give rise to the notion of 'I' and 'mine'. Just as a fast revolving firebrand gives the illusion of a circle of fire, these dynamic processes of physical and mental energy give rise to the illusion of I, self, ego, soul.

They are called aggregates of grasping because we cling to them passionately as 'I' and 'mine'. Just as an animal tied with a strap to a firm post runs round and round the post, stands, sits, and lies down beside the post, so the person who regards the five aggregates as his self cannot escape from the aggregates and the suffering, disappointment and anxiety which invariably accompany them (SN 22:99; S III 150).

The five aggregates constitute a real private prison for us. We suffer a great deal due to our attachment to this prison and our expectations of what the prison should be. As our perception of the external world and our relations with our fellow human beings are conditioned by the nature of this prison, interpersonal relations and communication become extremely complex, tricky, and problematic. Problems become more and more complicated to the extent that we identify ourselves with this private prison.

Now let us try to supplement our understanding of the canonical teachings in terms of our daily experience and see how we cling to each and every one of these aggregates as 'I' and 'mine', and continue to suffer in the private prison that we make for ourselves.

1. *The Aggregate of Body*

If someone were to ask us the question: "Who are you?" we would immediately respond by stating: "I am so-and-so." The name is but a label and it can be anything. We can also say: "I am a human being." By that we have only stated the species to which we belong. "I am a man or woman." This only affirms the sex of the person. "I am so-and-so's daughter, sister, wife, mother," etc. These describe relationships, but we have still not answered the question: "Who are you?" We produce the identity card to prove our identity, but the identity card shows only a picture of the body with the name label. Now we believe that we have satisfactorily answered the question: "Who are you?" Thus we identify ourselves with our bodies. When we say: "I am tall, I am fat, I am fair," etc., we really mean that the body is tall or fat or fair, but what we do is identify the body as I.

What is more, we decorate it in various ways and regard it as our beautiful self, "Am I not beautiful in this sari?" We regard the body as our precious possession—"my face, my hair, my teeth," etc. Thus it is very clear that we cling to the material body as our very own self. This identification is so widely accepted and thorough that it has crept in linguistic usages as well. In words such as 'somebody', 'everybody', and 'nobody', 'body' is used in the sense of person.

Now the Buddha, who analysed the body objectively under the microscope of mindfulness, realised the true nature of the body and found that there is nothing in it that can be called beautiful. It is made up of flesh, phlegm, saliva, blood, urine, and faeces, all very repulsive. Even what is generally considered beautiful such as hair, teeth, and nails, if found out of context, say for instance in one's food, becomes extremely repulsive. So too is the face of a beauty queen if closely looked at before an early morning wash. It is not necessary to dwell at length on the ravages of old age and the decomposition of the body at death. Therefore the Buddha says that this body is a bag of filth, a burden to be discarded rather than clung to as 'I' and 'mine'.

The body is composed of the material elements of solidity (earth), cohesion (water), heat (fire), and motion (air). There is nothing worth grasping in any of these elements. They are found abundantly in the external world too, but we cling to this fathomlong blob of matter as 'I' and 'mine'.

The Buddha defines the body, or 'form', as that which gets reformed and de-formed; it is afflicted with heat, cold and insects. The body is but a body-building activity. Modern medical science informs us that the body is composed of billions and billions of cells which are continually in a process of growth and decay. What is meant here can be explained with the help of a simile. We say that there is rain and use the noun 'rain'. But in actuality there is no 'thing' called rain apart from the activity of raining; the process of drops of water falling from the sky—that is what we call rain. Though we use the noun 'rain', there is in reality only the activity of raining which can be better described with a verb. Similarly, what we call the body is but a process of body building; therefore the Buddha defines the noun 'form' (*rūpa*) with its corresponding verb 'forming' (ruppati). This process of body-building is going on all the time and thus is always in a state of unrest. Therefore form is looked upon as impermanent (*anicca*). In this changing process of body-building activity there is absolutely nothing that can be regarded as a self, an unchanging ego, an 'I', a permanent soul. Thus our identification with the body as self is a big delusion.

During its lifetime the body passes through the stages of infancy, childhood, adolescence, youth, middle age and old age. Throughout this process there is a type of suffering which is characteristic of each particular age. Teething, learning skills in locomotion, communication add much frustration to infancy. Childhood is comparatively free of suffering if one is fortunate to have a healthy body, but coping with the growing body can become frustrating if energy is not channelled towards healthy play and creative work. Adolescence, when an individual is neither small enough to be a child nor mature enough to be an adult, is particularly troublesome. In youth the body can be quite problematic as sexual energy is at its peak. Unless it is wisely channelled, indulged in lawfully accepted ways, restrained with understanding, and sublimated, youth can lead to much misery. In middle age the body is prone to pressure-related diseases; for many it is a period of much anxiety. Suffering in old age is manifold; the body becomes too big a burden to carry. Thus at no stage in life does the body remain trouble-free; it is a source of suffering throughout life.

However much we pamper the body with all five strands of sense pleasures, the body is never grateful. It never behaves the way we would like it to behave. However much we wash it, it gets dirty. However much we feed it, it gets hungry and tired. It falls ill, it gets old, it loses its beauty and strength. It never stays within our control. Therefore it is not worth hankering after, calling it 'I' and 'mine'.

In the private prison of the five aggregates the body is the most tangible 'wall'. The body of each person is a unique combination of elements having particular biochemical and bioelectrical properties. Each body has strengths and weaknesses peculiar to itself. Each one is prone to certain types of diseases in a particular way. There is no individual who is completely healthy all through life. One person may be asthmatic, another diabetic. One may have a weak respiratory system, another a weak digestive system. Each one suffers individually, privately, by the body he has inherited.

Our bodies vary in size, shape, colour and appearance, and because of these differences we suffer various complexities. Our bodies may not be what we would like them to be. Then we get disappointed and depressed. A woman who had lost her sight in early childhood regained her sight after about thirty years as a result of the shock of a sudden fall. She was overjoyed to regain her sight, but her joy was short-lived, for she discovered through the mirror that she was not beautiful. Such is the disappointment the body brings when it does not come up to our expectations.

The body also changes from age to age: the once beautiful strong body becomes the haggard and infirm, and we suffer on account of that. We resort to various methods of making it beautiful and strong—we paint the face, dye the hair, use dentures and wigs; we take vitamins, tonics, and elixirs. Yet all the same the body defies our expectations and we continue to suffer within the confines of the private prison of our body.

Once a friend of mine related how he saw a child meddling with the rear bumper of a parked car. The owner started driving the car, and the child, clinging to the rear bumper, was yelling as he got dragged along. If only the child let go of his hold on the car his suffering would have ceased. Similarly, we cling to our body, and we grieve and lament when it goes according to its nature. If only we would learn to let go of it, our suffering would cease. Therefore the Buddha says: "Give up that which does not belong to you. The five aggregates of grasping do not belong to you."

2. *The Aggregate of Feelings*

Feelings demarcate the body from the rest of the environment and give the body the sense of self. The Khandhasaṃyutta (SN 22:47; S III 46) says that the uninstructed man, being impressed by feelings which are produced through contact with ignorance, thinks "I am this (body)." The body is strewn with an intricately woven network of nerve fibres, and there is no part of the body which is not sensitive to touch. The entire sensitive volume constitutes the I, the self, the ego.

When we say: "I am comfortable or happy or sad," we identify ourselves with feelings. Statements such as: "He does not care for my happiness, he hurt my feelings," also show how we establish a sense of possession for our feelings. There are three kinds of feelings, namely, pleasurable or happy feelings, unpleasant or painful feelings, and neutral feelings. No two types ever occur concurrently at any single moment. When pleasurable feelings are present the other two are absent; when painful feelings are there pleasant and neutral feelings are absent; similarly with neutral feelings. The Mahānidāna Sutta asks the question: when feelings are so complex in this manner, which feeling would one accept as one's self?

According to the Vedanāsaṃyutta, innumerable feelings arise in the body just as all kinds of winds blow in different directions in the atmosphere. We are hardly aware of these feelings for the simple reason that we do not pay enough attention to them. If we observe for a couple of minutes, how often we adjust our bodies and change the position of our limbs, we will be surprised to note that we hardly keep still even for a few seconds. What is the reason for this constant change of position and posture? Monotony of position causes discomfort and we change position and posture in search for comfort. We react to feelings, yearning for more and more pleasurable feelings, revolting against unpleasant feelings, and being generally unaware of neutral feelings. Therefore pleasurable feelings have desire as their latent tendency, unpleasant feelings have aversion as their latent tendency, and neutral feelings have ignorance as their latent tendency (MN 44; M I 303). Thus all feelings generate unskilful motivational roots and they partake of the nature of suffering (*yaṃ kiñci vedayitaṃ taṃ dukkhasmiṃ*, SN 36:11; S IV 216). Though the search for comfort and pleasure goes on constantly throughout life, pleasure always eludes us like a mirage.

Our feelings are extremely private and personal. A man may have a splitting headache, but the one next to him may not know anything about his painful sensations. We only infer the pain of another by his facial expressions, behaviour, and words, but we certainly do not know the feelings of another. We are each unique in the experiences of feelings: one may be sensitive to heat; another to cold, mosquitoes, or fleas; another to certain kinds of pollen. One may have a low threshold for pain, another a high threshold. Thus each one is so unique in the totality of his sensitivity that we are utterly and absolutely alone in our private prison of feelings.

The Buddha defines feeling as the act of feeling. There is no 'thing' called feeling apart from the act of feeling. Therefore feelings are dynamic, ever-changing, impermanent. They do not remain within our control either, for we cannot say: "Let me have or not have such and such feelings." They come and go as they please, we have no control or right of ownership over them. Therefore the Buddha exhorts us: "Give up that which does not belong to you." Trying to possess that which is fleeting and defies ownership causes grief. Giving up spells the end of sorrow.

3. *The Aggregate of Perception*

Saññā in Pali is translated as perception or ideation. Perception is nothing but the act of perceiving. Thus it is a dynamic process, an activity. What does it perceive? It perceives colours such as blue, yellow, red, white, etc. This definition of *saññā* seems to imply that the linguistic ability of man is associated with *saññā*. The word *saññā* also means symbol, and symbolization is closely associated with language. It is language that helps us to form ideas, and that is the reason why *saññā* is sometimes translated as ideation. According to one's perception, one forms a point of view, an idea.

We identify ourselves with our ideas too: "This is my point of view, this is my idea, this is my opinion, this is what I meant"—these are all expressions identifying ourselves with ideation and perception. Sometimes this identification is so strong that we are ready to sacrifice our lives for the sake of an idea. Many wars are waged in the world propagating or defending ideas. As this is such a dominant form of clinging it has been singled out by the Buddha as *diṭṭh'upādāna*, clinging to a particular view one chooses to believe in. Identifying ourselves with various points of view we call ourselves democrats, socialists, eternalists, annihilationists, positivists.

Our ideas change due to changing emotions and circumstances. A friend becomes a foe, an enemy becomes an ally, a stranger becomes a spouse. Therefore in ideation too there is nothing constant and permanent; it is not possible to hold them fast as 'I' and 'mine' without coming to grief.

Memory is also associated with *saññā*. That is why we are able to recognise a person we have met before. Through the faculty of memory we recall having existed in the past experiencing such and such events. By projecting the same kind of experience into the future we anticipate that we will exist in the future. Thus through the memory aspect of *saññā* we posit the illusion of a self continuing through the three periods of past, present and future. But we little realise that the retrospection of the past and the anticipation of the future are both in fact done in the present moment itself.

How does *saññā* form a wall in our private prison? Each one of us perceives the world around us through our own preconceived ideas. Let us take a very gross example. A doctor's perception of the world will be quite different from the perception of a politician or a businessman. A doctor looking at an apple might think of its nutritional value, a politician of the advantages and disadvantages permitting importation, the businessman of the commercial value. Thus we are so much conditioned by our interests and ideologies—some absorbed from upbringing, some from the culture we are exposed to, some from the academic and professional training we have acquired—that no two people can have identical perceptions. There are sufficient common factors in these aspects to allow us to form general superficial agreements with other individuals, but when we take into account all ramifications we have to conclude that as regards perception too each one of us lives in a private prison. If we wish to experience wisdom and happiness welling within ourselves, we have to give up clinging to our ideas, unlearn what we have spent years to learn, decondition ourselves and empty our minds.

4. *The Aggregate of Volitional Activities*

There are three types of volitional activities: physical, verbal, and mental. We identify ourselves so much with these volitional activities that we posit an agent behind them as the doer, the speaker, and the thinker. Therefore we say: "I do (walk, stand, sit, work, rest, etc.), I speak, I think." Because this egocentricity in activities is so much emphasised, we want to perform not only at our maximum efficiency but we also try to outdo others. Record breaking is a mania today. There are so many competitors vying with one another at the international level eager to earn a place in the Guinness Book of Records.

Because of our volitional activities we are involved in an endless process of preparation from womb to tomb. As infants we prepare ourselves for childhood, struggling and learning skills of locomotion and speech. As children we prepare ourselves for youth, and then we study various skills, arts, and sciences trying to become successful adults. Adults prepare for parenthood. At last in our old age too we do not give up preparation. We turn to religion in our old age to prepare for heaven. This same aspect of our personalities is expressed in different words as *cetanā*, intention, which in turn is said to constitute the moral force of *kamma* which propels life from birth to birth.

Repeated action has the cumulative effect of transforming character, and thus through repeated volitional activities we can shape our destinies. A little story taken from an Indian classical text illustrates how our destiny is affected by our behaviour. One day two young men who were lost in a forest chanced to meet a hermit living there who was able to predict the future. Before departing the young men requested the hermit to tell their fortunes. The hermit was reluctant, but the men pleaded. Then the hermit observed them closely and predicted that Vipul would be a king within a year and Vijan would die in the hands of an assassin. Vipul was very much elated and Vijan was naturally very sad. They went back to their homes and Vipul became very arrogant in his behaviour towards others, thinking he would soon be king. Vijan was a teacher and he performed his duties conscientiously; he became very virtuous and led a humble meditative life.

After about six months Vipul called his friend to go in search of a place to build a palace, and they went into a deserted area. When they were searching Vipul found a pot of gold and was very happy that his fortune was unfolding. When the two friends were examining the gold in great happiness and excitement, a bandit rushed in and snatched the pot. Vijan fought with the bandit and rescued the gold, but had to suffer a cut on the shoulder from the bandit's weapon. Vipul invited Vijan to share the gold, but Vijan declined the offer as he would die in a few months. Vipul took the gold and spent it in eating, drinking and enjoying himself in anticipation of becoming king. Vijan spent the time in meditation and humility. A year passed but the prediction did not come true. They revisited the hermit and asked why his prediction had not come to pass. The hermit explained that by the arrogant behaviour of Vipul his fortune was reduced to a mere pot of gold, while the virtuous behaviour of Vijan was powerful enough to mitigate his misfortune to a mere wound in the hands of a bandit.

The noun *saṅkhāra* is defined by its verbal counterpart thus: "Volitional activities are those (mental forces) which construct, form, shape or prepare the physical body into what it is, the feelings into what they are, perceptions, volitional activities and consciousness into what they are." This is a process that is going on all the time. What is meant can be understood in the following manner: the distinctive physical and mental characteristic features of each individual are determined by these volitional activities. To this category belong all our hopes, aspirations, ambitions and determinations, and we identify ourselves with them as my hopes, my ambitions, etc. No two people will be identical in this respect too. What one person will treasure and strive for, another may consider a trifle. When one person prefers to hoard money, another would prefer to spend it on education. Still another may consider both of these as insignificant and run after power, honour, and prestige. We shape our destinies alone, imprisoned as we are within the wall of volitional activities. If we want to free ourselves, we have to give up identification with this prison wall too.

5. *The Aggregate of Consciousness*

Consciousness is defined as the act of becoming conscious of objects through the instrumentality of the sense faculties. Therefore there is eye-consciousness, ear-consciousness, nose-consciousness, tongue-consciousness, body-consciousness, and mind-consciousness. This cognitive process takes place so rapidly and so continuously that we identify ourselves with the function of the sense faculties as: "I see, I hear, I smell, I taste, I feel, I think and imagine." According to the Buddha there is no I, ego, self, or soul who cognizes and enjoys these sense objects. Sense consciousness is but a causally produced phenomenon, dependent on sense faculties and sense objects. Each person's sense faculties are differently constituted. Some are blind, some have weak eyes, some have keen vision, some are deaf, some are short of hearing and some have sharp hearing. Because of the differences in the very constitution of the sense faculties our cognitive capacity too has to be different, however slight the differences may be. Moreover, our sense experiences are conditioned by our likes and dislikes, by our previous experiences and memories, by our aspirations and ambitions. As such, however much we value sense experience as authentic, no two people will experience the same sense object in exactly the same way. For example, suppose that three people are watching a fight between two boys. If the three people happen to be a friend, an enemy, and a parent of one of those involved in the fight, the three people will have entirely different views regarding it.

Our senses communicate to us what we prefer to see. Volitions condition consciousness throughout our day-to-day experiences. For instance, if we are looking for a pen on a crowded table, we may see the pen and take it away. We may have failed to see the glass that was next to it and we may have to make a fresh search for the glass, rather than look straight at the place where the pen was. This is because what we look for is predetermined by our will, which to a certain extent excludes from our field of attention and vision things irrelevant to our purposes.

If we gaze at a scene vacantly, only a few items which kindled our interest are registered in our memory. Interests are divergent, therefore different people see different things in the same situation. Thus it is extremely difficult to acquire impartial objective experience of sense objects, as each one of us is psychologically conditioned in a unique way. Therefore in sense experience too we lead a lonely private life imprisoned in a private cell.

Because each one of us is leading a secluded life within the confines of our individual personalities, interpersonal relations become extremely difficult and complicated. The way to be released from this self-imprisonment is to stop regarding the five constituents of personality individually or collectively as 'I' and 'mine'.

According to the Khandhasaṃyutta (SN 22:93; S III 137–38), a man carried down by the strong current of a river grabs at the grasses and leaves overhanging the river, but they give him no support as they are easily uprooted. Similarly, the uninstructed man grabs at the five aggregates as his self or ego, but as they are themselves evanescent and unstable they cannot support him. Being dependent on them the man only comes to grief and delusion. We have to realise the impermanent, ever-changing, conditional nature of these five factors of personality and become detached from them. It is only with this detachment that we can make ourselves free from the self-made private prison of our personality.

Why the Buddha Did Not Preach to a Hungry Man

Buddhist Reflections on Affluence and Poverty

Louis van Loon

Bodhi Leaves No. 121

First published: 1990

Why the Buddha Did Not Preach to a Hungry Man

Introduction

This essay is intended to explore from a Buddhist point of view the issue of affluence and poverty. At the outset it is necessary to point out that a Buddhist thinker would of necessity approach this issue from a different perspective than that which forms the basis of much Western thinking on the subject. In accordance with its philosophical outlook that all empirical phenomena are interdependently connected and causally related, Buddhism assigns no absolute value to any of them. There are thus no definite "objects" or "entities" in the Buddha's philosophy. Rather, the world is viewed as a dynamic pattern of events which appears as a collection of static "articles" and "things" only from the standpoint of an unenlightened observer. In the Buddhist view, a mountain is as much a "happening" as is the flame of a burning candle. It is just that our minds are conditioned to look upon the more slowly moving patterns of change as inert "objects."

This tendency—to assign a concrete and absolute status to situations that are essentially points of reference in a dynamic field of relationship—is at the core of our philosophical ignorance: we insist on confining to the particular that which is universal; we dichotomize things into good and evil whereas there is only a balancing continuum of positive and negative energies, actions and reactions, causes and effects. Similarly, from a Buddhist perspective affluence and poverty would be seen not as absolutes opposed to ("versus") each other, but as relative values in a complex and fluid psychic continuum of perceived needs and wants. Though we divide lifestyles into "affluent" and "destitute," in this area of human experience we are really dealing principally with a spectrum of psychological attitudes to needs and wants.

Affluence and poverty have to do with feelings of fulfilment and well-being rather than with an equation of goods and people.

Arrowheads from IBM Casings

In every society, simple or sophisticated, there are levels of subsistence below which people's lives are rendered virtually meaningless and inconsequential because their dominant experiences in life consist only of hunger, illness and unrelieved misery. We know only too well that such forms of "absolute" poverty exist in backward rural villages as well as in the slums and ghettos of New York and Johannesburg. Similarly, there are levels of "absolute" affluence in the world which enable a few people to live far beyond their real needs and reasonable wants. This level too may be found amongst the privileged members of primitive societies as much as it can be seen along Sunset Boulevard.

However, what makes one man poor and another rich is not only a question of material possessions, how much they consume or the extent to which they are able to satisfy their cravings. This is determined largely by the manner in which they subjectively experience and psychologically evaluate a feeling of well-being in the context of the environment in which they happen to be situated. Indeed, "poverty" and "affluence" are largely relative terms: quantitatively, a well-to-do member of a primitive Bushman society is still desperately poor compared with an urbanised African who may well own a radio, a guitar, a good suit and some cattle at his homeland kraal. He, however, is appallingly destitute when his lifestyle is contrasted with that of a white artisan who, in turn, envies the earning capacity—and everything that goes with it—of a Johannesburg business executive who, however, may well earn— and be able to afford only as much as a New York dockworker.

Between the "poor" bushman and the "affluent" Rockefellers there exists, indeed, an enormous quantitative difference in measurable, material wealth. But what is surely also important is to assess how each, in the compass of his particular socio-economic situation, qualitatively experiences this poverty/affluence level as a measure of intrinsic well-being. The acquisition of a set of new bronze arrowheads, for instance, may well be as much of a thrill to the primitive hunter as is the purchase of the latest IBM computer to the millionaire business tycoon. The computer, however, is a perfectly useless piece of equipment to the Bushman (who would probably wish to make arrowheads out of its casing) whereas the arrows may, at most, find a place in Rockefeller's Primitive Art collection. The two lifestyles are really nowhere in contact with each other. Their concepts of what constitutes wealth and affluence therefore bypass each other; each is irrelevant to the other.

In short, affluence and poverty are variables which may assume "absolute" values at various points on a sliding scale of socio-economic conditions which differ from society to society and which are relative to their adopted or accustomed lifestyles.

Snowmobiles to Tropical Countries

We tend to judge "unsophisticated" cultures from the point of view of our gadget-cluttered society. Because we are so preoccupied with "getting things out of life" (whatever that may mean) through a colossal expenditure of effort and use of natural resources, we pity any other society that does not have the benefit of our capacity to exploit and maim our natural environment and burden our lives with masses of silly contrivances and diversions.

Certainly, if these are the criteria by which one wishes to assess levels of affluence and well-being then, indeed, simple modes of existence are poverty-stricken. We demonstrate this view in our aid programmes to the nations we have designated as being "poor": Western nations are known to have donated sophisticated textile machinery to countries that have neither the executive or technical skills nor the raw materials to operate them; they have sent snow mobiles to tropical countries and fishing vessels to landlocked nations.

It is obvious that such an attitude to poverty and affluence is based on the wrong premises. The technologically advanced nations have taken it upon themselves to force their interpretation of well-being onto the "underdeveloped" communities, labelling them poor simply because they do not conform to their idea of an infinite-growth, consumer-oriented society. This has a self-fulfilling effect: increasingly, only the industrialised nations can afford to produce the goods needed to maintain their ever-expanding lifestyles, leaving the "poor" nations ever further behind in an acquisitive, hedonic race to consume the world's dwindling natural resources.

This race now embroils the entire globe to the extent that originally self-sufficient economies, by being so treated as poor are now, in fact, becoming truly destitute by not being able to afford even the most basic necessities of life. They are being drawn into a global scale of economic standards that is not of their making and find themselves automatically assigned to the lowest rungs. What used to be a local and relative form of well-being has been converted into a state of "absolute" poverty by having been forced to adopt an inflated socio-economic frame of reference that has been invented by, and is only applicable to, highly industrialised nations.

Even the boons of modern technology have a tendency to work against these "underdeveloped" nations. The reduction in their child mortality rate, for instance—however laudable in itself—curses them with an explosion in their population that runs well ahead of their capacity to feed the very same children saved by the miracle of twentieth-century preventive medicine, turning them, indeed, into walking skeletons. But high reproductive rates continue because that is how archaic societies, to a large extent, measure their sense of well-being. In too many cases the technological successes of the affluent nations have spelled nothing but disaster when transplanted into societies that had never felt the need nor the desire to be so materially ambitious in the first place. It is the penalty of having grafted the standard of well-being of one lifestyle onto that of another.

The Hedonic Principle

The experience of well-being, of meaningfulness and a sense of fulfilment, cannot be measured in dollar bills or handfuls of rice only. The sense of well-being is subjective. It reflects the extent to which an individual is able to express his or her creativity, the human potential. And that, again, is relative to the particular environment and the framework of socio-economic norms and values with which that individual happens to be integrated.

We cannot be sure that a simple, non-technological culture devoid of internal combustion engines and plastic milk bottles, however poor it may appear to be according to our standards, is spiritually, materially, psychologically less fulfilling than life in Hillbrow. We cannot compare experiences we have with ones we have never had, as little as we would crave for caviar if we had never tasted it.

Therefore, are we not unwise in pitying that poor Bushman because his desert lacks urban sprawl and freeways? Shouldn't we, instead, be envious of his atonement with his natural environment— something we try to re-enact so pathetically in our motorised safaris and gas-fired braais? How shall we ever know whether tribal dancers enjoy themselves more—or less—than our teenagers in their discotheques? Does the absence of tax-free savings accounts in his economic system really worry the Bushman?

It is an inborn human failing, however, dating back to man's earliest hominid days, that once we are presented with an opportunity to expand our sensual horizons we will unhesitatingly do so. It happened with the invention of the wheel; it happened again with the electric toothbrush. From stone axes to private jet planes, they are all part of an acquisitive syndrome that is basic to human nature; they define a hedonic principle that is the driving force behind man's psycho-social development; it is the golden—or perhaps the leaden?—thread that runs through our evolution and the pages of our history books.

This hedonic principle (the Buddhists call it *taṇhā* or "craving") is behind the experience of disappointment, dissatisfaction and frustration that is so fundamental to human existence. It drives us on and on in the pursuit of an impossible dream: the acquisition of a state of happiness in which all our desires are satisfied, in which there are no more needs and where our wants are painlessly realised. As this is impossible to attain, *taṇhā* inevitably gives rise to *dukkha*, "suffering."

Buddhism may well be defined as a religion that shows us not only how to come to grips with craving and suffering, but also how we may transcend them. This, the Buddha taught, can come about only when we have learned how to direct our mind, our awareness, away from its tendency to become emotionally entangled and attached to the objects contacted by our senses and towards a way of viewing things in their causal connectedness as they arise and fall away, with equanimity, insight and compassion. The world is then no longer perceived merely as a collection of objects and conditions from which one is forever attempting to extract the desirable entities and avoid the undesirable ones, but as a continuum of causal events, neither good nor bad by themselves, and arousing therefore neither greed, envy, aversion or attachment in us.

Only such a state of mind conduces to true happiness because it is not dependent on circumstances being this way or that. One is content because things are what they are—not because they happen to conform to one's specification for happiness. For the enlightened saint, every situation is essentially OK and workable. There is no judgement or regret or glee, blame or praise, just the joy of being clearly aware of "what is," the "suchness" of things, and the joy of interacting with things with understanding and compassion.

Being poor or affluent is a judgement based on comparisons. Like hot or cold and long or short, poverty and affluence are mental constructs, useful to demarcate the boundaries of a particular situation. They are relative to each other. Just as hot and cold describe a temperature range, so do affluence and poverty describe a range of needs and wants, or rather: attitudes to needs and wants. Depending on where one finds oneself within that range one feels oneself to be hot or cold—or poor or affluent. It depends on which way one is looking, which end of the scale one is comparing oneself with. But if one did not indulge in such judgements and comparisons, one would simply experience oneself the way one found oneself. This, by and large, is how the Buddha encouraged laypersons to train themselves: to be realistically in the here and now and make every circumstance ethically workable.

But there is yet another way of being neither poor nor affluent. If one lowers one's demands on the world, reduces one's needs to the merely necessary, and has no desire to have more than that (i.e. if one eliminates one's wants), then a scale of affluence and poverty would no longer affect one either. One would have opted out altogether. This, of course, applies to the lifestyle of the monk or nun.

The "Best Life"

A Buddhist monk who has renounced all worldly possessions and who devotes all his time to dissolving his sense of self and its many wants experiences, as a result, a degree of fulfilment, meaning and purpose in life that is in sharp contrast with that of the successful, popular, wealthy Hollywood star who contemplates—and often commits—suicide because life, to him or her, has become an unbearable ordeal: the ego and its wants has become a rampant, in*sati*able, all-consuming monster.

Quantitative affluence does not necessarily guarantee the experience of well-being. Wealth and status bring with them strife and competition, envy and ill will, and-yes—insecurity and anxiety. The feeling of living a meaningful life is subjective, psychological. It has to do with a spiritual dimension in man, a religious depth, rather than bank balances and yachts. Indeed, we may have to make up our minds which is the more important goal in our life: anxiety-ridden existence draped in glitter, or sack-cloth, tranquillity, contentment and purposefulness.

This does not mean, however, that only sack-cloth can produce peace of mind and that any form of wealth automatically leads to unhappiness. Buddhism teaches that it is not the lack or abundance of possessions as such that gives us the experience of poverty or affluence, only the extent to which we are attached to things and crave for them, whether they are needs or wants. It is not "bad" to appreciate enjoyable things; but one should refrain from craving for and clinging to them. Money, yachts and arrowheads are neutral entities by themselves; they only become "possessions" when the concepts of self and ownership enter our heads and with them, attachment, envy, and greed.

The Buddha's teachings were aimed primarily at the psychological upliftment and spiritual emancipation of man. But he knew, of course, that such upliftment is impossible in an environment that is so impoverished that all one's energies need to be channelled into mere physical survival. So he often indicated how his teachings could be applied to matters of state, economics and social welfare.

There were, he said, four "conditions" conducive to happiness for the layperson, so that the "best life" could be lived. The first was to become a useful, integrated member of society: to become "skilled and efficient, earnest and energetic" in a profession, craft or trade. The second was the opportunity to "safeguard" one's income and wealth, righteously earned, "by the sweat of one's brow," i.e. not to have it overtaxed, confiscated or in other ways eroded, devalued or "stolen." The third: to associate with intelligent, trustworthy, generous and virtuous friends. Fourth: a balanced lifestyle, where one spends and saves wisely, in proportion with one's income, i.e. one is neither a miser nor a spendthrift. In this respect, the Buddha once advised a young man to apportion his income in such a way that one quarter was spent on his daily expenses, one half used to run his business, and the remainder set aside for emergencies.

The "joys" that result from such prudent conduct are, he said, again of four kinds. The first three concern one s material wellbeing: the joy of being able to acquire, by just means and personal effort and skill, sufficient wealth to provide for one's economic security; the joy of spending this wealth liberally but wisely on meritorious deeds and on oneself, one's family, friends and relatives; and the joy of being without debts and able to meet one's liabilities. The fourth joy, the most important, is spiritual in nature: the joy of being able to live a blameless, virtuous life, free of evil in thought, word and deed.

Obviously, the first three joys make the fourth one possible. But the Buddha claimed the joys of material prosperity to be "not worth one sixteenth part" of the bliss that comes from a religiously meaningful life. This is so, of course, because a life lived free of evil in thought, word and deed dismantles the unwholesome kammic conditions that cause repeated rebirths and therefore liberates one from *saṃsāra*, the round of perpetual becoming. The way to Nibbāna is paved with virtue.

Yet it is clear that economic well-being is a necessary condition for the spiritual welfare of any society. Even monks and nuns—although their "best life" is measured entirely in spiritual terms—are utterly dependent on a reasonably affluent lay community to provide them with food, shelter and robes. The Buddha, therefore, placed the utmost stress on material welfare-not for its own sake, so that people would be happy simply because their bellies were filled—but as a condition that made truly enlightened, meaningful living possible.

Banyan Trees and Mango Groves

This principle is well expressed in one of the rock edicts of the great Buddhist king, Asoka (250 BC). In reviewing his "Rule of Righteousness" eighteen years after his conversion to Buddhism, he says that his principal aim has been to instruct his subjects in Buddhist "righteousness" so that they could enjoy the best life:

"I have had banyan trees planted along the roads to give shade to man and beast. I have planted mango groves, and I have had ponds dug and shelters erected along the roads at every eight kos. Everywhere, I have had wells dug for the benefit of man and beast. But this benefit is but small, for in many ways the kings of olden times also worked for the welfare of the world. But what I have done has been done so that men may conform to righteousness."

He goes on to relate how, as a consequence of his actions, virtue has increased in his kingdom: how there is obedience to parents and teachers; respect and care for the aged; kindliness to the monks and ascetics, to the poor and the weak, to slaves and servants.

Asoka clearly followed the Buddha's suggestions as to what he considered the duties of a king or a government to be. These were, first and foremost, the prevention of poverty. Poverty, the Buddha maintained, leads to a miserable, debilitated state of mind. The mind becomes clouded with worry and insecurity. Hatred and jealousy arise and theft and violence and deception follow. People need to go to great lengths to protect what they have, be that little or much, and learn to be callous and miserly and greedy. Thus, poverty causes immorality and crime. The "best life" has become impossible.

Therefore, a ruler's priority is to organise society in such a way that employment, food production and industry are generated: seeds and fodder should be made available to the farmers; capital to industries (in the Buddha's day, in 500 BC, the mining, metal working and textile industries were often parastatal institutions), and so on. This, the Buddha claimed, was the way to combat crime and immorality, not by repression and punishment.

The Greek traveller Megosthenes, writing in about 300 BC (before Asoka and thence before Buddhism had become an important element in Indian society) commented on the unusually harsh judgements that were meted out in Brahmanical India at the time. Petty criminals were often arbitrarily executed or severely maimed. Every aspect of public and private affairs was burdened by complex legislation and laws that required an enormous—and often corrupt—bureaucracy to administer. But 700 years later, after Buddhist moral principles had established themselves throughout the length and breadth of India, Chinese travellers wrote about the people of India as a nation that "… practises the teachings of the compassionate Buddha. It has become a habit with them not to kill and not to fight." These travellers marvelled that the death penalty had been abolished, that only the lower castes ate meat and that the people enjoyed an exceptional freedom of speech and movement. Indian society, it seems, enjoyed the best life that was possible at the time under the circumstances.

On a smaller scale, in areas that had come under the Buddha's influence, such enlightened ways of living had already become possible in his own time. The Vajji Republic, for instance, had adopted "seven principles leading to prosperity," suggested to them by the Buddha. There was "frequent assembly" amongst the Vajji elders and leaders of the community. Unanimity was aimed for in any decisions that affected the welfare of the people. Such decisions were carried out "as authorised and, as much as was possible, in keeping with established religious and social custom." The elders in the community were revered and asked for advice based on their more mature experience. Women and minors were protected from being exploited and abused. Due reverence was given to religious institutions and tithes encouraged to support them. The "worthy ones" (the sages, monks and nuns) were made to feel welcome wherever they went. It is to be noted that the

Buddha's own monastic order was guided by these same democratic principles redefined, where necessary, to suit the ascetic lifestyle of the monks and nuns.

It is clear that the Buddha felt that the welfare of a community is to be measured essentially in psychological terms: in a sense of community; in friendship and virtue; in a caring and responsible attitude to religious institutions, the elderly, the renunciates, women and children. Such a community would, as a consequence, enjoy material welfare: "increase in well-being can be expected in such a society, not decline."

Small is Beautiful

In one of the most significant books ever written on the subject of economics (E.F. Schumacher's Small is Beautiful: A Study of Economics as if People Mattered) the underlying theme is Buddhistic. Schumacher, a devout Christian himself, points out that a Buddhist would wish to plan his socio-economic environment in such a way that an optimum of well-being is obtained with a minimum of consumption, contrary to the prevailing Western view which suggests that the greater the amount of consumption the better off we ought to be.

The Buddhist outlook flows naturally from a concern to do the least possible harm to the environment and to interfere only as much as is necessary in the lifestyle of one's fellow creatures— plant, animal or human. The mindless squandering of irreplaceable natural resources and the devastation of our lived environment would, in a Buddhist-inspired economy, be considered as incredible follies; as acts of violence against one's natural habitat, equivalent to cutting one's wrist. Human labour would not be considered as a mere cost item, to be reduced to drudgery if profit or productivity so demand it, or to be eliminated altogether if possible through automation, but as the most immediate, natural and effective means through which a human being can express his or her humanity and usefulness the fact that he or she matters.

Equally important, a Buddhist economy would be highly adaptable and globally diversified to match, as much as possible, regional needs to local resources. This would avoid the frightful international power play which is, by and large, a contest between competing economic ideologies, locked in a deadly clash to acquire what are considered to be the world's sources of well-being: raw materials, cheap labour, agricultural land, industrial capacity, consumer markets, etc. In the process they inflict their conception of well-being onto a host of unwilling nations who are becoming increasingly powerless to resist this onslaught on their traditional lifestyles.

Such a Buddhist economic attitude may well mean that certain areas of the world will retain their man-drawn rickshaw carts as a means of mass transport whereas other regions have computer-run monorail hover-trains. But we should stop labelling the one poor and the other affluent, because a rickshaw may well have the same relative, economic utility value in that part of the world as the hover-train has in the other. Similarly, a mono diet of rice and dhal—provided enough of it is available—is not necessarily a sign of a low standard of living, one that should at all cost be replaced by a lifestyle in which steak and kidney pies are consumed.

Economics with a Human Face

In the Buddhist view, true civilization is exemplified when society functions in such a way that each man and woman has the optimum opportunity to ennoble his or her character and to live in harmony and peace with their fellows and their environment, whether that happens to be the Kalahari Desert or Fifth Avenue.

I have already indicated in what way the Buddha thought society—and an individual's attitude—could be shaped so as to make the "best life" possible. But there are many other elements in his teachings that show how each individual may go about structuring his or her actions and attitudes, so that practical conditions of well-being are created. One of the steps on the Buddha's Noble Eightfold Path, for instance, deals with "Right Livelihood." It is one of eight factors which, together, constitute the overall training of a Buddhist. This training covers the entire spectrum of our psychophysical constitution and aims at nothing less than the perfection of our virtue, gaining control over the workings of our mind and emotions, and developing a transcendental insight that is capable of perceiving the true nature of things behind their superficial appearance.

Right Livelihood isolates those trades and occupations that should be avoided if we are to demonstrate our wisdom and morality in the manner in which we acquire our daily bread and without which all other religious zeal would be spurious. It condemns specifically any activity that helps to keep people in bondage, demeaning servitude or drudgery; it considers it unworthy to be in any way involved in the manufacture of or trade in weapons and intoxicating or mind-deranging drinks and drugs or any other substances that can pollute or cripple our environment or harm our fellow creatures; it is consistent in its all-encompassing attitude of compassion and harmlessness in disapproving of the trade in animals for slaughter and food.

Another example of this type of simple but highly effective attitude to human welfare is the Buddha's suggestion that each man and woman should be in the habit of planting a tree every five years. Imagine the benefits that would result if such a policy was encouraged worldwide—especially if, at the same time, our agricultural policies were given a vegetarian orientation, another Buddhist predilection (vegetarian agricultural policies have been proven to yield ten times as much food value for the same use of land, capital and labour resources as agricultural methods that emphasise the production of animal protein). There is virtually no capital cost involved for even a child to obtain and plant a seed or seedling once every five years. No foreign exchange or development aid is required, no fancy equipment or expert advice, yet the countryside could be made to yield abundant fruit, nuts and other foodstuffs, building material and fibre, provide shade and conserve water, upgrade the capacity of the soil to carry crops, etc., all within a single generation.

These are just two examples out of many that can be found in the Buddha's teachings that show that an economic strategy based on Buddhist principles would have a human face. It may not have the neon-lit heroics of twentieth-century technology, but then it would not have its horrendous dehumanising effects either.

Golf Tournaments or Monasteries

In every Buddhist country, in ancient as well as modern times, there has always been enough surplus wealth—however poor the Western world may have labelled them—to make it possible for large numbers of men and women to live lives of religious dedication as monks and nuns. Buddhist monks and nuns (the Sangha) have no wants and their needs are so elementary that the lay community finds it no strain to provide them with a simple meal once a day and, occasionally, with a set of robes. Here, poverty has attained an elevated status because it implies that the "beggar" has become quite indifferent to his economic position and the beguiling attractions of worldly things, attractions which still entrap the (relatively) affluent layperson who, by the very act of almsgiving, silently and humbly acknowledges this fact.

The surplus wealth spent on the Sangha in Buddhist countries has existed in almost every civilization. The Egyptians spent it on pyramids; the Western world lavishes it on cosmetics, tobacco and alcohol, on missiles and an occasional war, on soap operas and golf tournaments, and on handouts to the poor nations. Yet some indulgence in contemplative religion would cost our community very little compared with what we are now prepared to spend on such hobbies as space research and high-energy particle physics.

Not only does the maintenance of a Sangha make it possible for many people who feel the need to withdraw from secular life to do so (a need which, when frustrated, produces dropouts and drug communes in our affluent society—a society that does not easily countenance even genuine contemplatives), it also removes from society those surplus members who may have joined the ranks of the unemployed and doledrawers. More significantly, perhaps, monks and nuns do not contribute to population explosions, apart from the fact that Buddhist countries have in any case no particular bias in favour of large families nor are they against the practise of birth-control. It is the quality of life that is important, not just the quantity.

Also, instead of having their senior citizens ignobly carried by state-run welfare programmes and assigned to penury and irrelevancy in chilly old-age homes, many of the aged in Buddhist communities retire only too willingly as contemplative monks and nuns to complete their lives meaningfully in the peaceful surroundings of monastic settlements and meditation centres. In fact, a Buddhist community can be deemed to have failed if it did not spontaneously produce, and support, a significant number of such "poor" contemplatives in their midst.

Conclusion

Although Schumacher has convincingly indicated how many of the world's economic ills may be eliminated or alleviated by the application of Buddhistic principles to such schemes as the establishment of small, rural agro-industrial units in impoverished regions; the use of a labour intensive "intermediate" technology; gifts of training and knowledge rather than handouts of money and fancy equipment, etc.; and although this paper has highlighted some additional human factors and religious attitudes that would play a part in a Buddhist-inspired economic system, it must be accepted that the success of such a globally applied Buddhist economic strategy would largely depend on vast numbers of people acquiring a Buddhist mentality. As this is highly unlikely (existing Buddhist communities cannot even apply these principles consistently) there is no doubt that "we shall have the poor with us always" (Matthew 26, verse 11).

The principal aim of this Buddhist contribution to the discussion on affluence and poverty has been to indicate that it would be a folly to treat these socio-economic situations simply as problems of "distributing wealth," "transferring technology to the poor," "educating the affluent to enjoy their leisure," etc. The real issues are far more complex and subjective and concern people rather than goods, the psyche of man more than his stomach.

However, as Schumacher has pointed out, even if we only physically handled these problems along Buddhist principles, the well-being of man could change dramatically within as little as a decade, leading, without a doubt, to a parallel improvement in man's morality, humanity and wisdom. After all, even the Buddha once refused to preach to a starving man until his hunger had first been appeased.

—§§§—

ABOUT PARIYATTI

Pariyatti is dedicated to providing affordable access to authentic teachings of the Buddha about the Dhamma theory (*pariyatti*) and practice (*paṭipatti*) of Vipassana meditation. A 501(c)(3) non-profit charitable organization since 2002, Pariyatti is sustained by contributions from individuals who appreciate and want to share the incalculable value of the Dhamma teachings. We invite you to visit www.pariyatti.org to learn about our programs, services, and ways to support publishing and other undertakings.

Pariyatti Publishing Imprints

Vipassana Research Publications (focus on Vipassana as taught by S.N. Goenka in the tradition of Sayagyi U Ba Khin)
BPS Pariyatti Editions (selected titles from the Buddhist Publication Society, co-published by Pariyatti)
MPA Pariyatti Editions (selected titles from the Myanmar Pitaka Association, co-published by Pariyatti)
Pariyatti Digital Editions (audio and video titles, including discourses)
Pariyatti Press (classic titles returned to print and inspirational writing by contemporary authors)

Pariyatti enriches the world by

- disseminating the words of the Buddha,
- providing sustenance for the seeker's journey,
- illuminating the meditator's path.

Made in the USA
Columbia, SC
01 August 2024

af4b6c4d-c09f-471b-80ad-f416230f3b9aR01